Microsoft® Office 2007 Business Intelligence: Reporting, Analysis, and Measurement from the Desktop

Doug Harts

New York Chicago San Francisco
Lisbon London Madrid Mexico City Milan
New Delhi San Juan Seoul Singapore Sydney Toronto

The McGraw-Hill Companies

Cataloging-in-Publication Data is on file with the Library of Congress

McGraw-Hill books are available at special quantity discounts to use as premiums and sales promotions, or for use in corporate training programs. For more information, please write to the Director of Special Sales, Professional Publishing, McGraw-Hill, Two Penn Plaza, New York, NY 10121-2298. Or contact your local bookstore.

Microsoft® Office 2007 Business Intelligence: Reporting, Analysis, and Measurement from the Desktop

1234567890 DOC DOC 01987

Microsoft® Office Business Intelligence: Reporting, Analysis, & Measurement from the Desktop
ISBN   978-0-07-149424-3
MHID   0-07-149424-3

Microsoft® Office Business Intelligence: Reporting, Analysis, & Measurement from the Desktop, Cizer Edition
ISBN   978-0-07-154551-8
MHID   0-07-154551-4

Sponsoring Editor	Wendy Rinaldi	Indexer	Kevin Broccoli
Editorial Supervisor	Jody McKenzie	Production Supervisor	Jim Kussow
Project Manager	Vastavikta Sharma, International Typesetting and Composition	Composition	International Typesetting and Composition
Acquisitions Coordinator	Mandy Canales	Illustration	International Typesetting and Composition
Technical Editor	Sean Boon		
Copy Editor	Robert Campbell	Art Director, Cover	Jeff Weeks
Proofreader	Paul Tyler	Cover Designer	Pattie Lee

About the Author

Doug Harts is the Chief Technology Officer at Cizer Software (www.cizer.com), a Microsoft Gold Partner focused on delivering packaged software and professional services to enhance the Microsoft Business Intelligence platform. Doug led Cizer's Joint Development Partnership with the Redmond SQL Server 2000 Reporting Services group, resulting in the Cizer.Net Ad-Hoc reporting toolset for Report Definition Language (RDL) that extends SQL Server 2005 Reporting Services and functions as a Trusted Report Source within PerformancePoint dashboards. He has been a participant on Microsoft's Business Intelligence Partner Advisory Council and is currently a member of the Excel Advisory Council. His experience encompasses 20 years of delivering BI solutions to large, geographically dispersed organizations. This work was responsible for the first sale of Microsoft's Business Scorecard Manager in the history of the product, which has progressed to the delivery of PerformancePoint solutions to government and corporate accounts in all aspects of monitoring, analysis, and planning. Doug maintains the Office Business Intelligence & Data Mining community web site at www.OfficeBIcentral.com.

About the Technical Editor

Sean Boon is a Program Manager at Microsoft and has ten years of experience in the business intelligence industry building data warehouses and designing software. Prior to working on the first version of Excel Services that ships as part of Microsoft Office SharePoint Server, Sean worked on the BI Practices team that developed the SQL Server Accelerator for Business Intelligence. He is currently working on the next release of SQL Server Reporting Services.

Contents

Foreword

Doug Harts and I have been colleagues in the Microsoft Business Intelligence Partner Advisory Council for years. We've been friends as long. Over those years we've compared notes as both fathers and as practitioners in business intelligence. When Doug told me he was writing this book, I was excited for him and for you, his readers. Doug's passion for business intelligence carries faithfully into this book. I believe you will find Doug's writing clear and concise. He uses practical examples with plenty of step-by-step instructions. Every chapter will help you grow your knowledge of business intelligence and Microsoft Office.

I have another reason to be excited about this book. We don't have many books on business intelligence in Microsoft Office. Given the very important role Office plays in the Microsoft BI offering, this surprises me. Over the years many customers have asked about successful patterns for implementing business intelligence. At Microsoft, our advice has been to start with the data layer and invest in "sound data." That is, make sure you know where your data comes from, how clean and consistent it is, and how your users access it. Sound data is so fundamental to sound business intelligence that we started our BI efforts in the SQL Server team at Microsoft.

Sound data alone is insufficient to improve companies. The next layer is just as critical. That layer supports personal and team insights. This is the role of Office in the Microsoft BI stack. I don't know any way to make people more insightful. But I do know that insights usually come from hunches. We have hunches all the time. A successful BI tool, built on sound data, lets employees explore their hunches and test them against facts. When the data is easily found and explored, using familiar tools, the process of going from hunch to insight is enhanced. Excel is simply the most natural tool for data work for huge numbers of people. The work the Excel team has done over many releases has provided our customers with a first-class business intelligence tool. SharePoint enables sharing of not just documents, but the insight our users develop using Excel—turning personal insight into team insight.

Business intelligence becomes truly impactful for corporations and organizations when it leads to better decisions. Insight alone is not enough; action leading to improved business performance is the true end goal. The top layer of the Microsoft stack is performance management. PerformancePoint Server 2007 is the Microsoft tool that builds on SQL Server and Microsoft Office (both Excel and SharePoint) and helps our customers measure and manage performance.

At Microsoft, we believe true business intelligence comes when you trust your data, trust your insights, and trust your decisions.

Regarding this book, check out Chapter 5, which introduces Microsoft Office SharePoint Server's (MOSS) role in business intelligence. This chapter may be acronym-laden (ODC, DCL, etc.), but it also provides an excellent overview of the Report Center, KPI lists, and other BI features of SharePoint.

Chapter 6 covers data mining. Data mining has been a practical, valuable, but relatively little-used analysis technique for years. SQL Server introduced data mining functionality in SQL Server 2000. With the Microsoft SQL Server 2005 Data Mining Add-In for Office 2007 (yes, two different years in that name), Excel users can easily add data mining to their analytic arsenal. All the details are in Chapter 6.

I hope you enjoy this book and profit from it.

Bill Baker
Distinguished Engineer and GM,
Business Intelligence Applications
Microsoft Corporation
Redmond, WA
October 2007

Preface

Microsoft Office has been the standard against which all other integrated office products have been measured since 1995. Throughout the years, we've watched Office, as everyone now knows it, go from being a somewhat simplistic word processor and spreadsheet to include capabilities such as desktop publishing, sophisticated e-mail and schedule management, and full-featured numeric data management, to the point that many organizations cannot operate on a day-to-day basis without it.

When MS Office 2007 was announced, many of us wondered what else Microsoft could add that would make it worth upgrading to the next version. And then we discovered the new business intelligence features that have been integrated into the fabric of the world's most popular business software.

This book was written for the business user who wants to be able to take advantage of this great new analytical feature set introduced in MS Office 2007. And it was written from the perspective of the non-technical business user, i.e., someone who knows their information and needs to be able to control it on an ad hoc basis without a great deal of training or the assistance of a full-time technical staff.

The examples in this book come from everyday business scenarios, and although the data used in the examples is entirely fictitious, it represents data that is used in real-world situations. For example, there are numerous examples of how you can take your Excel spreadsheets and turn them into analytical resources for your own use and to share with others.

In short, this book endeavors to transform the mystique of business intelligence into practical ways for you to use the information (data) you currently have in a whole new way that will make you better organized, more productive, and ultimately highly successful by managing your information on your own and allowing you to have the answers you need exactly where and when you need them.

Acknowledgments

I'd like to take this opportunity to thank all those who patiently listened to my stream-of-consciousness literary and technical exercises while I worked on this book. The time spent talking with two close friends, Jim Misgen and Mike Provines, who are savvy business users of information in their own fields of industry, helped me better reach my objective to empower the non-technical business person who needs to manage information. I'm also indebted to my co-workers at Cizer Software for helping me validate many of the examples I used in this book, particularly Mike Melzer and Trey Johnson, and to my family, who spent many long evenings reviewing chapters on a deadline.

My sincere thanks also to my technical editor and long-term colleague, Sean Boon, who took time from his busy schedule with the Microsoft Office Business Intelligence product team to work with me on this book, and who has provided excellent technical input throughout the project. And to Kaia Petin, who provided a constant stream of real-world advice on what people really want to understand with a book like this.

And finally, thanks to my extremely patient editor, Wendy Rinaldi, for her constant encouragement and support, without whom this text would not have gotten to press.

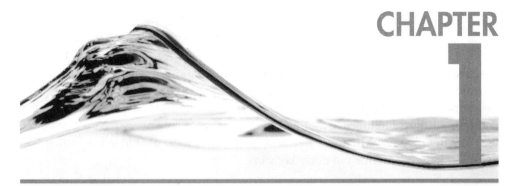

Introduction to Microsoft Office BI Concepts

IN THIS CHAPTER

The Scope of the Book
The Book's Purpose
Setting the Stage
Chapter Content

Thisbook is written for the business user, as well as for the information worker who would like to see working examples of the many features of business intelligence that we've heard about or seen. The chapters do not describe server operating system or database configurations in detail, but they do provide screenshots and exact descriptions to facilitate a comprehensive understanding of the server-based technology in the context of Microsoft Office 2007 as an end-user business intelligence toolset. This book should help everyone understand the "moving parts" of Microsoft Business Intelligence to be able to use reporting, analysis, and measurement in everyday work.

The Scope of the Book

Perhaps the first challenge of working with BI is to understand how different parts of the technology relate to each other, and work together in a "BI solution." This book will show you the details of how PivotTables work, for example—and show you where it is located on a map of Microsoft BI components. The following image will be used throughout the book with a "You are here!" notation to provide a sense of where the chapter pieces fit in the Microsoft Office and SQL Server technologies.

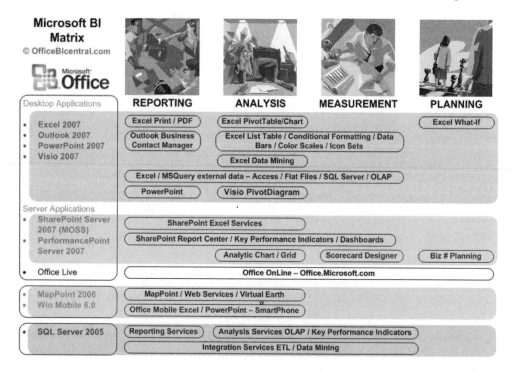

The Book's Purpose

If this book succeeds at one thing, it will be to introduce you to all aspects of Microsoft Business Intelligence, from back-end SQL Server servers to front-end Excel, Outlook, PowerPoint, Visio, and Word, in both stand-alone and collaborative SharePoint environments—using desktop and Windows Mobile Smartphone technologies. We will "push the envelope" with chapters on SQL Server data mining and PerformancePoint.

Setting the Stage

Today we live in a self-service world. We don't give a second thought to pumping our own gas or using an ATM to withdraw money from our bank account. And we've gained a comfort level with computers so that most of us use them practically without thinking. The standing joke when VCRs first came on the market was that anyone could set up their VCR—just put tape over the flashing display. Now special tools have been developed to block programs because even young children know how to access—and probably record—whatever they want.

We're comfortable with taking care of our own needs, both physical and mental. We like being independent and being able to get things done at the time it suits us. So why should business intelligence be any different?

Business intelligence used to conjure up visions of highly sophisticated calculations for financial or data modeling, resulting in stacks of reports streaming out of mainframe printers onto carts that were trundled around to the analysts' offices, sequestered somewhere on the top floor, to be interpreted for the rest of the workforce.

Next came the era of the spreadsheet, which certainly put informational tools at the fingertips of a much broader range of personnel. And most of us today use spreadsheets in some form as easily as we use word processing or e-mail. We've learned that keeping our own information at the ready is more productive and portable, and we've started down the road of personal business intelligence, possibly without even realizing we've done so.

With the advent of the Internet, information exploded into our lives. The world is now online, at our fingertips whenever we need it, and the only thing that may stand in our way is an Internet connection that's temporarily down for repairs. We can walk into an Internet café in almost any part of the world with modern conveniences and "log on." So now that we can access even more information, both from our internal data sources and external connections, how do we make the best use of all that information? And how do we manage to pick out the information we actually want, organize it, and put it to practical use in our everyday lives?

This book is designed to help; with the concepts described you can leverage your comfort with technology—particularly the new Microsoft Office 2007—to learn how to gather, organize, and utilize information to improve your daily performance in your job, and throughout the various aspects of your life, where having the right information in a useful format at the opportune moment will make a positive difference.

Today, you can enjoy self-service business intelligence.

Chapter Content

Every chapter can be read or referenced in a stand-alone manner because everything you need is contained in the chapter. The figures are captioned to help you scan the pages and find areas of interest using the figures as a graphical guide. Also, every chapter provides a BEST REFERENCE URL: "For further research on this topic, go to xxxxx". This is to help the reader quickly find the Internet resource the author found most helpful for the subject matter at hand.

Chapter 2: Excel PivotTables

This chapter provides a thorough exploration of PivotTables in Excel 2007, which is arguably the most popular business intelligence tool of all. The Microsoft Redmond Excel team put a lot of effort into making PivotTables a "mainstream Office experience" in Office 2007, and when combined with conditional formatting, the results are impressive.

The benefit of learning to work with PivotTables is immediate: you can use the interactive nature of a PivotTable and PivotChart to produce different displays of your data with automatic cross-tab subtotaling—which is much more flexible than the usual static spreadsheet rows and columns.

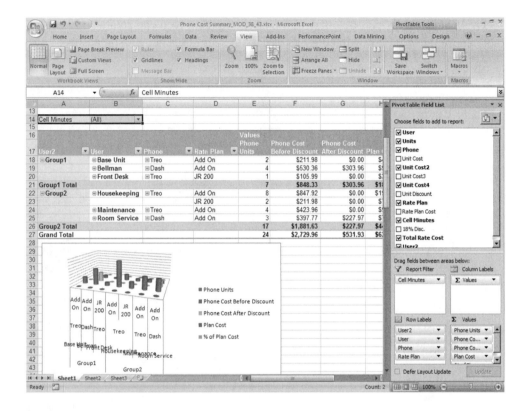

Chapter 3: Excel Tables

This chapter provides a complete exploration of Excel 2007 tables, which were known as Excel lists in previous versions of Office. As you'll see, data can be organized into sorted columns that make sense—and with data filters that make it easy to narrow the data visualization. This is perhaps the quickest way to work with data in Excel today; and whatever else we may think, "a million rows in Excel 2007" is something every Office user can appreciate.

The benefit of tables is that they are so easy and fast—you can create an Excel table in minutes to work with columns of data. It's simply a better "spreadsheet"!

	JAN	FEB	MAR	APR	MAY	JUN	JUL	AUG	SEP	OCT	NOV	DEC
	Column1	Column2	Column3	Column4	Column5	Column6	Column7	Column8	Column9	Column10	Column11	Column12
1957		-38.2	-53.7	-56.5	-55.8	-56.4	-60.8	-58.2	-62.4	-52.8	-37.2	
1958	-25.1	-35.3	-53.8	-62.1	-57.1	-61	-55.1	-61.6	-56.3	-49.3	-38.5	
1959	-28.9	-39.7	-54.7	-55.2	-56.3	-59.9	-59.1	-59.2	-62	-51.4	-41	
1960	-30.6	-39.9	-57.9	-56.6	-55.7	-58.4	-58.4	-62.4	-57.4	-52.1	-38.6	
1961	-30.6	-41.5	-57	-60.1	-57.4	-53	-60.5	-56.6	-57.6	-49.1	-38.5	
1962	-29.9	-41.8	-53.9	-58	-59	-53	-60.2	-60.7	-57.3	-50.7	-37.8	
1963	-29.1	-41.5	-54.4	-60.9	-55.8	-55.1	-59.7	-54.4	-54.4	-51	-41.1	
1964	-27.7	-41.5	-52.9	-61.3	-61.3	-53.9	-56.5	-57.9	-62.5	-53.3	-38.9	
1965	-29.1	-40.1	-52.1	-57.5	-56.4	-52.6	-64.4	-57	-63.1	-52.7	-40.6	
1966	-29.7	-41	-52.6	-56.7	-61.2	-61.5	-58	-61.4	-57.8	-51.3	-37.5	
1967	-24.7	-40.2	-54.8	-57.6	-58.4	-61.4	-56.9	-61.2	-57.8	-53.9	-38.2	
1968	-29.7	-40.1	-54.1	-54.2	-59.3	-58.7	-62.5	-62.1	-61.5	-47.2	-38.2	
1969	-27.9	-42.2	-58	-55	-56.6	-55.6	-64.2	-57.7	-56.9	-48.1	-40.8	
1970	-28.1	-40.7	-53.8	-59.6	-58.8	-60	-60	-59.9	-56.7	-49.1	-40.8	
1971	-25.1	-38.6	-54.9	-53.6	-56	-61.8	-61.5	-60.6	-62.1	-50.3	-37.8	
1972	-26.5	-39.3	-56.3	-57.9	-59.4	-58.6	-59.8	-54.7	-59.9	-47.2	-37.5	
1973	-29.3	-44.1	-55.1	-57.6	-55.4	-60	-59.6	-60.2	-58	-50.5	-35.7	
1974	-27.7	-41.7	-53.9	-57.7	-57.8	-58	-60.9	-55.8	-58.5	-50.8	-39.2	
1975	-27.5	-39.4	-51.8	-58.1	-54.4	-62.2	-62.3	-61	-60.1	-49.5	-38.1	
1976	-27.4	-40.8	-53.9	-59.9	-59.7	-59.1	-60.5	-65.1	-59.2	-51.2	-37.3	
1977	-25.1	-42.2	-53.9	-57.9	-54.7	-56.4	-56.8	-59.6	-62.3	-55.5	-40.1	
1978	-29.8	-40.9	-54.5	-50.4	-57.2	-60.2	-60.4	-62.6	-60.1	-50.1	-38.7	
1979	-28	-40.9	-51.7	-53.4	-61.5	-56.7	-63.6	-61.1	-55.6	-53	-37.9	
1980	-27.3	-40.1	-54.2	-56.7	-55.5	-57.9	-59.8	-62.7	-60	-51.2	-33.7	

Chapter 4: Excel and External Data

Let's face it, Excel is most often used with self-contained spreadsheets of data that business users have manually copied or entered from other sources. But what if we could connect Excel 2007, with its new million-row capability, to all kinds of external data both inside and outside our organizations? The result is shown in this chapter with many working examples of what it means to bring live data into Excel.

The benefit is that connecting to external data will empower you in your everyday work, whether the external data is on your desktop computer, somewhere in your organization, or out on the Internet. You don't have to wait for someone to get the data for you when you can simply use Excel's "Office Data Connection" features to get it yourself.

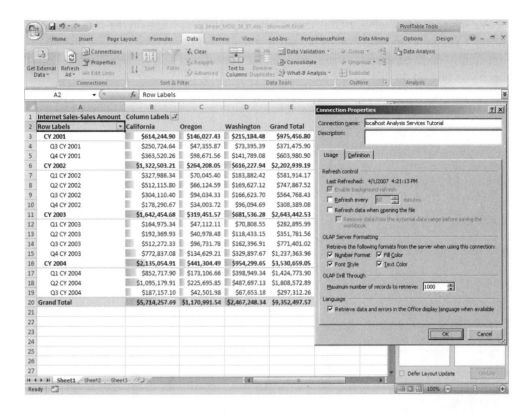

Chapter 5: SharePoint 2007 Dashboards and Reports

First of all, we need to say that SharePoint 2007 "is not the same as previous versions of SharePoint." SharePoint has reached a point of maturity with the 2007 version that actually makes it attractive and useful without endless customer programming! SharePoint is becoming the third ubiquitous Microsoft technology that we see everywhere, in addition to Windows and Office. When we add Office Excel Services to SharePoint we get "collaborative business intelligence," which, as we'll see, makes complete good sense in today's connected world of Microsoft Office application users. Frankly, the dashboards, reports, and Key Performance Indicators in SharePoint are compelling and can answer the business intelligence requirements of most organizations today.

The benefit of SharePoint BI is that it gets all of us "working on the same sheet of music." You don't have to e-mail the latest spreadsheet to everyone when, instead, you simply update the central copy of it on the SharePoint server. This chapter will teach you how to do this!

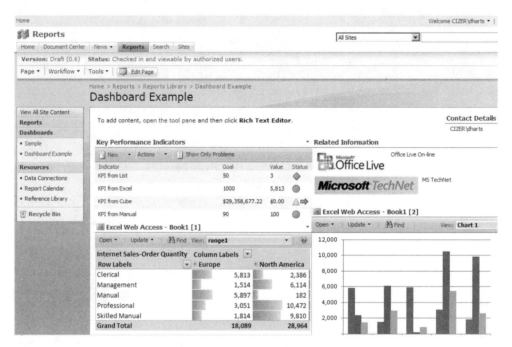

Chapter 6: Data Mining

Okay, so data mining is the ultimate "geek technology" that no one ever really sees in the working world. But what if we could present advanced SQL Server data mining statistical algorithms in Excel 2007? The results are amazing and just might succeed in getting Office knowledge workers to make use of true "data clustering" and "regression forecasting" analysis with Excel spreadsheet data!

The benefit of being able to connect to data mining really comes down to being able to discover clusters of data that, for whatever reason, affect each other and are the most significant parts of your data story. It just makes sense that we should be able to use the power of Excel to do this with huge spreadsheets—and this chapter proves that it's easy.

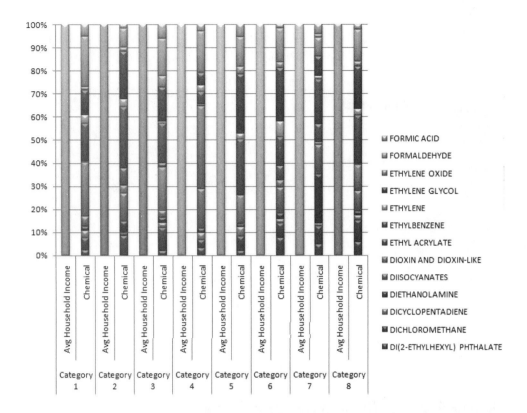

Chapter 7: PerformancePoint

Microsoft is aiming for the high end of enterprise business intelligence with PerformancePoint, which is really two technologies rolled into one server— monitoring and analysis, and planning (MAP). Together the technologies answer the "MAP" needs of geographically dispersed organizations that need to automate their Excel spreadsheet business processes with a server-based model that leverages Excel 2007.

The benefit of PerformancePoint is that it's a better scorecard for the enterprise than any other product on the market because it's built for the SharePoint environment. It's a great product from the Microsoft Office group with Office updates and support, and it can scale across the largest organizations in the world.

Sales Scorecard

| | Q1-06 | | | Q2-06 | | |
	Actual	Target	Actual	Target	Actual
(All) ▼	(All) ▼	(All) ▼	(All) ▼	(All) ▼	(All) ▼
Financial Objectives		●		●	
Revenue		△		△	
Sales Amt		△	$22,912,656	△	$30,663,750
Units	8,995	△	12,546	△	14,286
Margins		◉		◉	
Gross Margin %	18.06%	◉	21.03%	◉	15.02%
Gross Profit %	22.04%	◉	26.64%	◉	17.67%
Costs		◉		◉	
Cost	$13,502,265	◉	$18,092,994	◉	$26,059,138

Trailing 8 Quarter Sales by Product

Chapter 8: All the Other Microsoft BI Pieces

This is the "show and tell" chapter where we can provide working examples that really get everyone thinking about "BI for the masses," which is the central vision of Microsoft Business Intelligence. It's a fast-running and wide-ranging series of discussions that jump from Outlook to PowerPoint and Visio—grounded in a SharePoint environment that reaches to Windows Mobile Smartphone devices. The core foundation of SQL Server Integration Services, Analysis Services, and Reporting Services is explained in high-level terms. And finally, Microsoft's Virtual Earth is connected to Excel 2007 data in a quick working example of "geo-spatial BI"!

The benefit of seeing all these other Microsoft BI pieces is that you know they are real (not just something from a commercial); and in this chapter you'll learn what is involved in getting them to your desktop or Windows Mobile Smartphone. Also, the SQL Server foundation sections are a great way to understand Microsoft's BI server, which can be harnessed to provide reporting, analysis, and measurement for all of us with whatever end-user tools we choose.

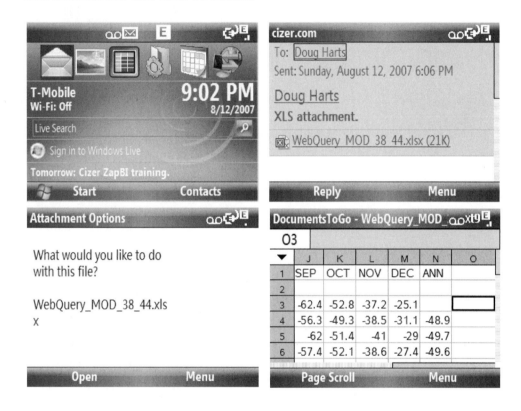

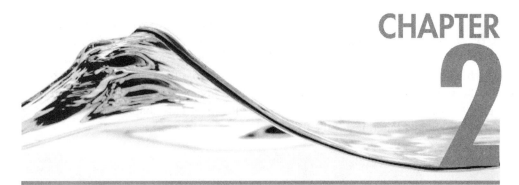

PivotTables, PivotCharts, and Conditional Formatting

This chapter starts with the basics of PivotTables to give you an understanding of this Excel analysis tool. It continues with a complete exploration of Excel 2007 PivotTable features, and then includes conditional formatting, which helps us see relative data values and ranges across thousands of rows of data. We'll discuss PivotCharts, along with some more advanced PivotTable data to round out this subject area of Microsoft business intelligence. This chapter will provide examples and explanations of the following:

- ▶ Creating a PivotTable

- ▶ Conditional formatting

- ▶ Adding a PivotChart

- ▶ Slicing and dicing the PivotTable and PivotChart

BEST REFERENCE

For further reasearch on this topic, go to http://office.microsoft.com/office/excel/training.

What Is a PivotTable?

In the working world of desktop business intelligence tools, Excel is used by millions of people for spreadsheets of text and numbers, row and column calculations, and meetings and sales presentations. But what if those rows and columns could provide

Technology Positioning Statement

PivotTables are probably the most improved area of the Excel product, particularly from a BI perspective. Most notable is the replacement of the old drag-and-drop interface with a new field well dialog box that enables users to simply check off which attributes they'd like to see—and Excel automatically provides a default layout. The display of the PivotTable and the available filtering options are different in Excel 2007 as well. For example, 2007 PivotTables have new value and date filtering options. There is also a new compact axis feature, which is the default on 2007 PivotTables, designed to improve the readability of PivotTables as members are expanded and collapsed.

—Sean Boon, Microsoft Excel Team

an interactive experience that would allow us to easily click and arrange the data cells on the computer screen for our own analysis or during meetings with other people—with automatic formatting and totaling on the fly?

That is the job of PivotTables, and Excel can provide this slice-and-dice capability right on the screen with the click of a mouse. It takes static presentations and turns them into dynamic analysis tools. And it's easy to make PivotTables and PivotCharts look good in Excel 2007! This chapter will present the beginning-to-end process of creating a PivotTable and a PivotChart in Excel 2007, with conditional formatting for analysis.

The following illustration shows an example of an Excel 2007 PivotTable, with the new PivotTable Field List selection pane. This chapter will explore the steps used to create this example PivotTable.

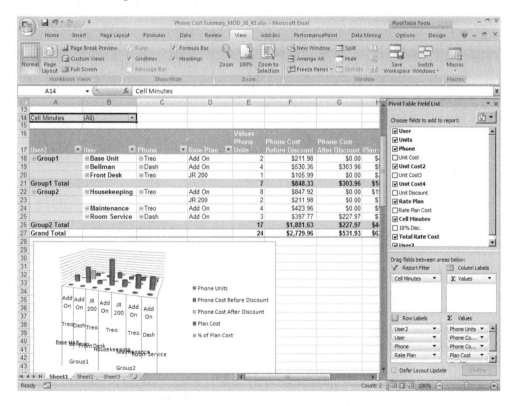

Where Do PivotTables Fit in the Microsoft BI Picture?

The following illustration shows a matrix view of Microsoft Business Intelligence technology (often referred to as BI). The Office, SharePoint, and SQL Server applications we see in the marketplace are shown on the left side of the matrix.

These applications are used in the real-world activities of reporting, analysis, measurement, and planning as shown across the top of the matrix. The top-down flow of the matrix starts with front-end BI tools we have in Office 2007 at our desktops—and goes down to back-end BI tools that run on servers such as SharePoint 2007 and Performance Point 2007, which provide an enhanced experience when connected to Office 2007.

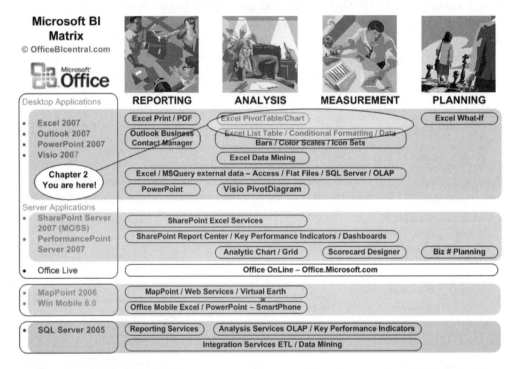

Learning about PivotTables makes more sense if we know where they fit in the Microsoft technology stack, and what they are used for in daily BI activities. The "You are here!" bubble in the illustration shows PivotTables as part of Excel 2007, which is part of Office 2007. We're going to use PivotTables and PivotCharts with conditional formatting for analysis work, as appears in the second column of the BI matrix.

PivotTables are one of the most commonly heard of, but least understood, mechanisms in spreadsheets because end users don't realize how easily they can be created. And yet as this chapter will show, everyday working spreadsheets can be significantly enhanced by using data you already have and putting it into Excel 2007 PivotTable tools. And you'll see that in Excel 2007, the new PivotTable interface makes it much easier for business users to understand what data should be placed where in the PivotTable to make a good presentation.

Opening an Excel 2003 Spreadsheet in Excel 2007

Figure 2-1 shows a real-world spreadsheet for cell phone plans from the telecommunications industry, used to present phone plans to prospective customers. This spreadsheet does not have an overly large amount of data because it is meant to represent the Excel 2003 files that are commonly a part of today's working environment. (It should be noted, however, that whereas Excel 2003 could hold 65,000 rows, Excel 2007 can hold up to a million rows of data!) This chapter will help you understand how to use PivotTables and PivotCharts with your working spreadsheets as well.

The spreadsheet in Figure 2-1 is not connected to any data sources; all data is contained in the cells shown. Because this spreadsheet is currently an Excel 2003 spreadsheet, the filename is displayed as Phone Cost Summary_MOD.xls [Compatibility Mode] on the title bar at the top of the Excel 2007 window. When you save spreadsheets created in previous versions of Excel, Excel 2007 saves them in their original formats unless you choose to Save As Excel 2007. This is a nice feature that helps keep compatibility with earlier versions of Excel for other users that might not yet be using Office 2007. Excel 2007 will prompt you to Save As Excel 2007 if you add version 2007 enhancements to your spreadsheet.

To open an Excel 2003 spreadsheet in Excel 2007, simply click an existing Excel 2003 XLS file; it will open in Excel 2007 if Office 2007 is installed on your desktop or laptop. You can also click the Office button in the upper-left corner of Office Excel 2007, choose File | Open, and browse to the file of your choice.

	A	B	C	D	E	F	G	H	I	J	K	L	M
1	Summary of Phone Costs												
2					Total	Discount	Total Discount						
3	User	Units	Phone	Unit Cost	Unit Cost	Unit Cost	Unit Cost	Unit Discount	Rate Plan	Rate Plan Cost	Cell Minutes	18% Disc.	Total Rate Cost
4	Front Desk	1	Treo	$105.99	$105.99	($105.99)	$0.00	($105.99)	JR 200	$45.98	400	$8.28	$37.70
5	Housekeeping	1	Treo	$105.99	$105.99	($105.99)	$0.00	($105.99)	JR 200	$45.98	400	$8.28	$37.70
6	Housekeeping	1	Treo	$105.99	$105.99	($105.99)	$0.00	($105.99)	JR 200	$45.98	400	$8.28	$37.70
7	Housekeeping	8	Treo	$105.99	$847.92	($105.99)	$0.00	($847.92)	Add On	$30.00	0	$5.40	$196.80
8	Maintenance	4	Treo	$105.99	$423.96	($105.99)	$0.00	($423.96)	Add On	$30.00	0	$5.40	$98.40
9	Room Service	3	Dash	$132.59	$397.77	$75.99	$227.97	($169.80)	Add On	$30.00	0	$5.40	$73.80
10	Bellman	4	Dash	$132.59	$530.36	$75.99	$303.96	($226.40)	Add On	$30.00	0	$5.40	$98.40
11	Base Unit	2	Treo	$105.99	$211.98	($105.99)	$0.00	($211.98)	Add On	$30.00	0	$5.40	$49.20
12		24			$2,729.96		$531.93	($2,198.03)			1200		$629.71

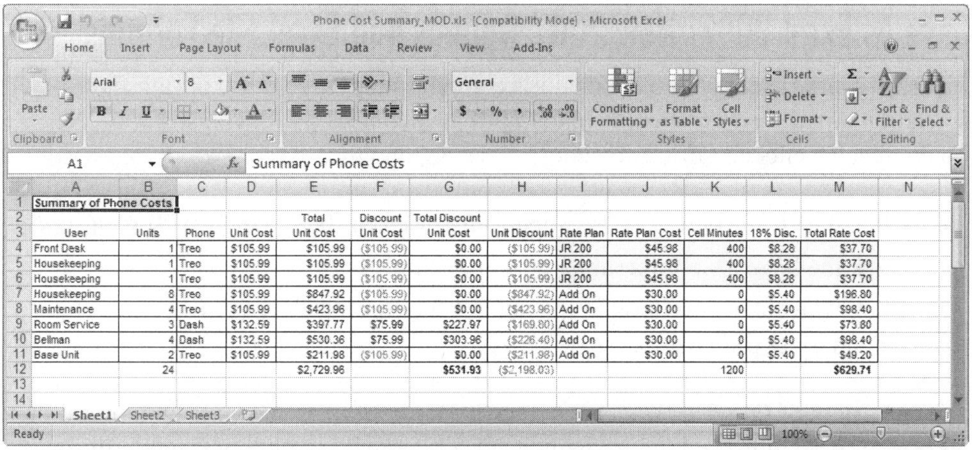

Figure 2-1 *A real-world Excel 2003 worksheet with no PivotTable*

The Business Reason for a PivotTable

The spreadsheet in our example is used to present unit and rate plan information to customers, but it has always required an explanation to help the customer see the value of the overall plan because the data was not easily understood, and the overall look was not compelling enough for presentations. The business purpose of adding a PivotTable and a PivotChart to this spreadsheet is to improve the look and feel of the information being presented. If we do our job right in this chapter, the pertinent data for cell phone users, cell phone plans, and costs will be easier to comprehend in a way that lets the customer see the various components at a glance and dynamically compare various data elements, such as rates versus plans.

BI TIP

Nicely formatted data that forms a good first impression in Excel and a clickable interactive presentation are part of the mission of business intelligence in the real world with Office 2007.

Note that a spreadsheet such as this may or may not come from a corporate library of examples, and it may or may not be connected to a central server of data. But that doesn't matter, since Excel 2007 makes it easy for you to add professional touches as a part of Microsoft Office right on your desktop or laptop—resulting in changes that will help convey information to the customer and deliver a compelling message. You won't need to ask an IT specialist for help, and you don't have to be connected to a database server! With Excel 2007 you have the power to make Business Intelligence work for you with spreadsheets you already have!

Save As Excel 2007: New 2007 Options and Excel File Formats

Figure 2-2 shows that we've decided it's a good time to save our working Excel spreadsheet in the new format of Excel 2007, which uses a file type suffix of .XLSX. To do this, we clicked Office and chose Save As, and then Excel Workbook.

1. Click the Office button in the upper-left corner of the Excel 2007 screen.
2. Click the Save As option in the pop-up menu.
3. Click "Save the workbook in the default file format" (.XLSX file type) on the secondary pop-up menu.

The variety of Excel 2007 save choices is less confusing if you keep in mind that all of your work will be done in the new XLSX format—which is the default for Excel 2007. XLSX is actually an XML format that supports the move toward open file formats for all of Microsoft Office 2007 that can be opened by either Microsoft

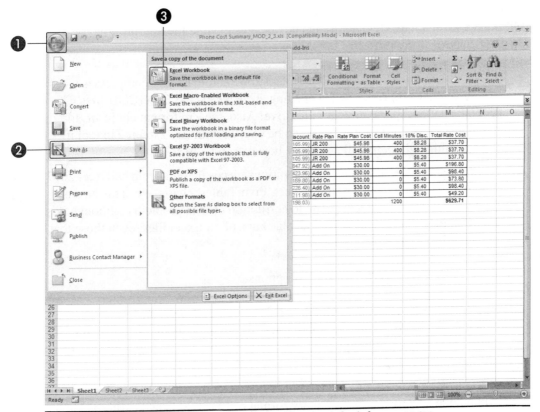

Figure 2-2   *Excel 2007 Save As | Excel Workbook; default format XLSX*

or non-Microsoft applications. XML formats in general have become the standard for data and files that exist outside of a database server, and it's worth noting that XML files can be opened in common tools such as Microsoft Notepad (although you don't get the Excel interface and toolset when the file is opened with Notepad).

Note that spreadsheets can be saved in a 97–2003 format as well for backward compatibility—to allow users of Office 97 through Office 2003 to open them as well. Or users of Office 2003 can download a free compatibility option from Microsoft that allows them to open the new XLSX 2007 files.

BI TIP

XML formats for Business Intelligence tools are increasingly popular with companies that favor the non-proprietary nature of XML files. And it makes sense that modern Business Intelligence tools support XML formats whose data can more readily be shared among multiple applications in companies today. So although the XML formats might not affect stand-alone users of Office 2007, it's something we expect with today's computer applications.

It's worth noting that the new Office 2007 XML formats, including the Excel 2007 XLSX format, have two additional advantages beyond the non-proprietary appeal of an XML format itself:

► XLSX is actually a Zipped file that Excel 2007 automatically compresses when saving, and decompresses when opening. This means the Excel 2007 files will take up less space on your hard drive! Also, the Zip format conforms to the industry standard format, so it can be opened with any Zip/un-Zip tool if desired (although there will not likely be a reason to do so).

► XLSX contains separate files for the various pieces that make up an Excel 2007 workbook, such as the base spreadsheet, PivotTables, charts, etc. This means the Excel 2007 files are less prone to corruption or data problems (although it is expected that you will make periodic backups of all Excel files, even those that are work-in-progress).

Note the other Excel 2007 Save format options:

► **Excel Macro-Enabled Workbook**   This is for workbooks that need to contain macros. As a security feature, macros are not contained in everyday Excel spreadsheets, although they can be a powerful way to add advanced or custom functionality.

► **Excel Binary Workbook**   This saves workbooks in a 2007 Binary format. Although this is like the XLS Binary format of Excel 2003 and earlier versions, it is only meant to be opened by Excel 2007, since it will contain Excel 2007–specific features.

► **Excel 97–2003 Workbook**   This saves workbooks in the older Excel 97, 2000, and 2003 format. Although 2007 features may be lost or not function in earlier Excel versions, this is important if you need to send an Excel workbook to someone who does not have Office Excel 2007.

BI TIP

Note that the PDF Save option is not available in Office 2007 until you download the free Microsoft Save As PDF or XPS file from the Microsoft.com/Office web site, where you'll find menu options to check for free updates or Office downloads.

► **PDF or XPS**   This saves workbooks in the Adobe Portable Document Format (PDF) format or the Microsoft XML Paper Specification (XPS). PDFs are a popular format that can be viewed by virtually everyone for free. Saving Excel workbooks as PDF files also allows you to share information with many other users without allowing them to modify the contents—which is a great way to distribute financial proposals or statements that need to remain unedited. XPS is a Microsoft XML format that provides a PDF-like experience. It can be output from all Office 2007 applications and can be viewed within Office 2007 or with a free XPS viewer from Microsoft.

Office 2007 Ribbon Menu: A Brand-New Look in 2007

Figure 2-3 shows our workbook open in the Excel 2007 format—note compatibility mode no longer appears at the top title bar of the Excel screen. To get this display, we actually closed the spreadsheet after saving it as a 2007 Excel workbook, and then reopened it. This is the best way to experience the Excel 2007 features, and in fact we don't want to be slowed down by the previous compatibility mode interface that uses some of the older Excel 2003 displays.

In Figure 2-3 note the Office button for file-level actions (sporting the Office 2007 logo) in the upper-left corner of the screen—clicking the Office button will show common file menu items such as Open, Save, and Print. Visually moving down to the Tabs part of the Ribbon menu, we see some appealing graphics that provide an intuitive guide to common tasks at four levels that follow the Figure 2-3 screen annotations (a, b, c, and d):

a. Looking at the Excel Ribbon, we see a top-level tab interface that organizes spreadsheet tasks into common areas; Home, Insert, Page Layout, Formulas, Data, Review, View, and Add-Ins.

b. Looking within the Options tab, we see a variety of submenu tasks: PivotTable, Active Field, Group, Sort, Data, Actions, Tools, and Show/Hide.

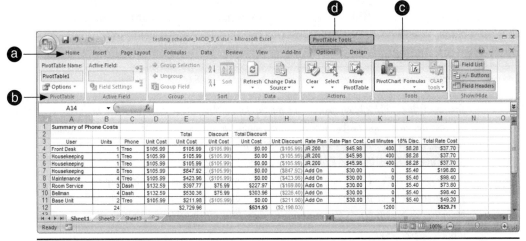

Figure 2-3 *Excel 2007 Ribbon menu, Office button, groups, icons, and context tabs*

    c. Looking within the Tools group, we see a variety of icon menu items for PivotChart, Formulas, and OLAP tools. These menu icons are really the foundation of working Business Intelligence in the context of Office 2007!

    d. When some menu icons are chosen, contextual tabs appear as more tabs along the top level of the Ribbon interface. In our working example, when we click the Insert tab and then click the PivotTable icon, we'll proceed to insert a PivotTable and end up working with PivotTable tools context tabs for options and designs that are available once we're working with a PivotTable on the screen.

BI TIP

You're well advised to open your existing spreadsheets in Excel 2007, save them in the new 2007 Excel workbook format, and then reopen them! You can always save your work in the Excel 97–2003 workbook format if you need to share the spreadsheet with other users that might not yet have Office 2007. In fact, Excel 2007 has a compatibility checker to show if any new 2007 items will be degraded when Saved As 97–2003 spreadsheets — this is available by clicking the Office button on the top left of the Excel 2007 screen, and choosing Prepare | Run Compatibility Checker.

It is worth pausing at this point for a brief discussion of the new Office 2007 menu layout. Microsoft has put a great deal of effort into consolidating the thousands of Office menu commands and choices into this new format. All of the Office 2007 applications use the new Ribbon menu approach for their user interface, notably Excel, Access, PowerPoint, Outlook, and Word.

Our step-by-step instructions in this chapter will primarily use the Ribbon menu icon-based tabbed/grouped interface to accomplish our work, for the purpose of consistency. Right-click and context-sensitive menus are also a significant part of the Office 2007 interface, however, and we'll use them whenever we go beyond the immediate options of the Ribbon menu. As you gain familiarity with the new Office 2007 interface, you'll probably develop your own favorite right-click menu paths in everyday work routines.

BI TIP

The new Office 2007 Ribbon menu is a big jump forward for Office applications — and it is perhaps the most important element of commonality to tie together Excel, Access, PowerPoint, Outlook, and Word since the early days of Office integration years ago. If you're a long-time power user of Excel, the new Ribbon menu will take some getting used to; although it honestly will be just a couple of days till you're comfortable with it, and then you probably won't ever want to return to the old way of doing work! And note the Ribbon menu look-and-feel is quickly becoming ubiquitous across Microsoft applications, from Microsoft Office SharePoint Server (MOSS) to Visio 2007.

The basic elements of the Ribbon menu are straightforward—the Office button, tabs, groups within the tabs, and icons within the groups. Office 2007 sports a much richer set of icons that display across the Ribbon menu and provide an intuitive idea of the actions that can be accomplished by clicking the icons.

Furthermore, many of the icons provide a live preview capability where the onscreen spreadsheet display will change as you hover the mouse over an icon but won't actually change the spreadsheet until you click and choose the icon action. This really makes working with Excel 2007 much faster, since you don't have to keep changing spreadsheet elements back and forth to get visual feedback on formatting and row-column arrangements. In fact, you can mouse over a gallery of choices that may have a large number of options, and very quickly find the appearance you want.

BI TIP

A very useful part of the new 2007 interface is the Zoom slider control that always appears at the lower right of the screen. It's amazing how often we find ourselves using this to zoom the display in or out—to bring whatever we want to see within the viewable screen.

Another helpful aspect of the Office 2007 Ribbon menu design is that the tabs and groups of icons follow your workflow of creating content. So with Excel 2007 we start at the Home tab with the common text and number formatting menu items, followed by the Insert tab, where we can start on a PivotTable / PivotChart inserted onto the spreadsheet, for example.

Subsequent tabs hold groups of icons for more advanced formulas and data work, and at the end of the default tab strip we find tabs for Review and View to help in the finalization of the workbook. Note we'll always wind up back at the Office button for saving and printing, and a surprisingly wide range of menu choices for Prepare, Send, and Publish, which hold some important capabilities that allow us to really control workbook content and delivery using e-mail or Microsoft Office SharePoint, for example.

BI TIP

One important thing to note about the new Ribbon menu is the location of the Properties menu item for a workbook. Click the Office button and choose Prepare | Properties to bring up a dialog box where you can edit the Author, Title, etc., of your workbook. This can be helpful to avoid surprises when someone else looks at your spreadsheet and sees information you didn't even know was there!

Getting Started: Selecting Data for the PivotTable

As shown in Figure 2-4 we're going to select all the data in the spreadsheet and see what we can do with the PivotTable tools in Excel. We're not going to worry about selecting just part of the data—we'll just go with everything and choose what we want from the PivotTable user interface. We can also just click the PivotTable icon itself instead of the drop-down arrow on the icon; we'll go immediately to the Create PivotTable dialog box and bypass the choice of PivotTable versus PivotChart.

1. Left-click the top-left corner of data Cell A2, and while holding down the left mouse button drag the cursor to the bottom-right corner of data Cell M11.

2. Click the Insert tab on the Ribbon menu, and then click the PivotTable icon in the Tables menu group, on the Ribbon menu Insert tab.

3. Click the PivotTable icon on the pop-up menu.

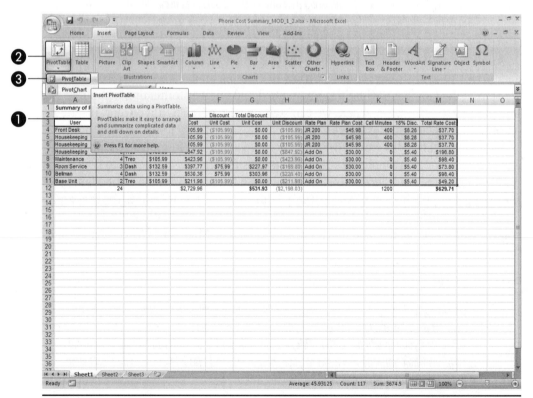

Figure 2-4   *Selected data for use in a PivotTable, choosing Insert | PivotTable*

Note we did not select the column totals on Row 12 because PivotTables by their very nature will automatically provide all the totals and subtotals we need. Note also that we did not worry about trying to select just part of the cell data—we'll take care of that with the PivotTable tools themselves.

Figure 2-5 shows the Create PivotTable dialog box that pops up when the Insert | PivotTable menu item is chosen. Note how in the area of the dialog box labeled "Choose the data that you want to analyze," the Select A Table Or Range option button is automatically chosen, and the Cell Range we selected is automatically showing in the text box as Table/Range: Sheet1!$A$3:$M$11.

1. Click the Existing Worksheet option button on the lower half of the Create PivotTable dialog box.

2. Click the cell-selection icon at the end of the Location text box, which allows you to directly click the spreadsheet.

3. Click Cell A16 on the spreadsheet itself to automatically place Sheet1!$A$16 in the text box for Location, and then click OK.

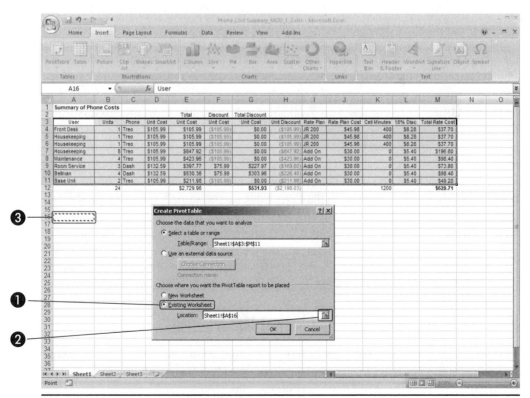

Figure 2-5   *Create PivotTable dialog box in Excel 2007*

Also note the Table/Range does not include Row 2, even though Row 2 was part of our selected data area. Excel automatically recognizes the text in Row 3 cells as possible data labels but does not know how to use the text in Row 2 cells, which are farther from the data cells.

This will not be a problem in the PivotTable interface because we can rename the data labels when working in the PivotTable interface (thus, we may rename the second Unit Cost data element to Total Cost if we make use of it in the PivotTable). This is typical of real-world scenarios where you'll want to change or improve text items in the PivotTable presentation for clarity.

BI TIP

It is typical of Business Intelligence work that we don't want to spend too much time improving an imperfect data source that is accurate enough to work with, when we can instead spend our time improving the Business Intelligence presentation with good Business Intelligence tools.

In this working example we are not going to "Use an external data source," which involves a different menu path that can bring in data from a wide variety of relational and multidimensional data sources. A wealth of data types and data manipulation techniques are available with external data sources, but for now we're going to learn how to deal with PivotTables on our own turf—our self-contained, stand-alone Phone Cost Summary Excel spreadsheet, which has data that anyone might have entered themselves in the course of a workday.

We are not going to use the New Worksheet option button, even though it is the default choice, because we don't want to have to go back and forth between separate sheets in our workbook to see the original spreadsheet and the PivotTable and PivotChart we are creating. Clicking the Existing Worksheet option button in the "Choose where you want the PivotTable report to be placed" area of the dialog box allows us to work with the PivotTable on the same Excel sheet as the original spreadsheet. This will help with the before and after comparisons we'll be discussing as we look at the standard cell data and its corresponding interactive presentation in PivotTable form. To create the Cell Reference, we simply click Cell A16 to automatically place the correct Cell Reference in the text box as Location: Sheet1!$A16. Then we can click OK to actually start the PivotTable design.

How to Choose PivotTable Fields That Make Sense

This section is where the concept of PivotTables first comes into focus. We're going to look carefully at the user interface to gain a high-level understanding of what we're building with PivotTable rows, columns, and values.

BI TIP

Frankly, a PivotTable is just rows, columns, and values in an automatic cross-tab spreadsheet! Once those are in place, we use the Excel 2007 PivotTable menu function to add sophistication.

And then, working within the concept of a PivotTable, all we have to do is choose the rows, columns, and values. Excel 2007 sports a new user interface for choosing and formatting the PivotTable elements. It is a big improvement over PivotTable interfaces in past versions of Excel—and many people in the Business Intelligence industry believe that Excel 2007 can finally bring PivotTables and PivotCharts into the mainstream of everyday business work.

The PivotTable 2007 Interface: Understanding Screen Components

Figure 2-6 shows a blank PivotTable anchored on Cell A16. As we choose the PivotTable elements in the PivotTable Field List pane on the right, the blank PivotTable will fill with data and put in place automatic cross-tab subtotaling.

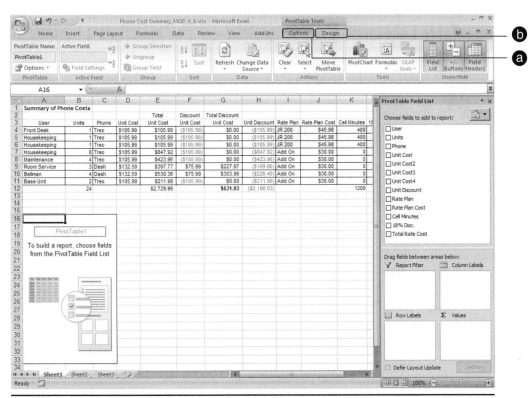

Figure 2-6 *Excel 2007 PivotTable interface and PivotTable tools context tabs*

This is the new Excel 2007 PivotTable user interface, and it's where we'll do most of our work in this chapter. And we'll find that the PivotTable elements can easily be arranged and rearranged using the PivotTable Field List pane.

Note that the top-level Ribbon menu has changed since we've started working with a PivotTable; two new context tabs are displaying under a top-menu heading of PivotTable Tools to provide items we'll need in working with PivotTables and PivotCharts. This is exactly how the new Office 2007 Ribbon menu is supposed to work; menu tabs with new choices are automatically made available to the user whenever we're working with Excel items that require additional tools. The following explanations correspond to the similarly labeled areas in Figure 2-6.

    a. **Options tab**   This is what we'll use for arranging the various elements of the PivotTable, such as Field display options and the +/− Expand/Collapse buttons. Excel is automatically displaying this tab, ready for us to start working with the PivotTable we are inserting onto the original spreadsheet.

    b. **Design tab**   Here we'll find tools to format the look and feel of the PivotTable, such as subtotals and overall styles to easily add color.

PivotTable Columns, Values, Rows, Filters: The New Look in 2007

In Figure 2-7 the blank PivotTable graphic has been expanded to help us talk about the main components of columns, values, and rows. The graphic is not an actual PivotTable; it is just a placemarker on the spreadsheet to give the user a sense of where the PivotTable will be located. As we select elements in the PivotTable Field List pane on the right, the actual PivotTable on the left will automatically expand to accommodate fields that we place in the areas of the PivotTable. The following explanations correspond to the similarly labeled areas in Figure 2-7.

    a. **Column Labels**   Fields placed here will become expandable columns. It can help to think of this as a way to categorize data, such as breaking out the cell phone data by Phone in our working example. It is also used to show a progression or trending of data, such as breaking out data by month. Column fields are normally text or date data.

    b. **Values**   Fields placed here will automatically be subtotaled by row and by column. It can help to think of this as a place to automatically add up numbers from the data, such as cell phone cost in our working example. Value items are normally numeric or currency data.

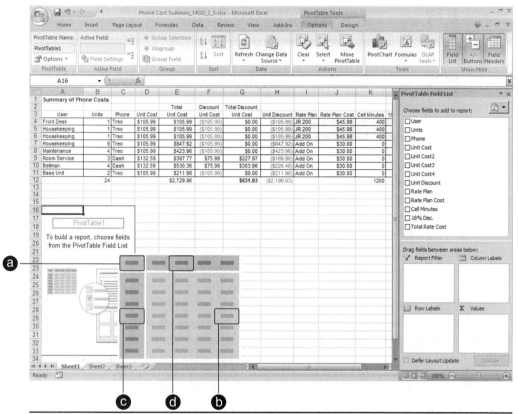

Figure 2-7   *Excel 2007 PivotTable interface and PivotTable field list elements*

c.   **Row Labels**   Fields placed here will become expandable rows. It can help to think of this as a way to group data, such as organizing the cell phone data by User in our working example. Row fields are normally text data.

d.   **Report Filter**   This is a fourth area of the PivotTable that will appear above the rows and columns. The distinct data values of Report Filter fields can be used to dynamically filter or narrow all the data in the PivotTable, without having to show the Report Filter fields in the main area of the PivotTable. In our working example we might use a Report Filter to show only cell phone data for plans with 400 minutes available.

The PivotTable Field List Pane: Data for the PivotTable

On the right side of the interface we see an area that contains the prompt "Choose fields to add to report"; the PivotTable Field List pane is the key to choosing fields for the PivotTable. Note that the original spreadsheet Column D Unit Cost appears in the PivotTable field list as Unit Cost, whereas the original spreadsheet Column E Total Unit Cost appears in the PivotTable field list as Unit Cost 2. Excel used just one row from the original spreadsheet to automatically create field names, and thus differentiated the various Unit Cost columns by adding sequential suffix numbers to the name. This won't be a problem, since we'll be able to change the names as we continue with our example.

The PivotTable Field List pane also has a drop-down button following the "Choose fields to add to report" label. This drop-down button is not used to choose fields—it just allows you to rearrange the working display order of the internal areas within the PivotTable Field List pane. We won't be using the drop-down button, since we're working with the default working display arrangement.

We also won't be using the Defer Layout Update checkbox at the bottom of the PivotTable Field List pane; in fact, it does not do anything when working with data that is internal, or self-contained with the spreadsheet. It is used when connected to external data, for arranging and formatting PivotTable fields without waiting for external data to be refreshed with each change.

Fields for the PivotTable will be chosen from the checkbox list of fields and placed into the four rectangles at the bottom of the PivotTable Field List pane where we see the prompt "Drag fields between areas below." Note there is no need to be concerned about whether you click the checkbox for a field from the checkbox list, or whether you drag and drop a field from the checkbox list into the "Drag fields between . . ." rectangles at the bottom of the PivotTable Field List pane. These mouse actions all have the same effect, and the filter, column, row, and values can be moved among the lower rectangles as desired.

PivotTable Fields: Choosing Data Elements in Excel 2007

In Figure 2-8 the User field has been added to the PivotTable by clicking the checkbox for the User field in the PivotTable Field List pane. Note that clicking the User field automatically placed it into the Row Labels rectangle within the PivotTable Field List pane—and it automatically placed it onto the actual PivotTable on the left side of the screen.

We're initially choosing this field simply because in looking at the original spreadsheet, it seems to be one of the base pieces of information upon which we can build our PivotTable presentation. Don't be too concerned about the order of PivotTable field placement, however, since we can change the fields at any time; we'll just go with the fields that seem to make sense as we proceed through this section and see what the actual PivotTable looks like.

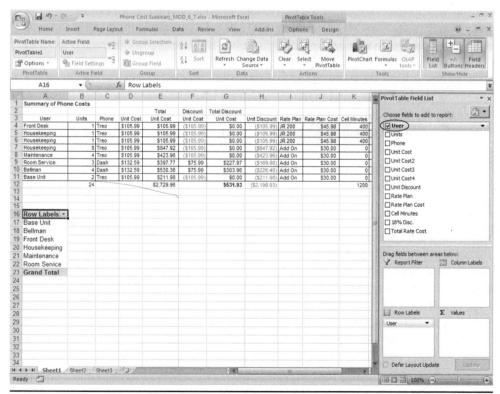

Figure 2-8   *PivotTable Field List User added to row labels*

To achieve a commonsense arrangement of data in PivotTables, it helps to think in order of general to specific when adding fields to the PivotTable. This will result in a hierarchical grouping that becomes apparent as you work with the PivotTable.

Excel 2007 automatically placed the User field into the Row Labels area to help us, as we normally think first in terms of Rows when looking at the actual PivotTable—and furthermore Excel automatically recognized the User data as text that typically belongs in PivotTable rows or columns. These helpful actions are typical of how the new Office 2007 menus and commands try to mirror our daily work flow—in this case to help everyday business people to start working with PivotTables—so we don't have to be Excel power users!

Also note that the User field on the PivotTable is showing distinct values in sorted order even though they were not sorted in the original spreadsheet. This is a helpful way to start looking at the PivotTable display; realizing we can reorder the field values in any way we choose later on—if, for example, it might help to show the Front Desk value first and the Base Unit last because that might be the order in which customers understand their business operation.

In Figure 2-9 the Phone field has been added to the PivotTable by clicking the checkbox for the Phone field in the PivotTable Field List pane. Note that Excel automatically placed it into the Row Labels rectangle within the PivotTable Field List pane—and it automatically placed it onto the actual PivotTable on the left side of the screen.

We chose this field next because, looking at the original spreadsheet, it makes sense to think of organizing the data by User, as we build this PivotTable presentation for a customer.

And look at how Excel is already organizing the fields on the actual PivotTable: the Phones are automatically matched with their Users—in fact the beauty of the PivotTable is that this can't be broken! So even if you're new to PivotTables, the data from various fields will be automatically related for you on the PivotTable. Excel has also added Collapse button controls to the PivotTable; so you can experiment with clicking the Collapse buttons to minimize the display of data. When a field row is collapsed, an Expand button appears to allow you to open up the row of data again. This is just the kind of click-and-change experience that gets people so enthused about PivotTables once they start using them.

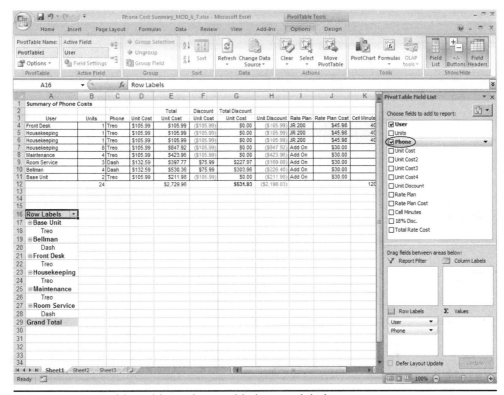

Figure 2-9   *PivotTable Field List Phone added to row labels*

BI TIP

PivotTables always arrange fields from either spreadsheet data or external data—in an order that correctly matches the original data relationships—no matter how you swap fields in or out of the PivotTable rows, columns, and values.

In Figure 2-10 the Rate Plan field has been added to the PivotTable by clicking the checkbox for the Rate Plan field in the PivotTable Field List pane. Note that Excel automatically placed it into the Row Labels rectangle within the PivotTable Field List pane—and it automatically placed it onto the actual PivotTable on the left side of the screen.

We chose this field next because our conversation with the customer might logically follow an explanation of Users, followed by Phone, and then Rate Plans

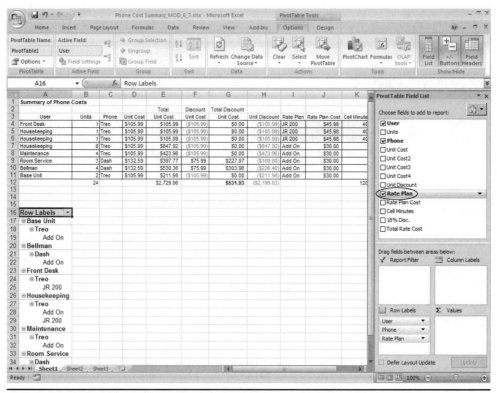

Figure 2-10 *PivotTable Field List Rate Plan added to row labels*

for those Users with Phones. We're trying to build the PivotTable in support of a customer meeting where Excel can be the primary presentation in the discussion, and the PivotTable can really show off with dynamic data visualizations for the customer.

BI TIP

Data presentations should be understandable at a glance with visually compelling mechanisms — this role is most commonly filled by Office 2007 Business Intelligence in the everyday working world.

At this point some of the automatic functionality of the PivotTable is becoming apparent on the screen:

▶ **Users** Users are row-grouped into Base Unit, Bellman, Front Desk, etc.

▶ **Phones** Phones are row-grouped, within each User value, into Treo and Dash. In our working example there is just one type of Phone for each User, such as a Treo for the Base Unit.

▶ **Rate Plans**   Rate Plans are row-grouped, within each Phone value, into Add On and JR 200. In our working example there are two Rate Plans, Add On and JR 200, for the Treo Phone that is assigned to Housekeeping.

In Figure 2-11 the Phone field has been swapped with the User field so that Phone shows first. As you can see, the PivotTable has automatically rearranged itself and the fields are displayed in the correct order! The ability to arrange data in Excel and to use drag-and-drop is familiar to Office users. What's new in Excel 2007 is that the menu-mouse methods work more consistently for the Business Intelligence tasks at hand; they are more intuitive and draw from lessons learned by Microsoft in previous versions of Office.

1. Locate the User field in the Row Labels rectangle of the PivotTable Field List pane on the right (if you click it and a pop-up menu appears; simply click the field again to close the pop-up).

2. Hold the left mouse button down over the User field, and drag it down past the Phone field (a thin black line will move with the field to indicate where it will drop).

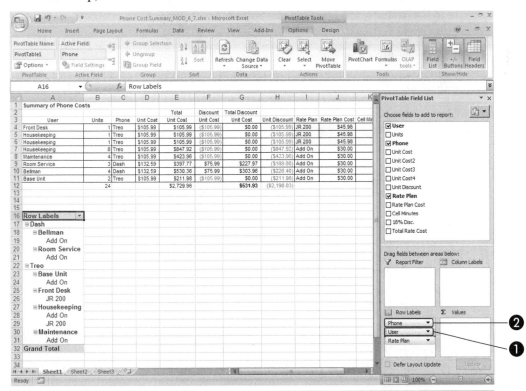

Figure 2-11   *PivotTable User field swapped to display after Phone field*

You can drag the User field back above the Phone field to reset the PivotTable display.

Note the PivotTable fields can be arranged in any order that makes sense! Thus we switched Users and Phone, perhaps because we want to talk about the great Phones available to the customer and then visually see how the Phones are distributed across the different Users. This can be done during our presentation to the customer. Furthermore, these PivotTable fields can be changed or swapped at any time—even by the customer themselves in Excel 2007 once they learn they can click the various PivotTable components—or by ourselves in front of the customer, where being able to manipulate the PivotTable live and in person can help tell a business story. This is part of the dynamic thought process that is supported by Excel's interactive PivotTables.

In Figure 2-12 we see the PivotTable is shaping up fast! The fields Units, Unit Cost2, Unit Cost4, and Total Rate Cost have been added to the PivotTable. Excel automatically placed these fields into the Values rectangle within the PivotTable

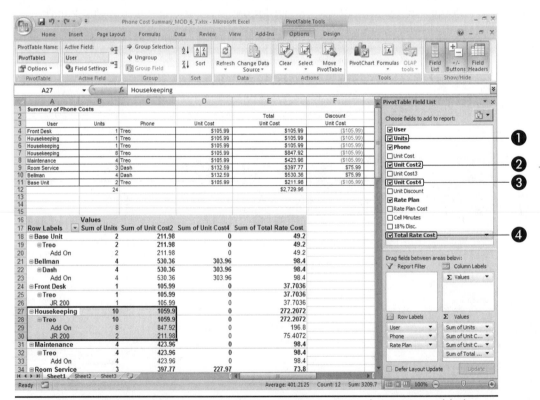

Figure 2-12 *PivotTable Field List Units, Unit Cost2, Unit Cost4, Total Rate Cost added to Values*

Field List pane because they are numeric—and it automatically placed them onto the actual PivotTable on the left side of the screen.

1. Click the checkbox for the Units field in the PivotTable Field List pane.
2. Click the checkbox for the Unit Cost2 field.
3. Click the checkbox for the Unit Cost4 field.
4. Click the checkbox for the Total Rate Cost field.

We chose these fields because in our presentation to the customer, it makes sense to show the number of Phones being provided in the scenario, the cost of the Phones before and after a discount is applied, and the cost of the Rate Plans. We're not going to worry about Unit Cost or Unit Cost3, because they are not part of the immediate discussion—we're selectively choosing fields to build a compelling customer presentation.

Figure 2-12 shows Housekeeping rows highlighted for the purpose of explanation. The PivotTable shows rows for each of the distinct User values such as Housekeeping. It then shows rows for each of the distinct Phone values; there are only Treo Phones assigned to Housekeeping.

Now within the Housekeeping | Treo group we see rows for Add On and JR 200. We have not designated any row sublevels of data beyond Rate Plan. The original spreadsheet number of Phones for Housekeeping matches the subtotal of 10 we see in the Pivot, but why does the PivotTable show Treos for Housekeeping broken out into eight Treos with an Add On plan, and two Treos with a JR 200 plan?

BI TIP

This is a key concept of PivotTables—PivotTables will do the totals for us, even when we place fields on the PivotTable in different ways!

Thus the PivotTable automatically consolidates the original spreadsheet Treos with JR 200 plans—which occupied two rows in the original spreadsheet—into one aggregate row in the PivotTable. There is no further differentiation in our working example that would break out the Housekeeping | Treo | JR 200 row, so Excel consolidates or aggregates it. This automatic aggregation and subtotaling is one of the powerful features of PivotTables, and we're beginning to see that we can add or remove fields to achieve the level of aggregation desired—for a rolled-up brief view of data, or an expanded-out view of our data.

Note the PivotTable can be placed on its own worksheet if it's easier to keep the data on one sheet and the PivotTable on another (but within the same workbook). This can be valuable with larger data sets where we need to focus on the PivotTable and have the data available but out of the way on another sheet.

BI TIP

Excel 2007 can handle up to one million rows—so PivotTables have become a fantastic tool for aggregating and looking across large data sets that would defy visualization by any other means. This concept works for both internal spreadsheet data sets such as we have in our working example, and external data sources such as database servers and data extract files.

Basic PivotTable Formatting and Data Element Placement

Figure 2-13 shows the PivotTable without the Rate Plan field. When we unchecked the field in the List pane, Excel automatically removed it from the Row Labels rectangle within the PivotTable Field List pane—and automatically removed it from the actual PivotTable. In removing the Rate Plan field, we removed the differentiating factor that made multiple Treos for Housekeeping break out as separate data items for Add On and JR 200—and the PivotTable automatically consolidated them. The remaining single row for Housekeeping accurately shows ten Treos—where before we showed two Treos and eight Treos, broken out by Plan.

1. Click the checkbox for the Rate Plan field in the PivotTable Field List pane to uncheck its selection.
2. Click the Rate Plan field again to check it and put it back into the Row Labels display.

Note also the PivotTable Grand Totals accurately shows 24 Phones, and the Unit Cost2 and Unit Cost4 Grand Totals match the original spreadsheet numbers as well. In fact, you can further remove the Phone field from the PivotTable (using the same procedure we used to remove the Rate Plan field)—and the Grand Totals are still accurate!

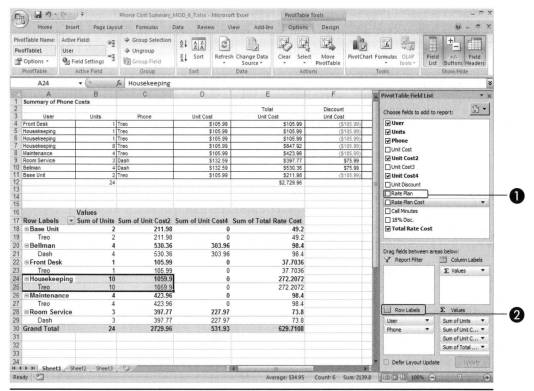

Figure 2-13 *PivotTable Rate Plan removed from row labels*

BI TIP

This is an important point that will help make PivotTables understandable; you can remove a field from the PivotTable rows and the PivotTable totals will further consolidate—and yet still be accurate. It almost seems that you can't break the PivotTable. Why? Because a PivotTable acts as an automatic cross-tab spreadsheet that will add up subtotals and Grand Totals for any combination of rows and columns!

In a dramatic reshaping of the PivotTable, we see in Figure 2-14 the Sum of Units, Sum of Unit Cost2, Sum of Unit Cost4, and Sum of Total Rate Cost labels are now showing as subrow areas of the PivotTable rows. The Σ Values field is a helpful item provided by Excel for Data Value header labels that normally show at the top of the PivotTable columns.

We're going to drag and drop the Σ Values field in the Column Labels rectangle of the PivotTable Field List pane on the right (if you click it and a pop-up menu appears, simply click the field again to close the pop-up).

1. Hold the left mouse button down over the Σ Values field.
2. Drag it down into the Row Labels rectangle below the Rate Plan field (a thin black line will move with the field to indicate where it will drop).

Note you can reset the PivotTable display by dragging the Σ Values field back into the Column Labels rectangle.

The Σ Values field automatically appeared in the Columns Label rectangle of the PivotTable Field List pane when we chose the multiple fields for the Values rectangle. It also provided the labels of Sum of Units, Sum of Unit Cost2, Sum of Unit Cost4, and Sum of Total Rate Cost for the actual PivotTable.

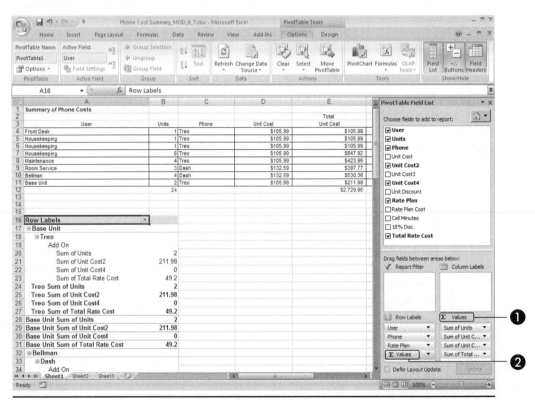

Figure 2-14 *PivotTable Values header labels moved from Column area to Row area*

As we continue to build our PivotTable, we can see the data taking shape in a nice hierarchical arrangement. As people work with PivotTables, this arrangement of data, and the interactive rearranging of the data, becomes surprisingly straightforward—even to those not initially familiar with the concept of PivotTables. Also, people that receive ready-made PivotTables are pretty quick to start clicking the various Collapse/Expand and Filtering drop-down arrows once they realize they won't hurt anything and they see the visually pleasing results with data that they care about.

BI TIP

A basic principle of Business Intelligence is that mechanisms such as Excel 2007 are not just about pretty displays—PivotTables can help us explain data in ways that are easy to understand, and they help us group and summarize large sets of data that would otherwise escape our control!

Report Filters on the PivotTable: How to Filter the Entire PivotTable

Figure 2-15 shows Cell Minutes added to the PivotTable as a Report Filter (the topmost area of the actual PivotTable). Figure 2-15 also shows the Cell Minutes Report Filter opened with Select Multiple Items checked to enable the checkboxes next to the Cell Minutes values: (All), 0, 400. This automatically filters the data being displayed in the entire PivotTable. It helps to think of Report Filters as top-level categorizations of data in PivotTables.

For this step we're not going to just click the Cell Minutes field (which would put it into the Values rectangle)—instead, we're going to drag it to the Report Filter rectangle.

1. Hold the left mouse button down over the Cell Minutes field in the PivotTable Field List pane.
2. Drag it down into the Report Filter rectangle (a thin black line will move with the field to indicate where it will drop).
3. Click the Cell Minutes drop-down arrow at the top of the actual PivotTable to display the Cell Minutes dialog box.
4. Check the Select Multiple Items checkbox.

It's amazing to see how easily we can manipulate the PivotTable with a Report Filter. Go ahead and try it; uncheck (All) and check 400, and then click OK. All of a sudden you're looking at all the data just as it pertains to cell Plans with 400 Minutes!

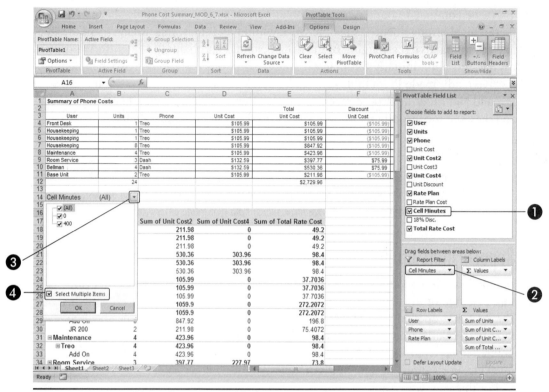

Figure 2-15 *PivotTable Cell Minutes added to Report Filter*

PivotTable Value Header Labels and a Percentage Column

Figure 2-16 shows that all four Values header labels have been edited to present more descriptive labels. Note that Excel changes the Values label in both the Field List pane Values rectangle and on the PivotTable itself. This part of the working example might look like menial work, but it avoids the troublesome situation where customers have to ask what the data means in a basic sense—and perhaps feel bad that they don't understand the data.

1. Click the Sum of Units field in the Values rectangle of the PivotTable Field List pane to display the Value Field Settings dialog box.

2. Change the text in the Custom Name text box to **Phone Units**, and click OK.

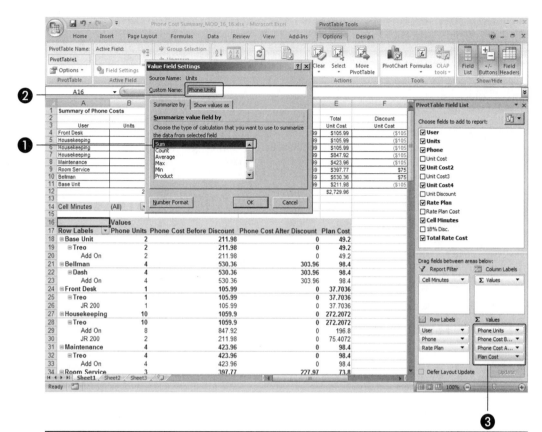

Figure 2-16 *PivotTable Value header label edit*

3. Click the Sum of Unit Cost2 field in the Values list box, and change the Name to **Phone Cost Before Discount**. Change the Sum of Unit Cost4 Name to **Phone Cost After Discount**. And change the Sum of Total Rate Cost Name to **Plan Cost**.

BI TIP

If the Business Intelligence presentation is clearly labeled, anyone with an appreciation of the data should be able to understand the story being conveyed. And all of us in the same situation can appreciate what it means to have a presentation with descriptive labeling that makes sense!

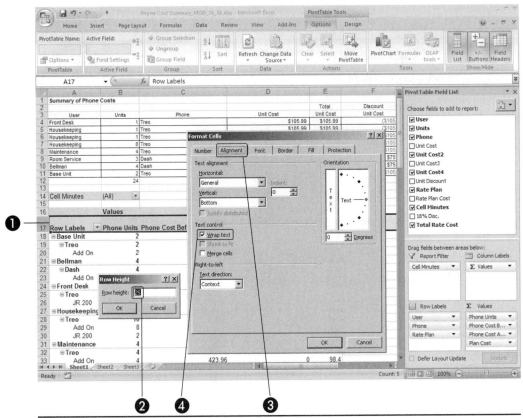

Figure 2-17 *PivotTable Row Height; Format Cells*

Figure 2-17 shows how we're continuing to format the PivotTable just as we would with a normal Excel spreadsheet. It's good to know that the same formatting menus and techniques we've always used with regular spreadsheets apply to PivotTables.

1. Right-click the PivotTable row left margin (holding the mouse over the 17 in our example) and from the pop-up menu choose Row Height.

2. Change the number in the Row Height text box to **25**; then click OK.

3. Right-click again on the PivotTable row left margin and from the pop-up menu choose Format Cells; then click the Alignment tab.

4. Click the Wrap Text checkbox; then click OK.

In Figure 2-18 we've right-clicked a PivotTable spreadsheet column to change the Column Width. Note the PivotTable Field List pane has disappeared on the right side of the screen, and the Ribbon menu top-level PivotTable Tools context tabs are gone!

1. Right-click the spreadsheet column top margin (holding the mouse over the D at the top of the column); and then choose Column Width from the pop-up menu.
2. Change the number in the Column Width text box to **15**; then click OK.

BI TIP

The disappearing PivotTable tool set is a surprisingly common and disconcerting effect that is easily handled by simply clicking anywhere on the actual PivotTable (such as on the User cell with the drop-down). People will open an Excel workbook that contains a PivotTable and not know how to get to the PivotTable menus—so remember, just click anywhere on the PivotTable itself to show the PivotTable Tools and Field List.

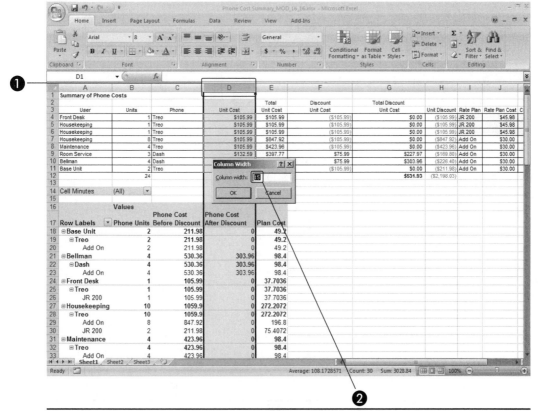

Figure 2-18 *PivotTable Column Width—no PivotTable field list or tools!*

In Figure 2-19 we see an important feature; a percentage column is being added to the PivotTable. This is an amazingly common part of spreadsheet displays that can be easily handled in Excel 2007 PivotTables. The % of Plan Cost column is really just a copy of the Plan Cost column with a different subtotaling format applied! In our working example, customers will appreciate being able to see at a glance both the Plan Cost and the % of Plan Cost as their eyes travel down the right side of the PivotTable.

For this step we're not going to just click the Total Rate Cost Field (which would put it into the Values rectangle)—instead, we're going to drag it to the Values rectangle and rename it.

1. Hold the left mouse button down over the Total Rate Cost field in the PivotTable Field List pane, and drag it down into the Values rectangle below the Plan Cost field (a thin black line will move with the field to indicate where it will drop).

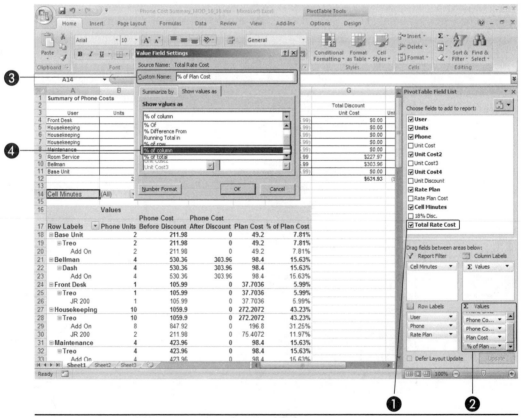

Figure 2-19 *PivotTable percentage column added*

2. Click the Total Rate Cost field in the Values rectangle, and choose Value Field Settings from the pop-up menu.

3. Change the text in the Custom Name text box to **% of Plan Cost**, in the Value Field Settings dialog box.

4. Click the Show Values As tab and select % of Column in the list box; and then click OK.

Note the PivotTable looks cluttered as we try to read through the values of Base Unit, Treo, Base Unit Total, etc. Also note how the percentages column shows the same percentage in a duplicate manner for Treo, Treo Total, and Base Unit Total— which is correct, as each percentage relates individually to the column 100% Grand Total. However, this can be confusing to people if they are looking at the duplicate percentages column entries and see they add up to more than 100%. We need to continue our formatting work to address this point of confusion.

PivotTable Field Settings: Suppressing Subtotals and Formatting

Now we see in Figure 2-20 the Subtotals for User and for Phone have been suppressed. It's interesting that this suppression of automatic subtotaling on these rows makes the User and Phone fields easier to read in their position next to each other because the Subtotal information is out of the way. In reality it was not adding anything substantial to the presentations, and besides, we can always bring the Subtotals back into the display if we wish by changing the Subtotals option back to Automatic in the respective dialog boxes.

1. Click the User field in the Row Labels rectangle of the PivotTable Field List pane, and choose Field Settings from the pop-up menu.

2. Select the None option button under Subtotals in the Field Settings dialog box; then click OK.

3. Click the Phone field in the Row Labels rectangle, choose Field Settings from the pop-up menu, and select the None option in the same manner.

BI TIP

An important task with Office 2007 Business Intelligence is the presentation of multiple relative values within a single screen of data.

Note the PivotTable is easier to comprehend as you read across to the percentages column where the distinct values add to 100%. And believe it; people will notice this!

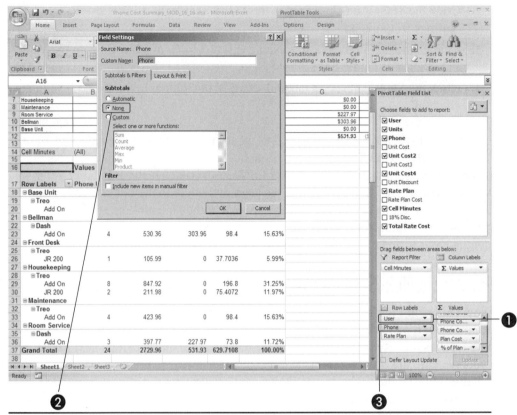

Figure 2-20   *PivotTable with Subtotals suppressed for User and Phone rows*

BI TIP

When working with Business Intelligence presentations, we should remove unnecessary information — but keep the right amount of information to help it read like a book from left to right.

In Figure 2-21 we've changed the dollar-value columns to a Currency format. Again, the normal formatting tools of Excel apply to PivotTable fields as well.

1. Click the Phone Cost Before Discount field in the Values rectangle of the PivotTable Field List pane, and choose Value Field Settings from the pop-up menu.

2. Click the Number Format button in the Value Field Settings dialog box.

3. Select Currency from the Category list in the Format Cells dialog box, and then click OK.

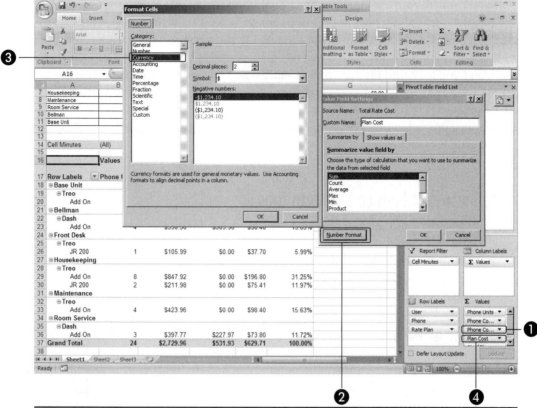

Figure 2-21 *PivotTable with Number Format set to Currency for the dollar-value fields*

4. Click the Phone Cost After Discount field in the Values rectangle, and change it to Currency format in the same manner—and then click the Plan Cost field in the Values rectangle, and change it to Currency format in the same manner.

Using the Ribbon Menu for More Advanced Formatting

Our working example PivotTable is looking pretty good now, but it's worth exploring the top-level Ribbon menu context tabs to add some further structure and color. This is a fairly important point—many people that work with Business Intelligence tools stop at a functional point of design and never finish the qualitative aspects of the presentation. Office 2007 gives us the ability to create professional-looking PivotTables, so why not go the extra distance—which in this case may make the difference in how the customer perceives the overall value of the phone plan?

If you find yourself looking at a functional PivotTable and simply don't have any creative ideas about how to improve something that frankly already works—take a step back and look through the top-level Ribbon menu. Microsoft has put a lot of effort into providing tools that can take everyday work to a professional level, and you may find they are more usable than you first thought. In fact, some people would say the new Excel 2007 formatting tools allow all business people to create polished PivotTables so that everyone can produce great-looking Business Intelligence presentations. For more information, see the sidebar "Business Intelligence Presentations."

Business Intelligence Presentations

Here are some good rules to remember for Business Intelligence Presentations:

▶ Make the presentation easy to see at a glance. This allows people to get an immediate idea of what we're trying to show with Business Intelligence data; so don't put too much information on the screen at once. First impressions are important.

▶ Arrange the data elements to tell a story in a top-down, left-to-right manner. This allows people to use their familiar skills of reading to explore the data in a Business Intelligence presentation. Realize the top-left information should start a story that can be followed in a logical manner across the screen.

▶ Titles and header labels should stand out and should tell people what they're looking at. So even though someone may be familiar with the data in the context of their business, they should not have to guess at the meaning of rows and columns of data, highlighted elements, and totals.

▶ Use a consistent color scheme throughout the presentation. People expect color today in Business Intelligence, and it is often used to convey a meaning of its own—or to highlight data elements. But don't use such a variety of colors that it looks confusing or jumbled. Also, use colors such as Green-Yellow-Red carefully, since they carry connotations of Good-Warning-Bad that we carry over from real life.

▶ Use your corporate colors or those from the customer's web site and perhaps a business logo if appropriate. People like to see themselves in the data presentation, and it helps deliver the message of data that becomes a compelling Business Intelligence story.

PivotTable Menu Options for the Entire PivotTable

In Figure 2-22, we're looking at the PivotTable Options dialog box. Most of the choices here are not significant to our working PivotTable—although on the Layout & Format tab it can be helpful to uncheck the Autofit Column Widths On Update checkbox, which will prevent PivotTable Column widths from arbitrarily changing as we apply different formats to various elements.

1. Click the Options icon in the PivotTable menu group, on the Ribbon menu Options tab.
2. Uncheck the Autofit Column Widths On Update checkbox.

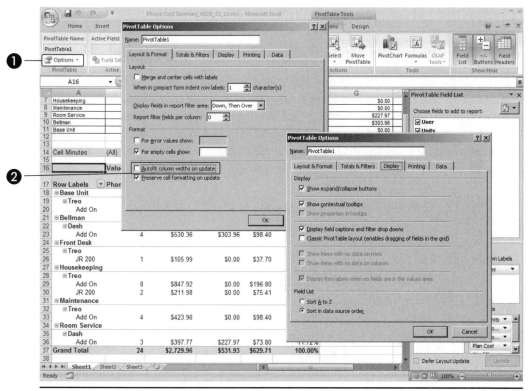

Figure 2-22   *PivotTable, uncheck Autofit Column Widths On Update*

The Display tab includes several options worth knowing about to control the dynamic nature of the PivotTable interaction with those with whom we share it:

▶   If you do not want to allow users to click the PivotTable plus/minus controls for collapsing the data display, you can uncheck the Show Expand/Collapse Buttons checkbox.

▶   If you do not want to allow users to click the PivotTable row drop-down arrows for data filtering, you can uncheck the Display Field Captions And Filter Drop Downs checkbox.

▶   If you want to allow users to rearrange rows and columns in an Excel 2003 manner by dragging and dropping within the actual PivotTable rows and columns (instead of using the PivotTable Field List pane) row-column-value areas, you can check the Classic PivotTable Layout checkbox.

PivotTable Active Field Menu Options: Collapse and Expand

Figure 2-23 shows the Field Settings dialog box for a PivotTable text field—a similar dialog box comes up when we first select a PivotTable numeric field (such as Phone Units)—with a title of Value Field Settings and menu choices that pertain to summary operations. Note these same Field Settings / Value Field Settings dialog boxes are available from the PivotTable Field List pane on the right side of the screen, by clicking any field in the lower rectangles.

1.   Click the Base Unit element in the actual PivotTable (which is a User field value).

2.   Click the Field Settings icon in the Active Field menu group, on the Ribbon menu Options tab.

3.   Click the Layout & Print tab in the Field Settings dialog box.

4.   Click the "Insert blank line after each item label" checkbox.

Most of the choices here are not significant to our working PivotTable—although many people like having a blank line as a separator between row values. On the Layout & Print tab this can accomplished by checking the "Insert blank line after each item label" checkbox.

In Figure 2-24 we see a different look for our PivotTable—where the text field elements for Phone and Rate Plan have been suppressed. Now we're starting to look at the dynamic nature of PivotTables, which can be used in a discussion with

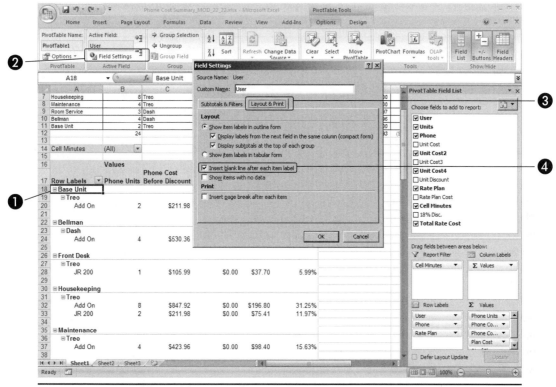

Figure 2-23 *PivotTable, Field Settings for row element*

the customer—where we might want to quickly show the cost data by User without displaying the Phone or Rate Plan information. We can just as quickly bring the Phone and Rate Plan data back onto the screen by clicking the Expand Entire Field icon, which is just above the Collapse Entire Field icon.

1. Click the Base Unit element in the actual PivotTable (which is a User field value).

2. Click the Collapse Entire Field icon in the Active Field menu group of the Ribbon menu Options tab.

Note that you can reset the PivotTable back to showing all fields, by simply clicking the Expand Entire Field icon (this icon is just above the Collapse Entire Field icon).

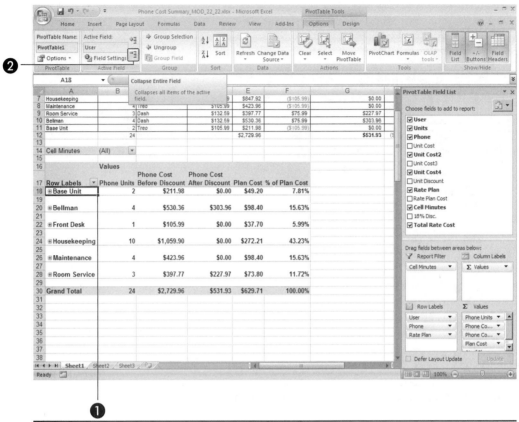

Figure 2-24   *PivotTable with row fields collapsed*

It's important to note that we don't lose any data when we manipulate the PivotTable in this manner; and we're able to rearrange the display of data to show more or less detail—with the same totals always showing, which keeps a consistent look on the screen so that we don't confuse people when we're collapsing or expanding fields.

BI TIP

Perhaps the most fundamental element of Business Intelligence presentations is a consistent data summarization and grouping, while allowing detail manipulation.

Figure 2-25 shows an important feature of Excel 2007 PivotTables that allows us to easily select a custom Group1, Group2 organization of row elements for subtotaling. The business case for this grouping springs from an understanding that

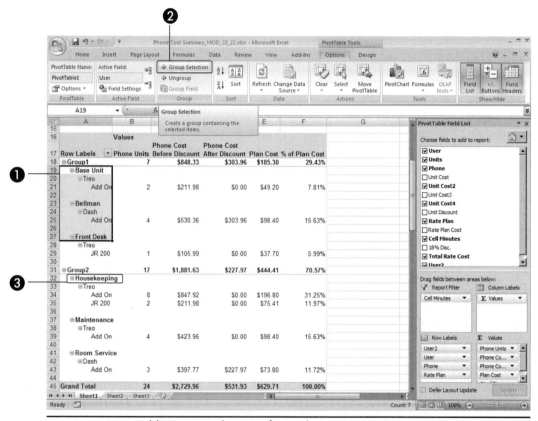

Figure 2-25 *PivotTable Group Selection of row elements*

the Base Unit, Bellman, and Front Desk are evaluated as a single cost center in the customer's place of business; and Housekeeping, Maintenance, and Room Service are a second cost center.

1. Click the Base Unit element in the actual PivotTable (which is a User field value) while holding the left mouse button down, and move the mouse down to the Front Desk element so the three elements of Base Unit / Bellman / Front Desk are selected.

2. Click the Group Selection icon in the Group menu, on the Ribbon menu Options tab to create a Group1.

3. Multi-select the Housekeeping through Room Service field elements in the same way, and click the Group Selection icon to create a Group2.

BI TIP

Instead of asking customers to change their way of thinking to follow a Business Intelligence display, we should arrange the Business Intelligence presentation to follow the customer's business process.

Now we're getting into PivotTable display preferences that are pretty subjective; you'll want to use the options shown in Figure 2-26 where you feel they are appropriate. The reasoning for the Group subtotaling is to show the relative importance of Group1 versus Group2 in the overall presentation. Thus Group1 has its own subtotal and Group2 has its own subtotal—and their subtotals can be compared to the bottom-level Grand Total.

1. Click the Group1 element in the actual PivotTable.
2. Click the Field Settings icon in the Active Field menu group, on the Ribbon menu Options tab.
3. Select the Automatic option button on the Subtotals & Filters tab of the Field Settings dialog box.

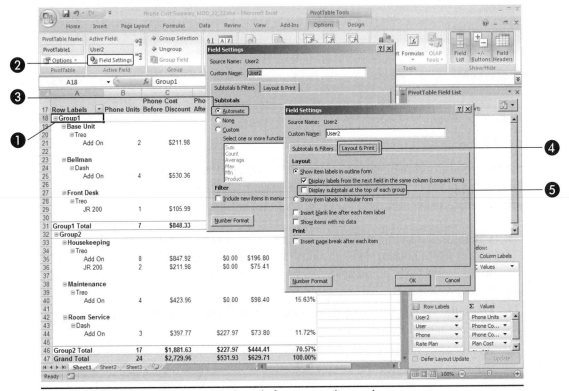

Figure 2-26 *PivotTable Automatic Subtotals for grouped row elements*

4. Click the Layout & Print tab.

5. Uncheck the "Display subtotals at the top of each group" checkbox.

Since most people follow a Business Intelligence presentation from left to right and top to bottom, we unchecked "Display subtotals at the top of each group." This moved the Group1 and Group2 subtotals to the bottom of the respective Groups and made them easier to see on their own lines with top and bottom borders.

PivotTable Sorting with On-screen Data

Figure 2-27 shows an arrangement of data that follows a business process. The Front Desk element has been moved up in the list of User elements because the customer thinks in terms of Front Desk operations preceding the Bellman operations.

1. Right-click the Front Desk element in the actual PivotTable (which is a User field value).

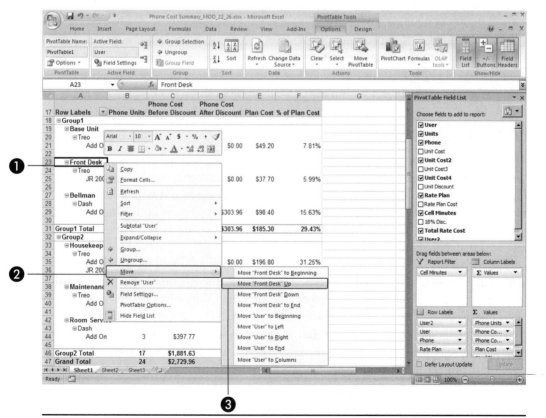

Figure 2-27 *PivotTable, Front Desk moved up to place elements in different order*

2. Choose Move on the pop-up menu.

3. Choose Move "Front Desk" Up on the secondary pop-up menu.

Note how the Sort icons in the Sort menu group on the Ribbon menu Options tab allow you to sort text, numeric, and date elements in an ascending or descending manner. However, the PivotTable field right-click functionality just described is actually more useful than the Sort menu group on the Ribbon menu.

PivotTable Data Menu Options

The Data group on the Ribbon menu is not something we'll use much, but it's worth a quick explanation.

The Refresh icon in the Data menu group of the Ribbon menu Options tab allows you to choose to refresh the PivotTable data if the original spreadsheet data has changed. However, it's probably more useful to note the PivotTable Options (far left menu group of the Ribbon menu Options tab) bring up a dialog box with a Data tab wherein we have a checkbox to refresh data when opening the file—if you wish to refresh the PivotTable data every time the workbook is opened.

The Change Data Source icon in the Data menu group of the Ribbon menu Options tab allows you to select different cells for the original spreadsheet data. We are not exploring the Use An External Data Source option in this section, since our data source is a spreadsheet within the current workbook.

PivotTable Actions Menu Options

The Actions group on the Ribbon menu is not something we'll use much, but it's worth a quick explanation. The Clear icon in the Actions group of the Ribbon menu Options tab is not something you normally want to click, since it wipes out the PivotTable Rows and Values! As we'd expect, though, the Excel 2007 Undo icon at the upper left of the screen will bring everything back as long as you have not saved any accidental changes.

The Select icon in the Actions group of the Ribbon menu Options tab allows you to quickly select/highlight area of the PivotTable, but it's more straightforward to simply click a cell in the actual PivotTable, and then SHIFT-click or CTRL-click subsequent cells to multi-select areas for formatting.

The Move PivotTable icon in the Actions group of the Ribbon menu Options tab is actually pretty handy for moving the entire PivotTable to another location on any sheet in the Excel workbook.

PivotTable Tools: Creating a PivotChart

In Figure 2-28 we've started to create a PivotChart that is based on the PivotTable. There is an amazing variety of chart types available in Excel 2007, but we're going to use the most common one in our working example so that we can proceed more quickly to a polished PivotTable/PivotChart combination for our Business Intelligence presentation.

1. Click the PivotChart icon in the Tools menu group, on the Ribbon menu Options tab.
2. Choose the 3-D Cylinder chart type on the Insert Chart dialog box, and then click OK.

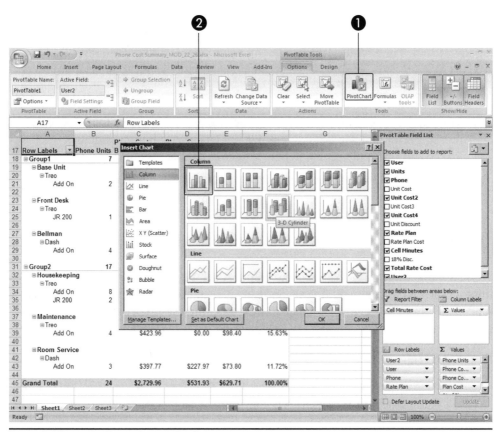

Figure 2-28 *PivotChart, 3-D Cylinder*

We selected the 3-D Cylinder chart type because it's one of the few types that can create an easy-to-understand chart from our PivotTable without spending too much time on formatting the chart. Also, 3-D chart types provide a more interesting display that looks appealing to people in general—in fact, a 3-D chart will really grab someone's attention even when it's just a 3-D version of what could be shown in a 2-D chart!

BI TIP

The PivotChart icon in the Tools group of the Ribbon menu Options tab creates a PivotChart that depends on the PivotTable, so keep in mind that the PivotChart data display will change as the PivotTable data is changed—and the PivotTable data display will change as the PivotChart data is changed.

In Figure 2-29 we've taken several important steps to improve the readability of the PivotChart. The PivotChart has been moved to display below the PivotTable. And the Vertical Axis label has been set to None and the Depth Axis label has been set to None.

1. Move the mouse over the PivotChart top-right corner to see a four-direction mouse-arrow, and while holding down the left mouse button, drag the PivotChart down the screen to below the PivotTable.
2. Click the Axes icon in the Axes menu group, on the Ribbon menu Layout tab.
3. Choose Primary Vertical Axis on the pop-up menu.
4. Choose None on the secondary pop-up menu.
5. Choose Depth Axis and None in the same manner.

We did this because the Vertical and Depth Axes were showing too much information on the chart and it was confusing. The numeric values for those axes (and data values in general) are much easier to read in the PivotTable—whereas the PivotChart does a good job of conveying the relative size of data values!

BI TIP

It's important in Business Intelligence design to use the right visual tool for the job, and keep the display simple enough for everyone to understand.

You can also close the PivotChart Filter pane, since it only allows us to filter the PivotChart values that display—which we'll accomplish instead with the Filter

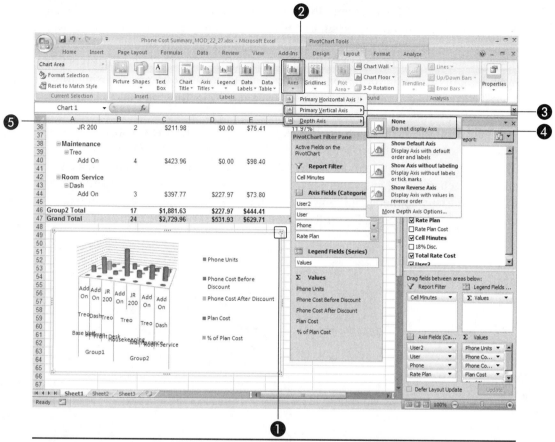

Figure 2-29 *PivotChart; no Vertical or Depth Axis labels*

drop-down controls on the actual PivotTable. Frankly, you'll find it's easier to use the PivotTable to change the data display.

This brings up an important point: in our working example the PivotChart and the PivotTable are connected to each other and use the same original spreadsheet data source. That is why we can't add or remove fields showing in the PivotChart using the PivotChart Filter pane! It's also why if we filter on the fields using the PivotTable drop-down controls, the PivotChart will automatically change to reflect the same data filtering.

Note that you could create a separate PivotChart that is not connected to the PivotTable, by going through the initial steps we followed to create a PivotTable—but instead choosing to create a PivotChart from the initial Ribbon menu Insert tab. We didn't do this, because it makes more sense to show a connected PivotTable and PivotChart to a customer and manipulate the data for both using the PivotTable controls.

Note also that the Layout tab of the Ribbon menu (for PivotChart tools) has many menu groups that are not important to our working example. In fact, most of those menu options will actually make the PivotChart look confusing or unreadable. It can be challenging to create a good PivotChart from a PivotTable because the PivotTable holds a lot of detailed information. It's important to note that we are choosing to keep the PivotChart simple and changing just a few formatting options to keep things easy to work with.

Figure 2-30 shows that with the PivotChart selected (click the PivotChart if you don't see the PivotChart Tools tabs on the Ribbon menu), the Design tab of the Ribbon menu shows quite a few menu groups with options that can be used to change the chart layout and style. This shows the wide variety of color combinations that can be easily applied to a PivotChart—although we're using the default that displays a reasonable color set for the PivotChart data series. The choice of color is

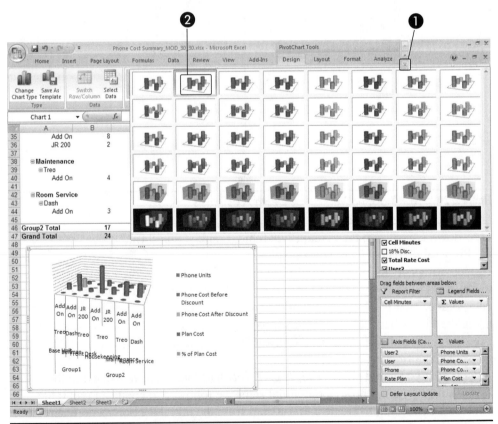

Figure 2-30 *PivotChart; chart styles*

a matter of personal taste, although it's good to stay away from color schemes that are too wild, since they distract from the data story being delivered to your audience.

1. Click the Chart Styles drop-down control (holding the mouse over it displays the tool tip More), on the Ribbon menu Design tab.

2. Place the mouse over the various Chart Styles to see the Live Preview on the actual PivotChart.

To make sure we're aware of some chart terminology involved, we should point out that the numeric sets of data in a chart are termed data series. In our working example we have a data series for each of the Value fields in the PivotChart—Phone Units, Phone Cost Before Discount, etc.—plotted against the row elements of Groups, Phones, and Plans. It's pretty impressive that we accomplished this somewhat automatically using the built-in structure of PivotTables and PivotCharts!

Figure 2-31 shows how to create a Calculated Field, which is simply an arithmetic formula that uses already-existing PivotTable fields. The example shows a new Field1

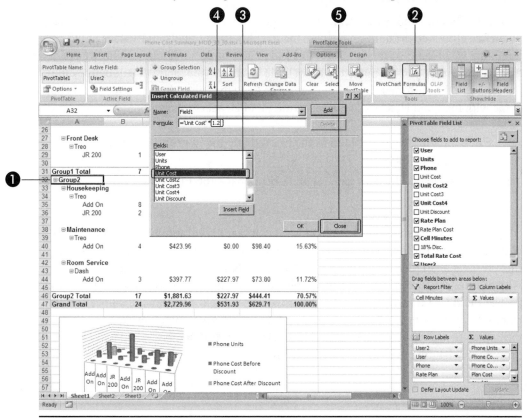

Figure 2-31 *PivotTable; creating a Calculated Field*

that will be 1.2 times the value of the Unit Cost field. For our working example we're not going to actually create a Calculated Field—but it's important to know that you can add such new Values to the PivotTable drawing from original data.

1. Click the actual PivotTable to make sure the PivotTable Tools tabs are displayed on the Ribbon menu.

2. Click the Formulas icon in the Tools menu group on the Ribbon menu Options tab, and from the pop-up menu choose Calculated Field.

3. Select Unit Cost as the base field desired for the calculation from the Fields list in the Insert Calculated Field dialog box, and then click the Insert Field button.

4. Enter the desired formula in the Formula text box, such as *** 1.2**.

5. For our working example, click Close to close the dialog box and not create the field.

PivotTable Show/Hide Group

Figure 2-32 shows another incremental change that we could make to the PivotTable—where we eliminate the column headers that display Row Labels and Values at the top of the PivotTable columns. Again this is a matter of personal choice, but we are trying different options to make the PivotTable easier to view and yet still convey the data story to the customer. Because we want to keep the Filter drop-down controls that come with the Field Headers, we'll leave the Field Headers display on.

1. Click the Field Headers icon in the Show/Hide menu group on the Ribbon menu Options tab.

2. Click the Field Headers icon again to bring back the Filter drop-down controls on the columns.

The Collapse/Expand (+/−) controls on the actual PivotTable could be hidden by clicking the +/− Buttons icon in the Show/Hide group on the Ribbon menu. While this presents a simpler PivotTable, it eliminates what people like best about them, which is the ability to click the PivotTable and dynamically change the data display.

The Field List icon simply makes the PivotTable Field List pane disappear on the right side of the screen. We'll go ahead and do this to give ourselves more room on the screen to work with the PivotTable and PivotChart. It can be redisplayed at any time if we wish by clicking the Field List icon again.

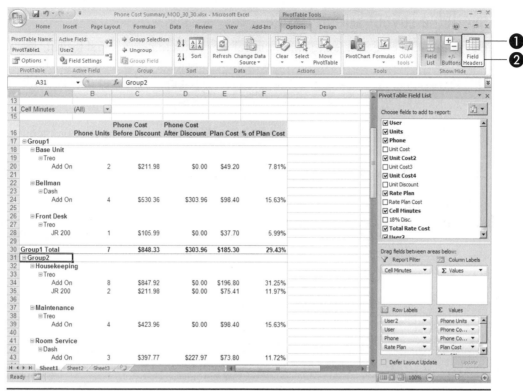

Figure 2-32 *PivotTable without Field Headers at the top of columns*

Ribbon Menu Design Tab: Power Formatting

In this section we'll add some final touches to the PivotTable/PivotChart. Adjusting the look and feel of a Business Intelligence presentation involves subjective judgment calls and is best explored through a trial-and-error process. Luckily, Office 2007 has a Ribbon menu feature called Live Preview, which is an incredible help in trying out different styles from the Ribbon menu.

Basically we can mouse over the various color combinations in the Style Gallery and see the effect on the PivotTable without having to actually choose any of them! We'll explore this Live Preview and other Ribbon menu Design options as we continue to hone the presentation quality of our Business Intelligence display.

PivotTable Layout Screen Design

In Figure 2-33 we've decided to apply the Tabular Form to the PivotTable. This is a significant change, and it's different from the Compact Form default for Excel 2007 PivotTables. In our case it makes sense to tighten up the look of the PivotTable because we don't have a large number of columns.

1. Click the Report Layout icon in the Layout menu group, on the Ribbon menu Design tab.
2. Click the Show In Tabular Form icon on the pop-up menu.

BI TIP

It should be noted the Compact Form for Excel 2007 PivotTables is best used when you have large amounts of data (especially columns) — the Compact Form was designed to fit many rows and columns on an Excel screen area.

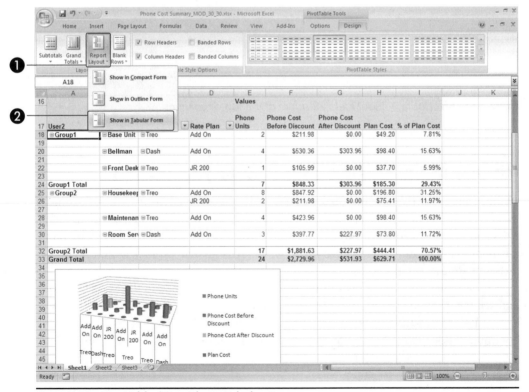

Figure 2-33 *PivotTable/PivotChart, Tabular Form*

If you click the icon for Subtotals and try clicking Do Not Show Subtotals, you'll see the Group1 Total and the Group2 Total Rows disappear. If you then click the icon for Show All Subtotals At Bottom Of Group, you'll see that every PivotTable Row field now has a Subtotal row! If you try this and want to return to our working display, simply click the Undo icon at the very top of the Excel screen to return to showing subtotals just for the Groups.

Note you can also show just the Group subtotals by right-clicking a Group column element and selecting Subtotal User2 on the pop-up menu that is just for the selected/highlighted PivotTable field. The Grand Totals icon on the Layout menu group simply causes the PivotTable Grand Total row to show or not.

In Figure 2-34 we've decided to remove the blank lines we previously inserted into the PivotTable. This is a matter of personal preference, and it's worth noting

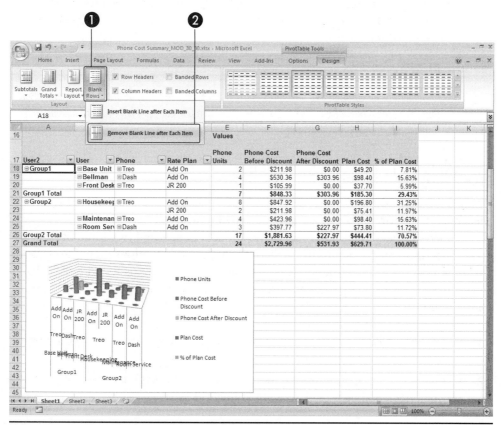

Figure 2-34 *PivotTable/PivotChart with blank lines*

that blank lines are more important with dense displays of data so that people are not faced with endless rows of data in a large display.

1. Click the Blank Rows icon in the Layout menu group, on the Ribbon menu Design tab.
2. Click the Remove Blank Line After Each Item choice on the pop-up menu.

Note we've also dragged the PivotChart up to fit right under the Tabular Form of the PivotTable. When you click the PivotChart you'll find the top Ribbon menu tabs change to show the context tabs for PivotChart operations. To change back to the Ribbon menu tabs for PivotTable operations—simply click anywhere on the actual PivotTable itself.

In our working example the intent is to tighten up the display because we'd like to show both the PivotTable and the PivotChart on the same screen when Excel is first opened—for maximum effect!

BI TIP

It's important for customers to be impressed right away with an initial Business Intelligence display that fits on the screen at the start of a presentation, and not wonder what they are missing with a display that stretches off the screen.

PivotTable Style Options: Banded Rows

Figure 2-35 shows an interesting display effect—checking the Banded Rows checkbox on the Ribbon menu actually does two things: it automatically applies every-other-row banding to the PivotTable, and it changes the PivotTable Styles graphics on the Ribbon menu (just to the right of the Style Options menu group)! Quite frankly, this is one of the most heavily used formatting tips with PivotTables; and users become familiar with various banded-row color combinations that work for their data.

1. Click the Banded Rows icon in the PivotTable Style Options menu group on the Ribbon menu Design tab.
2. Click the Banded Columns icon in the PivotTable Style Options menu group to see the effect, and then click it again to uncheck it.

This is an amazing example of Office 2007 Live Preview in action. The style options and the styles themselves work together to blend our menu choices. It is

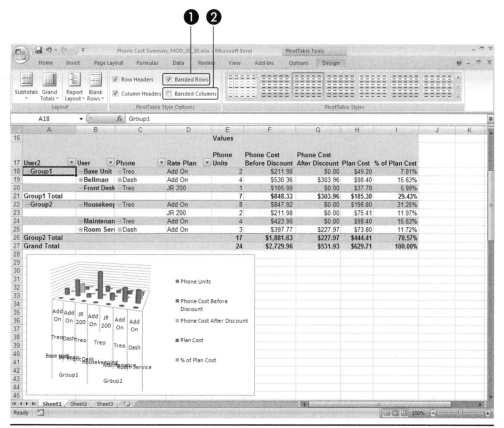

Figure 2-35 *PivotTable/PivotChart; with Banded Rows*

something normally seen in advanced graphics programs, and yet we're going to find that we come to expect it in the new 2007 user interfaces. These interactive menus make working with screen presentations much faster in everyday work, since they allow us to quickly try out many different design and style schemes without actually having to save or undo them as we view the screen results.

For our working example we'll choose Row Headers, Column Headers, and Banded Rows.

PivotTable Styles

And now, as Figure 2-36 shows, we're really putting the finishing touches on the PivotTable. It's clear a wide variety of color combinations can be easily applied to PivotTables—and you can preview the styles on the fly by hovering the mouse over the various styles in the Styles drop-down gallery—and the PivotTable will dynamically change to show what the style will look like if it's selected! This is another example of the Office 2007 Live Preview in action.

1. Click the PivotTable Styles drop-down control (holding the mouse over it displays the tool-tip More) on the Ribbon menu.

2. In the Medium area, choose the right-middle style (holding the mouse over it displays the tool tip Pivot Style Medium 14).

For our working example we'll choose Pivot Style Medium 14 because its colors are similar to the PivotChart colors—and we don't want to have clashing color styles. And although this may seem like common sense, it's worth stating the intent here is not too make use of many different color schemes, but rather to choose one that will help communicate the data picture and not distract the customer.

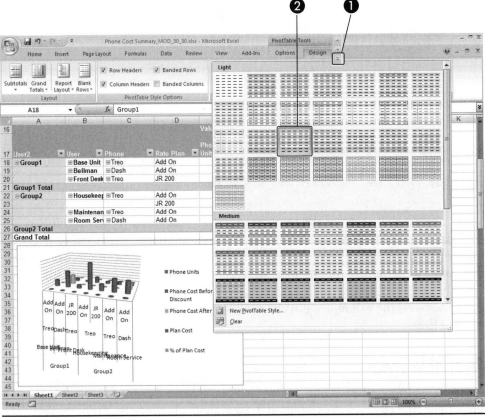

Figure 2-36   *PivotTable/PivotChart, style applied*

BI TIP

Choosing consistent colors and styles for Business Intelligence presentations helps end users understand the data, because the eye can quickly scan color-coded Table and Chart components without having to interpret different color schemes.

Figure 2-37 shows the finished product, with a picture of a phone inserted. It can actually be important (and persuasive) to include pictures, where appropriate, of the data elements involved in the Business Intelligence presentation.

1. Click the Picture icon in the Illustrations menu group, on the Ribbon menu Insert tab.
2. Browse to the appropriate image file and select it; then drag it into place on the Excel spreadsheet.

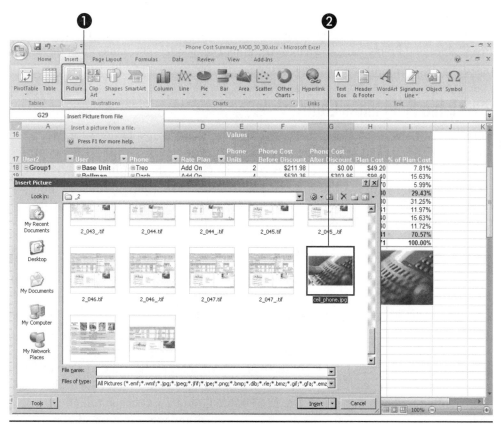

Figure 2-37 *PivotTable/PivotChart, final style with picture inserted*

BI TIP

A picture or illustration can connect people's understanding of objects in the real world with data in a Business Intelligence presentation, and really bring the data story to life.

The Right Data: Filters for PivotTable and PivotChart Data

And now for the fun part: we'll click the actual PivotTable controls to change the data display on the fly. It is amazing to see how quickly people learn how to do this in the real world when the data is something they care about. The result is a feeling of control over Excel data that can help drive business decisions.

This fits right into the monitor, analyze, and plan (MAP) categories that can be used to describe what we do with data every day—if we have easy access to it. We typically use reports and the dashboard to monitor our business activities, and we can use PivotTables and PivotCharts to analyze the data. Using filters on actual PivotTables is one of the best ways to analyze data, and it's available to anyone with Excel!

PivotTable Field Filter Controls

In Figure 2-38 the display data has been narrowed to show just Group1 for the purposes of discussion. And all we had to do was open one drop-down filter control on the PivotTable! This allows us to focus on the Group1 data during a customer meeting, live and in front of people. These PivotTable data filter controls are the fastest way to narrow the data display, which is often done during a meeting where the discussion needs to focus on a specific area of the data presentation.

1. Click the drop-down control on the actual PivotTable User2 element.
2. Uncheck the (Select All) checkbox to clear the checkboxes on the pop-up menu for filter choices.
3. Check the Group1 checkbox, and then click OK.

Note you can click again on the drop-down control for User2, and select Clear Filter From User2 to reset the PivotTable and PivotChart to the full data display.

Note the User2 header field drop-down icon has changed to indicate a filter has been applied to the field values. The PivotTable Grand Total has automatically changed to show the total for the displayed Group1 and the numbers add up correctly. Also, the PivotChart has changed in the same way and now shows just the Group1 data.

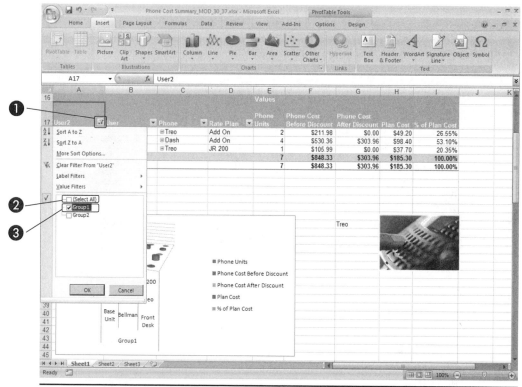

Figure 2-38 *PivotTable/PivotChart with field filtering applied to User2*

The entire data display can be restored by clicking the User2 header field drop-down control (which looks like a filter now) and choosing Clear Filter From User2. It's pretty easy to see that the PivotTable and PivotChart components all work together in this interface—and the automatic cross-tab behavior provides a consistent data display and subtotaling experience while we slice and dice the data.

Figure 2-39 shows filtering by Value Filter, where only those Users with more than three Phone Units are displaying. This makes it easy to bring out high-volume items in the display and focus a customer's discussion on those elements.

1. Click the drop-down control on the actual PivotTable User element.

2. Choose Value Filters on the pop-up menu.

3. Choose Greater Than on the secondary pop-up menu.

4. Enter **3** in the text-box of the Value Filter (User) dialog box, and click OK.

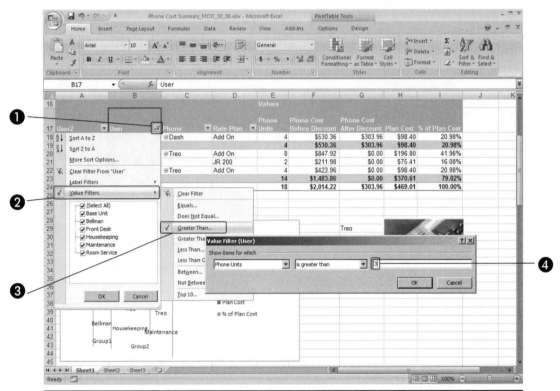

Figure 2-39   *PivotTable/PivotChart, filtering by Value Filters on User*

Note that you can click again on the drop-down control for User, and select Clear Filter From "User" to reset the PivotTable and PivotChart to the full data display.

However, note this Value Filter of Phone Units greater than 3 won't result in the same data display when applied to the User2 drop-down filter control. Why? The answer brings up a subtle and important point to understand about working with data in a more advanced tool such as a PivotTable!

Looking at the User2 elements of Group1 and Group2, we see that each group contains some rows with Phone Units greater than 3—so at this group level of the PivotTable, no rows are suppressed by a Value Filter of Phone Units greater than 3. All rows stay displayed!

Looking at the User elements of Base Unit, Bellman, etc., we see that some User elements contain rows that are below the filter of Phone Units greater than 3—so at this second level of the PivotTable some rows are in fact suppressed by a Value Filter of Phone Units greater than 3.

In Figure 2-40 we see another way to slice and dice the data display—which lends itself nicely to choosing text elements to narrow the PivotTable presentation.

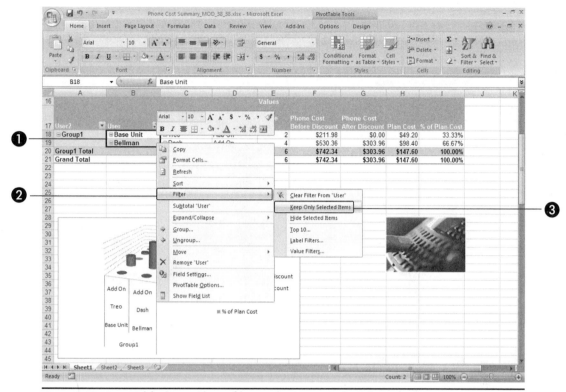

Figure 2-40 *PivotTable/PivotChart, filtering by Keep Only Selected Items*

Being able to simply drag the mouse across data elements to multi-select them, and then right-click to get appropriate menu options, is something we expect with modern software. The difference with Office 2007 is that these multi-select right-click actions work in a similar fashion across all the 2007 applications of Excel, PowerPoint, etc.

1. Click the Base Unit cell of the PivotTable, and while holding down the left mouse button, drag the selected area down to include Bellman.
2. Right-click the selected cells, and then choose Filter.
3. Choose Keep Only Selected Items on the secondary pop-up menu.

Note that you can click the drop-down control for User, and select Clear Filter From User to reset the PivotTable and PivotChart to the full data display. This capability to filter on just the selected cells really shows the fine level of control we can have with PivotTables.

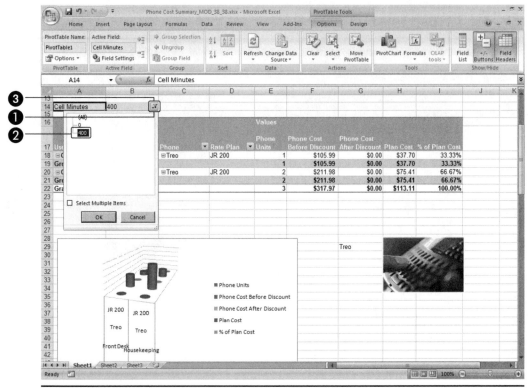

Figure 2-41 *PivotTable/PivotChart with Report Filter applied to all data*

Figure 2-41 shows a really fast top-level way to control the PivotTable data display; using the Report Filter for Cell Minutes that we made a part of the PivotTable when we first chose the fields. The top-level position implies that the Cell Minutes are an important part of the overall phone plan, which is exactly what we want to communicate to the customer.

1. Click the top-level drop-down Filter control for the Cell Minutes element on the PivotTable.

2. Select the 400 value, and then click OK.

3. Click again on the drop-down control for Cell Minutes, and select (All) and OK on the pop-up menu to reset the PivotTable and PivotChart to the full data display.

Figure 2-41 shows two interesting aspects of the Report Filter:

▶ The Report Filter appears above the main body of the PivotTable, where it helps us think of it as an overall aspect of the data presentation.

▶ The Report Filter data values do not appear in the main body of the PivotTable, which keeps it out of the detailed part of the discussion surrounding the data presentation.

As we've seen, there are many ways to slice and dice the data display of a PivotTable. You'll become familiar with the ones you need to support your data conversations in the workday world, but it's good to know there is a wide enough variety of display actions to complement the variety of business discussions you're likely to encounter.

PivotTable Field Collapse/Expand Controls

Figure 2-42 shows a dramatic change in display detail with the User2 group rows collapsed. With just two mouse-clicks you can simplify the data presentation and

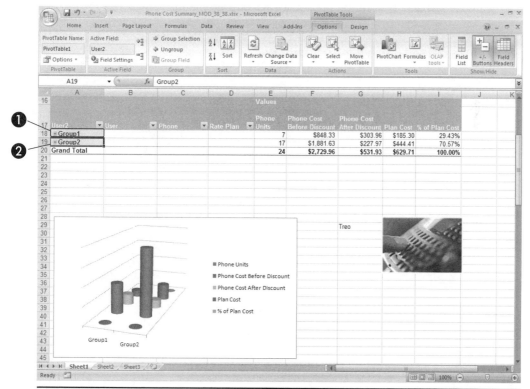

Figure 2-42 *PivotTable/PivotChart with collapsed fields*

focus the customer discussion on a very straightforward picture of the overall phone plan. This is a quick way to condense the data display.

1. Click the Plus/Minus control for the Group1 element.
2. Click the Plus/Minus control for the Group2 element.

Note that you can click again on the Plus/Minus controls for the User2 elements to reset the PivotTable and PivotChart to the full data display.

A more advanced Expand/Collapse option is demonstrated in Figure 2-43, where we've hidden all detail below the User level—on both the PivotTable and the PivotChart. Thus the Phone and Rate Plan detail is not showing!

1. Right-click the User2 column header to display the context-sensitive pop-up menu.
2. Choose Expand/Collapse on the pop-up menu.
3. Choose Expand To User on the secondary pop-up menu.

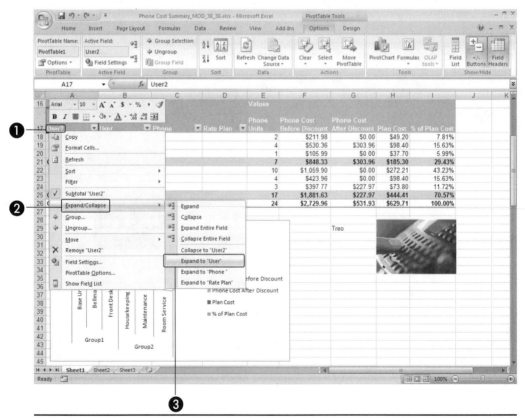

Figure 2-43 *PivotTable/PivotChart with a different kind of Expand to "User"*

Note that you can reset the PivotTable and PivotChart display, by simply right-clicking the User2 column header and choosing Expand/Collapse and Expand Entire Field.

This expand capability allows us to suppress any combination of fields looking across the PivotTable from left to right. In our working example we were able to hide the Phone and Rate Plan data, but keep the entire display area showing the same row-column layout. It also made it easy to show just the fields desired on the PivotChart.

Swapping Row and Column Fields in the PivotTable: Slice It and Dice It

And finally Figure 2-44 shows what is perhaps the most dramatic slicing and dicing example of all! We've moved the Phone field to the Columns area of the PivotChart, which created a series of repeating Value columns for the Dash and Treo phones.

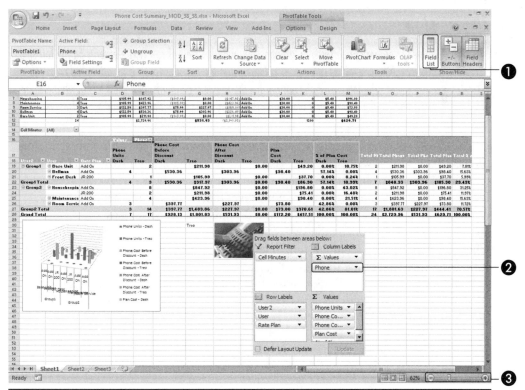

Figure 2-44 *PivotTable with Phone dragged and dropped to Columns area*

Essentially, the numeric columns are split out into groups for the Dash and Treo phones. At this point we're working with a pretty advanced PivotTable with both row and column subtotaling.

1. Click the Field List icon in the Show/Hide menu group, on the Ribbon menu Options tab.
2. Click the Phone field in the Row Labels rectangle, and while holding down the left button, drag it to the Column Labels rectangle.
3. Click the Zoom slider control on the bottom-right of the screen, and drag it down to 62% to see the entire PivotTable on the screen at once.

Note that you can click again on the Field List icon on the Ribbon menu to hide the PivotTable Field List pane and see the entire PivotTable screen. To reset the PivotTable and PivotChart to the previous data display, simply click again on the Field List icon on the Ribbon menu to open the PivotTable Field List pane, and drag the Phone field back into the Row Labels rectangle below the User field.

BI TIP

Value (or numeric) fields can be grouped by multiple levels of row text elements on the left side, and by multiple levels of column text elements on the top. The result is an advanced cross-tab matrix with subtotals across the bottom for the row text elements, and subtotals down the right-hand side for the column text elements. This is known as a multidimensional spreadsheet!

The PivotTable in Figure 2-44 has been zoomed out to fit the entire presentation on the screen so that we can see the visual effect of having both Row and Column text hierarchies—it's hard to read any detail, but it does show the overall look and feel of this result. People who work with PivotTables for a while become pretty familiar with the concept of dragging and dropping Fields from Rows to Columns and vice versa. This truly enables advanced analysis in a Business Intelligence sense, where we can visually see the arrangement of large data sets—in a way that seems to follow the way we're able to think of data.

And remember, the Undo icon at the top of the Excel screen will put the PivotTable and PivotChart back the way it was if you get lost in the slicing and dicing of data!

Conditional Formatting Inside a PivotTable

Excel 2007 takes the concept of conditional formatting to a new level. It's easy to apply color or icon schemes to selected cells of data (row or column) and produce a stunning visualization of the range of numeric values across the cells. We'll show some fast default ways to apply these color visuals—but we won't go into the sophistication of arithmetic rules that can be used to minutely control the conditional formatting. Suffice it to say that it's possible to take Excel conditional formatting to a level of statistical analysis if you explore these tools further!

Conditional Formatting Data Bars

Figure 2-45 shows the surprising result of adding data bars to a column of data. Longer data bars correspond to larger numbers, and the bars are automatically scaled against each other to show relative low-to-high values across the cells.

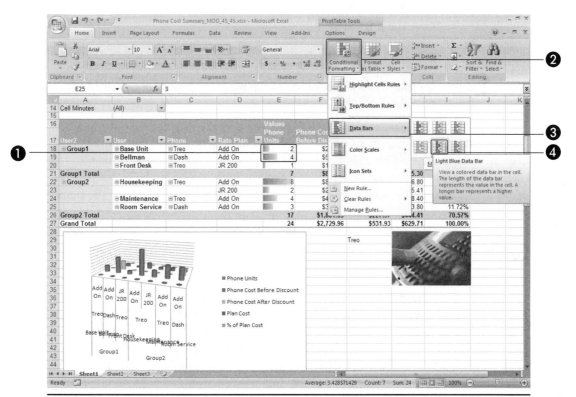

Figure 2-45 *PivotTable with Data Bars applied to Phone Units column*

You can even create your own color for a Data Bar by choosing the More Rules on the Data Bars menu gallery.

1. Click the top cell containing a number, in the Phone Units column, and then while holding the CTRL key down on your keyboard, click each of the other cells in the column—skipping over the Total row (thus cells with actual values will be multi-selected).
2. Click the Conditional Formatting icon in the Styles menu group, on the Ribbon menu Home tab.
3. Click the Data Bars icon on the pop-up menu.
4. Click the Light Blue Data Bar graphic on the pop-up gallery.

It's interesting to note that when you're choosing the conditional formatting and hover the mouse over various Data Bar graphics, you see a Live Preview of what they look like on the selected cells of the PivotTable. Again, Office 2007 is trying to help us work faster—and in this case it helped us choose a color scheme that fits the PivotTable style (the blue Data Bars stand out, but they don't clash with other colors).

BI TIP

Data Bars work best when applied to a single row or column of data, as opposed to large blocks of cells. They result in color gradients of cell background color that fill less or more of the cell, depending on relative cell values.

They can make an important part of the PivotTable stand out and guide discussion of the data. This makes sense when you think about using a Business Intelligence presentation as the visual centerpiece for a meeting where everyone needs to understand the data story and you want to make sure they notice the items with Data Bars.

Conditional Formatting Color Scales

Figure 2-46 shows the result of adding Color Scales to a column of data. Green corresponds to larger numbers, Red to smaller numbers, with Yellow in between— and the colors are automatically distributed against the data values to show relative low-to-high values across the cells. You can even create your own color combinations for a Color Scale by choosing the More Rules option on the Color Scales menu gallery. People really like the resulting color gradients of relative values, which adds immediate value to the data presentation.

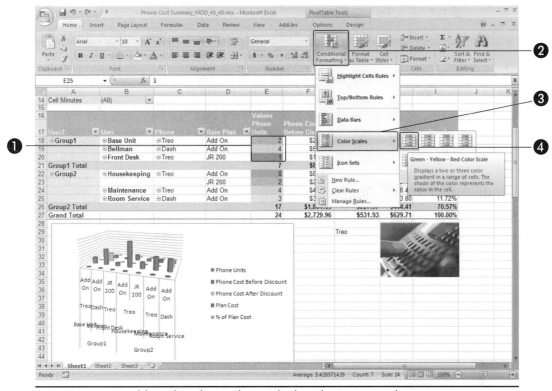

Figure 2-46 *PivotTable with Color Scales applied to Phone Units column*

1. Click the top cell containing a number, in the Phone Units column, and while holding the CTRL key down on your keyboard, click each of the other cells in the column—skipping over the Total row (thus cells with actual values will be multi-selected).

2. Click the Conditional Formatting icon in the Styles menu group, on the Ribbon menu Home tab.

3. Click the Color Scales icon on the pop-up menu.

4. Click the Green—Yellow—Red Color Scale graphic in the pop-up gallery.

As with the Data Bars, when you're choosing the Conditional Formatting and hover the mouse over various Color Scale graphics, you see a Live Preview of what they look like on the selected cells of the PivotTable. Office 2007 is trying to help us work smarter—and in this case it helped us choose a color scheme that made sense with the data we selected in the PivotTable (the green color, which has positive connotations, is applied to high numbers of Phones).

BI TIP

Color Scales work best when applied to large blocks of cells, as opposed to a single row or column of data. (This is the opposite of where Data Bars are best used!) They result in solid cell background colors that vary according to the relative cell values.

They can help you scan large spreadsheets of data and find large or small values. This makes sense when you think about using a Business Intelligence presentation for analysis in a data discussion.

Conditional Formatting Icon Sets

Figure 2-47 shows the result of adding Icon Sets to a column of data. Green corresponds to larger numbers, Red to smaller numbers, with Yellow in between—and the colors are automatically distributed against the data values to show relative

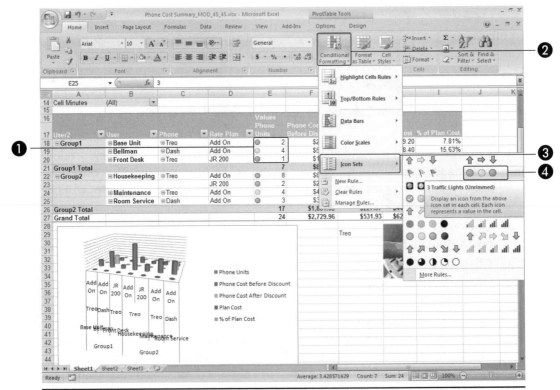

Figure 2-47   *PivotTable with Icon Sets applied to Phone Units column*

low-to-high values across the cells. It's important to note that if you choose the More Rules on the Icon Sets menu gallery, threshold values or formulas can be entered to guide when the icons show Green, Yellow, or Red!

1. Click the top cell containing a number, in the Phone Units column, and while holding the CTRL key down on your keyboard, click each of the other cells in the column—skipping over the Total row (thus cells with actual values will be multi-selected).
2. Click the Conditional Formatting icon in the Styles menu group, on the Ribbon menu Home tab.
3. Click the Icon Sets icon on the pop-up menu.
4. Click the 3 Traffic Lights (Unrimmed) graphic in the pop-up gallery.

Note that Conditional Formatting can easily be cleared on the spreadsheet, by clicking the Conditional Formatting icon again and choosing Clear Rules | Clear Rules From Selected Cells, or Entire Sheet.

As with the Data Bars, when you're choosing the Conditional Formatting and hover the mouse over various Color Scale graphics, you see a Live Preview of what they look like on the selected cells of the PivotTable. Office 2007 is trying to help us sort through the various graphic icons—and in this case it helped us choose a Traffic Light icon that seems to work with the PivotTable size and colors.

BI TIP

Icon Sets work best when applied to data that can act as indicators of business processes, which are sometimes called key performance indicators (KPIs). They can help point out data-related measures that show good things or bad things in an organization, such as the number of phones sold or the number of phones returned. This makes sense when you think about using a Business Intelligence presentation for measurement in a data discussion.

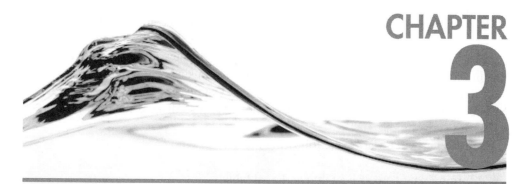

CHAPTER 3

Excel Tables: Conditional Formatting, What-If and Statistics, and Charts

T his chapter shows how the new Excel 2007 tables can be used to quickly turn a spreadsheet into columns that act like real database columns with top-level data filters and sorting. With Excel's new ability to hold up to one million rows, this becomes an important Office business intelligence tool. We show how conditional formatting is applied with Data Bars, Color Scales, and Icon Sets for a "dashboard" effect in the spreadsheet. We also discuss the new 2007 Chart features.

This chapter will describe the following topics:

▶   Turning your spreadsheet into an Excel table

▶   Excel table analysis

▶   What-If analysis and statistical tools

▶   Excel table charts

BEST REFERENCE

For further research on this topic, go to http://office.microsoft.com/office/excel/training.

Technology Positioning Statement

Excel tables in 2007 are the fastest way to format lists of data, especially with large data sets that have been imported into Excel. The conditional formatting is all done on the individual line items, and you can filter the rows based on column values to narrow down the set you are looking at. Tables and conditional formatting are easy to work with where the conditional formatting rules are comparing individual values in the selected cells.

The columns in a table have meaning—if we're referencing a column in a table, say using Structured References or via the Totals Row, we expect the table columns to reference real-world columns of data.

Tables are more about nonsummarized data, whereas PivotTables show aggregates. You can get aggregates in the Totals Row for an Excel table list, but the value of the table is in looking at the individual line items that make up the data.

—Sean Boon, Microsoft Excel Team

What Is an Excel Table?

Excel tables provide a way to keep your data in a coherent list format on an Excel spreadsheet. This list format is really somewhat like a database table, for those familiar with database terminology. It organizes the data into labeled columns with drop-down data-filtering controls that allow you reduce the data being displayed and to sort it in organized ways.

The tables are likely to be a popular tool with Excel 2007, since spreadsheets can hold one million rows in 2007! With all that data ending up in Excel, it really helps to be able to easily turn it into columns that help control the data display. It is in some ways an alternative to Excel PivotTables, which are not appropriate for all situations and, in fact, are sometimes limiting with the automatic PivotTable cross-tab behavior.

So we have two choices to handle large data sets in Excel 2007 (and support analysis or slicing and dicing of data in a business intelligence sense): PivotTables or Excel tables. This chapter will deal with Excel tables and subtotaling, adding conditional formatting and charting for analysis.

The following illustration shows an example of an Excel 2007 List, with the new conditional formatting. This chapter will explore the steps used to create this example List.

Where Do Excel Tables Fit in the Microsoft BI Picture?

The accompanying image shows a matrix view of Microsoft Business Intelligence technology (often referred to as BI). The Office, SharePoint, and SQL Server applications we see in the marketplace are shown on the left side of the matrix. These applications are used in the real-world activities of reporting, analysis, measurement, and planning, as shown across the top of the matrix. The top-down flow of the matrix starts with front-end BI tools we have in Office 2007 at our desktops—and goes down to back-end BI tools that run on servers such as SharePoint 2007 and PerformancePoint 2007, which provide an enhanced experience when connected to Office 2007.

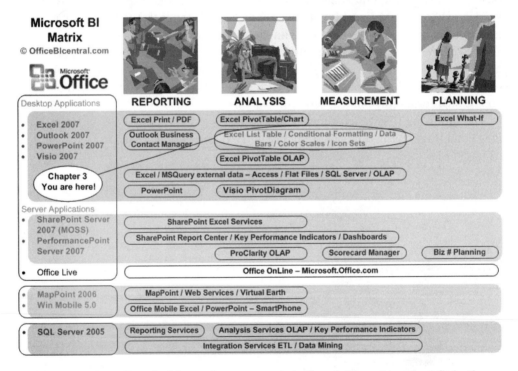

Learning about Excel tables makes more sense if we know where they fit in the Microsoft technology stack, and what they are used for in daily BI activities. The "You are here!" bubble in the image shows Excel tables as part of Excel 2007, which is part of Office 2007. We're going to use Excel tables, conditional formatting, and charts for analysis work, which is the second column of the BI matrix.

Excel tables are one of those capabilities that, if users knew how easy they are to work with, would be used much more often! Frankly, most of the spreadsheets used in everyday business can be turned into tables to do the things we'll show in this chapter.

In fact, the table can be turned back into its previous normal spreadsheet range at any time if desired. The new Excel 2007 Ribbon menu makes it fairly easy to work with tables and apply conditional formatting or add charts.

Opening an Excel 2003 Spreadsheet in Excel 2007

Figure 3-1 shows a real-world spreadsheet from a schoolteacher who tracks student reading levels and overall achievement scores. In this case, we have previous and current reading and full-scale scores, which is a simple representation of a year-to-year business process. The spreadsheet is not overly complex because it is from the real world of spreadsheets, and we're going to see how it can be enhanced with the business intelligence tools in Excel 2007.

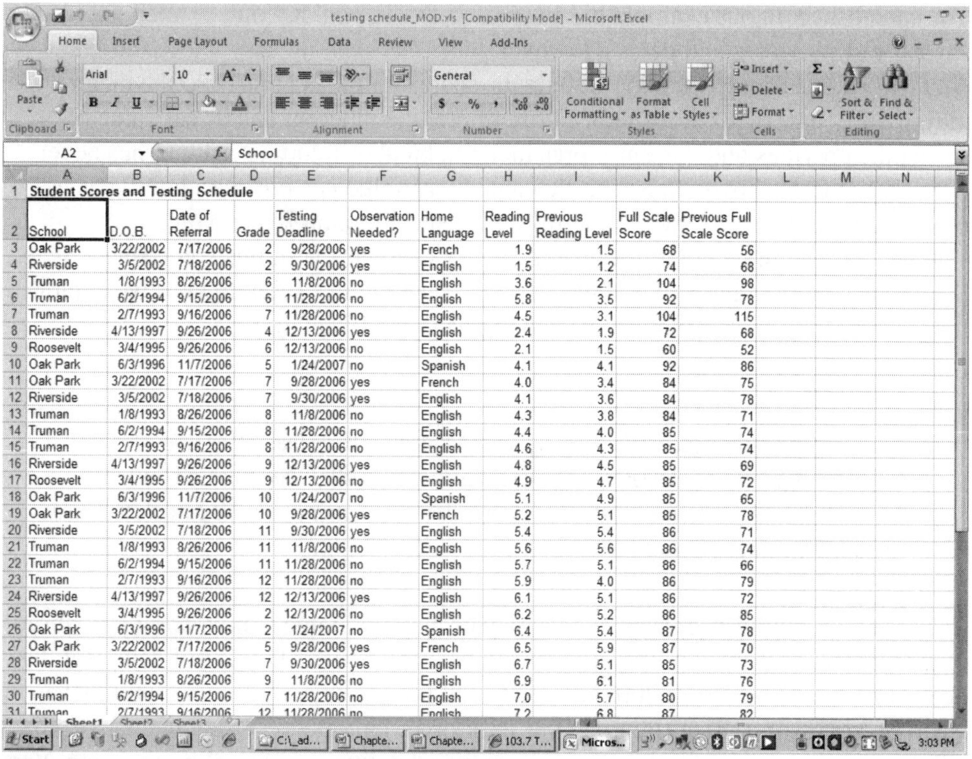

Student Scores and Testing Schedule

School	D.O.B.	Date of Referral	Grade	Testing Deadline	Observation Needed?	Home Language	Reading Level	Previous Reading Level	Full Scale Score	Previous Full Scale Score
Oak Park	3/22/2002	7/17/2006	2	9/28/2006	yes	French	1.9	1.5	68	56
Riverside	3/5/2002	7/18/2006	2	9/30/2006	yes	English	1.5	1.2	74	68
Truman	1/8/1993	8/26/2006	6	11/8/2006	no	English	3.6	2.1	104	98
Truman	6/2/1994	9/15/2006	6	11/28/2006	no	English	5.8	3.5	92	78
Truman	2/7/1993	9/16/2006	7	11/28/2006	no	English	4.5	3.1	104	115
Riverside	4/13/1997	9/26/2006	4	12/13/2006	yes	English	2.4	1.9	72	68
Roosevelt	3/4/1995	9/26/2006	6	12/13/2006	no	English	2.1	1.5	60	52
Oak Park	6/3/1996	11/7/2006	5	1/24/2007	no	Spanish	4.1	4.1	92	86
Oak Park	3/22/2002	7/17/2006	7	9/28/2006	yes	French	4.0	3.4	84	75
Riverside	3/5/2002	7/18/2006	7	9/30/2006	yes	English	4.1	3.6	84	78
Truman	1/8/1993	8/26/2006	8	11/8/2006	no	English	4.3	3.8	84	71
Truman	6/2/1994	9/15/2006	8	11/28/2006	no	English	4.4	4.0	85	74
Truman	2/7/1993	9/16/2006	8	11/28/2006	no	English	4.6	4.3	85	74
Riverside	4/13/1997	9/26/2006	9	12/13/2006	yes	English	4.8	4.5	85	69
Roosevelt	3/4/1995	9/26/2006	9	12/13/2006	no	English	4.9	4.7	85	72
Oak Park	6/3/1996	11/7/2006	10	1/24/2007	no	Spanish	5.1	4.9	85	65
Oak Park	3/22/2002	7/17/2006	10	9/28/2006	yes	French	5.2	5.1	85	78
Riverside	3/5/2002	7/18/2006	11	9/30/2006	yes	English	5.4	5.4	86	71
Truman	1/8/1993	8/26/2006	11	11/8/2006	no	English	5.6	5.6	86	74
Truman	6/2/1994	9/15/2006	11	11/28/2006	no	English	5.7	5.1	86	66
Truman	2/7/1993	9/16/2006	12	11/28/2006	no	English	5.9	4.0	86	79
Riverside	4/13/1997	9/26/2006	12	12/13/2006	yes	English	6.1	5.1	86	72
Roosevelt	3/4/1995	9/26/2006	2	12/13/2006	no	English	6.2	5.2	86	85
Oak Park	6/3/1996	11/7/2006	2	1/24/2007	no	Spanish	6.4	5.4	87	78
Oak Park	3/22/2002	7/17/2006	5	9/28/2006	yes	French	6.5	5.9	87	70
Riverside	3/5/2002	7/18/2006	7	9/30/2006	yes	English	6.7	5.1	85	73
Truman	1/8/1993	8/26/2006	9	11/8/2006	no	English	6.9	6.1	81	76
Truman	6/2/1994	9/15/2006	7	11/28/2006	no	English	7.0	5.7	80	79
Truman	2/7/1993	9/16/2006	12	11/28/2006	no	English	7.2	6.8	87	82

Figure 3-1 *A real-world Excel 2003 spreadsheet with no Excel table*

The spreadsheet in Figure 3-1 is not connected to any data sources; all data is contained in the cells shown. Because this spreadsheet is currently an Excel 2003 spreadsheet, the filename is displayed as Testing Schedule_MOD.xls [Compatibility Mode] on the title bar at the top of the Excel 2007 window. Excel 2007 saves earlier versions of Excel spreadsheets in their previous Excel version unless you choose to Save As Excel 2007. This is a nice feature that helps keep compatibility with earlier versions of Excel for other users who might not yet be using Office 2007. Excel 2007 will prompt you to Save As Excel 2007 if you add version 2007 enhancements to your spreadsheet.

To open an Excel 2003 spreadsheet in Excel 2007, simply click an existing Excel 2003 XLS file and it will open in Excel 2007 if Office 2007 is installed on your desktop or laptop. Or, click the Office button in the upper-left corner of Office Excel 2007, choose File | Open, and browse to the file of choice.

The Business Reason for an Excel Table

The spreadsheet in our example has been used day in and day out, to keep track of student testing scores and dates. However, there has been no easy way to add new data to the spreadsheet when new students, scores, or dates come into the picture during the course of a school year. Furthermore, the inherent analytical value of seeing the previous and current scores in a graphical or trending manner has never been shown from this spreadsheet; this analytical value is a business intelligence aspect that we'll explore by turning the spreadsheet into an Excel table.

If we succeed in taking a few analytical steps forward with this spreadsheet, it should spark some innovative thinking by everyone with similar data as we explore the value of the analysis that can be accomplished in Excel 2007.

BI TIP

Every spreadsheet used in the working world has analytic value that can be unlocked with just a few steps into the business intelligence features of Excel 2007. And it doesn't have to be sophisticated; just an organized list or Excel table with a chart is a valuable part of the business intelligence way of looking at data.

Note that a spreadsheet such as this may or may not come from a corporate library of examples, and it may or may not be connected to a central server of data. But that doesn't matter, since Excel 2007 makes it easy for you to add professional touches as a part of Microsoft Office right on your desktop or laptop—resulting in changes that will help convey information to the customer and deliver a compelling message. You don't need to ask an IT specialist for help, and you don't have to be connected to a database server! With Excel 2007 you have the power to make business intelligence work for you with whatever spreadsheets you already have!

Save As Excel 2007: New 2007 Options and Excel File Formats

Figure 3-2 shows that we've decided it's a good time to save our working Excel spreadsheet in the new format of Excel 2007, which uses a file type suffix of .XLSX. To do this, we clicked Office, chose Save As, and then chose Excel Workbook.

1. Click the Office button in the upper left of the Excel 2007 screen.
2. Click the Save As option in the pop-up menu.
3. Click "Save the workbook in the default file format" (.XLSX file type) on the secondary pop-up menu.

The variety of Excel 2007 save choices is less confusing if we keep in mind that all of our work will be done in the new XLSX format, which is the default for Excel 2007. XLSX is actually an XML format that supports the direction of open file formats for all of Microsoft Office 2007 that can be opened by either Microsoft or

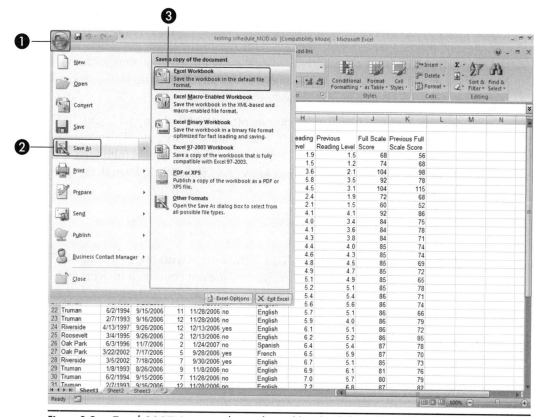

Figure 3-2 *Excel 2007 Save As | Excel Workbook: default format XLSX*

non-Microsoft applications. XML formats in general have become the standard for data and files that exist outside of a database server, and it's worth noting that XML files can be opened in common tools such as Microsoft Notepad (although you don't get the Excel interface and toolset when the file is opened with Notepad).

BI TIP

XML formats for business intelligence tools are increasingly popular with companies that favor the nonproprietary nature of XML files. And it makes sense that modern business intelligence tools support the saving of content in XML formats whose value can more readily be shared among the multiple applications we find in companies today. So although the XML formats might not affect stand-alone users of Office 2007, it's something we expect with today's computer applications.

It's worth noting that the new Office 2007 XML formats, including the Excel 2007 XLSX format, have two advantages beyond the nonproprietary appeal of an XML format itself:

▶ XLSX is actually a Zipped file that Excel 2007 automatically compresses when saving, and decompresses when opening. This means the Excel 2007 files will take up less space on your hard drive! Also, the Zip format conforms to the industry standard format, so it can be opened with any Zip/Unzip tool if desired (although there will not likely be a reason to do so).

▶ XLSX contains separate files for the various pieces that make up an Excel 2007 workbook, such as the base spreadsheet, Excel tables, charts, etc. This means the Excel 2007 files are less prone to corruption or data problems (although it is expected that you will make periodic backups of all Excel files, even those that are a work in progress).

The other Excel 2007 Save formats are

▶ **Excel Macro-Enabled Workbook**   This format is for workbooks that need to contain macros. As a security feature, macros are not contained in everyday Excel spreadsheets, although they can be a powerful way to add advanced or custom functionality.

▶ **Excel Binary Workbook**   This format saves workbooks in a 2007 binary format. Although this is like the XLS binary format of Excel 2003 and earlier versions, it is meant to be opened only by Excel 2007, since it will contain Excel 2007–specific features.

▶ **Excel 97–2003 Workbook**   This format saves workbooks in the older Excel 97, 2000, and 2003 formats. Although 2007 features may be lost or not function in earlier Excel versions, this is important if you need to send an Excel workbook to someone who does not have Office Excel 2007.

BI TIP

Note the PDF Save option is not available in Office 2007 until you download the free Microsoft Save as PDF or XPS file from Microsoft's web site. It's easy to find on the Microsoft.com/Office web site, where you'll find menu options to check for free updates or Office downloads.

▶ **PDF or XPS**   This saves workbooks in the Adobe Portable Document Format (PDF) format or the Microsoft XML Paper Specification (XPS). PDFs are a popular format that can be viewed by virtually everyone for free. Saving Excel as a PDF also allows you to share information with many other users without allowing them to modify the contents, which is a great way to distribute financial proposals or statements that need to remain unedited.

XPS is a Microsoft XML format that provides a PDF-like experience. It can be output from all Office 2007 applications, and it can be viewed within Office 2007 or with a free XPS viewer from Microsoft.

Office 2007 Ribbon Menu: A Brand-New Look in 2007

Figure 3-3 shows our workbook open in the Excel 2007 format. Note that compatibility mode no longer appears in the top title bar of the Excel screen. To get this display, we actually closed the spreadsheet after saving it as a 2007 Excel workbook, and then reopened it. This is the best way to experience the Excel 2007 features, and in fact we don't want to be slowed down by the previous compatibility mode interface that uses some of the older Excel 2003 displays.

In Figure 3-3 note the Office button for file-level actions (sporting the Office 2007 logo) in the upper-left corner of the screen. Clicking the Office button will show common file menu options such as Open, Save, and Print. Visually moving down to the tabs part of the Ribbon menu, we see some appealing graphics that provide an intuitive guide to common tasks at four levels, as shown in the figure.

    a. Looking at the Excel Ribbon, we see a top-level tab interface that organizes spreadsheet tasks into common areas; Home, Insert, Page Layout, Formulas, Data, Review, View, and Add-Ins.

    b. Looking across the tabs, we see a variety of submenu tasks: Connections, Sort & Filter, Data Tools, Outline, and Analysis.

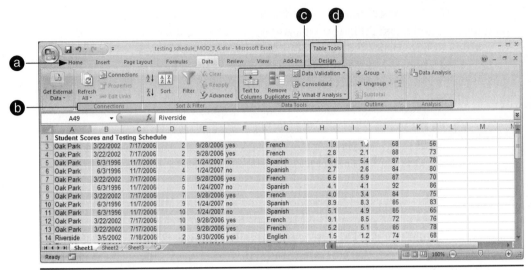

Figure 3-3 *Excel 2007 with the new Office 2007 Ribbon menu*

c. Looking within the Data Tools group, we see a variety of menu options for Text To Columns, Remove Duplicates, Data Validation, Consolidate, and What-If Analysis. These menu options are really the foundation of working business intelligence in the context of Office 2007!

d. When some menu options are chosen, contextual tabs appear as more tabs along the top level of the Ribbon interface. In our working example, when we go to the Styles group and click the Format As Table option, we'll proceed to transform the data into an Excel table and end up working with a new Table Tools context tab for Design that is available once we're working with an Excel table on the screen.

BI TIP

You're well advised to open your existing spreadsheets in Excel 2007, save them in the new 2007 Excel workbook format, and then reopen them! You can always save your work in the Excel 97–2003 workbook format if you need to share the spreadsheet with other users that might not yet have Office 2007. Excel 2007 has a compatibility checker that automatically shows any new 2007 items that might be degraded when Saved As 97–2003 spreadsheets. The compatibility checker is also available by Clicking the Office button at the top left of the Excel 2007 screen and choosing Prepare | Run Compatibility Checker.

It is worth pausing at this point for a brief discussion of the new Office 2007 menu layout. Microsoft has put a great deal of effort into consolidating the thousands of Office menu commands and choices into this new format. All of the Office 2007 applications use the new Ribbon menu approach for their user interface—notably Excel, Access, PowerPoint, Outlook, and Word.

Our step-by-step instructions in this chapter will primarily use the Ribbon menu icon-based tabbed/grouped interface to accomplish our work for consistency. However, right-click and context-sensitive menus are also a significant part of the Office 2007 interface, and we'll use them whenever we go beyond the immediate options of the Ribbon menu. As you gain familiarity with the new Office 2007 interface, you'll probably develop your own favorite right-click menu paths in everyday work routines.

BI TIP

The new Office 2007 Ribbon menu is a big jump forward for Office applications, and it is perhaps the most important element of commonality to tie together Excel, Access, PowerPoint, Outlook, and Word since the early days of Office integration years ago. If you're a long-time power user of Excel, the new Ribbon menu will take some getting used to; although it honestly will be just a couple of days until you're comfortable with it, and then you probably won't ever want to return to the old way of doing work! And note the Ribbon menu look and feel is quickly becoming ubiquitous across Microsoft applications, from Microsoft Office SharePoint Server (MOSS) to Visio 2007.

The basic elements of the Ribbon menu are straightforward: the Office button, tabs, groups within the tabs, and icons within the groups. Office 2007 sports a much richer set of icons that display across the Ribbon menu and provide an intuitive idea of the actions that can be accomplished by clicking the icons.

Furthermore, many of the icons provide a live preview capability where the on-screen spreadsheet display will change as you hover the mouse over an icon but won't actually change the spreadsheet until you click and choose the icon action. This really makes working with Excel 2007 much faster, since you don't have to keep changing spreadsheet elements back and forth to get visual feedback on formatting and row-column arrangements. In fact, you can mouse over a gallery of choices that may have a large number of options, and very quickly find the appearance you want.

BI TIP

A very useful part of the new 2007 interface is the Zoom slider control that always appears at the lower right of the screen. It's amazing how often we find ourselves using this to zoom the display in or out—to bring whatever we want to see within the viewable screen.

Another helpful aspect of the Office 2007 Ribbon menu design is that the tabs and groups of icons follow your workflow of creating content. So with Excel 2007 we start at the Home tab with the common text and number formatting menu options, followed by the Insert tab, where we can start with a PivotTable/PivotChart inserted into the spreadsheet, for example.

Subsequent tabs hold groups of icons for more advanced Formulas and Data work, and at the end of the default tab strip we find tabs for Review and View to help in the finalization of the workbook. Note we'll always wind up back at the Office button for saving and printing, where we'll find a surprisingly wide range of menu choices for Prepare, Send, and Publish, which hold some important capabilities that allow us to really control workbook content and delivery using e-mail or Microsoft Office SharePoint, for example.

BI TIP

One important thing to note about the new Ribbon menu is the location of the Properties menu option for a workbook. Click the Office button and choose Prepare | Properties to bring up a dialog box where you can examine or edit the Author, Title, etc. of your workbook. This can be significant to avoid surprises when someone else looks at your spreadsheet and sees information you didn't even know was there!

Selecting Data for the Excel Table

As shown in Figure 3-4 we're going to jump right in and turn the spreadsheet into an Excel table. We're not going to worry about arranging the data beforehand, because we'll be able to use the tools of an Excel table to sort and group the data. It's amazing to see how quickly we can change an ordinary spreadsheet into a much better-looking table in Excel 2007.

1. Click the Format As Table icon in the Styles menu group, on the Ribbon menu Home tab.
2. Click the Table Style Medium 14 icon in the pop-up gallery.
3. Click the cell-selection icon in the Format As Table dialog box, which allows you to then click directly on the spreadsheet.
4. Click the spreadsheet cell A2 and then hold the right mouse button down and drag the mouse to select the entire desired spreadsheet area. Click again on the cell-selection icon in the Format As Table dialog box, which will automatically place =$A$2:$K$48 into the text box. Then click OK.

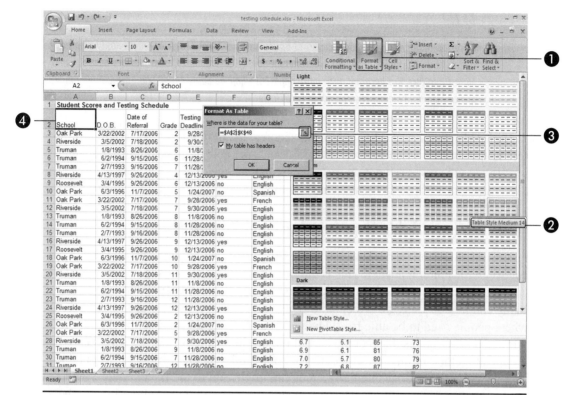

Figure 3-4   *Selected data for use with an Excel table; choosing Format As Table*

Figure 3-4 gives us the opportunity to look at a couple of interesting points about Excel tables in Office 2007. First, the Format As Table icon brings up a gallery of format styles that make it easy to color-arrange spreadsheet data. These Office 2007 galleries offer a Live Preview feature as well. After selecting one of the gallery styles and applying it to spreadsheet data, you can go back to the Format As Table icon again to bring up the gallery of styles. As you hover your mouse over each style, Excel automatically changes the colors of the spreadsheet data outside the gallery so that you can get a quick idea of the color formatting results from among a large variety of choices without ever clicking a style unless until you know it's the one you want! You might want to think about your organization's color schemes, such as those used in logos or web sites, in choosing a gallery style that resonates with the people that will be viewing the Excel table result.

Notice also that Excel 2007 was fairly accurate in automatically selecting the entire spreadsheet of data when we clicked the Format As Table icon. We adjusted it slightly by changing the row designation from $A1 to $A2 in the dialog box, which allowed us to more exactly specify the row and column range of data for the Excel table.

Using the Excel Table User Interface and Ribbon Menu

Figure 3-5 shows our spreadsheet as an Excel table. Each column has a drop-down control in the column header. This is the new 2007 Excel table user interface, and it's where we'll do most of our work in this chapter. And we'll find that we can easily add new rows to the Excel table. This mirrors the real world of Excel work, where people need to be able to add new data to their spreadsheet with minimal effort and have the results become part of the original data that can be sorted and grouped together. In fact, we'll see that building an Excel chart from an Excel table automatically incorporates new rows that you might add to the Excel table.

Note the top-level Ribbon menu has changed since we've started working with an Excel table; a new Design context tab is displaying under a top-menu heading of Table Tools to provide items we'll need in working with Excel tables. This is exactly how the new Office 2007 Ribbon menu is supposed to work; menu tabs with new choices are automatically made available to the user whenever we're working with Excel items that require additional tools. The following explanations (a through e) correspond to the similarly labeled areas in Figure 3-5.

a. **Properties group** This is where you can change the table name (not important to us) or resize the table to incorporate more rows or columns. We'll see later in this section that it's easier to simply click the bottom-right cell of the table, and press your TAB key to automatically add a new row to the Excel table.

b. **Tools group** This is where you can create a PivotTable from the Excel table (see Chapter 2), or remove duplicates, which is not recommended, since the duplicates are invariably a legitimate part of the original data. The Convert To Range option is actually useful, since it allows you to change the Excel table back to the original spreadsheet format at any time (and you can then change it back to Excel table form as well). This could come in handy if you become

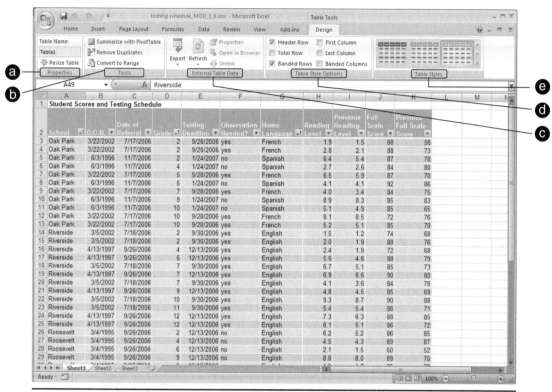

Figure 3-5 *Excel 2007 table, showing the Ribbon menu and Table Tools context tab*

frustrated in working with the Excel table and need to revert back to the original data format.

c. **External Table Data**   This is potentially a valuable part of the Excel table interface, but we won't be using it in this chapter, since we're working with a stand-alone spreadsheet that mirrors a common part of the real world and does not draw its data from external sources. For external data, see Chapter 4.

d. **Table Style Options**   This menu group sports a nice-to-have set of options that allow us to toggle display elements on or off. The most useful one is the Total Row checkbox, which adds a grand total row to the bottom of the Excel table. The grand total cells that appear at the bottom of each column have drop-down controls that support Sum, Count, Mix, Max, etc. as totaling options. However, we'll see later in this section that the Excel table Subtotal menu options are actually more useful, since they allow us to place Sum, Count, Average, etc., for each group of data in the Excel table.

e. **Table Styles** This holds the menu options to choose different table styles. It's interesting that checking or unchecking display options in the Table Style Options menu group automatically changes the appearance of the Excel table style in both the Excel table and the menu group. This is an example of the Live Preview capability that is built into Office 2007 applications.

BI TIP

If you find the Excel table Design tab has disappeared while working on the overall spreadsheet, simply click anywhere on the Excel table itself to bring back the Design context tab. This tip can really be helpful, since it's surprisingly disconcerting to suddenly lose Ribbon menu options you've learned to depend on—a common but temporary point of frustration for Excel users!

Sorting Data in the Excel Table

Figure 3-6 shows the next step we're going to take with the Excel table: sorting the various columns of data so that they make sense. This, combined with the

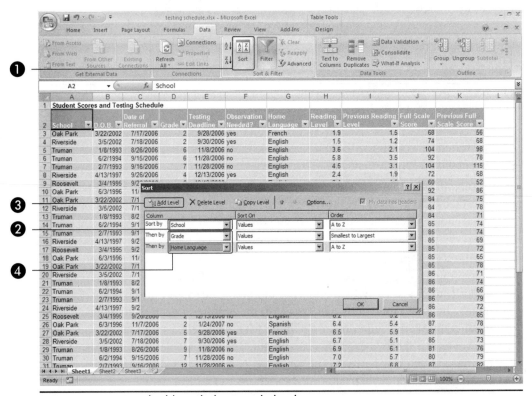

Figure 3-6   *An Excel table with the Sort dialog box*

Data Filter drop-down controls at the top of each column, will bring the Excel table into a structure that is truly useful. Note we're now using the Data tab of the top-level Ribbon menu, which has the main options we'll now be using to work with the Excel table.

1. Click the Sort icon in the Sort & Filter menu group, on the Ribbon menu Data tab.
2. Choose School in the Sort By drop-down control, on the Sort dialog box.
3. Click the Add Level menu option at the top of the Sort dialog box.
4. Choose Grade for the second Sort By drop-down. Repeat the Add Level menu click, and choose Home Language for the third Sort By drop-down, and click OK.

Note the powerful sorting capabilities of the Excel 2007 table. Frankly, this is the feature that most business users find to be an immediate value. We can quickly turn any data into an Excel 2007 table and then use the table as a list to sort and subsort the rows of data.

Entering Data into Excel Tables with Data Validation

Figure 3-7 shows that we're going to take another step with the Excel table now that it's sorted in a logical manner (it certainly helps that we can now visualize the data grouped by School, for example). In everyday work we often need to add data to our Excel spreadsheets—and Excel tables can make this a reasonable process with the use of Data Validation.

1. Click the Data Validation option in the Data Tools menu group, on the Ribbon menu Data tab.
2. Choose List in the Allow drop-down menu control, in the Data Validation dialog box.
3. Click the cell-selection icon at the right end of the Source text box, which allows you to directly click any area of the actual spreadsheet!
4. Click the top of the first column of the Excel table (column A) to automatically place =$A:$A into the Source text box of the Data Validation dialog box. Then click OK.

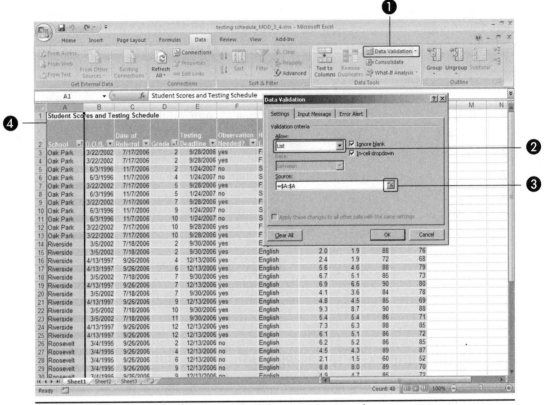

Figure 3-7   *Excel table with Data Validation to support new data entry on new rows*

Figure 3-8 shows the working result of adding Data Validation to our Excel table. Basically, we can add a new row to our original data without having to retype (or incorrectly type) recurring spreadsheet data. This is a big step forward, since using existing data for new rows, where appropriate, avoids the problems of manually typing the desired data and eliminates data entry errors.

This is a brute-force use of Excel data to help us with data entry, and we'll see in a subsequent step how to limit this to unique data values. For now, however, this use of the Data Validation feature provides a quick way to avoid manual data entry.

1. Click the bottom-right cell in the Excel table, and then press the TAB key on your keyboard.

2. Click the drop-down control that automatically displays on the new cell in the first column, and choose the desired data value.

	School	D.O.B.	Date of Refer	Grade	Testing Deadli	Observation N	Home Languag	Reading Le	Previous Re	Full Scale	Previous Full	L	M	N
22	Riverside	3/5/2002	7/18/2006	10	9/30/2006	yes	English	9.3	8.7	90	88			
23	Riverside	3/5/2002	7/18/2006	11	9/30/2006	yes	English	5.4	5.4	86	71			
24	Riverside	4/13/1997	9/26/2006	12	12/13/2006	yes	English	7.3	6.3	88	85			
25	Riverside	4/13/1997	9/26/2006	12	12/13/2006	yes	English	6.1	5.1	86	72			
26	Roosevelt	3/4/1995	9/26/2006	2	12/13/2006	no	English	6.2	5.2	86	85			
27	Roosevelt	3/4/1995	9/26/2006	4	12/13/2006	no	English	4.5	4.3	89	87			
28	Roosevelt	3/4/1995	9/26/2006	6	12/13/2006	no	English	2.1	1.5	60	52			
29	Roosevelt	3/4/1995	9/26/2006	9	12/13/2006	no	English	8.8	8.0	89	70			
30	Roosevelt	3/4/1995	9/26/2006	9	12/13/2006	no	English	4.9	4.7	85	72			
31	Truman	1/8/1993	8/26/2006	5	11/8/2006	no	English	4.1	3.2	78	79			
32	Truman	6/2/1994	9/15/2006	5	11/28/2006	no	English	5.3	4.4	89	82			
33	Truman	1/8/1993	8/26/2006	6	11/8/2006	no	English	3.6	2.1	104	98			
34	Truman	6/2/1994	9/15/2006	6	11/28/2006	no	English	5.8	3.5	92	78			
35	Truman	2/7/1993	9/16/2006	6	11/28/2006	no	English	6.5	5.6	104	⌴			
36	Truman	2/7/1993	9/16/2006	7	11/28/2006	no	English	4.5	3.1	104	115			
37	Truman	6/2/1994	9/15/2006	7	11/28/2006	no	English	7.0	5.7	80	79			
38	Truman	1/8/1993	8/26/2006	8	11/8/2006	no	English	4.3	3.8	84	71			
39	Truman	6/2/1994	9/15/2006	8	11/28/2006	no	English	4.4	4.0	85	74			
40	Truman	2/7/1993	9/16/2006	8	11/28/2006	no	English	7.7	7.4	90	87			
41	Truman	2/7/1993	9/16/2006	8	11/28/2006	no	English	4.6	4.3	85	74			
42	Truman	1/8/1993	8/26/2006	9	11/8/2006	no	English	6.9	6.1	81	76			
43	Truman	1/8/1993	8/26/2006	11	11/8/2006	no	English	5.6	5.6	86	74			
44	Truman	1/8/1993	8/26/2006	11	11/28/2006	no	English	9.4	9.4	92	81			
45	Truman	6/2/1994	9/15/2006	11	11/28/2006	no	English	5.7	5.1	86	66			
46	Truman	2/7/1993	9/16/2006	12	11/28/2006	no	English	5.9	4.0	86	79			
47	Truman	2/7/1993	9/16/2006	12	11/28/2006	no	English	7.2	6.8	87	82			
48	Truman	6/2/1994	9/15/2006	12	11/28/2006	no	English	9.6	9.2	102	84			
49														
50	Truman													
51	Truman													
52	Truman													
53	Truman													
	Truman													

Figure 3-8   *Excel table with Data Validation applied—supporting data entry in a new row*

As Figure 3-8 shows, we now have a controlled data input environment. It's not as perfect as a data entry screen that we might expect in an enterprise application used by many users, but it's a lot better than no entry mechanism at all, and you can configure and control it as an end user without help from anyone else!

BI TIP

There are many situations in business intelligence projects where a coherent data entry mechanism is not available, so the BI analysis depends on data that is manually entered into an Excel spreadsheet. In an ideal setting, a true data entry application would be added to the business process, but this is often not practical, so we need to know how to use Excel as a data entry mechanism. Excel 2007 tables provide one way to do this.

Now suppose we'd like to provide a data input mechanism for the Excel table that does not show all the duplicate values that are contained in an Excel column. Figure 3-9 shows how we can configure just such a mechanism, which may be important when we consider that an Excel column could have thousands (or millions!) of rows of data, and we just want to choose from unique values for data input on new rows.

1. Click the column A header of the Excel table to designate it as the source column for this Advanced filter.

2. Click the Advanced option in the Sort & Filter menu group, on the Ribbon menu Data tab.

3. Choose the "Copy to another location" option button in the Advanced Filter dialog box.

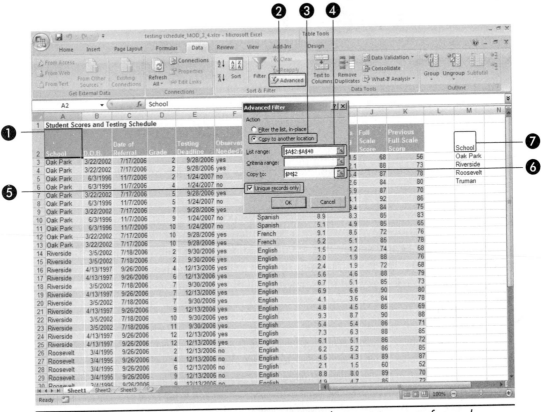

Figure 3-9   *Excel table; Advanced menu option to produce a unique set of records*

4. Look at the value in the List Range text box. If it does not already show the cells from column A, click the cell-selection icon at the right end of the List Range text box, which allows you to click directly on the header for column A in the spreadsheet Excel table.

5. Click the Unique Records Only checkbox.

6. Click the cell-selection icon at the right end of the Copy To text box.

7. Click directly on cell M2 of the spreadsheet. Click the cell-selection icon again at the right end of the Source text box to automatically place **$M$2** into the text box, and click OK.

It's pretty amazing that we are able to produce a separate unique list of column values so easily, from an Excel table column. We are now going to use this unique list of values as the Data Validation List source for new rows that we might want to add to the Excel table. Figure 3-10 shows that we can now apply Data Validation to the first column with a unique set of data values that is much more reasonable to choose from.

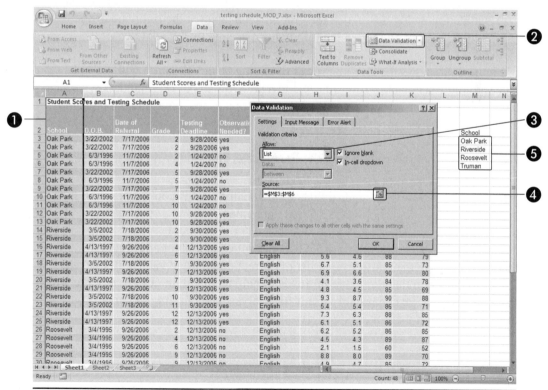

Figure 3-10 *Excel 2007 table—data input validation using a unique list*

The advantage to this approach is that we achieve a data-input mechanism for our Excel table that draws from unique values so that we don't have to manually retype data values. The integrity of the Excel 2007 table is preserved with valid data that can be sorted, aggregated, and charted with consistency.

1. Click the column A header of the Excel table to designate it as the column for this Data Validation.

2. Click the Data Validation option in the Data Tools menu group, on the Ribbon menu Data Tools tab.

3. Choose List in the Allow drop-down control, on the Data Validation dialog box.

4. Click the cell-selection icon at the right end of the Source text box, which allows you to then click/select any area of the actual spreadsheet!

5. Click cell M3 of the spreadsheet, and while holding the left mouse button down drag the mouse down to include cell M6 to select the list of unique values. This automatically places =$M$3:$M$6 into the Source text box of the Data Validation dialog box. Click the graphic icon again at the right end of the Source text box to reopen the full dialog box, and then click OK.

Figure 3-11 shows the working result of adding Data Validation with unique values to our Excel table. Now we can add a new row to our original data without having to retype (or incorrectly type) recurrent spreadsheet data, and we have the unique list of values from which to choose!

1. Click the bottom-right cell in the Excel table, and then press the TAB key on your keyboard.

2. Click the drop-down control that automatically displays on the new cell in the first column, and choose the desired data value.

As Figure 3-11 shows, we now have a controlled data input environment that makes it easy to choose from a list of correct and unique values. It's worth emphasizing again that the value of this is to help us maintain our Excel table with valid data so that we can reliably use it for analysis and charting to support our everyday decision making.

	School	D.O.B.	Date of Refer	Grade	Testing Deadli	Observation Ne	Home Languag	Reading Le	Previous Re	Full Scale	Previous Full	L	M	N
22	Riverside	3/5/2002	7/18/2006	10	9/30/2006	yes	English	9.3	8.7	90	88			
23	Riverside	3/5/2002	7/18/2006	11	9/30/2006	yes	English	5.4	5.4	86	71			
24	Riverside	4/13/1997	9/26/2006	12	12/13/2006	yes	English	7.3	6.3	88	85			
25	Riverside	4/13/1997	9/26/2006	12	12/13/2006	yes	English	6.1	5.1	86	72			
26	Roosevelt	3/4/1995	9/26/2006	2	12/13/2006	no	English	6.2	5.2	86	85			
27	Roosevelt	3/4/1995	9/26/2006	4	12/13/2006	no	English	4.5	4.3	89	87			
28	Roosevelt	3/4/1995	9/26/2006	6	12/13/2006	no	English	2.1	1.5	60	52			
29	Roosevelt	3/4/1995	9/26/2006	9	12/13/2006	no	English	8.8	8.0	89	70			
30	Roosevelt	3/4/1995	9/26/2006	9	12/13/2006	no	English	4.9	4.7	85	72			
31	Truman	1/8/1993	8/26/2006	5	11/8/2006	no	English	4.1	3.2	78	79			
32	Truman	6/2/1994	9/15/2006	5	11/28/2006	no	English	5.3	4.4	89	82			
33	Truman	1/8/1993	8/26/2006	6	11/8/2006	no	English	3.6	2.1	104	98			
34	Truman	6/2/1994	9/15/2006	6	11/28/2006	no	English	5.8	3.5	92	78			
35	Truman	2/7/1993	9/16/2006	6	11/28/2006	no	English	6.5	5.6	104	84			
36	Truman	2/7/1993	9/16/2006	7	11/28/2006	no	English	4.5	3.1	104	115			
37	Truman	6/2/1994	9/15/2006	7	11/28/2006	no	English	7.0	5.7	80	79			
38	Truman	1/8/1993	8/26/2006	8	11/8/2006	no	English	4.3	3.8	84	71			
39	Truman	6/2/1994	9/15/2006	8	11/28/2006	no	English	4.4	4.0	85	74			
40	Truman	2/7/1993	9/16/2006	8	11/28/2006	no	English	7.7	7.4	90	87			
41	Truman	2/7/1993	9/16/2006	8	11/28/2006	no	English	4.6	4.3	85	74			
42	Truman	1/8/1993	8/26/2006	9	11/8/2006	no	English	6.9	6.1	81	76			
43	Truman	1/8/1993	8/26/2006	11	11/8/2006	no	English	5.6	5.6	86	74			
44	Truman	1/8/1993	8/26/2006	11	11/8/2006	no	English	9.4	9.4	92	81			
45	Truman	6/2/1994	9/15/2006	11	11/28/2006	no	English	5.7	5.1	86	66			
46	Truman	2/7/1993	9/16/2006	12	11/28/2006	no	English	5.9	4.0	86	79			
47	Truman	2/7/1993	9/16/2006	12	11/28/2006	no	English	7.2	6.8	87	82			
48	Truman	6/2/1994	9/15/2006	12	11/28/2006	no	English	9.6	9.2	102	84			

Figure 3-11 *Excel table with Data Validation applied; unique data entry in a new row*

Excel Tables and Data Filtering on Columns

The next step is an easy one with our working Excel 2007 table. Because it's now a table, we have Data Filtering drop-down controls at the top of each column. Figure 3-12 shows how quickly we can change the data display to show unique sets of data within the Excel table.

Note that by default the (Select All) choice is checked whenever an Excel Data Filtering dialog box is displayed; simply uncheck it to allow the selection of individual choices below the (Select All) choice. This is a simple point but it sometimes confuses first-time users of Excel Data Filtering controls.

1. Click on the School drop-down control to display the Sort dialog box.
2. Click the (Select All) choice to deselect all the choices.
3. Click the Oak Park checkbox, and click OK.

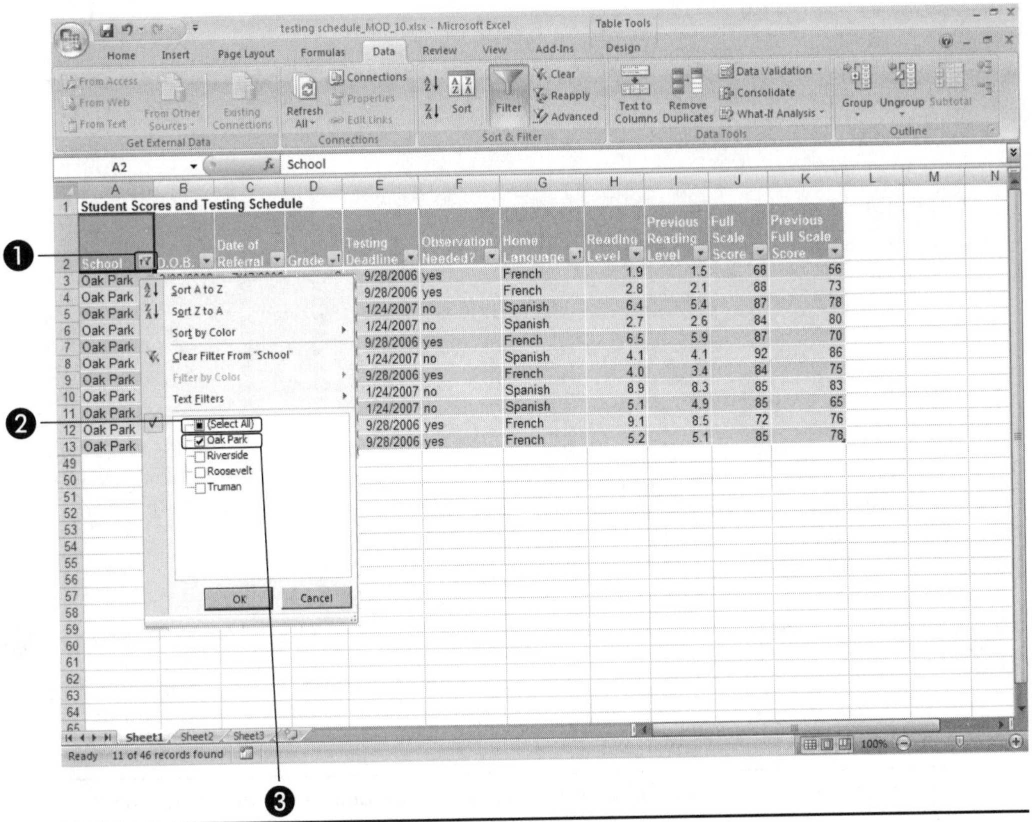

Figure 3-12 *Excel table with column filtering by unique data elements*

It's easy to see that Excel tables provide an automatic list of unique values for each column, and then allow us to choose which elements to display in the Excel table. Note this can be done for any column(s) in the Excel table, and it can be done on the fly in the middle of discussions during the workday. All of the data is still contained in the Excel table (it has not been erased or deleted), and it can be redisplayed with the same Data Filter drop-down arrows used in this example.

Data Filters are particularly important with large data sets where we might have so many rows (remember, Excel 2007 can hold one million rows of data!) that we need to narrow the display just to understand what we're working with.

Excel Tables with Groups and Subtotals

In this section we're going to take Excel tables to their limit by adding subtotals. This may sound simple enough, but in Excel 2007 tables and subtotals are a bit difficult to get working together. However, the result is worth the menu steps involved, since we will find our working example is much more versatile with subtotal outline controls added to the spreadsheet.

Figure 3-13 shows how we start the process of adding subtotals by changing the Excel table back to a regular spreadsheet. This must be done because subtotals cannot be added to an Excel table, but a spreadsheet that already has subtotals can be turned into a table!

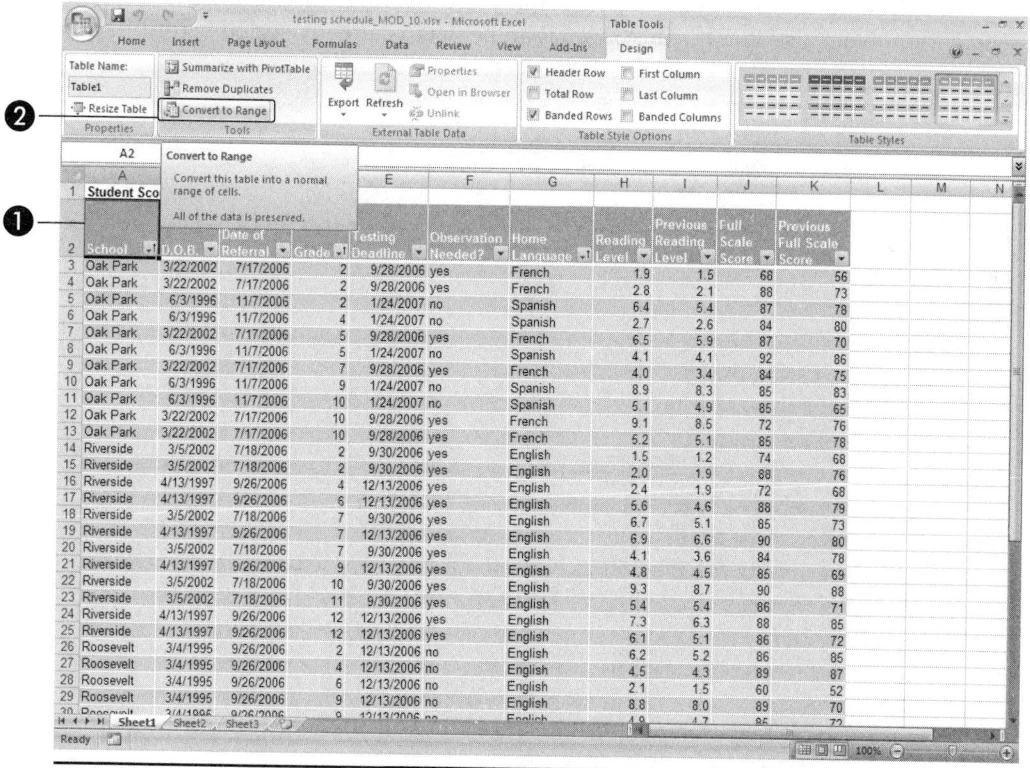

Figure 3-13 *Excel 2007 table; converting it back to a regular spreadsheet*

To do this, simply we use the Convert To Range option in the Tools menu group, on the Ribbon menu Design tab (which displays when the Excel table is selected by clicking anywhere on the table).

1. Click anywhere on the Excel table to select it, and make sure the Ribbon menu Table Tools context tab is showing.

2. Click the Convert To Range option in the Tools menu group, on the Ribbon menu Design tab.

Figure 3-14 shows how we apply Subtotals to the spreadsheet (which is no longer an Excel table). Note how the Subtotal icon in the Outline group of the Ribbon menu was dimmed and not available when the data was displaying as a table. Now that we're in normal range mode for the data display, we can make use of the Subtotal menu option. Note also that it's important that the data is already sorted before

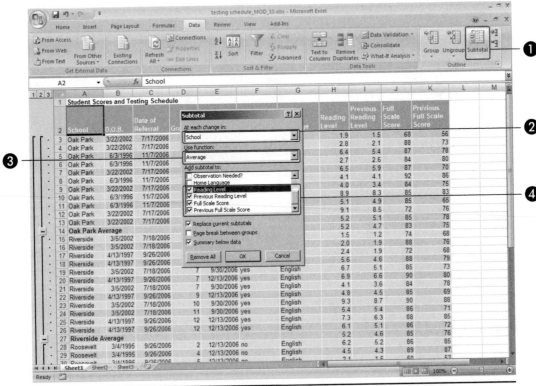

Figure 3-14 *Excel 2007 subtotals applied to a normal range (not in table form)*

applying subtotals (otherwise, the subtotals will not follow a logical grouping sequence in the first column, and the result will not make sense).

1. Click the Subtotal icon in the Outline menu group, on the Ribbon menu Data tab.
2. Choose School in the At Each Change In drop-down box, in the Subtotal dialog box.
3. Choose Average in the Use Function drop-down box.
4. Click the checkboxes for Reading Level, Previous Reading Level, Full Scale Score, and Previous Full Scale Score, and make sure the other checkboxes are unchecked. Then click OK.

The result of applying subtotals is rather striking; the outline controls on the left side of the Excel screen allow us to dynamically collapse and expand the data display by School grouping. Figure 3-15 shows what this looks like with the outline

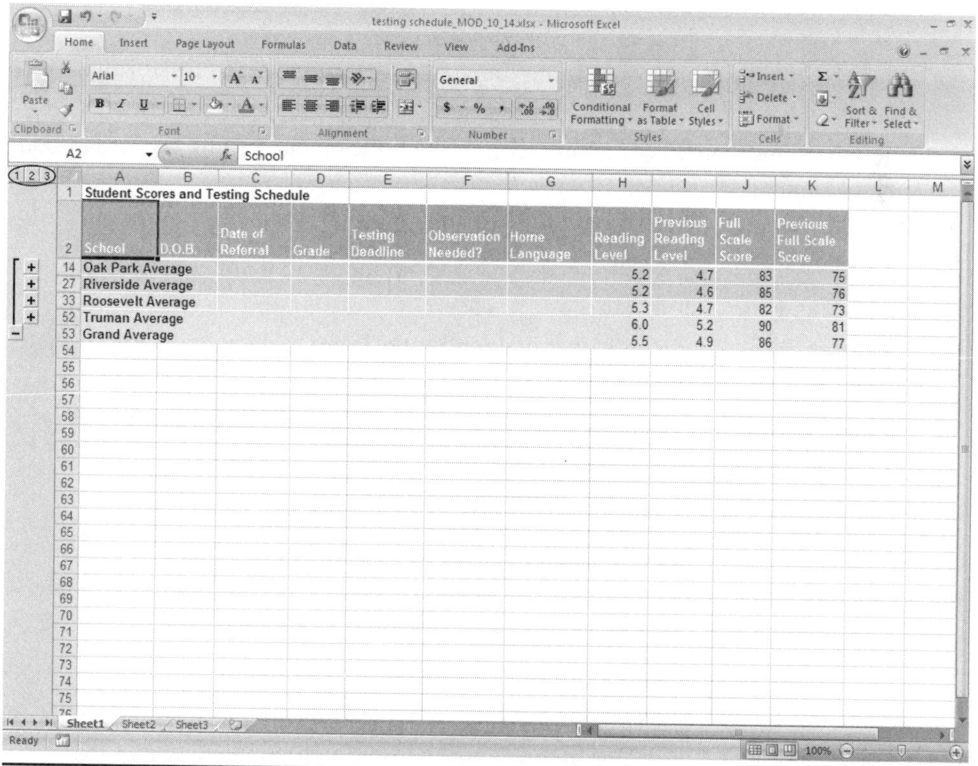

Figure 3-15 *Excel 2007 subtotals—with all groups collapsed*

controls all collapsed, which can be done by simply clicking the control labeled 2 at the top of the outline controls margin on the left side of the screen. Clicking on the Expand plus-sign icons will open the subtotaled groups into the detail data display. Notice the Subtotaled Average nicely displays at the bottom of each group but just for the columns chosen for the summary operation.

Excel Tables with Conditional Formatting

While we have the spreadsheet data in normal range form (not in table form), we'll apply the new Excel 2007 conditional formatting techniques to the data. Conditional formatting can be applied to either a normal range or an Excel table. This will add the strong visual effect of using color combinations to understand the data. Remember, this is very important when working with the large data sets we'll find in Excel 2007, which can hold huge amounts of data.

Figure 3-16 shows how to apply conditional formatting to our working spreadsheet example, using the Styles menu group in the Ribbon menu (the same menu group where we found the Format As Table menu option).

1. Click the column header for Home Language to designate it as the format column.
2. Click the Conditional Formatting icon in the Styles menu group, on the Ribbon menu Home tab.
3. Click the Highlight Cells Rules option on the pop-up menu.
4. Click the More Rules on the secondary pop-up menu, to display the New Formatting Rule dialog box.
5. Click the "Format only cells that contain" Rule Type, to display the appropriate display options for this text rule.
6. Choose Specific Text in the Format Only Cells With drop-down control.
7. Choose containing in the second drop-down box.
8. Enter **english** in the subsequent text box, which is not case-sensitive.
9. Click the Format button to display the Format Cells dialog box.
10. Click the Fill tab.
11. Choose the Light Blue color rectangle.
12. Click the Fill Effects button to bring up the Fill Effects dialog box, where desired gradient effects can be chosen.
13. Choose the Light Blue color in the Color 2 drop-down box, and click OK.

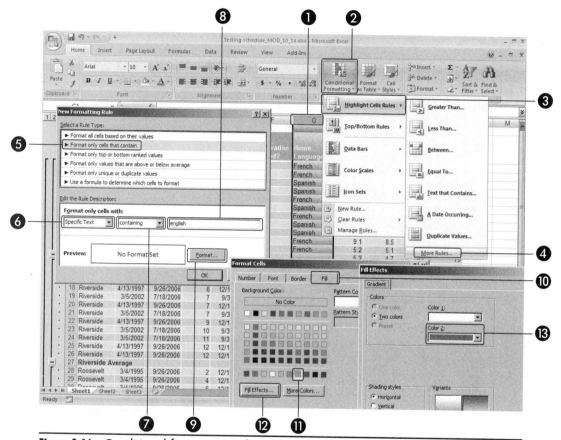

Figure 3-16 *Conditional formatting with a rule "Format only cells that contain English"*

The result of this conditional formatting is easy to see—all student scores associated with non-English backgrounds are highlighted. This might be of interest, since in some cases a translation expert may be needed to help bridge language gaps in understanding or interpreting standardized test results. At the very least it can help users of our working spreadsheet to understand the diversity of primary languages among various schools.

Figure 3-17 shows how we can clean up the formatting of column header or blank cells to really polish the conditional formatting presentation. While this might not seem overly important, a little extra care in formatting can make a big improvement in the first impression people form when looking at such a spreadsheet.

1. Click the cell(s) to be cleared of formatting, in this case G1 and G2.

2. Click the Conditional Formatting icon in the Styles menu group, on the Ribbon menu Home tab.

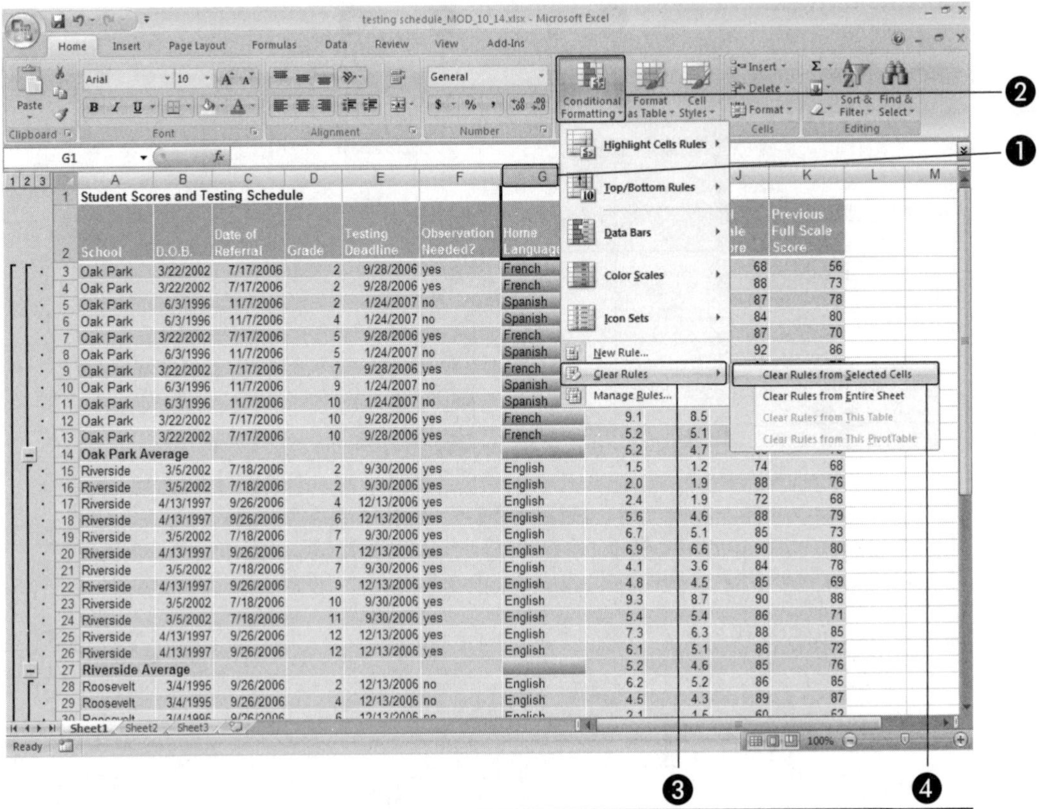

Figure 3-17 *Excel 2007 conditional formatting—clearing rules from selected cells*

3. Click the Clear Rules option on the pop-up menu.

4. Click the Clear Rules From Selected Cells icon on the secondary pop-up menu.

> **BI TIP**
>
> *Cleaning up the formatting of specific cells can be important in business intelligence presentations. It helps decision-makers form a positive first impression, it eliminates the visual confusion of formatting anomalies, and it guides the focus to the data being displayed.*

At this point in our formatting of data, it makes sense to turn the subtotaled and conditionally formatted spreadsheet into a table again (see Figure 3-18). Experience has shown that we often need to jump back and forth between a normal range and an Excel table to use the different features of each format. It's actually pretty quick once you get used to it!

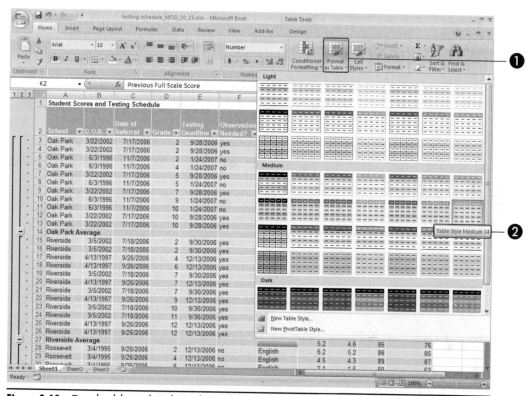

Figure 3-18 *Excel table with subtotals and conditional formatting*

1. Click the Format As Table icon in the Styles menu group, on the Ribbon menu Home tab.
2. Click the Table Style Medium 14 icon in the pop-up gallery.

Adding a Calculated Column to an Excel Table

This next step is fairly important; it is common to require that a calculated column be added to an Excel table, usually to show simply combinations of other columns such as a difference or percentage change. Excel 2007 is helpful in this case, but the steps must be followed quite carefully, since the calculated column will refer to the named columns inherent to Excel tables.

Figure 3-19 shows how we start the process of adding a new column to the right side of our working Excel table, which will show the difference between the Full Scale Score and the Previous Full Scale Score columns.

1. Click the header cell for the new column, in this case cell L2.
2. Type the column header label **Full—Previous Full Score**, and press ENTER.

After you enter a new column header immediately to the right of the Excel table and pressing ENTER to locate the mouse on the cell below (which in this case is L3), the Excel 2007 table automatically assumes the new column to be part of the existing table. This is one way in which Excel tables help with the changing needs of spreadsheets in the working world—by automatically acquiring new columns and rows, and adding them to the overall formatting of the table.

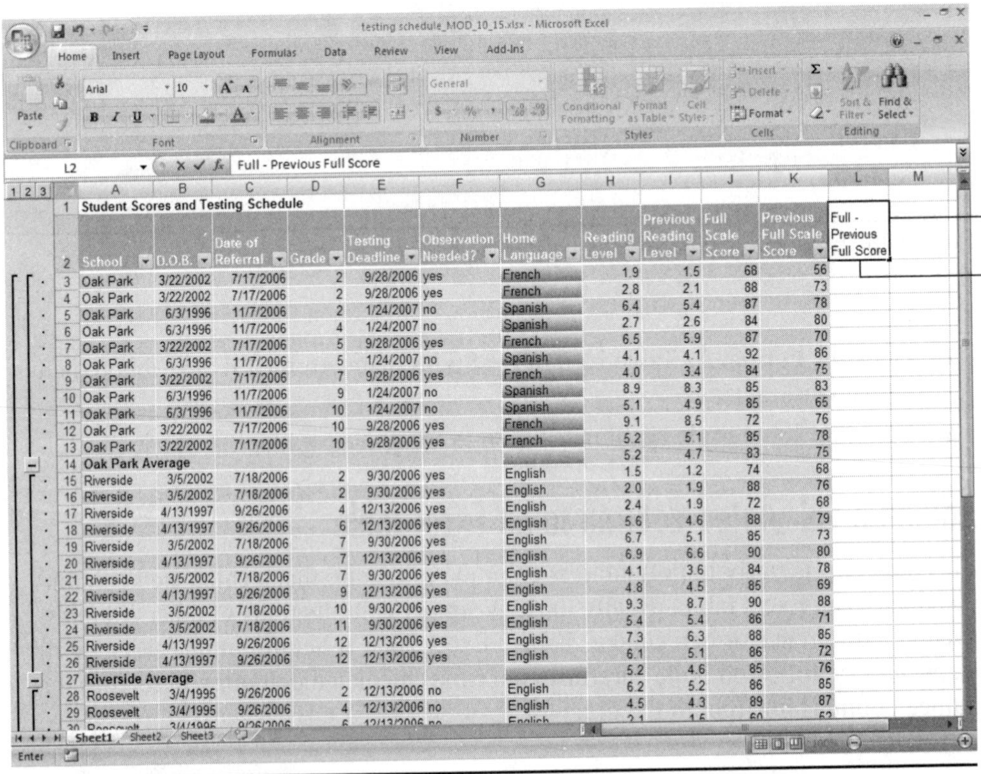

Figure 3-19 *Excel 2007 table—adding a calculated column*

Figure 3-20 shows the next steps that should be followed to make this new column a calculated column that will refer to values in other columns of the Excel table. Pay careful attention to the steps involved because they are a bit tricky the first time, but they'll allow us to create a calculated column without having to figure out any of the cell formulas involved.

1. Click the topmost data cell in the new column, which in this case is L3, and enter an equal sign to designate the following as an Excel formula.

2. Press the LEFT ARROW key twice so that the dashed rectangle is on the Full Scale Score column.

3. Type a minus sign to separate the Full Scale Score column selection from the following column selection.

4. Press the RIGHT ARROW key once so the dashed rectangle is on the Previous Full Scale Score column, and press ENTER to finish the formula.

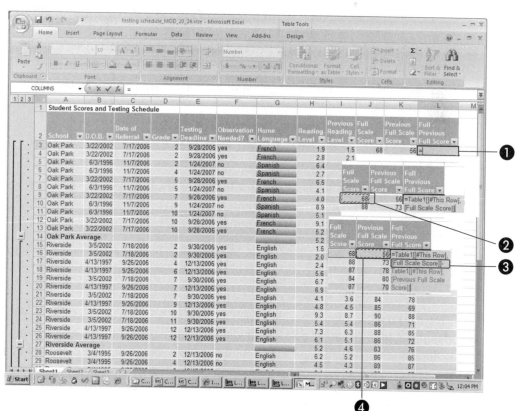

Figure 3-20 *Excel 2007 table—adding a calculated column with references to other columns*

It's pretty amazing to realize you can create Excel formulas in this manner, without having to decipher the code that is contained within the formula itself. Furthermore, the result of this calculated column is automatically part of the Excel table and thus displays a Data Filter drop-down arrow in the column header.

This is valuable in the use of Excel with business intelligence because so much of our work involves everyday working spreadsheets that we manually maintain. Excel tables make it possible to maintain regular spreadsheets with some semblance of order, which means we can make use of them with data analysis techniques such as conditional formatting and charting. What starts as a regular rectangular spreadsheet becomes a column-oriented table with consistent rows of data!

Excel Tables and Conditional Formatting

At this point it's worth taking a couple more steps to show off conditional formatting with our working Excel table. Figure 3-21 shows how we can add an icon set to the calculated column we just created to show increasing versus decreasing test scores.

1. Click the column header for Full—Previous Full Score to designate it as the format column.
2. Click the Conditional Formatting icon in the Styles menu group, on the Ribbon menu Home tab.
3. Click the Icon Sets option on the pop-up menu.
4. Click More Rules on the secondary pop-up menu.
5. Click Format All Cells Based On Their Values in the Select A Rule Type list box to display the appropriate configuration options in the Rule Description area.
6. Choose 3 Traffic Lights (Unrimmed) in the Icon Style drop-down control, to display the appropriate icon rule definitions.
7. For the Green definition, choose > and enter a value of **0** with Type Number.
8. For the Yellow definition, choose >= and enter a value of **0** with Type Number, and click OK.

The result of the three-level Icon Set you chose here for the Calculated Column is a red dot in cells with negative values, a yellow dot in cells with zero, and a green dot for all cells with positive values. Although it can be a bit confusing to explore the Icon Set configuration rules, it doesn't hurt to go with a trial-and-error approach to find a combination that works. It should be noted that in this rule set, yellow displays only for zero elements because the entire configuration line reads "when <= 0 AND >= 0," which is only satisfied when the value is exactly 0.

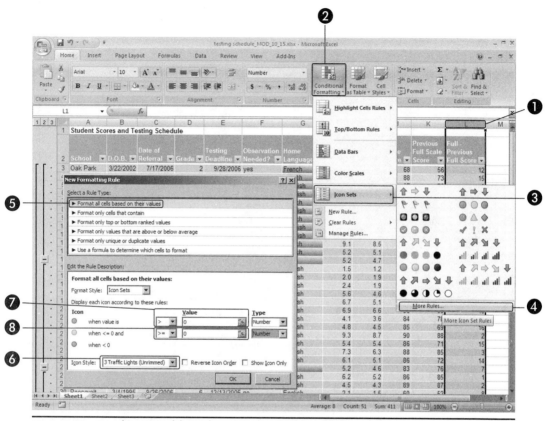

Figure 3-21 *Excel 2007 table with conditionally formatted icon sets*

Figure 3-22 shows how to add a color scale to the Reading Level column of our working Excel table. This is added to illustrate the main variations of conditional formatting.

1. Click the Reading Level column header to designate it as the format column.
2. Click the Conditional Formatting icon in the Styles menu group, on the Ribbon menu Home tab.
3. Click the Color Scales option on the pop-up menu.
4. Click the Green-Yellow Color Scale icon on the pop-up gallery.

It's worth mentioning that we chose the Green-Yellow color scale because it makes sense to associate Green with high test scores. As you choose the color scale color scheme in the gallery of choices, note that you can mouse over the various

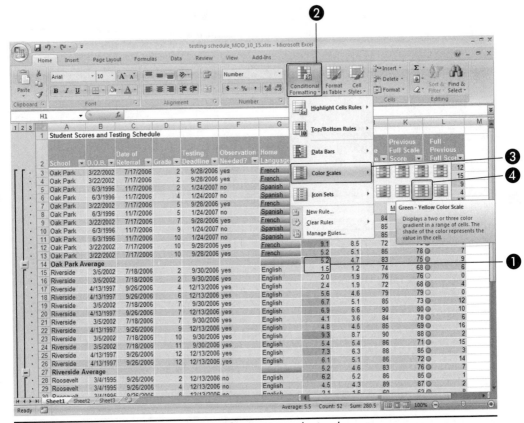

Figure 3-22 *Excel table with conditional formatting color scales*

color scale schemes and the Excel 2007 Live Preview will automatically show the effect on the selected column of data! New in 2007, this allows users to try out various color schemes to choose one that will highlight data in the best way.

BI TIP

Color schemes are critical to business intelligence. Since people automatically associate certain colors with preconceived ideas of good and bad, you must be careful to select color combinations that will convey an accurate image of good and bad data elements, especially when visually scanning dense arrays of data elements that are located in close proximity to each other in an Excel table.

Figure 3-23 shows the end result of three types of conditional formatting that have been applied to our working Excel table. It's interesting that we can apply

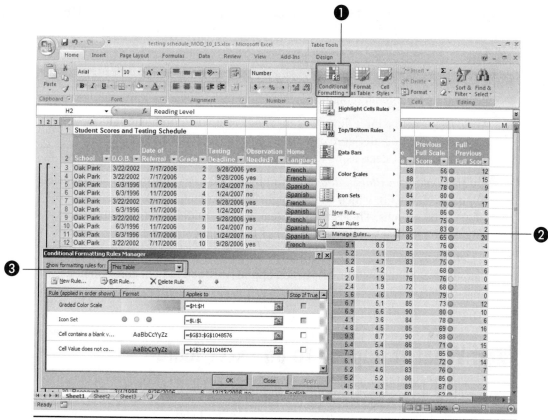

Figure 3-23 *Excel table; Conditional Formatting Rules Manager*

multiple conditional formatting rules to an Excel table and then manage them with the Manage Rules menu and dialog box. This is an Excel-based form of key performance indicator threshold display, and it's a powerful new capability in Excel 2007.

1. Click the Conditional Formatting icon in the Styles menu group, on the Ribbon menu Home tab.
2. Click the Manage Rules option in the pop-up menu.
3. Click the Show Formatting Rules For drop-down box, and choose This Table.

Highlight Cell rules have been applied in four ways; the rules can be edited by clicking on a rule to select it, and then clicking the Edit Rule icon above the list of rules.

▶ A *Graded Color Scale* with a Green-Yellow shading combination—for the Reading Level column (column H) that indicates high versus low reading scores.

▶ An *Icon Set* with a three-level Green-Yellow-Red dot combination—for the Full-Previous Full Score calculated column (column L) that indicates increasing versus decreasing test scores.

▶ A *Cell Contains A Blank Value* is a Highlight Cell rule—for the Home Language column (column G), which simply applies an Automatic color (effectively no color) to blank cells. This is used to clean up the conditional formatting of the column so that blank cells are not part of the visual color scheme.

▶ A *Cell Value Does Not Contain* is a Highlight Cell rule—for the Home Language column (column G), which applies a Blue gradient color on non-English data entries.

Excel What-If Applied to an Excel Table

Excel's What-If capability is a good example of the advanced statistical tools that are available to anyone that is willing to explore Excel features. Forecasting is not always a part of everyday office work, but on the other hand, we can all envision projections of data into months and years ahead—we just need to know how it works at our desktop.

Figure 3-24 shows how we start this process of What-If. Excel needs a column and a row of data that follow a pattern, any kind of pattern. Excel will do the job for us of projecting the pattern to fill in What-If cells that line up with the row value progression, and with the column value progression.

1. Click the School subtotal averages in the original spreadsheet (for Truman, cell H52), and copy them to create column headers of averages on a clear area of the spreadsheet.

2. Create a column of percentage values (1%, 2%, etc.) for an increasing forecast value.

3. Create a formula that uses the column and row values (=B56+A58*B56 in our example).

	A	B	C	D	E	F	G	H	I	J	K	L	M
37	Truman	6/2/1994	9/15/2006	6	11/28/2006	no	English	5.8	3.5	92	78	14	
38	Truman	2/7/1993	9/16/2006	6	11/28/2006	no	English	6.5	5.6	104	84	20	
39	Truman	2/7/1993	9/16/2006	7	11/28/2006	no	English	4.5	3.1	104	115	-11	
40	Truman	6/2/1994	9/15/2006	7	11/28/2006	no	English	7.0	5.7	80	79	1	
41	Truman	1/8/1993	8/26/2006	8	11/8/2006	no	English	4.3	3.8	84	71	13	
42	Truman	6/2/1994	9/15/2006	8	11/28/2006	no	English	4.4	4.0	85	74	11	
43	Truman	2/7/1993	9/16/2006	8	11/28/2006	no	English	7.7	7.4	90	87	3	
44	Truman	2/7/1993	9/16/2006	8	11/28/2006	no	English	4.6	4.3	85	74	11	
45	Truman	1/8/1993	8/26/2006	9	11/8/2006	no	English	6.9	6.1	81	76	5	
46	Truman	1/8/1993	8/26/2006	11	11/8/2006	no	English	5.6	5.6	86	74	12	
47	Truman	1/8/1993	8/26/2006	11	11/8/2006	no	English	9.4	9.4	92	81	11	
48	Truman	6/2/1994	9/15/2006	11	11/28/2006	no	English	5.7	5.1	86	66	20	
49	Truman	2/7/1993	9/16/2006	12	11/28/2006	no	English	5.9	4.0	86	79	7	
50	Truman	2/7/1993	9/16/2006	12	11/28/2006	no	English	7.2	6.8	87	82	5	
51	Truman	6/2/1994	9/15/2006	12	11/28/2006	no	English	9.6	9.2	102	84	18	
52	Truman Average							6.0	5.2	90	81	8	
53	Grand Average							5.5	4.9	86	77		
54													
55			Oak Park	Riverside	Roosevelt		Truman						
56			5.2	5.2	5.3		6.0						
57	Avg Reading Level Increase What If												
58		5.158442											
59		1%											
60		2%											
61		3%											
62		4%											
63		5%											
64													
65													

Figure 3-24   Excel 2007 What-If column and row preparation

Now this may look a little strange, but we're simply configuring a miniature spreadsheet area to show a projection of average school scores—starting with each school's average score today and increasing by 1%, 2%, 3%, 4%, and 5%. The intent is to see the projection of each school's average score.

Figure 3-25 shows the next step in configuring the spreadsheet area of average scores, where we copy the first formula we just created into the subsequent cells. This creates a base of actual average scores as column headers, which will allow Excel to create a projection of average scores in the cells below them.

1. Click the first column header cell formula, which in our case is B58, and right-click and choose Copy.

2. Click the second column header C58, and while holding the left mouse button down, drag the mouse across all desired column headers, and right-click and choose Paste.

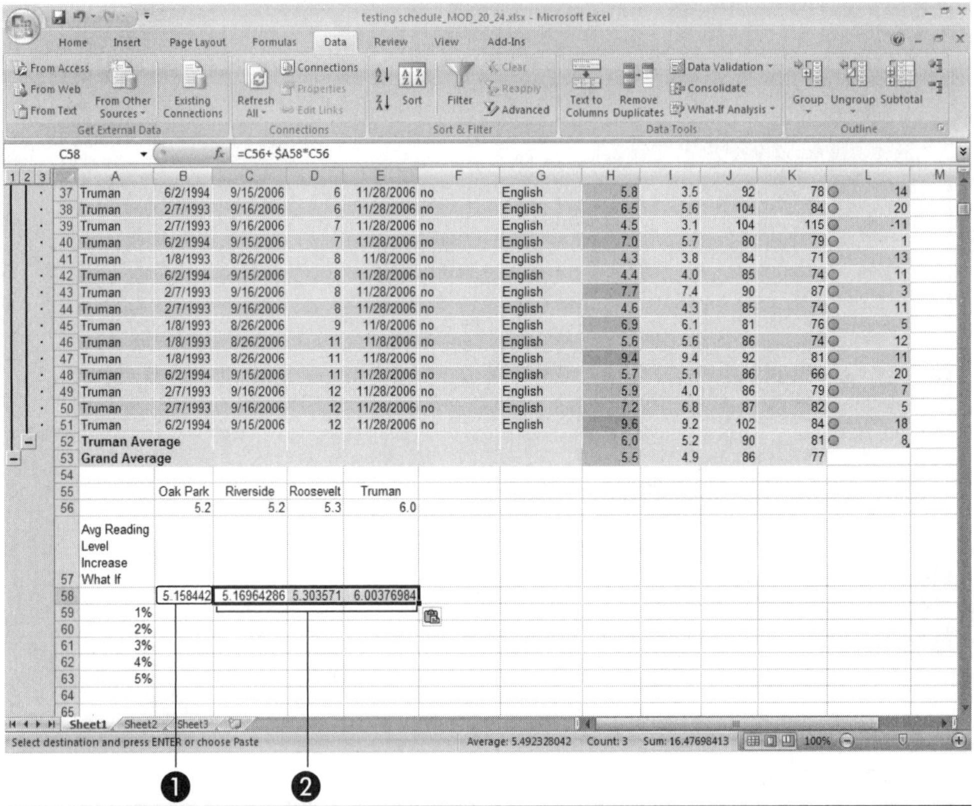

Figure 3-25 *Excel 2007 What-If column header values*

Now we're going to see the magic of Excel's What-If capability in Figure 3-26. By selecting the rows and columns of our spreadsheet area that have a pattern of increasing changing values, we can ask Excel to infer forecast values!

1. Click the top-left cell of the spreadsheet area with the pattern of changing values (A58), and hold the left mouse button down to drag across and select all entire row-column area.

2. Click the What-If Analysis option in the Data Tools menu group, on the Ribbon menu Data tab.

3. Click the Data Table option on the pop-up menu.

4. Enter the top-left cell in the Column Input Cell text box, in the Data Table dialog box (A58), and click OK.

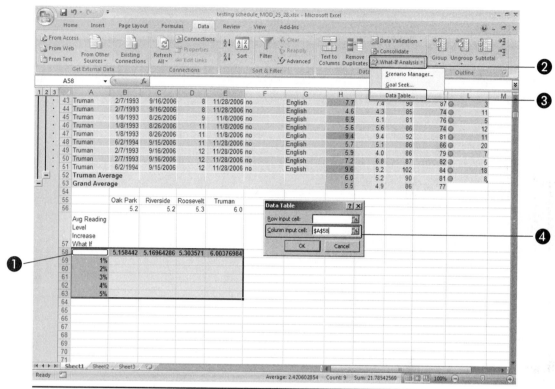

Figure 3-26 *Excel 2007 What-If Analysis menu steps*

The result of this is simply astounding; as we see in Figure 3-27, Excel will accurately fill in the projected values in a What-If manner. The projected values show the school average test scores, assuming an increase of 1%, 2%, etc. While we used this with a relatively simple example, Excel will project values in the same manner for large spreadsheets as well. This eliminates the burden of creating formulas or manually creating projection What-If data values.

Excel Statistical ToolPak Add-In

Many business users of Excel know that Microsoft has built in some real statistical tools, but they are not sure where to find them or how to use them. In this section we'll take the What-If projections created previously and show how to quickly see the advanced 2007 Statistical Analysis tools that come with Excel.

	A	B	C	D	E	F	G	H	I	J	K	L
43	Truman	2/7/1993	9/16/2006	8	11/28/2006	no	English	7.7	7.4	90	87	3
44	Truman	2/7/1993	9/16/2006	8	11/28/2006	no	English	4.6	4.3	85	74	11
45	Truman	1/8/1993	8/26/2006	9	11/8/2006	no	English	6.9	6.1	81	76	5
46	Truman	1/8/1993	8/26/2006	11	11/8/2006	no	English	5.6	5.6	86	74	12
47	Truman	1/8/1993	8/26/2006	11	11/8/2006	no	English	9.4	9.4	92	81	11
48	Truman	6/2/1994	9/15/2006	11	11/28/2006	no	English	5.7	5.1	86	66	20
49	Truman	2/7/1993	9/16/2006	12	11/28/2006	no	English	5.9	4.0	86	79	7
50	Truman	2/7/1993	9/16/2006	12	11/28/2006	no	English	7.2	6.8	87	82	5
51	Truman	6/2/1994	9/15/2006	12	11/28/2006	no	English	9.6	9.2	102	84	18
52	Truman Average							6.0	5.2	90	81	8
53	Grand Average							5.5	4.9	86	77	

	A	B	C	D	E
55		Oak Park	Riverside	Roosevelt	Truman
56		5.2	5.2	5.3	6.0
57	Avg Reading Level Increase What If				
58		5.158442	5.16964286	5.303571	6.00376984
59	1%	5.210026	5.22133929	5.356607	6.06380754
60	2%	5.26161	5.27303571	5.409643	6.12384524
61	3%	5.313195	5.32473214	5.462679	6.18388294
62	4%	5.364779	5.37642857	5.515714	6.24392063
63	5%	5.416364	5.428125	5.56875	6.30395833

Figure 3-27 *Excel What-If table with projected values*

Figure 3-28 shows how we make sure the Excel 2007 Statistical ToolPak is part of our working Excel environment. It's an add-in that can easily be added to the 2007 Ribbon menu.

1. Click the Office button at the upper left of the Excel interface.
2. Click the Excel Options button at the bottom of the pop-up menu.

Note the range of menu choices we see when the Office button is clicked. Many of these are central to everyday work with Excel 2007, and experience has shown that once business users understand how to access these high-level menu choices, the actual spreadsheet work with the 2007 Ribbon menu proceeds fairly smoothly.

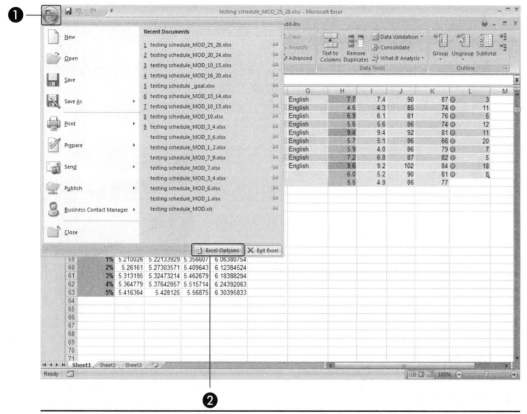

Figure 3-28 *Excel 2007 options for add-in programs*

BI TIP

A consistent user interface is of paramount important to people working with business intelligence tools for reporting, analysis, and measurement. And Excel 2007, with its Office button and Ribbon menu, sets the standard for these BI interfaces simply because of the global use of Microsoft Office and the power of Excel as the most commonly used BI tool.

Figure 3-29 shows how we find the Analysis ToolPak Add-In package for Excel. Add-ins are simply additional packages with specialized functionality that are not part of the default Excel installation. The market actually has many Excel add-ins that are available to Excel users to extend Excel into specialized areas of analysis, particularly into vertical business areas that involve business processes that are germane to given industries.

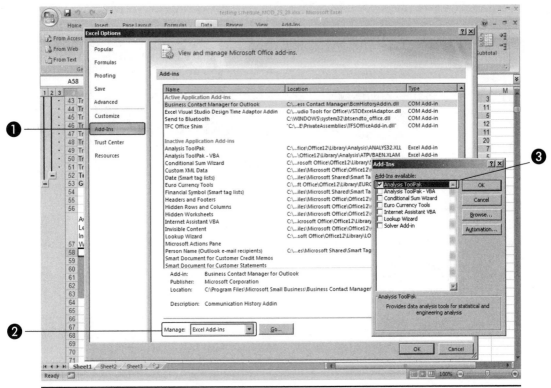

Figure 3-29 *Excel 2007 add-ins—Analysis ToolPak*

1. Click the Add-Ins menu option on the left side of the Excel Options dialog box.
2. Choose Excel Add-ins in the Manage drop-down control, and click Go.
3. Click on the Analysis ToolPak checkbox in the Add-Ins Available list box, and click OK.

Figure 3-30 shows a nice result of adding the Analysis ToolPak to the Excel environment: it shows up as a new menu option in the Ribbon menu! This is a consistent use of the Office 2007 Ribbon menu design, where specialized or new menu options are displayed in separate tabs that extend the normal tab functions of Excel.

1. Click the Data Analysis option in the Analysis menu group, on the Ribbon menu Data tab.
2. Click the Descriptive Statistics choice in the Data Analysis dialog box, and click OK.

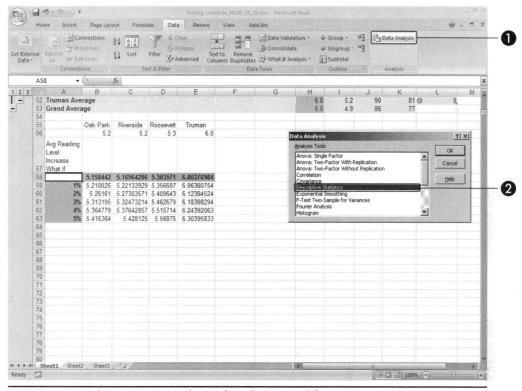

Figure 3-30 *Excel 2007 Data Analysis tab with statistical functions*

Figure 3-31 shows the remarkable variety of statistical functions that can be applied to spreadsheet data in Excel 2007. We're choosing the Descriptive Statistics because it's an easy way to show off these analytical functions without delving into a scientific exploration of statistical tools.

1. Click the Input Range icon in the Descriptive Statistics dialog box, to choose the spreadsheet data for analysis (B59 through E63).

2. Click the Output Range icon to choose a blank area of the spreadsheet to display the statistical functions (B65).

Note that the cell-selection icons in the Descriptive Statistics dialog box can be clicked, which minimizes the dialog box to allow you to mouse over any desired cells and select them. When the cell-selection icon is again clicked, the dialog box redisplays with the just-selected cell range automatically showing next to the selection icon.

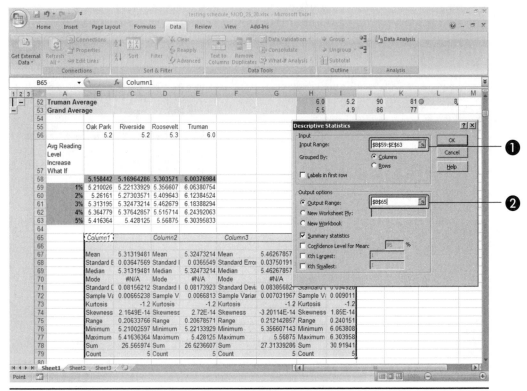

Figure 3-31 *Excel 2007 Analysis ToolPak—descriptive statistics*

This section is not meant to provide a discussion of the various statistical functions we see in Figure 3-31, but we can certainly mention the presence of Mean and Standard Deviation calculations. The Descriptive Statistics output shows these and many others for each of the columns from the selected cell range now labeled Column1, Column2, and so forth. Business users who need statistical functions generally have a specific statistical need in mind, and with the preceding procedure everyone can access Excel's Analysis ToolPak to find the appropriate function.

Excel 2007 Charts with Excel Tables

The need to understand Excel charts is almost universal among business users, and yet most people don't know how to take advantage of Excel's sophistication in this area. In this section we'll use our working example of school test scores to show

how to create a compelling chart story that can be used in a presentation or meeting to truly convey information about the various school scores.

Figure 3-32 shows how we start this process, using the Office 2007 Ribbon menu options to choose a chart type.

1. Click the Other Charts icon in the Charts menu group, on the Ribbon menu Insert tab.

2. Click the Line chart type in the Insert Chart dialog box.

3. Click the first Line icon in the gallery of chart types.

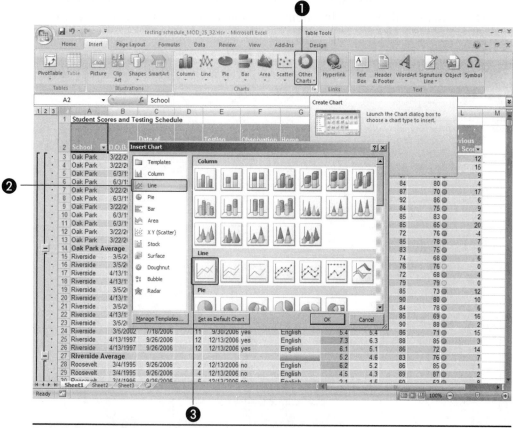

Figure 3-32 *Excel 2007 Other Charts to see all chart types*

Let's pause for a moment to look at the wide variety of chart types. There are so many that it can be challenging to choose one that will look good with the data we have in mind. One way to help with this challenge is to try the simpler charts first and examine the results. That way we can try others like the Radar chart when we have experience with the basics.

Excel Chart Axis Labels and Data Series

Figure 3-33 shows the first step in formatting the chart so that it displays the data in a reasonable manner. We'll use the various menu options on the Ribbon menu Chart Tools tab that have appeared in the Excel 2007 interface now that we're doing chart work. This feature of Office 2007 is called context tabs. They do not display until we need them to work with the functions they contain; this keeps the Office 2007

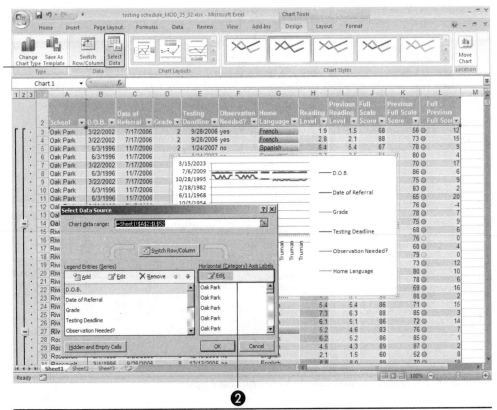

Figure 3-33 *Excel 2007 Chart Tools—selecting the chart data*

user interfaces to a reasonable set of menu choices so that users can more easily navigate the thousands of menu options as needed.

1. Click the Select Data icon in the Data menu group, on the Ribbon menu Design tab.
2. Click the Edit icon on the right-side list box, in the Select Data Source dialog box.

The steps shown in Figure 3-33 are fairly important in being able to create good Excel charts. Working with the Select Data Source menu dialog box alone can change a bad chart to a good one. In this case we're editing the horizontal axis labels to get the desired chart display.

Figure 3-34 shows how we can interactively select the cells that provide the horizontal axis labels.

1. Click the cell-selection icon in the Axis Labels dialog box.

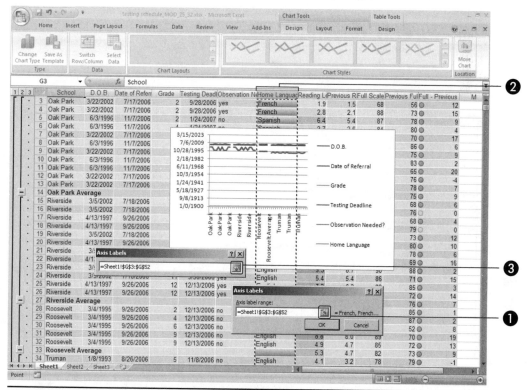

Figure 3-34 *Excel 2007 charts—changing the axis labels*

2. Click the upper data cell in the School column of the spreadsheet, and holding the right mouse button, drag it down to select the data cells in the column.

3. Click the cell-selection icon again, and then click OK.

Note that as you get used to using the interactive nature of Excel's cell-selection icon, you'll probably use it whenever it's available instead of manually typing cell addresses.

Figure 3-35 shows the next step in cleaning up the chart display, where we're eliminating unwanted Legend Entries (or Data Series).

1. Click the D.O.B. item to select it in the Legend Entries list box.

2. Click the Remove option on the Legend Entries list box. Repeat this for the Legend Entries items until only the Reading Level and Previous Reading Level items are left.

The work we're doing in Figure 3-35 is important because it is defining the data series for the chart. A data series is simply a set of Excel cell values we want to

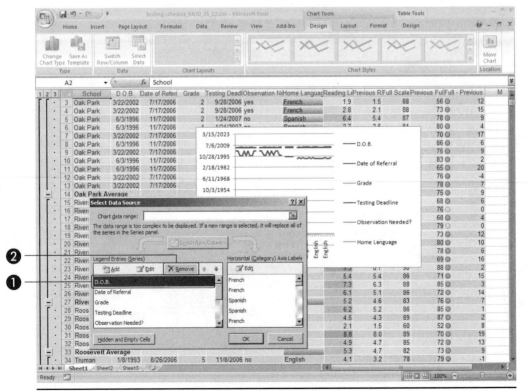

Figure 3-35 *Excel 2007 charts—changing the legend entries (data series)*

chart, and in our working example we're narrowing the series until we have just the two left that we want.

Multiple Data Series are responsible for the multiple lines we'll see in a line chart, or for multiple rows of columns in a columnar chart. The good news is that once we learn to work with the horizontal axis labels and the legend entries (or data series), we have the most important parts in hand to create informative charts in Excel.

Formatting Excel Charts

Figure 3-36 shows how to start arranging the elements of the chart for a better display. We'll be using the Ribbon menu icons for this work, which appear on the Chart Tools context tabs.

1. Click the Chart Title icon in the Labels menu group, on the Ribbon menu Layout tab.

2. Click the Above Chart option in the pop-up menu.

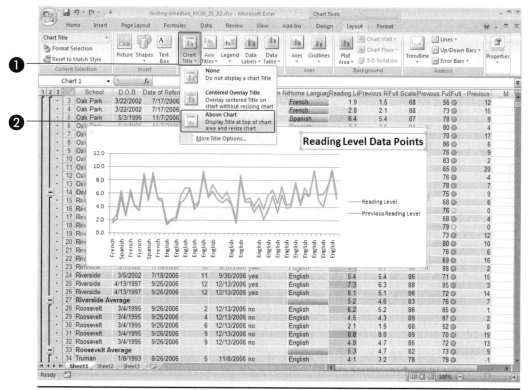

Figure 3-36 *Excel 2007 charts—changing the chart title*

At this point we're really working on the cosmetic display aspects of the chart. However, this is important, since people who see the charts will make a quick first judgment of the quality of the data by the quality of the chart presentation.

Figure 3-37 shows the continuing process of formatting the chart, using the Ribbon menu icons.

1. Click the Axis Titles icon in the Labels menu group, on the Ribbon menu Layout tab.
2. Click the Primary Vertical Axis Title option in the pop-up menu.
3. Click the Rotated Title option in the secondary pop-up menu.

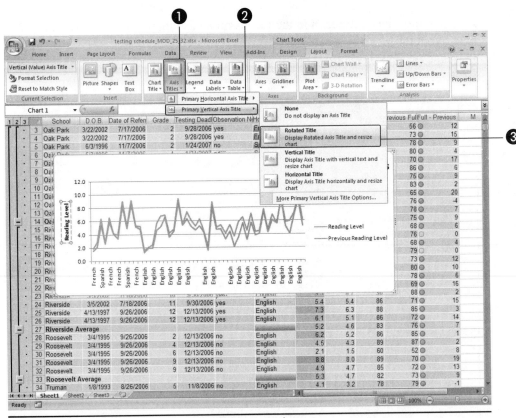

Figure 3-37 *Excel 2007 charts—rotating the axis title*

By now it's becoming clear that the Ribbon menu has the functions we need to control the display of the chart. We're going to continue this formatting process with Figure 3-38 by introducing a new element—a picture background image for the chart.

1. Click the Plot Area icon in the Background menu group, on the Ribbon menu Layout tab.
2. Click the More Plot Area Options option in the pop-up menu.
3. Click the Fill menu choice in the Format Plot Area dialog box.
4. Click the Picture Or Texture Fill button.
5. Click the Clip Art button.

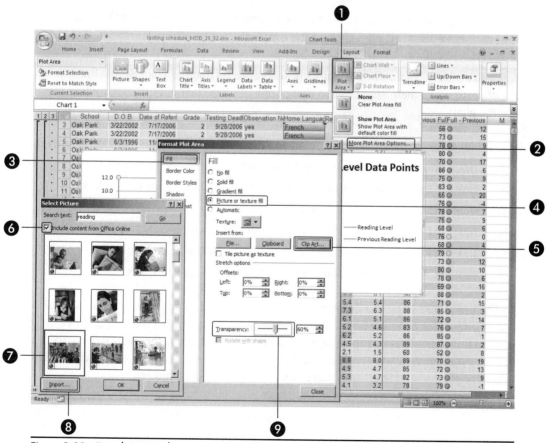

Figure 3-38 *Excel 2007 charts—importing a picture for background fill*

6. In the Select Picture dialog box, click the checkbox called Include Content From Office Online.

7. Click the Class Students picture to select it.

8. Click the Import button.

9. Click the Transparency slider control to change the transparency to 60%.

The effect of adding a picture for the background is actually done to help convey the message of the chart data, which in our working example is a data story about students and their test scores.

BI TIP

It may seem superfluous to cosmetically arrange the elements of a chart and to add pictures, but it really does help deliver a business intelligence message. The formatting results in a good first impression that carries over to analysis of the data, and a picture can immediately convey the real-world context within which the data is to be interpreted or acted upon.

Figure 3-39 shows an important step, where we format the Data Series lines in the chart to make them stand out so that people look at the data lines first when they see the chart.

1. Click a line in the Chart to select it, and then right-click to open the pop-up menu.

2. Click Format Data Series on the pop-up menu.

3. Click the Line Color menu choice in the Format Data Series dialog box.

4. Click the Solid Line option button.

5. Click the Color drop-down control to open the color palette, and choose Blue.

6. Click the Line Style menu choice in the Format Data Series dialog box.

7. Click the Width text box control, and change the value to 1.5 pt.

The preceding steps should be repeated for the send line in the chart, and a contrasting color can then be chosen to make it easier to discern the two distinct lines in the chart. This is important so that people who look at the chart can easily see the different data series (although they might not know the term data series). This avoids confusion and leads to a more compelling chart presentation.

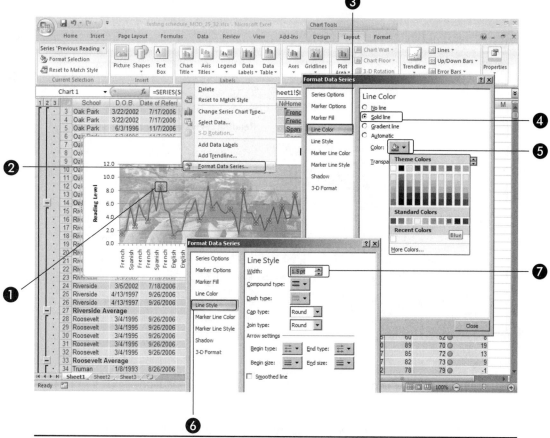

Figure 3-39 *Excel 2007 charts—formatting the data series lines*

Figure 3-40 shows a final and really interesting Excel 2007 chart feature—the ability to quickly mark up a multiple data series line chart to show relative differences between the series.

1. Click the Up/Down Bars option in the Analysis menu group, on the Ribbon menu Layout tab.

2. Click the Up/Down Bars option on the pop-up menu to show the bars.

The result of the up/down bars would be hard to explain without being able to see it in a chart such as Figure 3-40. Note that while it only works on a line chart, it certainly adds a unique visual element of analysis that makes it easy to see the

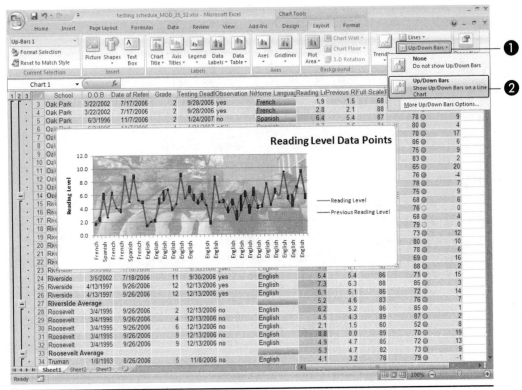

Figure 3-40 *Excel 2007 charts—up/down bars for data differentiation*

parallel data points that have the greatest differences in value between the two data series. This kind of feature exploration is typical of working with Excel 2007, and using the features with real-world spreadsheets can really set the spreadsheets apart so that they become presentations that accurately and quickly convey a data story to audiences!

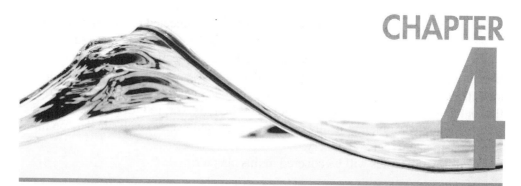

Excel and External Data: Files, Databases, Cubes, and Data from the Internet

T he real power of Excel is realized when it's connected to external data. This chapter explores in some detail the various data sources that are supported from within Excel 2007 using Office Data Connections. As an example, Excel's Text Import Wizard is so powerful that database experts often use it to bring miscellaneous data files into an Excel table where it's easy to work with data. You'll find out how to connect to Access, Oracle, and SQL Server; to OLAP cubes, which are a great source of hierarchically organized data; and even to web site data on the Internet using an Excel Web Query.

The following topics will be covered in this chapter:

▶ Turning your files into Excel data, and Office trusted locations

▶ Converting MS Access, Oracle, and SQL Server files into Excel

▶ Multidimensional SQL Server OLAP cubes and Excel

▶ Converting web queries from the World Wide Web into Excel

BEST REFERENCE

For further research on this topic, go to http:// blogs.msdn.com/excel.

Technology Positioning Statement

Excel 2007 Office Data Connections (ODCs) offer a great way to connect the new features in Excel to all kinds of external data. ODCs can be shared and reused among Excel users to look at data from SQL Server or Access, Oracle, or DB2, and the Text Import ODC has a really good Text Import Wizard. Once someone has connected to external data, it's easy to format and sort it in an Excel table or PivotTable.

The new million row capability of Excel will likely encourage users to connect Excel to all kinds of data they may have in their organizations, and it positions Excel 2007 to continue as the most popular data analysis tool in the world.

—Sean Boon, Microsoft Excel Team

What Is an External Data Connection?

Excel provides the ability, out of the box, to connect to data outside of Excel. Realizing this opens a whole new world to Excel users, since you can then connect to almost any data lying around in files or to database servers in your organization if you have permission to do so. Excel is one of the best ways to connect to OLAP cubes as well (we'll see what this looks like later in the chapter). When you connect to external data from within Excel, the external data can easily be imported into an Excel spreadsheet, where all the great tools of Excel 2007 can be used to analyze and arrange the data.

In fact, Excel can connect to data on the Internet, and we'll show how to do this in the chapter as well. Imagine, connecting to the entire world's data available to you in Excel 2007, which can hold one million rows in a spreadsheet!

Importing data into Excel typically results in an Excel table, which provides a way to keep your data in a coherent list format on an Excel spreadsheet. This list format is really somewhat like a database table, if you are familiar with database terminology. It organizes the data into labeled columns with drop-down data-filtering controls that allow you reduce the data being displayed—and to sort it in organized ways.

Tables are likely to be a popular tool with Excel 2007, since spreadsheets can hold one million rows in 2007, and with all that data ending up in Excel, it really helps to be able to easily turn it into columns that control the data display. Excel tables provide a list of all data elements, whereas Excel PivotTables provide aggregates of data elements. PivotTables are not appropriate for all situations, and in fact they are somewhat specialized with their automatic cross-tab behavior (although PivotTables are the norm when connecting to OLAP cubes, as we'll see in this chapter).

Both Excel tables and PivotTables can handle large data sets and support slicing and dicing of data in a business intelligence sense, and both work with conditional formatting and charting.

The following illustration shows an example of an Excel 2007 PivotTable, with an External Connection to a SQL Server Analysis Services cube. This chapter will explore the steps used to create this example PivotTable.

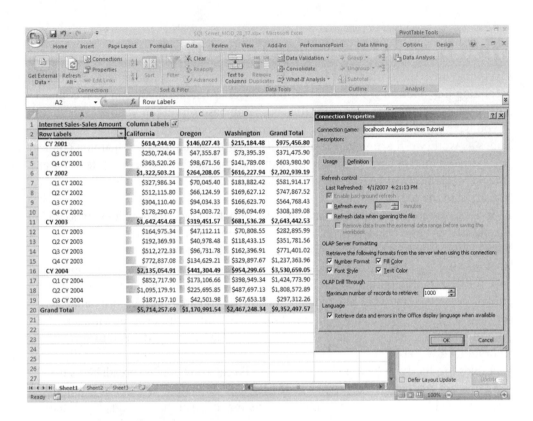

Where Do Excel External Data Connections Fit in the Microsoft BI Picture?

The following illustration shows a matrix view of Microsoft Business Intelligence technology (often referred to as BI). The Office, SharePoint, and SQL Server applications we see in the marketplace are shown on the left side of the matrix. These applications are used in the real-world activities of reporting, analysis, measurement, and planning as shown across the top of the matrix. The top-down flow of the matrix starts with front-end BI tools we have in Office 2007 at our desktops, and goes down to back-end BI tools that run on servers such as SharePoint 2007 and PerformancePoint 2007, which provide an enhanced experience when connected to Office 2007.

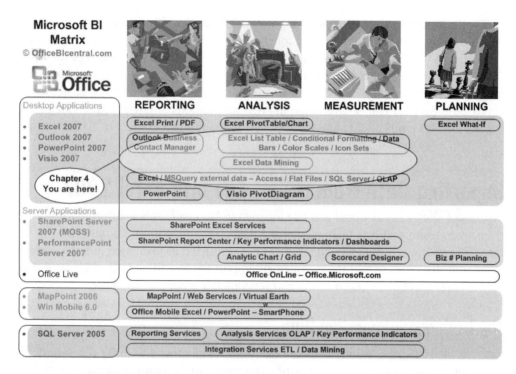

Learning about Excel Data Connections makes more sense if we know where they fit in the Microsoft technology stack and what they are used for in daily BI activities. The "You are here!" bubble in the illustration shows Excel External Data Access as part of Excel 2007, which is part of Office 2007. We're going use Excel Connectors and MSQuery (the Office SQL query tool) to connect to Flat Files, Access, SQL Server, and OLAP cubes for Analysis work, which is the second column of the BI matrix.

Note that a much more sophisticated data import technology is also shown in the BI matrix illustration; looking at the base of the diagram, we see Integration Services, which is commonly referred to as extraction, transformation, and loading software (or ETL as an acronym). Integration Services is part of the SQL Server 2005 product from Microsoft and is sometimes called SSIS by those who work with it on a daily basis.

There are many ETL tools on the market, but it's interesting to see that we can accomplish simple data connection and import ETL work just using Excel 2007, as we'll see in this chapter, or jump into a sophisticated ETL toolset with Integration Services to move large amounts of data between database servers or applications, as we'll see in Chapter 8.

Excel data connections are one of those capabilities that, if users knew how easy they are to work with, would be used much more often! Frankly, most of the data in our everyday working life can be imported into Excel tables to do the things we'll show in this chapter. Alternatively, the tables can be turned into normal spreadsheet ranges at any time if desired. The new Excel 2007 Ribbon menu makes it easier to get to these external data sources than in previous versions of Office, which means we can grab all kinds of data and work with it in the familiar context of Excel.

Importing Data from a Text File into Excel 2007

Figure 4-1 shows a real-world text file, opened in Notepad. This is information from swim teams that lists team names and dates for competition. Looking at it in Notepad, we can see valuable data, but it's not organized or formatted in any usable manner. It makes sense that if we can easily import the text file into Excel, we could then arrange and list the swim teams and schedules in a coherent manner.

The Truth about Importing Data

Our text file is a simple example of data that we have all around us in the real world. It is a single file of swim team information (important to the swim team participants!), but working with it will help us see the Excel 2007 Data Connection and Import tools that we can use right on our desktop computer without any special software or training.

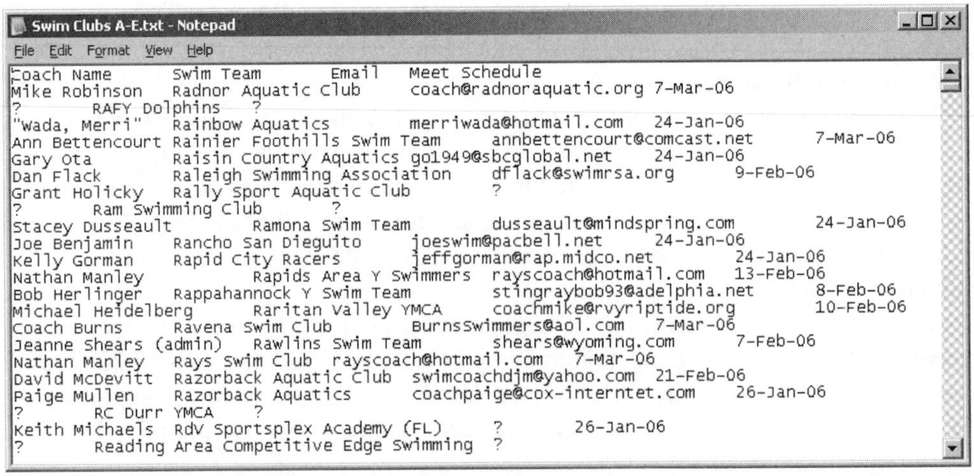

Figure 4-1 *A typical text file of data, swim teams and schedules*

In the professional world of database analysis and design, importing data is a large part of the hours spent by people in charge of databases. This work is known as extraction, transformation, and loading (ETL), and it is accomplished with a wide variety of ETL tools—tools that can be very sophisticated. However, sophisticated ETL is really an extension of the relatively simple ETL we can do with Excel 2007, as we'll see in this chapter.

The value to business users of Excel is the ability to bring external data into Excel, where we have familiar and powerful tools to analyze the imported data, and in so doing, business users can gain an appreciation for the work that database professionals do with the more sophisticated SQL Server Integration Services (SSIS) toolset used by database professionals to move millions of rows of data around organizations every day.

BI TIP

Data connection and import, also known as ETL, is often the most time-consuming part of business intelligence projects in the real world. Easily half of the hours for any BI project can be consumed by extracting data from application databases and files, and transforming the data into an organized data structure to support BI analysis.

Get External Data from Text

Note that a text file such as we have for our example can come from anywhere on any computer. It does not necessarily come from a formal corporate data store, and you don't have to ask the IT shop for help in importing it—everything we need is contained within Excel 2007.

Figure 4-2 shows how we start the process of importing data from a text file.

1. Click the Get External Data icon on the Ribbon menu Data tab, to the left of the Connections group of options.
2. Click the From Text icon on the submenu for Get External.
3. Browse to the desired text file, and click Import.

Figure 4-2 gives us an opportunity to look at the new Excel 2007 menu, especially the Ribbon menu, which is new across the Office 2007 applications. Notice the menu options are logically arranged with helpful icons. Looking at the Get External menu group, for example, we can intuitively see several good options for connecting to data, notably Access and Web for bringing data into Excel from web sites.

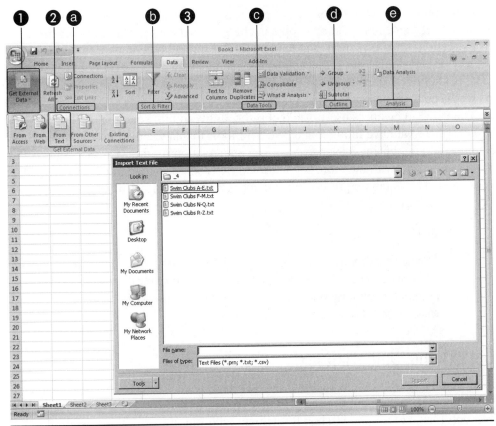

Figure 4-2   *Excel 2007—get external data from text file*

Understanding Screen Components in the Excel User Interface

This is the new 2007 Excel table user interface, and it's where we'll do most of our work in this chapter. The top-level Ribbon menu is divided into tabs that provide a reasonable grouping of menu options. For some work in Excel we'll find that new context tabs become available to the right of the original Ribbon menu tabs to provide special items needed in working with Excel features that have been selected. This is exactly how the new Office 2007 Ribbon menu is supposed to work; menu tabs with new choices are automatically made available to the user whenever we're working with Excel items that require additional tools. The following explanations (a through e) correspond to the similarly labeled areas in Figure 4-2:

a. **Connections Group** This is where you can choose which kind of data you'd like to connect to and import into Excel. The most interesting choices are in the From Other Sources menu, which includes connections for SQL Server relational data and SQL Server Analysis Services OLAP cubes, and for Microsoft Query, which is the well-known SQL query visual design tool.

b. **Sort & Filter Group** This is where you can choose menu options to sort the data displaying on the spreadsheet, and to filter or narrow the data being displayed.

c. **Data Tools** This is a valuable part of the Excel 2007 interface; and we'll use some of these menu options to clean up and manipulate the data being displayed on the spreadsheet.

d. **Outline** This menu group sports a nice-to-have set of options that allows us to group the data being displayed on the spreadsheet using Excel outline controls to collapse and expand rows and columns. It is particularly useful for inserting subtotals on the spreadsheet.

e. **Analysis** This holds the menu options to perform advanced statistical analysis on the spreadsheet data, with tools such as Regression and Correlation.

It is worth pausing at this point for a brief discussion of the new Office 2007 menu layout. Microsoft has put a great deal of effort into consolidating the thousands of Office menu commands and choices into this new format. All of the Office 2007 applications use the new Ribbon menu approach for their user interface, notably Excel, Access, PowerPoint, Outlook, and Word.

Our step-by-step instructions in this chapter will primarily use the Ribbon menu icon-based tabbed/grouped interface to accomplish our work for the purpose of consistency. However, right-click and context-sensitive menus are also a significant part of the Office 2007 interface, and we'll use them whenever we go beyond the immediate options of the Ribbon menu. As you gain familiarity with the new Office 2007 interface, you'll probably develop your own favorite right-click menu paths in everyday work routines.

BI TIP

The new Office 2007 Ribbon menu is a big jump forward for Office applications, and it is perhaps the most important element of commonality to tie together Excel, Access, PowerPoint, Outlook, and Word since the early days of Office integration years ago. If you're a long-time power user of Excel the new Ribbon menu will take some getting used to, although it honestly will be just a couple of days till you're comfortable with it and probably won't ever want to return to the old way of doing work!

And note the Ribbon menu look-and-feel is quickly becoming ubiquitous across Microsoft applications, from Microsoft Office SharePoint Server (MOSS) to Visio 2007 (and the new PerformancePoint Server 2007).

The basic elements of the Ribbon menu are straightforward—the Office button, tabs, groups within the tabs, and icons within the groups. Office 2007 sports a much richer set of icons that display across the Ribbon menu and provide an intuitive idea of the actions that can be accomplished by clicking the icons.

Furthermore, many of the icons provide a live preview capability where the on-screen spreadsheet display will change as you hover the mouse over an icon but won't actually change the spreadsheet until you click and choose the icon action. This really makes working with Excel 2007 much faster, since you don't have to keep changing spreadsheet elements back and forth to get visual feedback on formatting and row-column arrangements. In fact, you can mouse over a gallery of choices that may have a large number of options, and very quickly find the appearance you want.

BI TIP

A very useful part of the new 2007 interface is the Zoom slider control that always appears on the lower right of the screen. It's amazing how often we find ourselves using this to zoom the display in or out—to bring whatever we want to see within the viewable screen.

Another helpful aspect of the Office 2007 Ribbon menu design is that the tabs and groups of icons follow your workflow of creating content. So with Excel 2007 we start at the Home tab with the common text and number formatting menu items, followed by the Insert tab, where we can start on a PivotTable/PivotChart inserted onto the spreadsheet, for example.

Subsequent tabs hold groups of icons for more advanced formulas and data work, and at the end of the default tab strip we find tabs for Review and View to help in the finalization of the workbook. Note that we'll always wind up back at the Office button icon for saving and printing, and a surprisingly wide range of menu choices for Prepare, Send, and Publish, which hold some important capabilities that allow us to really control workbook content and delivery using e-mail or Microsoft Office SharePoint, for example.

BI TIP

One important thing to note about the new Ribbon menu is the location of the Properties menu item for a workbook. Click the Office button and choose Prepare | Properties to bring up a dialog box where you can examine or edit the author, title, etc. of your workbook. This can be significant to avoid surprises when someone else looks at your spreadsheet and sees information you didn't even know was there!

Excel 2007 Text Import Wizard

As shown in Figure 4-3, Excel pops up a very handy set of dialog boxes to help us import and format the text data file. This is an important part of the chapter because the Excel Text Import Wizard is fairly powerful, and if you know how to use it, you'll find it becomes a permanent part of the tools you use with Excel. In the database professional world, the following text import process is commonly termed ETL.

BI TIP

Data professionals have long known that Excel's Text Import Wizard is one of the easiest ways to get data files into a coherent table format. It's amazingly flexible, and once the imported data is in Excel, you can subsequently use SQL Server to import the Excel data into a true relational database format.

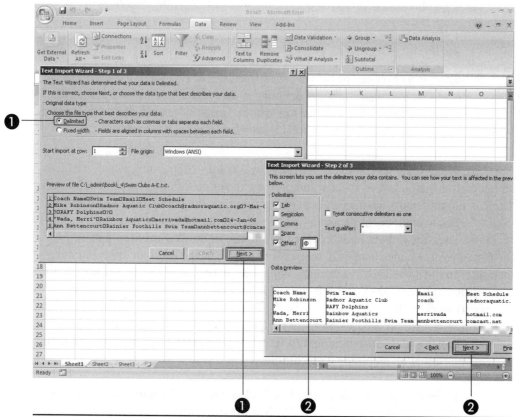

Figure 4-3 *Excel Get External Data Text Import Wizard, Steps 1 and 2*

1. Accept the default of Delimited and click Next on the Text Import Wizard – Step 1 of 3 dialog box.

2. On the Text Import Wizard – Step 2 of 3, check the Other checkbox for Delimiters, type an @ symbol in the associated text box, and click Next.

In Figure 4-3, Text Import Wizard – Step 1 of 3, we chose the Delimited option button because we can see some interesting characters in the Preview pane that might be separators for the text elements (in fact, we're able to choose the separator characters in the subsequent Text Import Wizard dialog box). This intuitively makes sense, since the Preview pane shows text that is not aligned in a columnar fashion (which would indicate a Fixed Width format for the text file).

Note that if we chose the Fixed Width option button, we would be able to interactively choose the column widths in the subsequent Text Import Wizard dialog box (Step 2 of 3). This is important because the ability to preview and click-and-choose text elements or text separators is what makes Excel such a great tool for importing data files!

BI TIP

Data files are a common part of real-world information; and even though it would be nice to have all data in coherent relational databases, we need to be able to work with business data in whatever form we find it. The two most common formats for data outside a database such as SQL Server are Delimited and Fixed Width, which Excel is well able to import.

Figure 4-3 also shows the Excel Text Import Wizard – Step 2 of 3, where we have an interactive dialog box to specify and preview the effect of different data delimiters. There is nothing really advanced about data delimiters; they are just text characters used to separate columns of data in a text file such as the one in our example.

As we click the Other checkbox for Delimiters, in the Wizard Step 2 of 3, the Data Preview pane changes dynamically to show us the result of applying the Delimiter to the data. This live preview capability is typical of the data manipulation capabilities in Excel 2007, and it is part of what makes the import text feature so easy to work with.

In Figure 4-4 we proceed with the text import and use a couple of the features that allow us to manipulate data coming into Excel. We'll eliminate an incoming column of data and format an incoming date column.

1. On the Text Import Wizard, Step 3 of 3, click the Email column to select it in the Data Preview pane. Click the Do Not Import Column (Skip) option button in the Column Data Format choices.

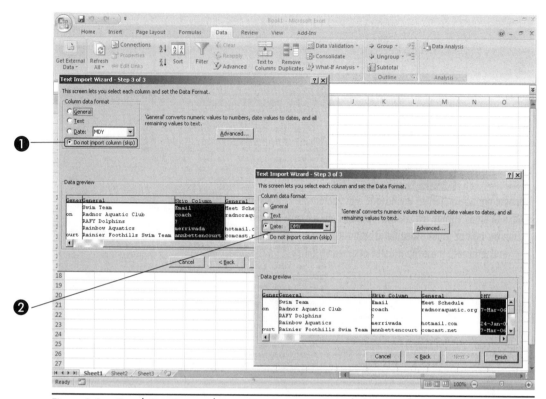

Figure 4-4 *Excel Get External Data Text Import Wizard, Step 3 of 3*

2. Click the General last column to select it in the Data Preview pane. Click the Date option button in the Column Data Format choices, choose DMY in the drop-down box, and click Finish.

In Figure 4-4 we have an interactive user-interface that allows us to select columns of incoming data in the Data Preview pane and apply import rules. Since we don't want to import the names, which were part of the e-mail addresses (we only want to bring in the e-mail organization information), we applied the Do Not Import Column (Skip) choice to it. To make sure the date column is imported correctly, we were able to examine the dates in the Data Preview pane, and we decided to apply a Day-Month-Year format to the column.

The Advanced button on the Text Import Wizard allows the designation of decimal and thousands separators for incoming data. We did not use it for our working example.

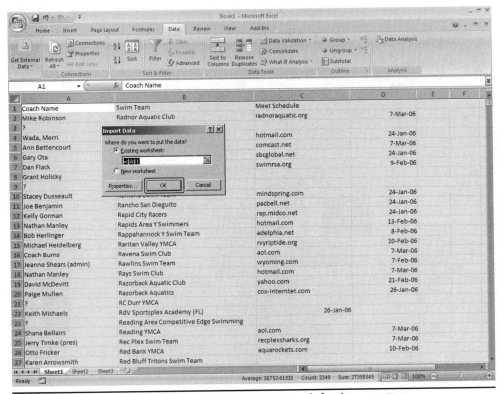

Figure 4-5 *Excel Get External Data Text Import Wizard, final Import Data*

And as Figure 4-5 shows, we have data to work with in Excel by simply clicking OK in the Import Data dialog box! This is significant because so many people are comfortable with analyzing and formatting data in an Excel spreadsheet. Excel 2007 can hold a million rows of data, so we're likely to see a lot more of this Excel extraction, transformation, and loading of data, since it's available to us in Office 2007.

If we save the Excel spreadsheet and reopen it as shown in Figure 4-6, we will see the Security Alert warning dialog box that tells us the spreadsheet has a link to external data. This is a good safeguard, since anyone could send us a spreadsheet that is ready to connect to outside data (that we might not be aware of)—and Microsoft realizes that external data import should not be allowed without asking the user for permission.

1. Click the Enable This Content option button.

2. Click OK to allow the data connection.

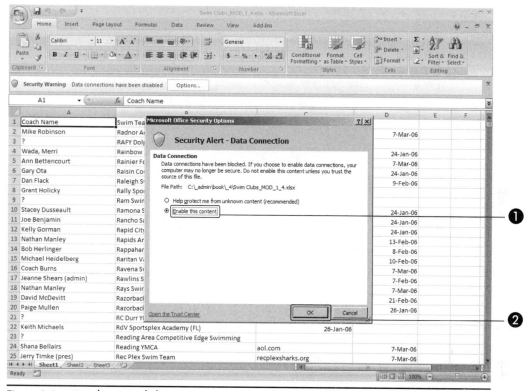

Figure 4-6 *Excel external data connection Security Alert warning*

Note that in Figure 4-6, clicking to Enable This Content in the dialog box does not actually import any data; it just enables the previously configured text import data connection so that we can subsequently import more text data. Be aware that a malicious spreadsheet could contain a data connection that is configured to automatically import data if the user chooses to enable this content, so you should be careful to only allow external data that you have personally created, or that come from someone you know or work with (and you know the reason for the data import!).

Office 2007 Trusted Locations

In Figure 4-6 we could have clicked the Open The Trust Center link at the bottom-left corner of the Security Alert – Data Connection warning dialog box, which would

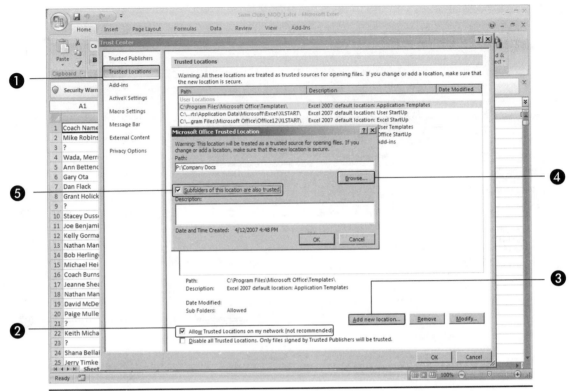

Figure 4-7   *Microsoft Office Trusted Location configuration*

display the screen shown in Figure 4-7. For the purposes of this chapter we won't explore all Trust Center options, but it's worth understanding that we can designate Microsoft Office Trusted Locations as we see in Figure 4-7.

1. Click the Trusted Locations menu choice in the left pane of options.
2. Click the checkbox for Allow Trusted Locations On My Network (not recommended).
3. Click the Add New Location button.
4. Browse to the known network or file location for trusted data files, and click OK.
5. Check the checkbox for "Subfolders of this location are also trusted," and click OK.

The procedure outlined with Figure 4-7 can actually be pretty helpful in a company setting. If your company has text file exports that are regularly saved to a network location (perhaps on a public drive or folder), you can connect Excel 2007 to those text files and work with the data. If this is done on a regular basis, it makes sense to designate the source of the text files as a trusted location whereby you won't get the Security Alert – Data Connection warning dialog box when re-opening Excel workbooks with connections to the trusted location.

Our next step of working with data that we've imported into Excel is pretty mundane: actually cleaning up miscellaneous items on a cell-by-cell basis as shown in Figure 4-8, where we cut and paste a DATE field into the correct column for dates. Admittedly this is not an optimal situation, but real-world data is not optimal either, and at some point we need to decide to finish our work with some manual cleanup! In truth this is one reason people import data into Excel—because it's easy to look it over and clean up miscellaneous items.

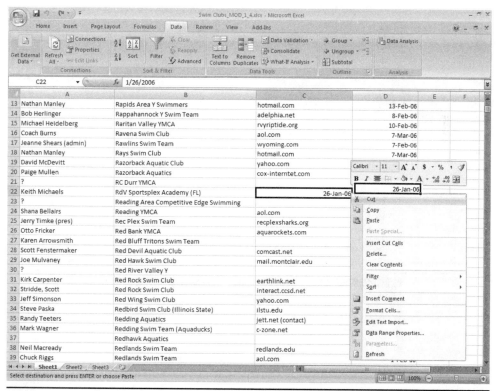

Figure 4-8   *Excel cut and paste manual data cleanup*

Importing Additional Text Data: Concatenation

The next step in our text import process gets interesting again; as shown in Figure 4-9, we can import an additional text file and add it onto the data already imported. This is actually known as concatenating data, because we're adding the new data onto the end of the previous data. The benefit of this will be a solid set of data in Excel that can be sorted and formatted as one big list or Excel table.

1. Scroll down to the first empty row, and click the first column blank cell.
2. Click the Get External Data icon on the Ribbon menu Data tab, to the left of the Connections group of options.
3. Click the From Text icon on the submenu for Get External Data.
4. Browse to the desired text file, and click Import.

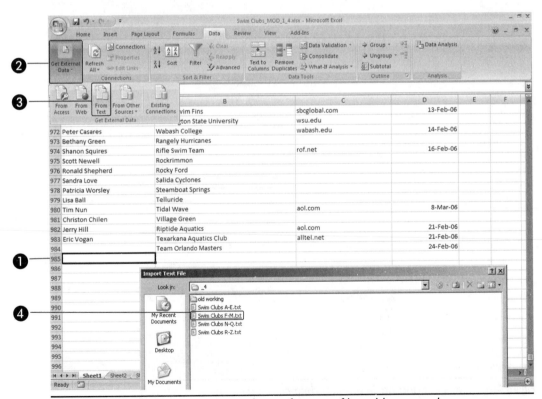

Figure 4-9 *Excel 2007—Get External Data from text file; adding new data*

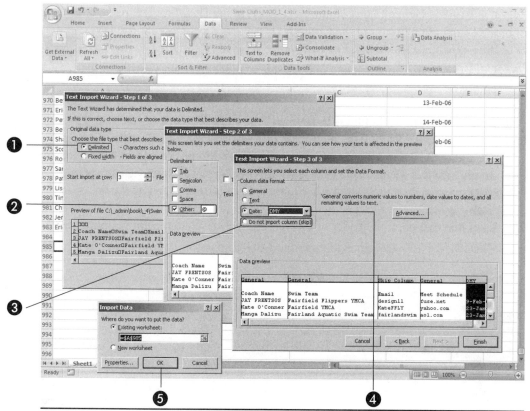

Figure 4-10 *Excel Get External Data Text Import Wizard, Steps 1, 2, and 3*

As Figure 4-10 shows, the Text Import Wizard pops up just as it did before, and we choose the same text import options to make sure the new data matches the columns and date format of the earlier data import.

1. Accept the default of Delimited and click Next on the Text Import Wizard – Step 1 of 3 dialog box.

2. On the Text Import Wizard – Step 2 of 3, check the Other checkbox for Delimiters, and type an @ symbol in the associated text box, and click Next.

3. On the Text Import Wizard – Step 3 of 3, click the Email column to select it in the Data Preview pane. Click the Do Not Import Column (Skip) option button in the Column Data Format choices.

4. Click on the General last column to select it in the Data Preview pane. Click the Date option button in the Column Data Format choices, choose DMY in the drop-down box, and click Finish.

5. Click OK on the Import Data dialog box, to place the data starting in the empty cell.

The menu steps shown in Figure 4-10 mirror the steps followed for the first text import; we choose the Delimited data format; we separate the e-mail strings using the @ symbol, skip the name column, and designate a Day-Month-Year format for the date column. The result is a single spreadsheet of imported data, to which we can apply the Excel data manipulation tools shown in Figure 4-11, to further clean up the data.

1. Click the first column header of the spreadsheet to select the entire column.

2. Click the Text To Columns icon, in the Data Tools group of the Data tab.

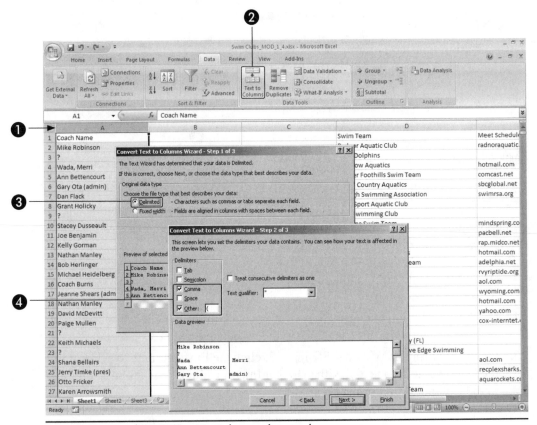

Figure 4-11 *Excel 2007 Text To Columns data tool*

3. Accept the default of Delimited and click Next on the Convert Text To Columns Wizard – Step 1 of 3 dialog box.

4. Uncheck the Tab checkbox, check the Comma checkbox, check the Other checkbox, and enter a left parenthesis in the adjacent text box, and then click Next.

Using Excel Tools to Clean Up Imported Data

The next part of our text import process will use some of the Excel tools to clean up the data. This is pretty simple, but it's worth showing in our example, since it's part of the real world of data cleanup. Figure 4-12 displays the often-used Find And Replace feature of Office 2007; in this case we're going to get rid of the extraneous parentheses in the second column of the spreadsheet.

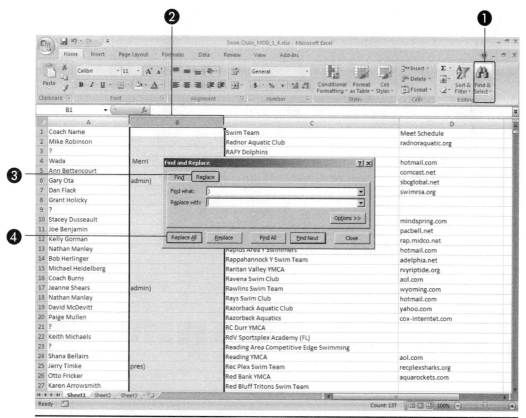

Figure 4-12 *Excel Find & Select to remove unwanted characters*

1. Click the Find & Select icon in the Editing menu group, on the Ribbon menu Home tab.

2. Click the column header for the second column in the spreadsheet, to select the entire column.

3. Click the Replace tab in the Find And Replace dialog box, and enter a left parenthesis in the Find What text box.

4. Click Replace All.

Formatting the Imported Data as an Excel Table

Now it makes sense to do something interesting with the data we've imported into Excel, and an Excel table is an easy and quick way to format the data. Figure 4-13 shows how we use the Format As Table feature of Excel 2007 to take a big jump forward in terms of being able to manipulate the imported data.

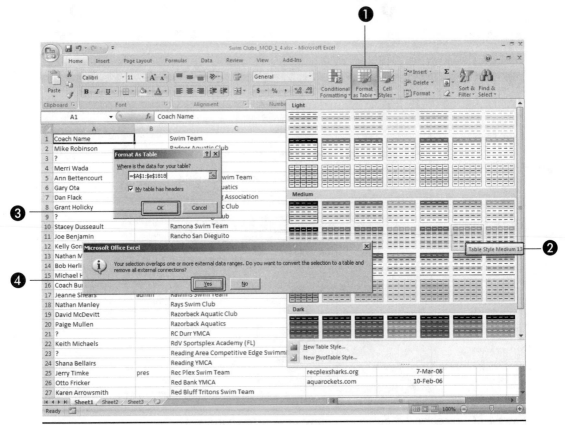

Figure 4-13 *Excel 2007 Format As Table*

1. Click the Format As Table icon, in the Styles menu group on the Ribbon menu Home tab.

2. Click Table Style Medium (or whatever style you wish).

3. Click OK on the Format As Table dialog box.

4. Click Yes on the dialog box to proceed with the conversion to Excel table form.

Note that in this case we've decided we don't need to stay connected to the external text file data—and it's more important that we be able to work with data as an Excel table. Since we've cleaned up the data, it would be easier to re-import new data from scratch than to try and refresh through a data connection onto the same data sheet.

Figure 4-14 shows off the new look of our data in an Excel table. This is an improved part of Excel 2007, and we're going to explore it further. A table is simply the same data in a more organized list form, and as a table the data can be filtered

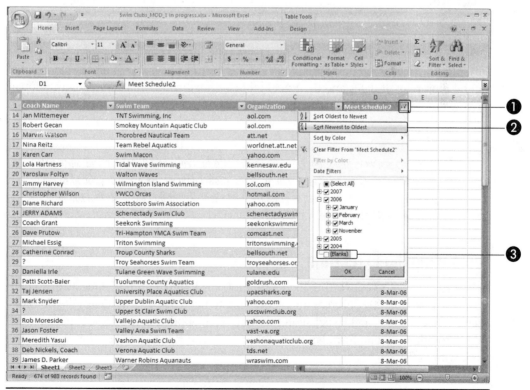

Figure 4-14 *Excel 2007 table sorting and filtering*

and sorted. We'll also see that Excel 2007 automatically customizes the Data Filter choices according to the type of data—in the case of a Date type, the elements are sorted newest-to-oldest (Descending), and the Date type is automatically broken out by Date hierarchy (Year-Month-Day). This is new in Excel 2007!

Furthermore, the data rows of an Excel table enjoy alternate row color banding. This required formulas in previous versions of Excel. Note how much easier it is to scan a large quantity of data with this helpful formatting in Figure 4-14.

1. Click the Meet Schedule drop-down control.
2. Click the Sort Newest To Oldest menu option.
3. Click the Blanks checkbox.

Our thought process in this working example is that we'd like to explore the data by ordering its date column, and we'd like to suppress the Date fields that are blank. As we can see in Figure 4-14, it's easy to sort any column of the Excel table; in fact, we can narrow the data display as well by simply clicking the Date Filters checkboxes that automatically break the Date data in the column into Year and Month elements.

Since we imported the Date data as a Date type (and specified the format as Day-Month-Year), Excel 2007 (and yes, *this is new in Excel 2007*) understands the natural hierarchy of dates and the Excel table automatically breaks the column down into the date parts of Year, Month, and Day!

BI TIP

Date data is always important in manipulating data for real-world understanding, since date and time are so often associated with the transactional data we use every day. Good BI tools understand Date data and help to organize it into Year-Month-Day elements that can be individually chosen for display and analysis.

Subtotaling the Excel Data

In Figure 4-15 we're converting the Excel table back into a normal data sheet so that we can use Excel 2007 subtotaling to consolidate the data rows by Date. We do this because Excel tables and Excel subtotals cannot be applied at the same time, so we simply toggle back and forth between Table form and Range form so that we can work with both.

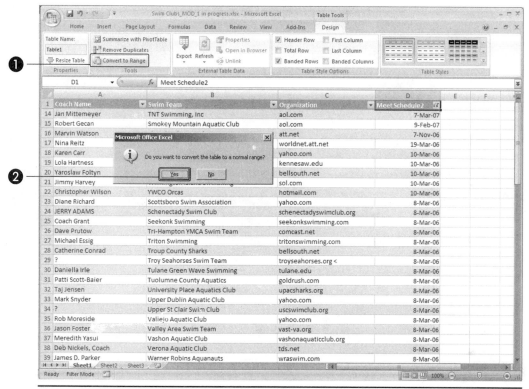

Figure 4-15 *Excel 2007 table Convert To Range*

1. Click on the Convert To Range icon, in the Tools menu group on the Ribbon menu Design tab.
2. Click Yes on the dialog box to convert the table.

Figure 4-16 shows the interesting steps we take to subtotal the data and consolidate the rows by Date. Note this is being done on the data in Range form, not Table form.

1. Click the Subtotal icon, in the Outline menu group on the Ribbon menu Data tab.
2. Click the At Each Change In drop-down control to select the Meet Schedule column.
3. Click the Use Function drop-down control to select a Count operation.
4. Click the Meet Schedule checkbox, make sure the other checkboxes are unchecked, and click OK.

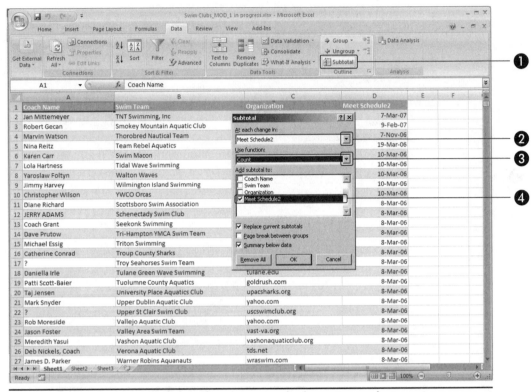

Figure 4-16   *Excel 2007 Subtotal configuration, applied to a Date column*

The subtotaling results in a dramatically different-looking spreadsheet, with Outline controls on the left margin. We can click the Plus and Minus symbols to collapse and expand the subtotal groups, which is exactly what we want to do in order to collapse the rows to only show the subtotals as we see in Figure 4-17.

1. Click the 2 button at the top of the Plus symbol Outline controls on the left margin.
2. Click the top cell to be graphed in the Meet Schedule column, and while holding the left mouse button down, drag the mouse down to include the rest of the Subtotal cells.
3. Click the Column icon, in the Charts menu group on the Ribbon menu Insert tab.
4. Click the 2-D Column icon in the Chart Types gallery.

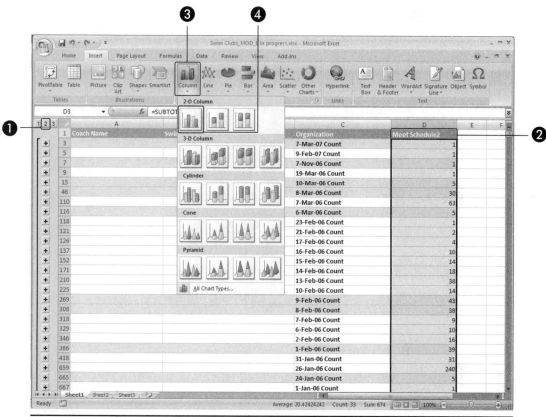

Figure 4-17 *Excel 2007 subtotals and subsequent chart*

Figure 4-17 shows how quickly we can condense a spreadsheet using the Outline controls—it is an important way to get a view of the data that is above the detail level! Figure 4-18 also shows how to quickly create a Chart in the Excel spreadsheet. Excel charting is one of the fastest-changing areas of Office technology which could be explored in multiple chapters—but for the purposes of this discussion we'll just take the most direct route to creating a usable Excel chart.

Charting the Excel Data

Next we're going enhance and manipulate the Chart in the Excel spreadsheet. In Figure 4-18 we continue our Chart configuration and correct the Horizontal Axis labels to reflect the Meet Schedule dates.

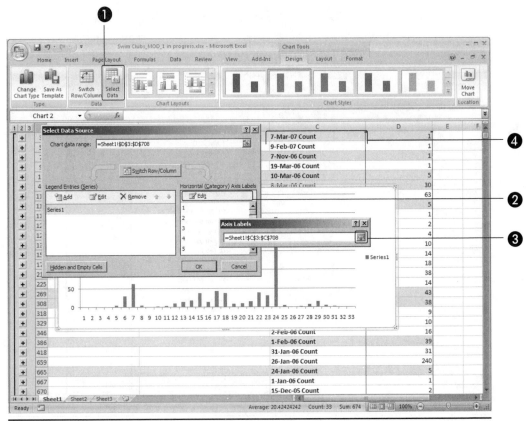

Figure 4-18 *Excel 2007 chart Select Data Source dialog box*

1. Click the Select Data icon, in the Data menu group on the Ribbon menu Design tab.
2. Click the Edit icon in the Select Data Source dialog box for the chart.
3. Click the icon at the end of the Axis Labels text box.
4. Click the top cell of the Date labels column, and while holding the right mouse button down, drag the mouse down to select the cells for Date labels. Then click OK.

Figure 4-19 shows the final result of our text import process, with a bar chart that clearly shows the spread of Meet Schedules across various dates. This is certainly a better portrayal of the Swim Team activity and scheduling that we had with the text files, and with the data in Excel 2007 we can support a entire season of managing the various team schedules.

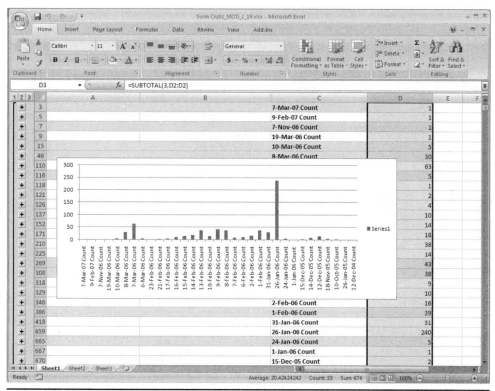

Figure 4-19 *Excel text import, Date values in a bar chart*

There are many different ways to organize and highlight the data imported, and as you gain a working familiarity with the Excel 2007 import mechanisms, it can become quite comfortable to bring almost any external data into Excel and analyze or format it—with results that can be used in meetings and presentations.

Importing Access Data into Excel 2007

It is amazing to see how much data resides in Access databases around the world. This makes sense when you realize that Access has been the de facto departmental database for many years now—and it is part of the Office suite of products. Excel 2007 makes it easy to connect to Access data, and we'll start with a direct connection to Access, as shown in Figure 4-20.

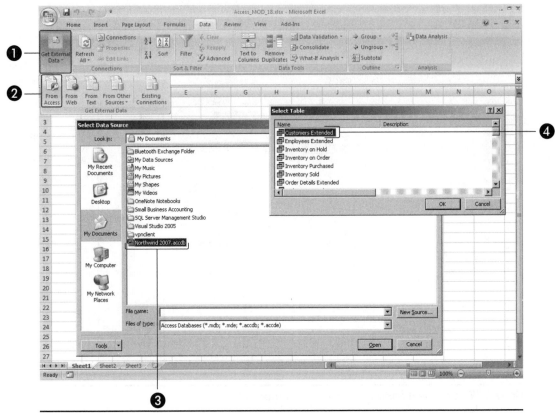

Figure 4-20 *Excel 2007 get external data from Access*

1. Click the Get External Data icon, in the Connections menu group on the Ribbon menu Data tab.

2. Click the From Access icon, in the Get External Data pop-up menu.

3. Browse to any Access database file mdb or accdb, and click Open.

4. Select the view or table desired from the Select Table dialog box, and click OK.

Figure 4-20 highlights an interesting point about Access data: we are able to directly choose Access views or tables without having to go through a SQL interface that would require us to join or link tables of data together. This is significant because many end users don't know how to work with SQL (Structured Query Language) to get to databases, and with Excel and Access we don't have to deal with SQL.

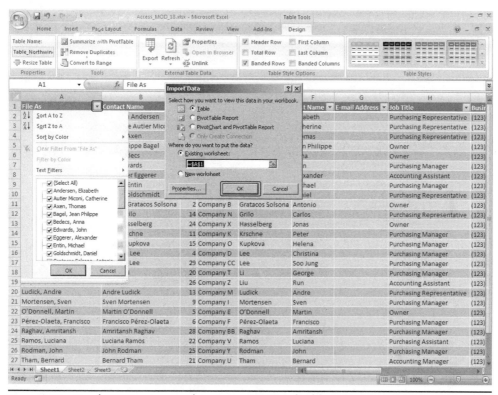

Figure 4-21 *Excel 2007—Access data import to Excel table*

Figure 4-21 shows what the Access data looks like when we import it into Excel by simply clicking OK to place the data onto a spreadsheet.

Note in Figure 4-21 that the incoming Access data could come into a table, PivotTable, or PivotChart. For our working example, we'll go with the default table choice, which is very easy to work with in Excel 2007. The advantages of an Excel table are easy to see; the columns can be sorted and data-filtered by clicking the drop-down controls that appear at the top of every Excel table column.

Using MS Query SQL to Join Tables and Import Data

Figure 4-22 shows a different approach to importing Access data; in this case we're going to use MS Query to connect to an Access database. This approach is more sophisticated than our previous direct connection to Access, which did not involve MS Query or SQL. As we'll soon see, using MS Query is a more flexible way to connect to Access, but it involves more choices as well.

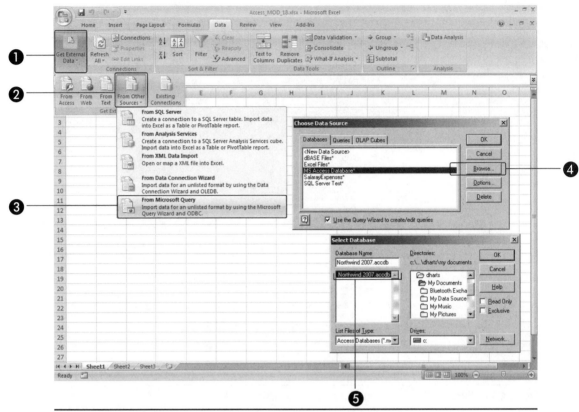

Figure 4-22 *Excel 2007—Get External Data | Microsoft Query | Access*

1. Click the Get External Data icon, in the Connections menu group on the Ribbon menu Data tab.

2. Click the From Other Sources icon, in the pop-up menu choices dialog box.

3. Click the From Microsoft Query choice in the pop-up menu dialog box.

4. Click the MS Access Database choice in the Choose Data Source dialog box, and Browse to the Access database files.

5. Choose the desired Access database file in the Select Database dialog box, and click OK.

BI TIP

Database query tools can offer connections to database tables in two ways: directly to the tables or to views that contain already-joined tables, or through a SQL tool that then connects to the database tables. The first, direct connection requires that tables be previously joined in a database view (thus the end user does not have to deal with SQL); the second, SQL connection requires the use of a SQL query tool such as MS Query that will join or link tables, and then provide data from the joined tables.

It's important to realize that MS Query can be used to join tables from any modern database such as SQL Server, Oracle, DB2, or Informix—if you have the client connection software that is required to access these database servers. SQL Server is the easiest to configure because Excel 2007 includes the SQL Server client connection software (it's already built into Excel).

Excel 2007 also includes the Access client connection software, which is what allows us to use MS Query to connect to the Access database. Figure 4-23 shows

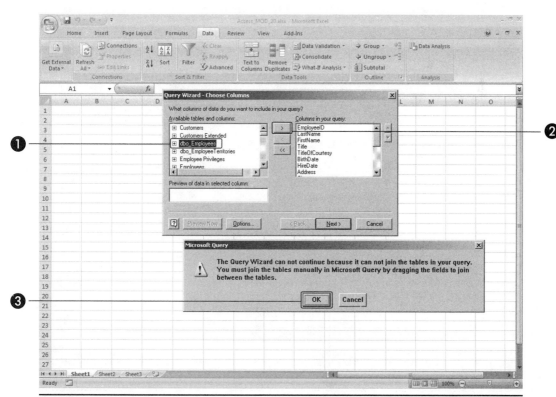

Figure 4-23 *MS Query—Query Wizard to generate SQL for data retrieval from Access*

how we can proceed to select information from Access, using MS Query, which is Microsoft's visual query design tool for Office 2007.

1. Click the desired database table in the Available Tables And Columns list.

2. Click the > button to copy the chosen table fields into the Columns in your query list, and click Next.

3. Click OK on the Microsoft Query dialog box to continue and manually join the tables involved.

Now, don't be concerned that MS Query won't automatically join the tables required for the data we've chosen in the MS Query Wizard—it's actually a good thing that we can move forward into the actual MS Query visual query designer. As we see in Figure 4-24, we can intuitively make a connection between the tables offered up by the MS Query Wizard.

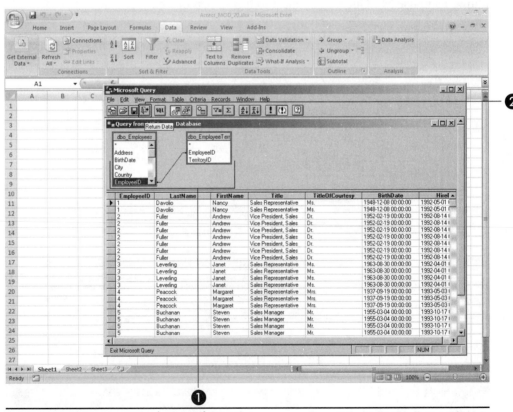

Figure 4-24 *MS Query visual query designer*

1. Click the EmployeeID field in the dbo_Employees table list. Hold the right mouse button down, and drag the mouse to the EmployeeID field in the dbo_Employee Territories table list.

2. Click the Return Data icon (the open door with a left arrow) at the top of the MS Query screen.

Let's pause for a minute and look at the MS Query screen in Figure 4-24. The concept of joining or linking tables is not really complicated; it's the knowledge of the data that determines this process. In our working example, we can guess that the EmployeeID field might connect data between the two tables involved, and trying it out in MS Query is easy.

It's not important that we understand SQL, or how to join tables in general. The concept here is that it can be done with a visual linking mechanism such as MS Query, and the resulting data from two tables can be seen in the MS Query preview pane. Most business users will not be using SQL, but MS Query can provide a visual guide for those people that need this capability.

Many business users instead rely on database professionals to have previously joined tables into views to be presented to end users. We saw the results of this with our earlier direct connection to Access, where we did not use MS Query; we simply connected directly to an Access view that someone had already created in the Access database.

BI TIP

Database views provide some of the best values in the BI world. They offer coherent data from tables that have been prejoined by database professionals, and end users can obtain data directly from the view with everyday tools such as Excel 2007.

Figure 4-25 shows that the end result of importing Access data using MS Query is the same as the end result of importing Access data using a direct connection to a view that has been predefined. The MS Query route offers more flexibility of choice in deciding which table to join or link, and to return data—while the direct-to-view route offers a faster business user experience to import data into Excel.

As we've seen before, Figure 4-25 shows that once we have the data imported into Excel 2007, we're in a familiar world of tools to arrange, format, and aggregate data. The same column-header-level drop-down controls are presented as part of the Excel table format that is automatically displayed for imported data. Furthermore, Excel 2007 provides a toolset that allows us to Get External Data directly from text files or Access, or to use MS Query and the power of SQL to query the data and bring it into Excel.

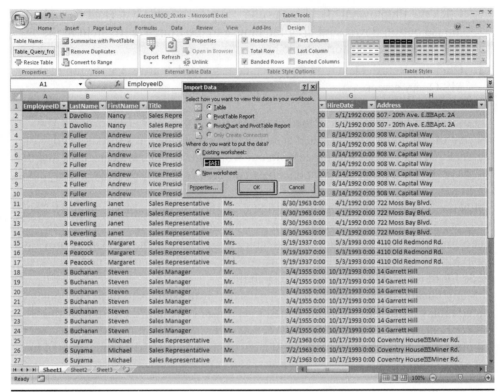

Figure 4-25 *Excel 2007—Get External Data | From Other Sources | From Microsoft Query*

Importing Oracle Data into Excel 2007

Excel 2007 can be connected to a wide variety of non-Microsoft data sources. People often ask if Microsoft Business Intelligence tools work with Oracle or IBM DB2 databases—and the answer is yes! This is important because organizations usually have a wide variety of databases and formats—and yet most of us have Office. So if we realize that Office 2007 applications such as Excel can connect to these data sources, then we can use Office as a common front end to the data sources in our everyday work.

BI TIP

Front-end business intelligence tools—whether they are reporting, analysis, or measurement tools—should be able to connect to any modern data source such as a relational database or text file. And the mechanisms used to connect to the data sources should follow the standards of OLE-DB or ODBC connectors, or built-in text file connectors that are provided as part of the business intelligence toolset.

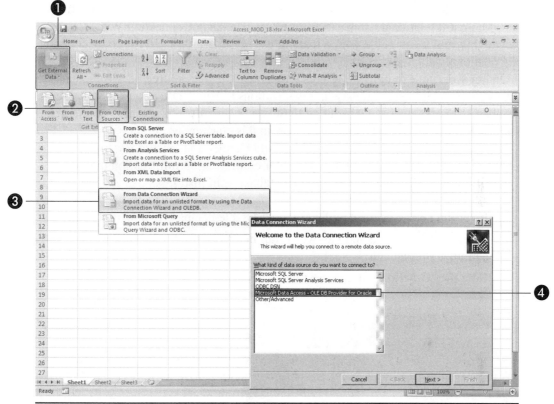

Figure 4-26 *Excel 2007—Get External Data | From Data Connection Wizard | Oracle*

Figure 4-26 shows how we start the process of connecting to an Oracle data source. If you're not sure what kinds of databases your organization has in place, don't be too concerned; the purpose here is to briefly show what is involved in connecting to a non-Microsoft relational database. We are not actually going to complete the process of importing data from Oracle; rather, we will explain the Excel process and the required Oracle components.

1. Click the Get External Data icon in the Connections menu group, on the Ribbon menu Data tab.

2. Click the From Other Sources icon in the Get External Data pop-up menu.

3. Click the From Data Connection Wizard in the From Other Sources pop-up menu.

4. Click the Microsoft Data Access—OLE DB Provider For Oracle choice in the Data Connection Wizard dialog box, and then click Next.

Figure 4-26 is important because it shows the most common way of connecting to non-Microsoft relational databases from Excel. The Data Connection Wizard is the key to this, and it can guide you to making use of OLE-DB or ODBC connectors to the relational database servers.

In our working example we're choosing an Oracle data source because it's a prevalent non-Microsoft database in organizations today. Please note that SQL Server databases are prevalent as well, and SQL Server is actually a bit easier to configure for data import into Excel, as we'll see later in this chapter.

Figure 4-27 shows the next step of the Data Connection Wizard for an Oracle connection, which is where we have to enter configuration information that is typically provided by the organization's database administrator.

1. Enter the Server Name supplied by your Oracle database administrator.

2. Enter the User Name and Password supplied by your Oracle database administrator, and click Next.

3. Note the "Oracle client. . ." message, and click OK.

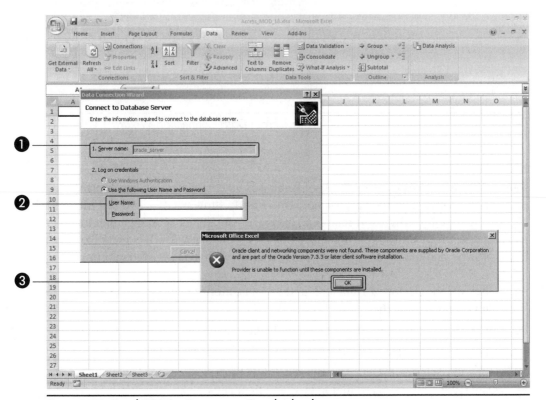

Figure 4-27 *Excel 2007—Connect to Oracle database server*

Oracle Client Requirements for Excel Connection

Figure 4-27 shows the point at which data import from non-Microsoft databases requires information from a database administrator (DBA) that is responsible for the database in your organization. In this case an Oracle client is required, and it must be installed to your computer for Excel to make use of it and connect to an Oracle database server.

This is actually an important point of understanding; for connection to non-Microsoft database servers, Excel requires client components from the company that publishes the database server. This is not a surprise when we realize that only the software company that publishes the database application (in this case Oracle) can provide the licensed and up-to-date components required to connect to their database server.

In support of our working example, Figure 4-28 shows the Oracle Instant Client Downloads web page that is available on the Oracle web site. The steps to install and configure the Oracle client are beyond the scope of this book—and really should be done with the help of an Oracle database administrator that knows the server name, user ID, and password for proper setup.

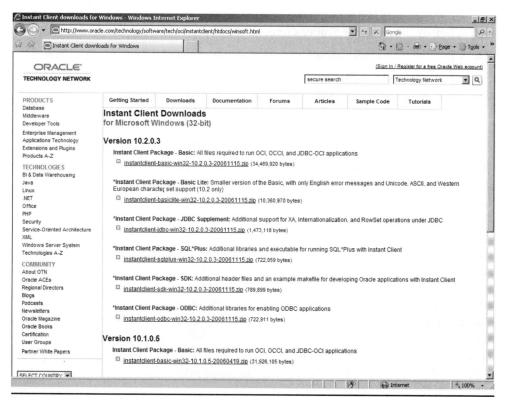

Figure 4-28 *Oracle Instant Client Downloads for connection to Oracle databases*

This section on Oracle connectivity is not meant to provide detailed instructions on Oracle client configuration, but rather to help us understand that Excel 2007, through the Data Connection Wizard, can connect to an Oracle database if the proper Oracle connection components are installed and configured on the computer that is running Excel. This is known as a client connection to a database source.

Importing SQL Server Data into Excel 2007

Our exploration of Excel Data Connection to external data now proceeds to SQL Server. Since SQL Server is published by Microsoft, it makes sense that Microsoft Excel comes with the client components required to connect to a SQL Server database server—there are no other connectivity components needed.

Figure 4-29 shows how we start the process of connecting to SQL Server. Excel 2007 makes it easy, since it's the first choice in the From Other Sources menu.

1. Click the Get External Data icon in the Connections menu group, on the Ribbon menu Data tab.
2. Click the From Other Sources icon on the pop-up menu.
3. Click the From SQL Server choice in the pop-up menu.
4. Enter the Server Name where the SQL Server database resides.
5. Choose Use Windows Authentication or enter a User Name and Password, then click Next.

As Figure 4-29 shows, it is a relatively straightforward process to connect to SQL Server. You need to know the Server name, which in our working example is localhost because the SQL Server database resides on the same machine where we're running Excel. Also, you need to use the Log On credentials of either Windows Authentication or an ID and Password.

Windows Authentication automatically uses your Windows Network ID and Password to connect to SQL Server, which works if the SQL Server database has been configured to accept Everyone and/or your ID for connection. The Everyone logon access to SQL Server is commonly used with non-sensitive data where your previous Windows Network logon provides an acceptable validation of credentials. The user name (ID) and password are more often used with SQL Server database servers that contain data that should only be available to specific users on the network. In either case, the actual databases on the SQL Server can be further configured to be available only to selected users or roles.

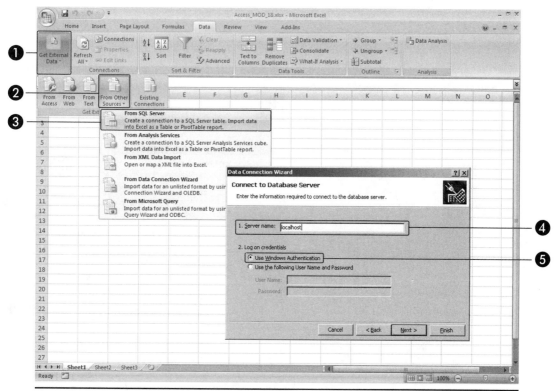

Figure 4-29 *Excel 2007—Get External Data | From SQL Server*

Excel Direct-Connect to SQL Server

Figure 4-30 shows that—after we've provided the appropriate server, ID, and password information—we have a choice of databases, tables, and views within each database.

1. Click the desired database in the Select The Database drop-down box.
2. Click Finish.

Note that the double-rectangle icons in the list of Tables and Views indicate a view (which is a preconfigured combination of tables connected by a SQL join). We chose not to check the Connect To A Specific Table checkbox, because we'll choose the actual tables (or views) in a subsequent step. For our working example, we're using the AdventureWorks database because it is commonly available as a sample database from Microsoft.

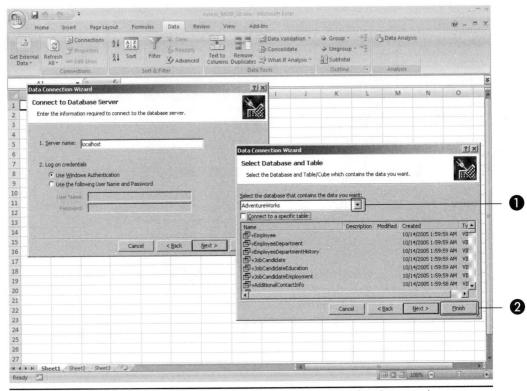

Figure 4-30 *Excel 2007 Data Connection Wizard | SQL Server | Select Database and Table*

Figure 4-31 shows the prompt to save an Excel 2007 data connection and select a table to work with from the SQL Server database chosen previously.

1. Click Finish on the dialog box to Save Data Connection File And Finish.
2. Click the Table desired in the Select Table dialog box list.
3. Click OK.

Figure 4-31 shows an interesting piece of information about the Excel external data connection—Excel saves the connection information as a file for later reuse when importing again into Excel. In our working example we're simply using the default File Name and Description.

The Select Table dialog box is displayed because we previously elected not to choose a specific table to work with in this data connection; thus the Data Connection Wizard prompts us to choose a Table (or View) for import into Excel.

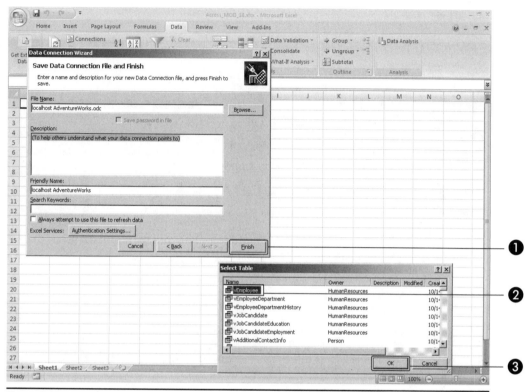

Figure 4-31 *Excel 2007 Data Connection Wizard—Save Data Connection, Select Table*

This is an important point; we must choose a table or a view, since we're not creating a SQL query to bring data in from the SQL Server database.

BI TIP

We can connect directly to a SQL Server table or view without creating a SQL query, but this effectively means we are depending on the database administrator (DBA) to create views for data sets that combine data from more than one table. This is perfectly fine for users who don't know how to create SQL queries. The alternative is to use the From Microsoft Query External Data Connection mechanism in Excel, which provides a Visual Query Builder to create SQL and retrieve data.

In Figure 4-32 we see the results of importing the SQL Server view in Excel by simply clicking OK to create an Excel table. This is fairly important when we realize we're able to bring data into Excel without creating SQL; we just have to

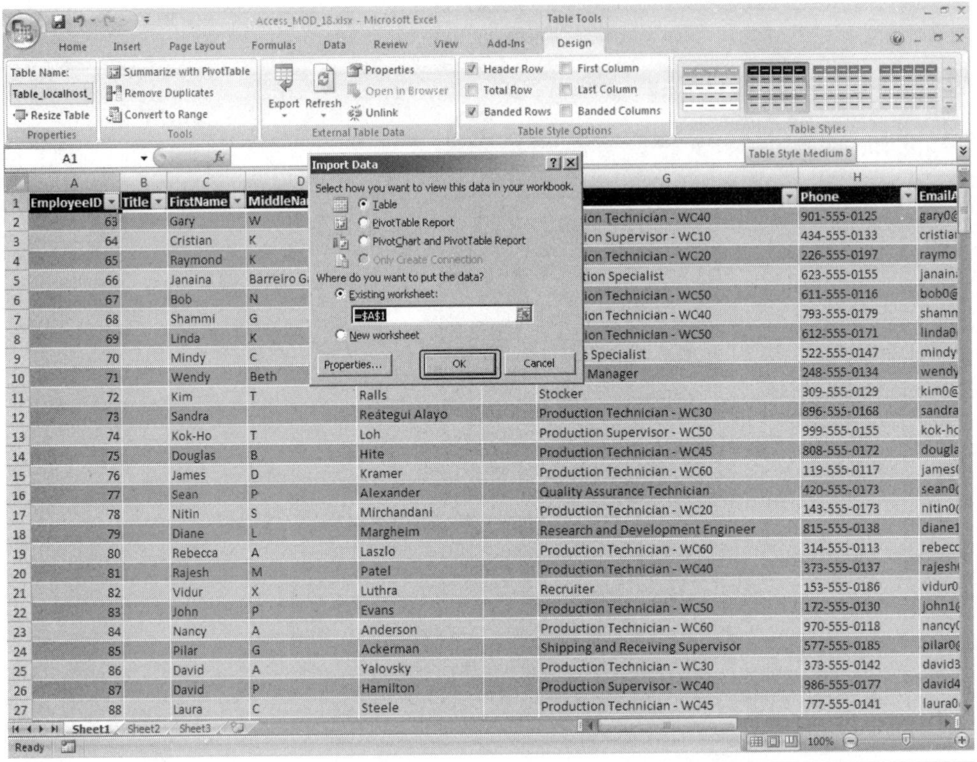

Figure 4-32 *Excel 2007—an Excel table created from a SQL Server import*

choose views that have been created for us by the SQL Server database administrator (DBA). This process is good for business users, because it relies on a DBA to create accurate SQL queries and save them as views, to then be available for us to import into Excel.

Importing SQL Server OLAP Data into Excel 2007

This section is a fairly exciting look at one of the advanced business intelligence aspects of SQL Server: Analysis Services. Most business users do not know what Analysis Services is, or OLAP in general. But it can have a profound benefit when business users connect to Analysis Services OLAP cubes with Excel 2007. In fact, some people might say that Excel and OLAP cubes, together, are the leading edge of business intelligence on the desktop.

What Is an Analysis Services OLAP Cube?

When people need to evaluate summarized data in a flexible manner, online analytical processing (OLAP) can provide the fastest way to look at the data and create totals/subtotals on the fly. One of the classic examples is credit card customer spending rates. Suppose you want to look at total credit card transactions for all people, of all ages, across the country. Then you decide to break it down by gender and look at male versus female card totals—and then within gender, by age groups—and then on a state-by-state basis. And we want to do this with millions of rows of data!

This slicing and dicing is known as online analytical processing, or OLAP, and we can envision an OLAP cube with one edge of the cube showing gender, one edge of the cube showing age, and one edge of the cube showing states. As we ask questions of the cube data, we are really asking for totals and subtotals on the fly, which require the speed of an OLAP cube that is designed to return fast answers.

BI TIP

OLAP cubes are an increasingly common part of business intelligence, where we require fast totaling and subtotaling of data according to different groupings of data that we choose in an ad hoc manner. OLAP cubes require a special database server that is designed to host OLAP cubed data.

Microsoft SQL Server includes a special database server function called Analysis Services that hosts OLAP cubes and returns very fast summations of data, particularly when we use Excel 2007 to connect to the SQL Server OLAP cube.

Excel Direct-Connect to SQL Server OLAP Cubes

Figure 4-33 shows how we start the process, from within Excel 2007, of connecting to a SQL Server Analysis Services cube that resides on a server running SQL Server. As we'll see, the connection process is quite similar to other Excel data connections to relational databases, and in our example the Analysis Service connection results in an Excel PivotTable.

1. Click the Get External Data icon in the Connections menu group, on the Ribbon menu Data tab.
2. Click the From Other Sources icon in the pop-up menu.
3. Click the From Analysis Services choice in the pop-up menu.

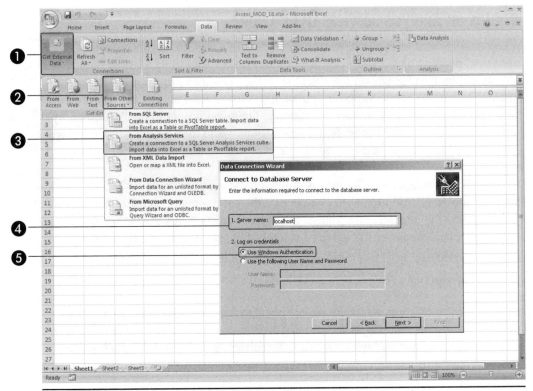

Figure 4-33 *Excel 2007—Get External Data | From SQL Server Analysis Services*

4. Enter the desired Server Name.

5. Choose Use Windows Authentication for the Log On Credentials, and click Next.

In Figure 4-33 we're using **localhost** for the Server Name because the SQL Server Analysis Services cube resides on the same machine where we're running Excel. Windows Authentication is the most common way to connect to SQL Server OLAP cubes, so we'll simply continue with it as the default, and click Next.

If you're not sure whether your organization has any Analysis Services cubes on a SQL Server, you might ask an available database administrator (DBA) if Analysis Services is being used anywhere in the organization. Analysis Services is not something you typically find on end-user desktops, and not all organizations use it. But those organizations that do implement Analysis Services cubes can offer the slice-and-dice capability shown in this section.

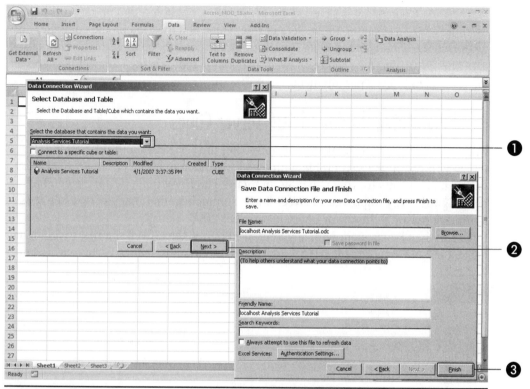

Figure 4-34 *Excel 2007 Data Connection Wizard—to SQL Server Analysis Services cube*

Figure 4-34 shows the process of using the Excel Data Wizard to choose the Analysis Services database or cube.

1. Click the drop-down box of Analysis Services databases in the Data Connection Wizard, and choose the Analysis Services database desired.

2. Click Next.

3. Click Finish to use the defaults on the Save Data Connection File And Finish dialog box.

Note in Figure 4-34 that we chose a Microsoft sample Analysis Services database because it is a readily available example of an OLAP cube. Don't be confused by the term *database* in this case when we're connecting to a cube; the two terms are interchangeable here, since cubes are actually contained in Analysis Services databases (although they are special OLAP databases).

The Data Connection is saved to the file location of choice, and in our working example we're just saving to the default File Name and location on the computer where we're running Excel. Data Connections can actually be reused when importing data into Excel, and they can be viewed by clicking the Existing Connections icon on the Get External Data pop-up menu.

Excel PivotTable Display of SQL Server Cubes

Figure 4-35 shows the final step of importing the OLAP data into Excel 2007, which will result in a PivotTable with a user interface that makes it easy to select cube data elements for row and column totals. The PivotTable design screen has been significantly improved in Excel 2007, so much so that many people see it as a primary reason to install or upgrade to Excel 2007.

Excel PivotTables work with any kind of imported data, from flat file, to relational data tables and views, to OLAP cubes. This is important to realize because as Excel

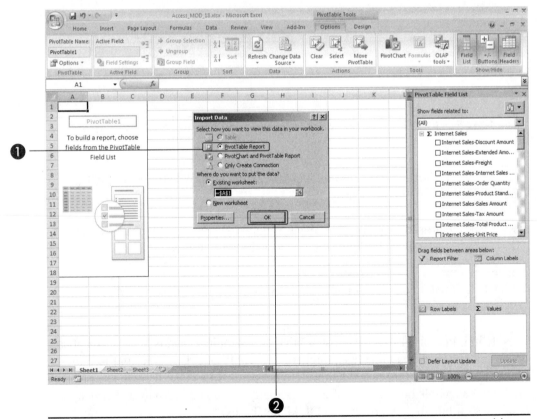

Figure 4-35 *Excel 2007—importing an Analysis Services OLAP cube into a PivotTable*

business users become familiar with PivotTables, they turn to them more and more often to work with external data. The automatic cross-tab subtotaling of PivotTables can be used to arrange any of the imported data; however, imported OLAP cube data provides a particularly compelling PivotTable display, since OLAP cube data is intrinsically hierarchical in nature.

You should feel free to work with either Excel PivotTables, favoring a hierarchical cross-tab display, or Excel tables, favoring a data list display. And frankly, you can try both Excel mechanisms because either one can be created in minutes, once you're connected to the external data.

1. Click the PivotTable Report option button on the Import Data dialog box.
2. Click OK to see the PivotTable design interface.

BI TIP

Excel is by far the most common tool used to connect to OLAP cubes, and an Excel PivotTable is the most common way to manipulate the OLAP cube data. Furthermore, there are many tools on the market that provide a very advanced experience in working with OLAP cubes, and they also follow the familiar Excel PivotTable way of working with totals and subtotals.

Figure 4-36 shows the result of choosing data from the Analysis Services cube, where we're choosing cube data elements for our PivotTable rows. As we work with the data elements from the OLAP cube, it becomes clear why Excel is the most-used tool for displaying such data: Excel has a built-in understanding of the nature of cube elements and provides an easy-to-understand interface to choose and format the data.

1. Click the Location field in the PivotTable Field List, to expand the Location hierarchy.
2. Click the State-Province field in the PivotTable Field List.
3. Click the City field in the PivotTable Field List.

Figure 4-36 shows how the new Excel 2007 PivotTable design interface helps us by making intelligent assumptions about the placement of fields in PivotTable rows, column, and values. When we clicked the State-Province and City fields, Excel automatically placed them in the Row Labels list box, which makes them display as hierarchical rows in the actual Excel PivotTable display.

Note that working with OLAP cube fields is really not much different from working with the usual database fields we've seen before in Excel's external connection to data. In this case we're using Excel to connect to external data in a cube data source, and the resulting fields behave much the same as all other data elements we might bring into an Excel spreadsheet.

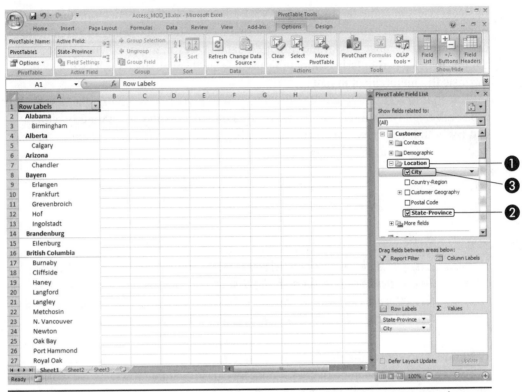

Figure 4-36 *Excel 2007 PivotTable design interface for Analysis Services OLAP cubes*

Note also that the incoming OLAP cube fields automatically arrange themselves into a hierarchical display. This is because the Excel 2007 PivotTable designer understands how cube data is organized and helps us visualize it by placing fields above and below each other in a hierarchical manner on the PivotTable spreadsheet. In our working example, we chose State-Province first so that it displays as the higher level of data in the PivotTable; we chose City second so that it displays as the lower level of data in the PivotTable.

Furthermore, we can use the mouse to drag the State-Province and City fields around in the Row Labels list box, and view the data with City above State-Province—although the resulting hierarchical display is not useful, because every City will be listed with just one State-Province below it. However, the PivotTable display will be accurate no matter how we arrange the PivotTable fields among the rows or columns; this is part of the automatic organized nature of a PivotTable!

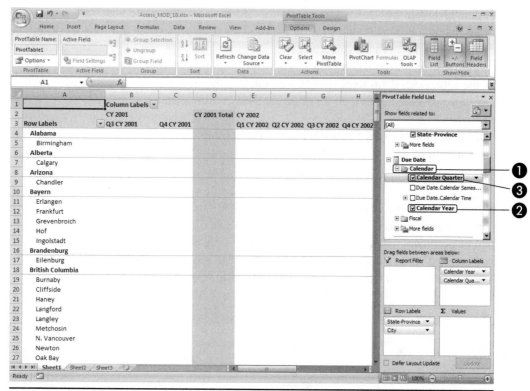

Figure 4-37 *Excel 2007 PivotTable row and column display for OLAP cubes*

Figure 4-37 shows how we continue to populate the PivotTable with OLAP cube fields, where we're choosing data elements for the Column display.

1. Click the Calendar field in the PivotTable Field List to expand the Calendar hierarchy.

2. Click the Calendar Year field in the PivotTable Field List.

3. Click the Calendar Quarter field in the PivotTable Field List.

Figure 4-37 shows how quickly the PivotTable becomes an interesting display of OLAP cube data elements. In this case, we chose the Year field first because it's naturally at a higher data level than the Quarter field. Note the Excel 2007 PivotTable design interface automatically placed the date type fields in the Column Labels list box, which produces a PivotTable columnar arrangement of the Year-Quarter data hierarchy.

Date fields are a very common part of information analysis in our everyday world because so much of our activity is date-driven. Thus we often need to look at data arranged by year, quarter, month, and day, and these elements are most often placed across the columns of a spreadsheet display (which in our working example is a PivotTable spreadsheet).

Figure 4-38 shows a complete PivotTable display with rows, columns, and values as the actual cell data. Realize that we took just three large steps to get to this point; we chose rows in a previous set of steps, then columns, and now values.

1. Click the Internet Sales field in the PivotTable Field List, to expand the Sales hierarchy.

2. Click the Internet Sales – Sales Amount field in the PivotTable Field List.

Figure 4-38 shows a PivotTable in Excel 2007 that is displaying data values, arranged and automatically subtotaled by State and City, and by Year and Quarter. This is pretty amazing when we realize the rows and columns can actually be arranged in any way we wish, using the PivotTable field list to move fields around or deselect and select different data fields from the overall field list box.

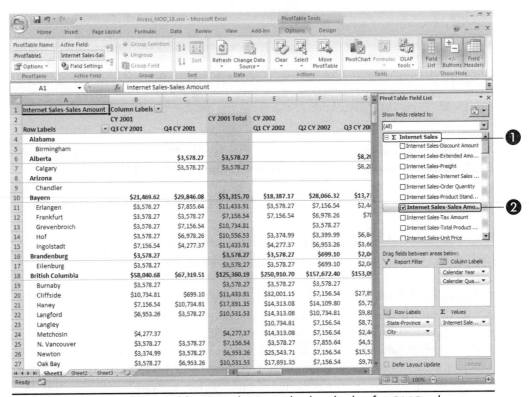

Figure 4-38 *Excel 2007 PivotTable row, column, and value display for OLAP cubes*

Excel Slice and Dice with PivotTables

The PivotTable interface is clickable; the user can click the drop-down controls next to the Row and Column labels on the actual PivotTable and choose which states or cities, or which years and quarters, to display. The automatic subtotals will rearrange themselves around whichever row and column elements are chosen for display.

BI TIP

PivotTables are perhaps the most commonly used analysis tool in the working world of business intelligence. And the ability to arrange and rearrange the rows, columns, and values, and to select or deselect the categories of data to display, is known as slicing and dicing the data.

Figure 4-39 shows how we can click the PivotTable drop-down boxes to choose the data values to display. It's nice to see that the PivotTable interface provides the

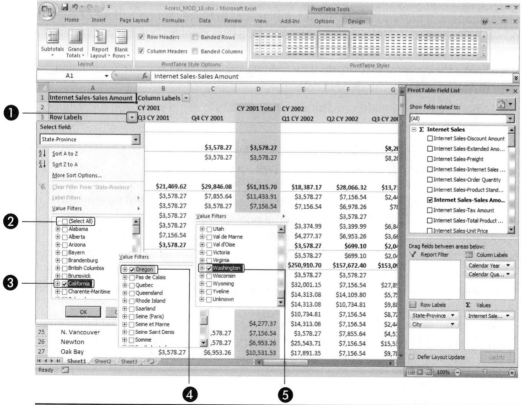

Figure 4-39 *Excel 2007 PivotTable row drop-down controls and list boxes of cube data*

actual row and column data values in a list box format, so we can see the data and choose exactly what we want to display.

1. Click the Row Labels drop-down control on the actual PivotTable.
2. Click the (Select All) checkbox to deselect all values in the list box.
3. Click the California checkbox to select California data.
4. Click the Oregon checkbox to select Oregon data.
5. Click the Washington checkbox to select Washington data, and then click OK.

Excel Conditional Formatting with PivotTables

Figure 4-40 shows a quick way to dress up the data display of the PivotTable. We're using the new conditional formatting feature of Excel 2007 to add some color to the PivotTable, and to automatically accentuate the higher and lower data values in the cells! This use of color to support a quick visual interpretation of data is becoming more common in the world of business intelligence, and when properly done, it allows people to immediately grasp the overall nature of a data display.

1. Select the cells to be formatted, by holding the right mouse button down and dragging it across the desired cells.
2. Click the Conditional Formatting icon in the Style menu group, on the Ribbon menu Home tab.
3. Click the Data Bars icon in the pop-up menu.
4. Click the Green Data Bar icon in the pop-up gallery.

Note that Excel 2007 provides a live preview capability as you hold the mouse over different data bar color schemes in the pop-up gallery; the cells in the PivotTable change color dynamically to show the effect of the different data bar color schemes. Not only does this live preview feature allow us to choose the color scheme that best highlights the data; it also helps us visually analyze the data in the PivotTable because it so quickly adjusts the color and size of the shaded color bars in the PivotTable cells.

The live preview capability allows us to connect Excel to external data (and bring it into a PivotTable or an Excel table) and then try out the different data bar and color scales color combinations to best highlight the incoming data values.

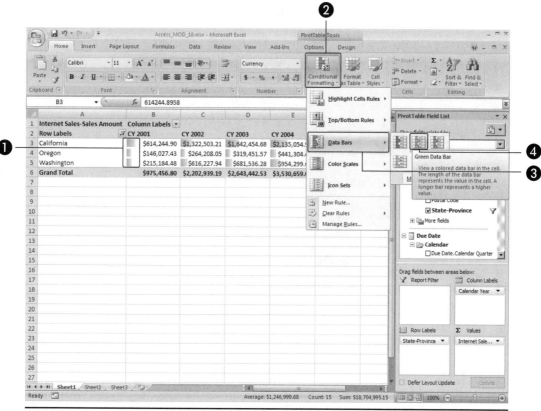

Figure 4-40 *Excel 2007 PivotTable row conditional formatting of cube data*

Excel PivotChart with PivotTables

In Figure 4-41 we take a couple of quick steps forward in our visual analysis of the external OLAP cube data in our Excel 2007 PivotTable. To focus our analysis on a subset of the data, we narrow it to just State and Year values by deselecting the City and Quarter fields in the PivotTable Field List pane. To create a graphical representation of the data subset, we insert a chart and see what the default chart shows us.

1. Click the City checkbox in the PivotTable Field List pane to deselect it.

2. Click the Calendar Quarter checkbox in the PivotTable Field List pane to deselect it.

3. Click the Area icon in the Charts menu group, on the Ribbon menu Insert tab.

4. Click the first 3-D Area icon on the pop-up Charts gallery.

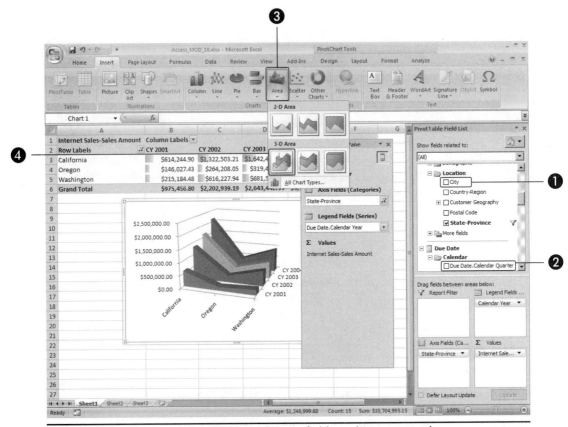

Figure 4-41 *Excel 2007 PivotTable—deselecting fields and inserting a chart*

Note in Figure 4-41, the PivotChart Filter pane that displays next the PivotTable Field List pane. Clicking the drop-down controls in the PivotChart Filter pane allows us to choose the data elements to be displayed in the PivotChart in the same way we choose data elements for display using the drop-down controls on the actual PivotTable. In fact, changing the PivotChart Filter elements changes both the PivotChart and the PivotTable, and changing the PivotTable Filter elements changes both the PivotTable and PivotChart display!

Figure 4-41 also shows a change in the list box titles, in the PivotTable Field List pane. Row Labels are changed to Axis Fields, and Column Labels are changed to Legend Fields. This is not really a change at all; the interface is dynamically reflecting whether we're working on the PivotTable or the PivotChart, but there is actually no change in function.

Clicking the PivotTable, clicking the PivotChart, and clicking the spreadsheet outside the PivotTable and PivotChart areas will change the user interface to follow our mouse actions and area of selected work. Sometimes people are not sure how to get the PivotTable or PivotChart Field panes to display because the panes disappear when the spreadsheet is clicked outside the PivotTable and PivotChart areas. The PivotTable and PivotChart Field panes redisplay as soon as you click the actual PivotTable or PivotChart.

It's amazing to see how quickly we can change the data display, with automatic subtotaling, and add a chart on the PivotTable user interface. Four mouse clicks dramatically narrow the data displayed and create a 3-D chart that clearly shows the relative sizes of the sales data by state and year!

This slicing and dicing of data is what leads people to depend on Excel PivotTables, and in this case we're seeing how powerful this is when connected to external data. Quite frankly, Excel 2007 allows us to arrange, subtotal, and chart the data as fast as we can think about it.

BI TIP

PivotTables quickly become a part of everyday decision making because they provide a fast way to visually interpret data from the business processes that run our organizations. Excel PivotTables can be connected to external data of any kind regardless of whether the data is a relational database or a multidimensional OLAP cube.

In Figure 4-42 we take a final step with our PivotTable analysis of external cube data by swapping the Row and Column fields. Again, this slicing and dicing of data in a PivotTable produces a visual display that can be dramatically different with a few mouse clicks. As people work with PivotTables to look at their own data, they learn to slice and dice the fields in a surprisingly short time because when working with data we care about, we quickly learn to use a tool such as Excel that has an intuitive user interface.

1. Click the State-Province field, and drag it from the Row Labels (Legend Fields) to the Column Labels (Axis Fields) list box.
2. Click the Calendar Year field, and drag it from the Column Labels to the Row Labels list box.
3. Click the Calendar Quarter field, and drag it from the Column Labels to the Row Labels list box.

In Figure 4-42, the PivotChart changed the same way as the PivotTable, and they are working together to support our visualization of dates down the rows and states

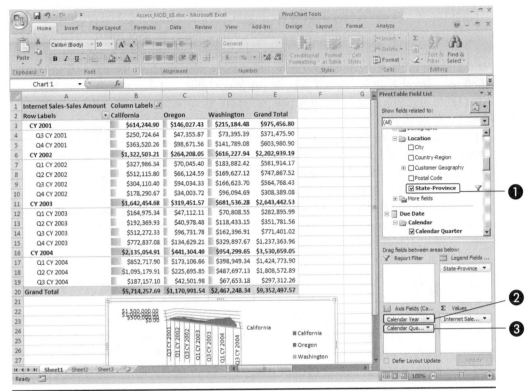

Figure 4-42 *Excel 2007 PivotTable—swapping the rows and columns*

across columns. Also, the conditional formatting followed the rearrangement of data to provide a truly fluid way of looking at the information in whatever way helps us see what is going on with our organization's business process.

Connecting Excel to the Internet with Web Queries

This section will illustrate one of the more glamorous abilities of Excel 2007, the capability to retrieve data from web sites from anywhere in the world using Excel's Web Query mechanism. When it comes to connecting Excel to external data, this is a feature that really brings a world of information into a familiar and powerful toolset.

Figure 4-43 shows how we start this process from the same External Data Connections menu that we've used for files, databases, and OLAP cubes. This time, however, we'll be guided through the Excel Web Query process, which is fairly flexible.

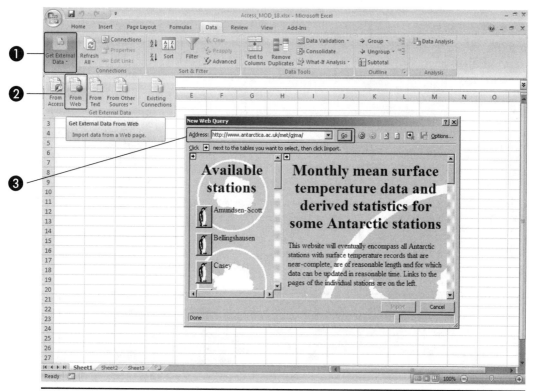

Figure 4-43 *Excel 2007 Web Query connecting to external Internet data*

1. Click the Get External Data icon in the Connections menu group, on the Ribbon menu Data tab.
2. Click the From Web icon on the pop-up menu Get External Data choices.
3. Enter the desired web address URL (**www.antarctica.ac.uk**) in the browser Address text box, and click Go.

The web site in our working example contains the Monthly Mean Surface Temperature Data for various Antarctic scientific research stations. This example was chosen because it represents data on the World Wide Web that is available to anyone with Excel 2007 and an Internet connection. Our goal is to bring it into Excel and apply a trend line to see where the temperature changes are headed in an era of global warming!

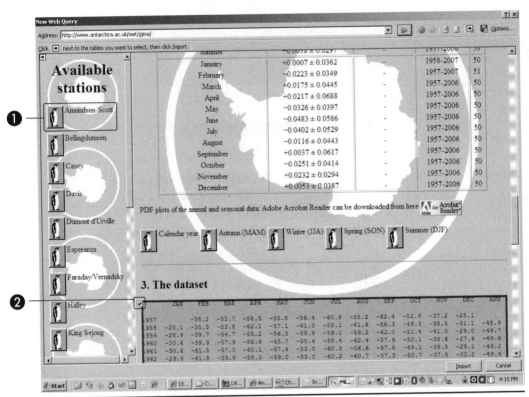

Figure 4-44 *Excel 2007 Web Query selection of HTML table data*

Figure 4-44 shows how we configure the Web Query once we've browsed to the desired web site. The Web Query is pretty flexible and will try to interpret and import almost any table or HTML arrangement of data (the results may have to be cleaned up in Excel, but at least we can do so in the familiar environment of Excel).

1. Click the Admundsen-Scott icon of Available Stations.
2. Click the yellow arrow next to the tables you want to select. Then click Import.

Note that we chose a fairly clean and coherent data display for our example import. Many of the HTML tables that can be imported by the Excel Web Query are not as nicely arranged as this but can still be imported and then cleaned up in Excel.

Figure 4-45 shows the data in Excel, where we've simply finished the Import Data step. This will bring us to a point where we can display the data in a chart.

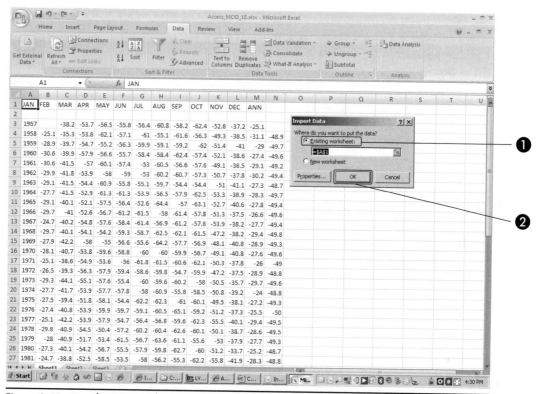

Figure 4-45 *Excel 2007 Web Query Import Data*

1. Click the option button for Existing Worksheet.
2. Click OK.

As we see in Figure 4-45, the data looks very familiar once we have imported it into our familiar working environment, and we can now arrange and save it to our desktop computer for further analysis and future trending comparison. Now that we have the data in Excel, the Web Query URL connection string has actually been stored for the spreadsheet as an external data connection.

Figure 4-46 shows how one could refresh the external data import at any time, by simply using the Refresh All option on the Ribbon menu.

1. Click any cell or select a cell set, and delete it.
2. Click the Refresh All icon in the Connections menu group, on the Ribbon menu Data tab.

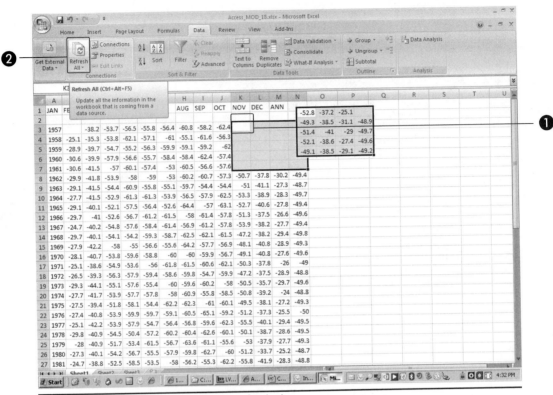

Figure 4-46 *Excel 2007 Web Query refresh data*

As we see in Figure 4-46, the deleted data is simply replaced (actually, all the data is replaced) by the Refresh All menu action. It's nice that Excel has remembered the Internet query for us, but note the Refresh All option overwrites the existing spreadsheet data and should be used only when we don't need to keep the prior external data import results.

The prior external data could easily be copied to another sheet within the Excel workbook, and then a refresh of data would not cause us to lose the previous results. This might be important to us if we've done analysis with the previous external data import as we see next in Figure 4-47.

Excel X Y Scatter Chart with Trendline

1. Click the labels and data to be selected, and drag the mouse over the actual data cells (starting with A1 in our working example).

2. Click the Scatter icon in the Charts menu group, on the Ribbon menu Insert tab.

3. Click the Scatter With Straight Lines icon on the pop-up Chart gallery.

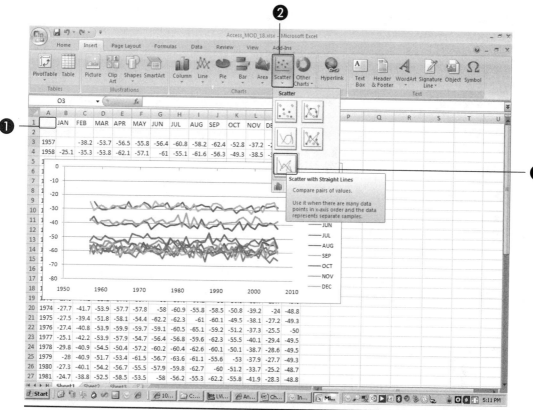

Figure 4-47 *Excel 2007—insert scatter X Y chart for trend line analysis*

It is important to note that we're choosing a scatter chart, which is also known as an X Y chart. An Excel X Y chart supports the addition of a trend line, which in our working example is of interest in exploring the problem of global warming! You can resize the chart by dragging the left edge to make the chart larger and more clearly see the horizontal axis values and data lines.

Figure 4-48 completes our journey into Internet data with the Excel external data connection. We can apply a trend line and extrapolate the data to any number of additional periods (time frames).

1. Click the Trendline icon in the Analysis menu group, on the Ribbon menu Layout tab.

2. Click the Linear option button in the Trend/Regression Type menu box.

3. Enter **40** in the Forward text box for periods.

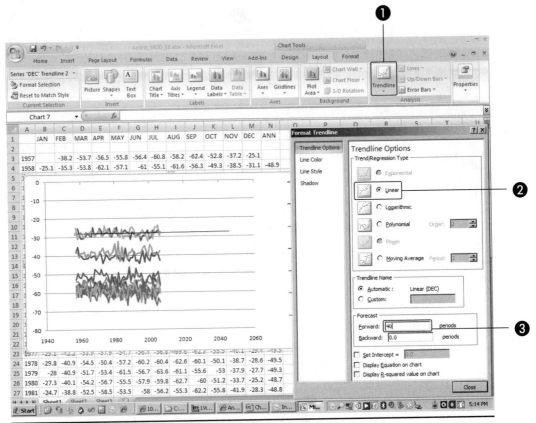

Figure 4-48 *Excel 2007 scatter X Y chart with trend line*

Figure 4-48 shows the graphical results of being able to apply a trend line to data we've imported from the World Wide Web. This is fairly significant when we realize that much of the world's statistical analysis is done in Excel, and with this connection to Internet data we can use the full power of Excel 2007, with its charting and trend line analysis tools.

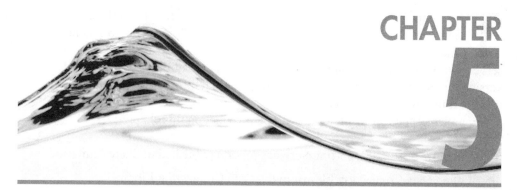

Excel and SharePoint: Reports, Key Performance Indicators, and Dashboards

This chapter shows how to use Excel 2007 with SharePoint 2007 and Excel Services to achieve a collaborative business intelligence environment. Imagine the latest spreadsheets and reports, always available on a central server with real-time data connections and automatic control over editing and version history. Excel Services is explored in depth to provide an understanding of what it provides as an "Excel server."

Examples of the following topics will be provided in this chapter:

▶ Excel reports and Reporting Services reports published to SharePoint

▶ Office Data Connection files from the Data Connection Library

▶ Key Performance Indicators from SharePoint lists, Excel, and OLAP cubes

▶ SharePoint dashboards

BEST REFERENCE

For further research on this topic, go to http://msdn2.microsoft.com/en-us/library/ms546696.aspx.

Technology Positioning Statement

New in SharePoint 2007 is the Report Center, where you can create rich and interactive BI dashboards that display data from multiple sources, and bring them into the place where people are already collaborating on documents and projects. The great thing about it is that building dashboards can be as easy as adding a workbook that tracks project metrics to a document library.

Anyone that can build a report in Excel can now make their report available on a web page. For example, a workbook that tracks event attendance can be turned into a web page just by publishing the workbook to SharePoint Excel Services, and as you update the spreadsheet, everyone sees one version of the truth. You can also add Key Performance Indicators and Reporting Services reports right on the same pages.

—Sean Boon, Microsoft Excel Team

What Is a SharePoint Portal?

SharePoint 2007, also known as Microsoft Office SharePoint Services (MOSS), is truly different than previous versions of SharePoint from Microsoft. Earlier versions of SharePoint required significant work by SharePoint programmers to get the site up and running, whereas SharePoint 2007 comes ready to do work out of the box. We are most interested in the new Reports site, which is really a dashboard that includes Excel spreadsheets (we'll call them reports in this chapter) and Key Performance Indicators, or KPIs for short.

But first, let's define what we mean when using the term SharePoint portal. A *portal* is really just an Internet (World Wide Web, external) or intranet (within your organization) web site location that provides a convenient gathering point for documents, news, reports, etc. So we might have a portal for a project that involves collaborative work among several people, or a portal for current news about our organization, or a portal for reports that we need to access every day.

It is this last example of a portal that interests us in this chapter—a convenient gathering point for reports, charts and spreadsheets with live data, and Key Performance Indicators. And as you might have guessed, SharePoint 2007 makes it easy for everyday users of Microsoft Office 2007 to share business intelligence information through a reports site. Note that when we're dealing with SharePoint terminology, the term portal is synonymous with site.

Having a collaborative web site opens a whole new area of productivity to Excel users, since you can "publish" your Excel spreadsheets to a SharePoint reports site and share the live-data-connected results with anyone that has permission to connect to the reports site. The Excel workbook that you create on your client computer is, in this SharePoint process, published to the reports site, where it then resides independently from your original Excel workbook. Furthermore, a SharePoint-published Excel workbook can automatically refresh to external data such as a database or OLAP cube, whenever it's accessed in the SharePoint reports site.

Ideally, the Excel workbook that has been published to the SharePoint document (report) library will be considered the master copy that can be opened from the SharePoint library for editing and maintenance. Keeping master Excel workbooks in SharePoint allows you to apply SharePoint permissions that control who can view it and who can update it—and you can make use of SharePoint's versioning to automatically keep previous versions of the workbook in the SharePoint repository.

This helps to eliminate the proliferation of important Excel spreadsheets across multiple desktop machines—where no one really knows which copy is the up-to-date, validated report source for decision making.

BI TIP

SharePoint provides a server-based storage mechanism for documents and spreadsheets that is easier to use than a shared public file folder, and much safer than local desktop drives. It makes sense that businesses today keep business intelligence content produced by Office workers in such a repository, which provides check-in and check-out control, along with automatic historical versions of changed documents and workbooks.

The concept of Key Performance Indicators, or KPIs, comes into play with a SharePoint reports site as well. KPIs are simply a measure that we choose to track our progress or success for any organizational effort. They are an increasingly popular part of Office 2007 Business Intelligence, because they are easy to configure and share with others through SharePoint. KPIs provide a common basis for working toward organizational goals, and they help teams work in a common direction when everyone can see live-data KPIs on a reports site.

And finally, dashboards will be explored as a tangible concept in this chapter. A dashboard can have anything on it that you think is worth seeing—it's simply a screen to showcase business intelligence reports, analysis, and a measurement graphics. A SharePoint dashboard, as you'll see, is easy to configure with Excel spreadsheets (we'll often call these reports) and Key Performance Indicators that can be created with several Office 2007 tools.

The following illustration shows an example of a SharePoint 2007 dashboard with a new Excel Services PivotTable. This chapter will explore the steps used to create this example dashboard.

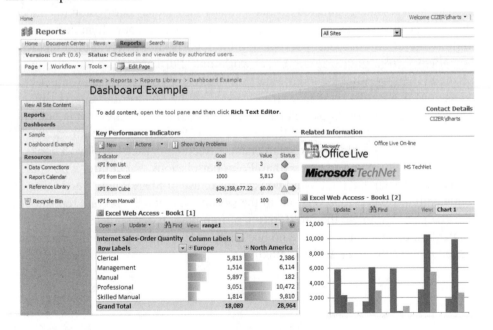

Where Does a SharePoint Portal Fit in the Microsoft BI Picture?

The next image shows a matrix view of Microsoft Business Intelligence technology (often referred to as BI). The Office, SharePoint, and SQL Server applications we see in the marketplace are shown on the left side of the matrix. These applications are used in the real-world activities of reporting, analysis, measurement, and planning as shown across the top of the matrix. The top-down flow of the matrix starts with front-end BI tools we have in Office 2007 at our desktops and goes down to back-end BI tools that run on servers such as SharePoint 2007 and PerformancePoint 2007, which provide an enhanced experience when connected to Office 2007.

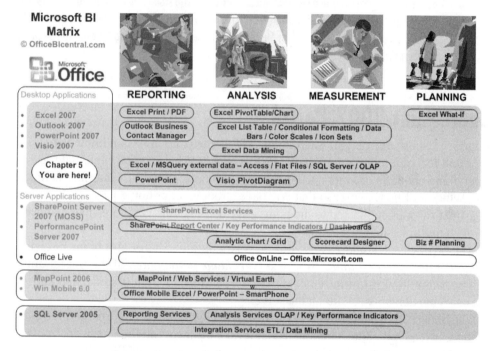

Learning about SharePoint dashboards makes more sense if you know where they fit in the Microsoft technology stack, and what they are used for in daily BI activities. The "You are here!" bubble in the image shows SharePoint dashboards and Key Performance Indicators—which are typically part of a SharePoint Report Center. Excel Services is a special component of SharePoint that allows Excel spreadsheets to be published for shared use in SharePoint. SharePoint and Excel Services are server applications from the Microsoft Office group of products.

You're going use Excel 2007 to publish workbooks (we might also call them reports) to Excel Services for display in a SharePoint dashboard, and you'll create SharePoint KPIs for display in the same SharePoint dashboard. The Excel reports and SharePoint KPIs can be stand-alone or connected to external data from almost any file or database server, or from SQL Server Analysis Services (SSAS) OLAP cubes, which are part of the SQL Server 2005 foundation of the BI matrix.

SharePoint 2007 is a Microsoft technology that has achieved a new maturity with business intelligence collaboration. It looks good even in its out-of-the-box installation—and as Excel users realize they can publish spreadsheets to SharePoint, they'll use it for all kinds of group project work. It provides a good in-house display capability for organizational performance metrics as well (Key Performance Indicators).

BI TIP

Business intelligence has evolved from isolated PC users with stand-alone spreadsheets, to today's network-connected "information workers" connecting to external data and sharing spreadsheets through collaboration portals such as SharePoint. This new way of working together can be called collaborative BI.

SharePoint 2007 Portal

Figure 5-1 shows the default SharePoint 2007 home page. It has an immediate look and feel of a modern web site, which is exactly what it is—for internal use. Everything about SharePoint can be changed and customized. It's interface is much like Windows File Explorer in that you have a root level or home page, and you can construct subsites connected to the home page and click in a explorer-like manner through multiple site levels.

The browser URL address used to display a default SharePoint home page is simply "http://*server_name*," where *server_name* is the name of the SharePoint server. SharePoint essentially takes over the server on which it's installed and becomes the default web site on the server.

The SharePoint site in Figure 5-1 is being accessed through Internet Explorer—nothing is required on the client machine for the business intelligence work you'll be doing in this chapter. You'll use Excel 2007 to publish to the SharePoint site, but once a workbook is published, it requires nothing on the client to view within SharePoint (not even Excel!).

Looking at Figure 5-1, you see the main navigation points of the user interface:

a. Top-level menu tabs behave as tabs do in other Office user interfaces. Clicking a tab typically brings up a different SharePoint screen or site that is on the same level (in other words, a peer-level site).

b. Side-level menu items provide sublevel options to the SharePoint top-level menu tabs. At the home page level, the side-level menu mimics the top-level menu tabs—this will change, however, as we navigate to subsites from the home page.

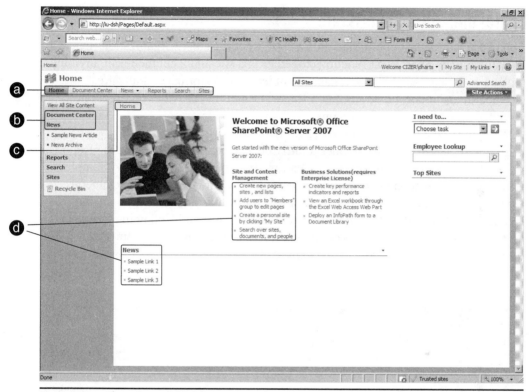

Figure 5-1 *SharePoint 2007 home portal page*

c. Page-level header labels show the current SharePoint site or subsite. As you click to other sites and subsites, this page-level header label will display the navigation path you take to get to the subsites—and it is clickable if you wish to use it to go back along the navigation path.

d. Embedded links appear throughout the SharePoint sites, for whatever document, function, or navigation link is appropriate for the content.

BI TIP

Collaborative business intelligence in the Microsoft context requires SharePoint Enterprise version—which includes Excel Services to allow publishing Excel spreadsheets. Excel 2007 stand-alone, Office Professional Plus, Office Enterprise, or Office Ultimate is required to be able to publish to Excel Services!

Office Standard and Office Professional will allow you to publish to a SharePoint Document Management Server but not to SharePoint Excel Services.

SharePoint 2007 Reports Site

Figure 5-2 shows the default SharePoint 2007 Report Center. Organizations can actually put any SharePoint functions together in a site and label the result anything they wish. In this case Microsoft has assembled Key Performance Indicator, dashboard, and report functions into a Report Center that provides an excellent working example for our discussion.

Navigate to the Report Center by clicking the Reports tab.

In Figure 5-2, Microsoft provides a fairly decent explanation of what the Report Center includes: Key Performance Indicators, dashboards, and reports. A Sample KPI display appears on the right side of the Report Center screen. Miscellaneous elements can be added to a Report Center site (in fact, any SharePoint item can be added), as implied by the Contact Details, Highlights, and Upcoming Events areas—but we're going to focus on the main Business Intelligence elements of KPIs, dashboards, and reports. We'll also examine the concept of the Data Connection

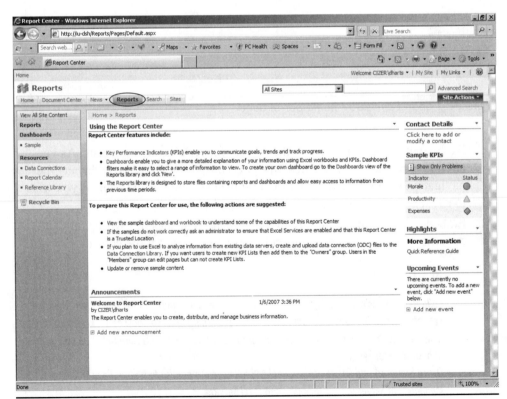

Figure 5-2   *SharePoint 2007 Report Center*

Library, which provides a SharePoint repository of trusted Office Data Connection (ODC) files for use with Office 2007 BI.

Note that the left-side menu has changed to show items that pertain to the Report Center subsite within SharePoint. We'll explore these as we discuss the BI components of the Report Center.

BI TIP

SharePoint screen components are known as web parts. Web parts have a common graphical user interface for adding the web part into an existing SharePoint page. In the context of SharePoint BI, the web part provides a standardized way to include spreadsheets and KPIs in a SharePoint page.

Report Center Reports Library Excel Workbooks

Figure 5-3 shows the main screen for the SharePoint Reports Library. Notice the similarity with a Windows File Explorer Library. As has been mentioned before, the top-page navigation tracking shows Home | Reports | Reports Library, which clearly

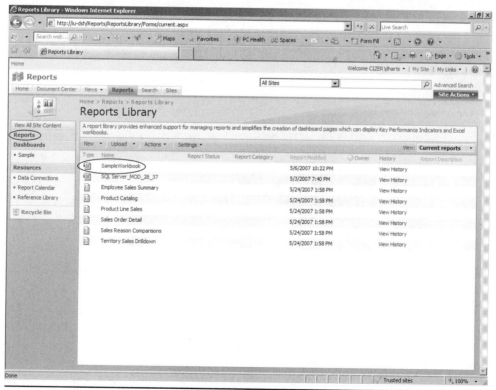

Figure 5-3   *SharePoint 2007—Reports | Reports Library*

shows our location in the SharePoint site (and it's clickable for navigation purposes). The following discussion will explore the contents and menu options in the Reports Library.

Navigate to the Reports Library by clicking the Reports left-side menu option.

In Figure 5-3, in the New column, you see Excel icons designating Excel workbooks that have been published to the Reports Library. You also see Report icons designating Microsoft Reporting Services reports that have been published to the Reports Library. Although any document or file can be uploaded to this SharePoint site, it's more appropriate that we have Excel workbooks and Reporting Services reports (both of which are typically thought of as reports in the context of SharePoint) in this site that has a title of Reports Library.

The SampleWorkbook was installed as part of the default Report Center. If you click the SampleWorkbook name itself (or the Excel icon) as shown in Figure 5-3, a full-screen rendering of the spreadsheet is presented as shown in Figure 5-4.

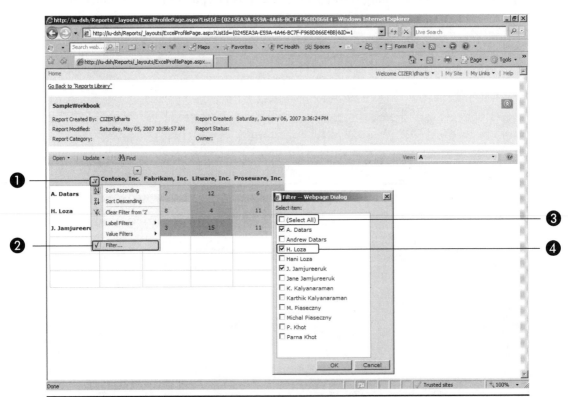

Figure 5-4 *SharePoint 2007 Excel Services rendering of a SampleWorkbook*

Furthermore, Figure 5-4 shows that you can click the PivotTable Filter icons to slice and dice the Excel data as shown in the steps that follow. And this clickable screen interaction with the PivotTable is occurring in SharePoint without any Excel desktop client involved!

Excel Services is a very cool feature because we can play with the data, just as in Excel, but here the interaction is on the SharePoint browser page. You can save the Excel Services spreadsheet to your own desktop computer, change it or add data, and publish it as a new workbook to Excel Services or overwrite the original workbook if you have permission to do so. This supports the scenario where you may have a different perspective on the data to better illustrate an idea that you'd like to share with others.

1. Click the Excel Filter drop-down control.
2. Choose Filter on the pop-up menu.
3. Click the (Select All) checkbox to allow individual filter selections.
4. Click the individual checkboxes to choose the data filter values for display, and then click OK.

Figure 5-4 shows something you have not seen before—a pure-browser rendering of an Excel PivotTable! This is really important because it shows what Excel looks like when it's rendered to HTML through Excel Services in SharePoint. You'll explore how to place Excel workbooks into this environment, but for now we can say that an Excel 2007 desktop client published this SampleWorkbook to SharePoint Excel Services.

Note that the Excel Services rendering of the SampleWorkbook in Figure 5-4 does not require any connection or reference back to the original Excel file—on whatever client machine it may have come from. This is because once an Excel workbook is published to Excel Services, a server-only copy of the workbook is stored in a SharePoint library on the SharePoint server.

BI TIP

Server-based reports and server-based data connections are the most important elements of report servers such as the SharePoint 2007 Report Center. This allows users to connect to the Report Center and run reports that are on the server for everyone to use with appropriate permissions—and the reports use server-based data connections so that user client machines don't have to create or maintain their own connections to external data.

Figure 5-5 takes another look at the SampleWorkbook in Excel Services. This time we've clicked the View drop-down control to see a different view of the

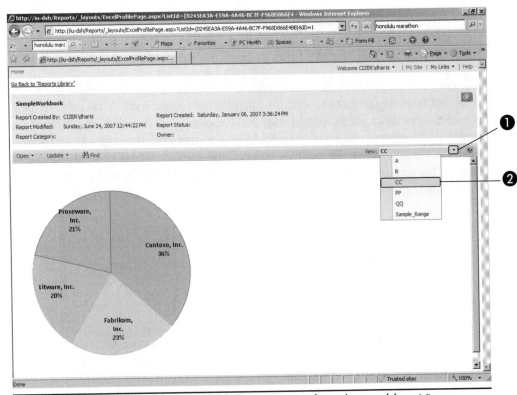

Figure 5-5   *SharePoint 2007 Excel Services rendering of Excel spreadsheet Views*

same spreadsheet. This allows us to look at one area or component of a busy or sophisticated spreadsheet instead of looking at the entire presentation, which might be too much to reasonably fit on a screen.

1. Click the View drop-down control.
2. Click the CC pop-up menu choice.

   Views are an interesting feature of Excel Services—they allow us to display the different "published items" in a workbook that is published to Excel Services. Published items can be any spreadsheet component such as PivotTables, charts, and named ranges that have been designed into a spreadsheet. The spreadsheet author can decide which items will be available as published items, when publishing the workbook to Excel Services. You'll explore this later as you work with a spreadsheet in Excel 2007, edit the named ranges, and then publish the spreadsheet to Excel Services.

Basically, Views allow us to display one portion of the spreadsheet at a time (a named range from the spreadsheet)—which allows us to place the various portions of the spreadsheet into different places on a SharePoint dashboard screen. Thus a sophisticated spreadsheet can support multiple views for use in SharePoint. This results in a significantly reduced maintenance burden, since we have fewer source spreadsheets to maintain as we keep the SharePoint Excel views up-to-date.

You may notice that the Excel Services spreadsheet has a slightly different screen display than we see on Excel 2007 desktop client spreadsheets. This is because Excel Services provides a pure-browser rendition of Excel workbooks that might not always have the rich-screen feel of Excel on a client machine. It's important to note that Excel Services does not require any client software to show its workbooks—but Excel Services does require a SharePoint browser window displayed in Internet Explorer or Firefox.

In Figure 5-6 you can see how to open the Excel Services workbook in desktop Excel on our client machine for personal work. Note this will open the entire

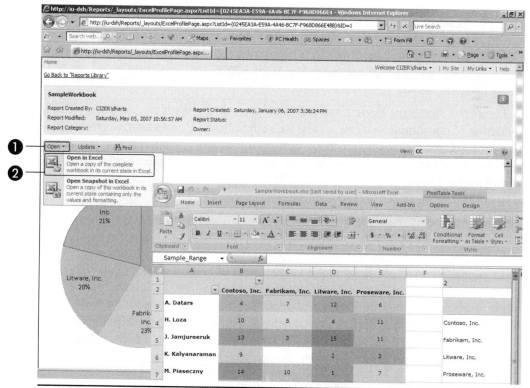

Figure 5-6   *SharePoint 2007 Excel Services HTML Open In Excel to desktop Excel*

workbook, which includes the previously shown PivotTable and the chart showing on the current screen.

1. Click the Open menu bar option.
2. Choose Open In Excel on the pop-up menu, and click OK when prompted to load it into Excel on your computer.

Figure 5-6 shows how easy it is to open a copy of the Excel Services workbook in our Excel 2007 client application—and continue working with it on our desktop computer. This allows us to use the Excel Services workbook as a trusted spreadsheet source—and yet download spreadsheets for personal use to our own local Excel environment outside of SharePoint.

The menu option for Open Snapshot In Excel would simply open a copy of the Excel Services workbook, but without any formulas—just the data and formatting.

BI TIP

It's important to users of business intelligence that we do not take away the familiar tools that have long been a part of Microsoft Office. Rather, server-based BI can provide a trusted source of data and reports (Microsoft calls this "a single version of the truth") that users can easily run or "open" to work with on their own desktops in Office 2007.

Figure 5-7 shows the Update menu options for working with the Excel Services rendering of our sample workbook. The Refresh Selected Connection, Refresh All Connections, and Calculate Workbook options mimic their counterparts in Excel to refresh data or recalculate the spreadsheet. The workbook data can be refreshed as shown in these steps:

1. Click the Update menu-bar option.
2. Choose Refresh All Connections on the pop-up menu.

In Figure 5-7 we chose Refresh All Connections because it refreshes all components of the workbook (PivotTable, Chart, etc.), so we don't have to use the Views drop-down control to find components that have data connections. Note the Reload Workbook option does not republish the workbook from its original point of origin on the local desktop machine—it simply reloads it from the SharePoint repository to the Excel Services screen display, which discards any screen arrangement or manipulation that you might have done in the SharePoint screen.

It's important to understand that we're working with a read-only Excel workbook of data. Although we're able to change the screen display and use the PivotTable controls to manipulate the row-column display, we're not actually changing any

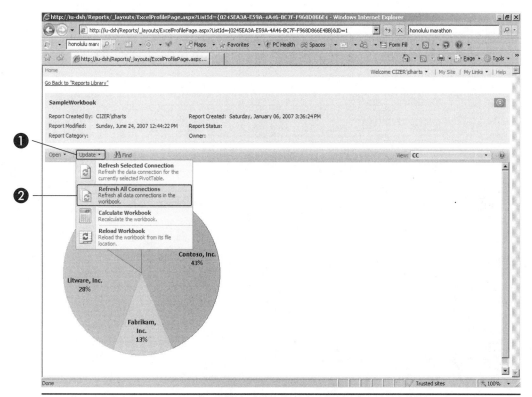

Figure 5-7   *SharePoint 2007 Excel Services HTML refresh data*

source data (nor are we changing the SharePoint repository workbook itself)! This is consistent with the concept of an Excel spreadsheet in a SharePoint Reports Library, since reports are typically read-only representations of data, not able to write back to or change data at the source.

BI TIP

Business intelligence reports and spreadsheets are typically read-only mechanisms. The primary purpose of BI is to present data in formats that can be manipulated on the screen or printed for analysis and monitoring, not to write changes back to data sources. Data source changes can be accomplished by any number of mechanisms (including Excel macros) but this falls into the realm of data input mechanisms which might feed information into systems that ultimately are presented in BI reports.

Report Center Reports Library Excel Properties and Permissions

By clicking the Go Back To "Reports Library" link at the top left of the Excel Services display screen shown in Figure 5-7, we return to the Reports Library as shown in Figure 5-8. The following discussion will explore the drop-down menu choices

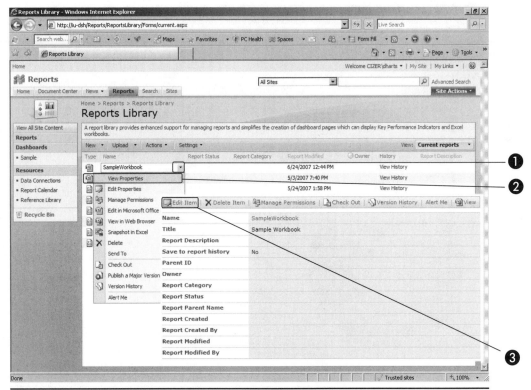

Figure 5-8   *SharePoint 2007 Reports Library—View Properties | Edit Item*

available on Excel reports in the Reports Library. This will touch many of the fundamental capabilities of reports (and documents) that are stored and maintained in SharePoint; from permissions (who can update the report) to versioning of current and historical copies of reports.

1. Hover the mouse over the SampleWorkbook name, and click the drop-down list control.

2. Choose View Properties.

3. Click the Edit Item icon on the Properties page.

In Figure 5-8 you are looking at the drop-down menu choices available for the SampleWorkbook Excel Services item. By choosing View Properties, you are able to edit the properties of the Excel report and manage permissions using the menu bar on the Properties page. We're going to jump right to the Edit Item page for the SampleWorkbook Excel report, as shown in Figure 5-9.

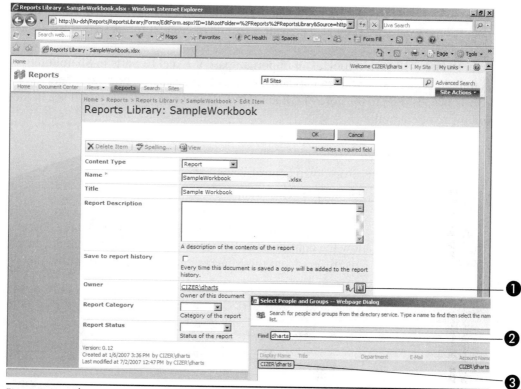

Figure 5-9   *SharePoint 2007 Reports Library—Excel Report Properties page*

1. Click the Owner icon.
2. Type the desired Owner's network ID in the Find text box and press ENTER.
3. Click the Owner name in the Display Name list, and click OK.

Selecting the Owner of the document does not impart any special privileges or document control; it's simply a property that can be used in an informational manner for document management and workflow. It does not drive permissions. In the same manner, you can select a Report Category and a Report Status to help in tracking the document (which is actually an Excel report in this case).

The Content Type drop-down at the top of the Properties page is more important, in that the Report choice shown in Figure 5-9 enables the display of report-specific properties. If you were to choose Dashboard instead, for example, you'd see a different set of properties on the Properties page.

Next, click SampleWorkbook in the navigation links shown at the top of Figure 5-9. This is a good time to note the Home | Reports | Reports Library |

SampleWorkbook navigation links that make it easy to click back to a desired page in the SharePoint site. They also provide a feeling of context for us so that we always know where we are in the site pages.

In Figure 5-10 you'll look at an important part of Excel Reports in SharePoint permissions that guide who can update the SharePoint Excel Report for others to see. This goes right to the core of collaborative BI in SharePoint, as you'll see in the following discussion.

1. Click the Manage Permissions icon.
2. Click the Actions drop-down control.
3. Choose Manage Permissions Of Parent.

In Figure 5-10 note the Manage Permissions and Edit Permissions menu choices. The Edit choice will allow the configuration of permissions for the current document (report in our case). This differs from the Manage choice, which will allow the

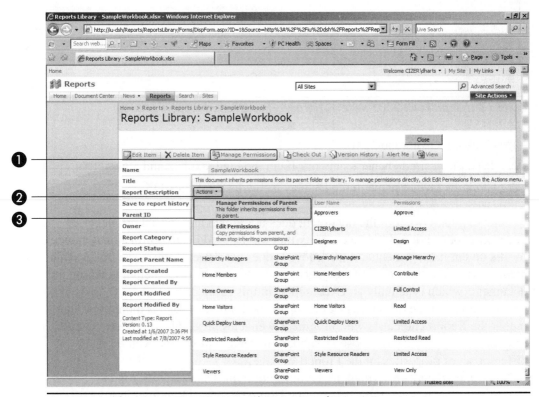

Figure 5-10   *SharePoint 2007 Reports Library—Excel Report Permissions page*

configuration of permissions for the current Reports Library site—it is usually a better choice, since it avoids having special permissions for each document that can be difficult to track with many documents involved.

A complete discussion of SharePoint permissions is beyond the scope of this section, but we'll keep it simple and look at site-level permissions in Figure 5-11.

1. Click the Designers checkbox.

2. Select the Manage Hierarchy checkbox and click OK.

Figure 5-11 shows how straightforward SharePoint permissions can be. Each of the Users/Groups listed on the page have their own permissions that are chosen from the standard Permissions checkbox list that is also shown in Figure 5-11. In this case we checked Manage Hierarchy, which gives the Designers group the ability to create sites within the SharePoint environment. When we clicked OK, the Manage

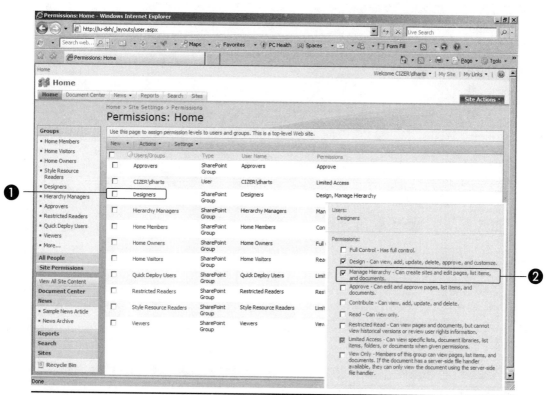

Figure 5-11   *SharePoint 2007 Groups and Permissions page*

Hierarchy permission was added to the Permissions displayed on the Designers group display row.

In Figure 5-12 we see the screens that allow us to add or remove users from a group, and to add a new group.

1. Click the Designers link in the Groups list.
2. Click the New drop-down control.

Figure 5-12 displays the users that are members of the Designers group (in our working example there is just one user). And clicking the page-level drop-down menus provides a fairly intuitive set of choices for managing users that belong to groups.

Again, the concept of users and groups is reasonably easy to grasp if we think of users belonging to groups, and groups having permissions to add, edit, and

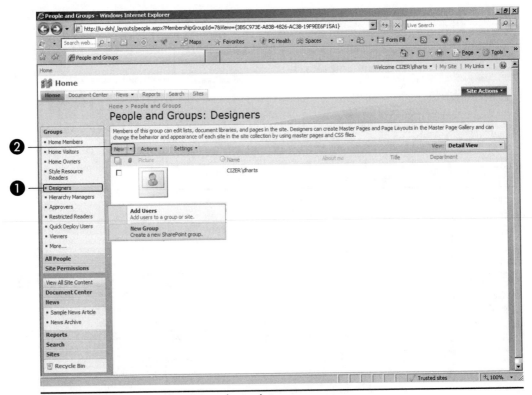

Figure 5-12 *SharePoint 2007 People And Groups page*

delete content in the SharePoint sites or pages. We'll finish our brief discussion of SharePoint permissions with Figure 5-13 and a quick look at site settings.

1. Click the Site Actions drop-down control.
2. Choose Site Settings.
3. Choose Modify All Site Settings.

As you see in Figure 5-13, there are many elements of SharePoint that can be configured. Although this might seem like an overwhelming set of choices, they are really organized in a commonsense manner. In Figure 5-13 we see a columnar organization of site settings that will usually be configured by a SharePoint administrator, not end users. However, it helps for all users to have an idea of how SharePoint is made up of sites (also called pages) with documents and reports in the sites that are governed by permissions.

And as you've seen, users belong to groups—and groups have permissions by site or by document(s) within the site. This is the Office 2007 world of collaboration that is much improved with Excel and Word being able to directly publish to SharePoint.

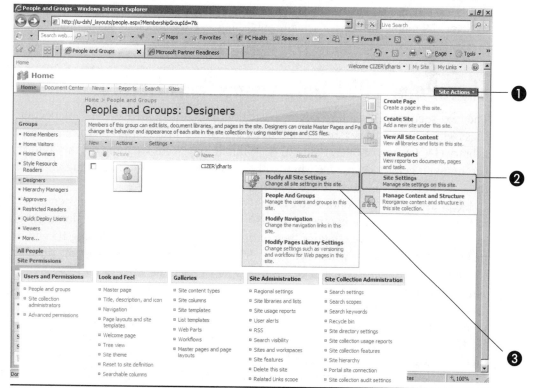

Figure 5-13 *SharePoint 2007 site settings*

BI TIP

In much the same way that desktop productivity applications became an integrated suite of products in Office years ago, those same applications are today able to share content (documents and reports, for example) in a controlled manner when connected to SharePoint. In the case of Excel 2007 publishing to SharePoint 2007 we are able to realize the connected and controlled benefits of collaborative business intelligence.

SharePoint document library permissions determine what workbooks are visible, and to which users. Excel Services relies on this SharePoint permissions structure, which can provide Reader rights for viewing spreadsheets, Contributor rights for viewing, changing, and adding to spreadsheets, or Administrator rights for full control.

Reader rights allow users to download the Excel workbook into Excel 2007 and access the formulas and any built-in logic of the spreadsheet. This can be further controlled by providing only View Item rights, which prevent downloading the spreadsheet—it can only be viewed through Excel Services and the browser.

Again, we should emphasize this is not a complete discussion of SharePoint configuration and permissions, which would take an entire book to fully explore. Rather, we've just touched on the overall design of sites, content, users, and groups. In the next section we'll follow the steps of actually publishing an Excel report to SharePoint.

SharePoint 2007 Data Connections Library

The next section will run through the basic configuration of Office Data Connection files (which have a file extension of .ODC) in a SharePoint 2007 Data Connection Library (DCL) area of SharePoint 2007. While it may seem we jump quickly into acronyms, it helps to know the Microsoft terminology when you're reading about these technologies and find references to ODCs and DCLs.

Excel uses ODCs to connect to external data; and an ODC connection is created in Excel, as you've seen in other chapters in this book. The ODC connection is saved as a stand-alone file that contains the configuration information (including ID and password for the data)—which is a good thing in a SharePoint environment, since we can store previously created ODCs in a Data Connection Library for reuse by other Excel users.

This benefits those other Excel users, since they don't have to worry about configuring external data connectivity (they just select ODCs from a SharePoint DCL) when working with Excel on their desktop computer. Imagine the productivity gain in being able to use the SharePoint DCL repository of ODCs to get to data across the enterprise, without having to continually ask database administrators for server and database location information!

BI TIP

A long-standing benefit of server-based reporting tools has been the availability of data connections that are maintained on the server by database experts. This keeps the maintenance of data connection configurations in the hands of people that know the data, and allows end users to access data through the server-based connections without having to keep track of data connections on their own desktop computers.

Figure 5-14 takes us right into a SharePoint 2007 Data Connection Library (DCL) where we can upload an already-existing Office Data Connection (DCL) file into the SharePoint site.

1. Click the Data Connections link on the left side of the screen.
2. Click the Upload drop-down control.
3. Select the Upload Document menu choice.
4. Click Browse on the subsequent Upload Document screen.

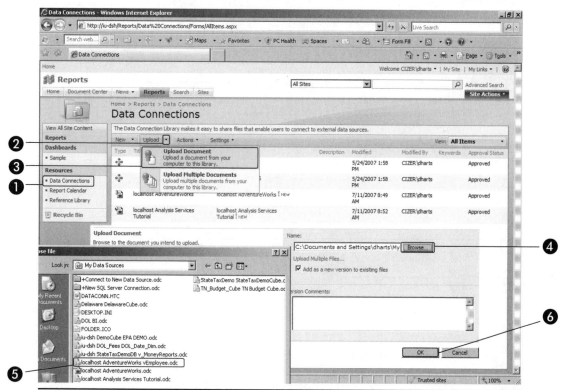

Figure 5-14 *SharePoint 2007 Data Connections Library*

5. Browse to any desired .odc file in the pop-up dialog box.

6. Click OK.

Uploading documents into SharePoint is a common practice, and the term document refers generically to any file that we wish to place in SharePoint. In Figure 5-14 we followed the familiar Windows File Explorer paradigm of browsing to a file. In this case the Browse File dialog box displayed files with .ODC extensions, which are typically going to be found on whatever computer-drive-folder the database personnel have used to save ODC files they created in Excel for uploading into SharePoint.

In Figure 5-15 we see how to make the uploaded data connection available for public use.

1. Hover over the newly uploaded Data Connection, and click the drop-down control.

2. Select Approve/Reject on the pop-up menu list.

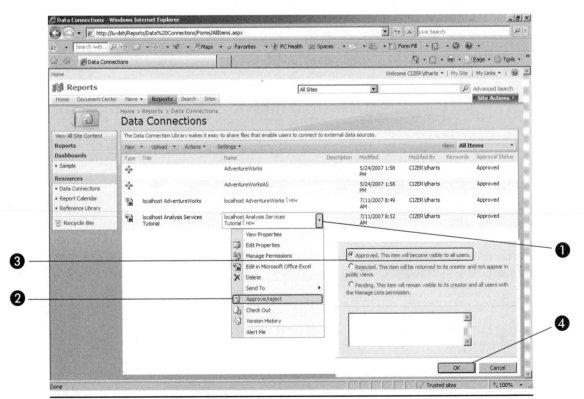

Figure 5-15 *SharePoint 2007 Data Connections Approval Status*

3. Select the Approved option button on the subsequent Approval screen.
4. Click OK.

The steps in Figure 5-15 may seem like unnecessary busy work, but they actually highlight SharePoint's important theme of content control. It makes good sense that uploading an Office Data Connection goes through an Approval step, since it requires the SharePoint library administrator to think about the validity of the data connection before releasing it for use by many people across the organization.

Office Data Connections Available to Excel on End-user Computers

The next step in our Data Connection Library process is to make the ODCs available to end users in Excel on their local desktop client machines. There are two ways to accomplish this; we'll show how to use the registration key method:

1. A SharePoint Server 2007 site administrator defines a SharePoint DCL to be available for use on client computers and then associates each user's SharePoint "My Site" with the SharePoint Connection Library. The ODCs in the DCL are then available from within Excel on the end user's computer.

2. A registration key is configured on the end user's computer, which refers to the SharePoint DCL. The ODCs in the DCL are then available from within Excel on the end user's computer.

Figure 5-16 shows the client computer Registry entry that makes the data connections available from within Excel on the client. It should be noted that manually editing the computer's Registry is not considered to be a "best practice" in most organizations (although it can be automated with scripts)—but the Registry modification is presented here as a practical way to make the ODCs known to Excel clients without going through the configuration of multiple "My Site" personal SharePoint configurations for all end users.

Please note the following instructions come from the Microsoft TechNet guidance for "Plan external data connections for Excel Services." To edit the Windows Registry on the client desktop, first follow these steps:

▶ From the Windows desktop screen choose Start | Run, enter **regedit** in the text box, and click OK to bring up the Registry Editor as shown in Figure 5-16.

▶ Open the left-pane tree view to HK_CURRENT_USER\Software\Microsoft\Office\12.0\Common\Server Links\Published

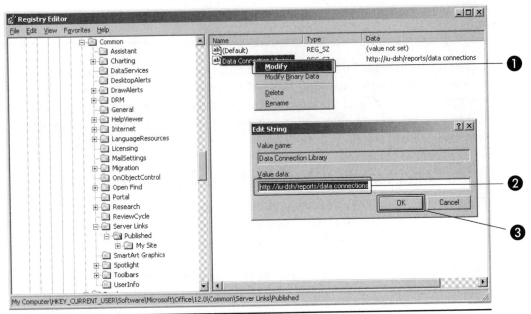

Figure 5-16 *RegEdit client computer configuration for use of SharePoint ODC files*

Here, modify the Published Registry entry as shown in Figure 5-16.

1. Right-click the Data Connection Library text, and choose Modify on the pop-up menu.

2. Enter **http://*your_server_name*/reports/data connections** in the Value Data text box.

3. Click OK, and close the Registry Editor by clicking the close box at the top right of the window.

The result of editing your client computer Registry is immediately available to Excel on your computer. It simply tells Excel to show the SharePoint Data Connection Library (DCL) in the dialog box for Existing Connections within Excel 2007.

Creating an Excel Report with a SharePoint Office Data Connection

The benefit to you as an end user is in being able to make use of SharePoint 2007 Office Data Connections to connect Excel to external data of all types from Microsoft servers such as SQL Server, and from non-Microsoft data sources such as

Oracle, DB2, and Informix. Figure 5-17 shows how we make use of the SharePoint ODC from within Excel 2007.

1. Click the Get External Data icon, in the Connections group of the Data tab on the Ribbon menu.
2. Click the Existing Connections icon in the pop-up menu choices.
3. Double-click the Data Connection Library folder in the Existing Connections dialog box.
4. Select the desired Office Data Connection in the subsequent Folder dialog box.
5. Click Open.

The steps in Figure 5-17 lead right to the result in Excel 2007 shown in Figure 5-18, where we are ready to create an Excel report using the ODC. In this case we're

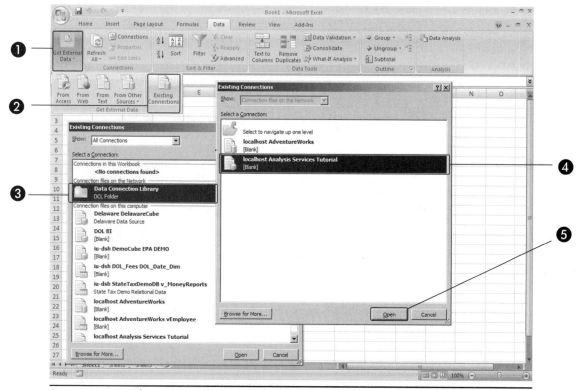

Figure 5-17 *Excel 2007—making use of a SharePoint Data Connection Library*

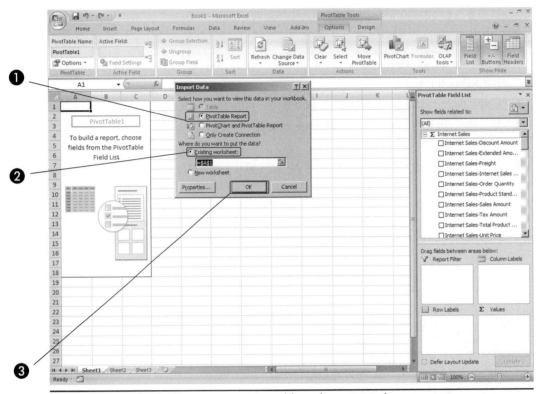

Figure 5-18 *Excel 2007—creating a PivotTable with an ODC data connection*

connecting to a SQL Server OLAP cube, which is explained in Chapter 8. For now we'll quickly create a PivotTable and Chart.

1. Choose the PivotTable Report option button.
2. Choose Existing Worksheet with the default cell reference.
3. Click OK.

Figure 5-18 shows use of the Excel 2007 PivotTable design interface to create a cross-tab report against the ODC connection to a SQL Server data source. In Figure 5-19 we arbitrarily choose a few data elements for the PivotTable.

1. Choose Internet Sales-Order Quantity and place it in the Values list box.
2. Choose Occupation and place it in the Row Labels list box.
3. Choose Sales Territories and place it in the Column Labels list box

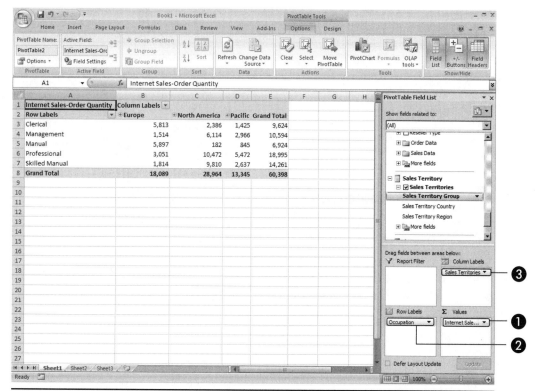

Figure 5-19   *Excel 2007—creating a PivotTable from the PivotTable field list*

Figure 5-19 shows how easy it is to create a PivotTable in Excel 2007 with a connection to external data. This is one of the most improved areas of Excel 2007, and it makes for a nice demonstration, since the PivotTable automatically has data filter drop-down and expand-collapse controls that will still work when we publish to SharePoint Excel Services!

Figure 5-20 continues this process by adding a PivotChart to the same worksheet. The PivotChart uses the same data as the PivotTable.

1. Click the PivotChart icon, in the Tools menu group on the Options tab of the Ribbon menu.
2. Click OK to use the default Column chart type.

Figure 5-20 shows how easy it is to add a PivotChart in Excel 2007, after we already have a PivotTable in place on the worksheet. We'll see how this PivotChart displays in SharePoint Excel Services as well.

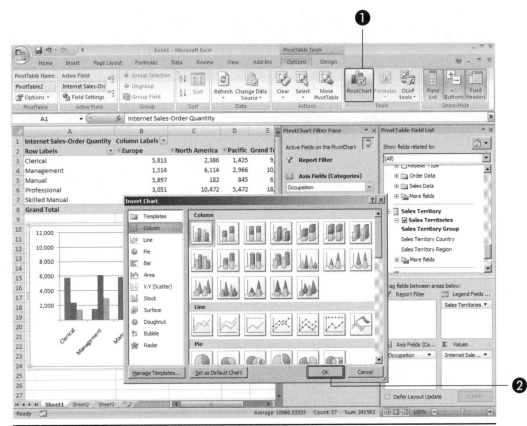

Figure 5-20 *Excel 2007—creating a PivotChart based on a PivotTable*

In Figure 5-21 we're going to use the Excel Range feature to give a name to a selected set of cells in the spreadsheet; in this case the PivotTable we've already created. Range names provide a handy way to keep track of various parts of an Excel spreadsheet, especially when the spreadsheet has multiple tables or charts—each of which might be considered to be an individual report for later use in our SharePoint displays.

The benefit here is that we are able to create and maintain a single Excel spreadsheet with multiple tables and charts from one Office data source selected from a SharePoint Data Connections Library—and yet we can publish the tables and charts as individual reports for display in SharePoint Excel Services!

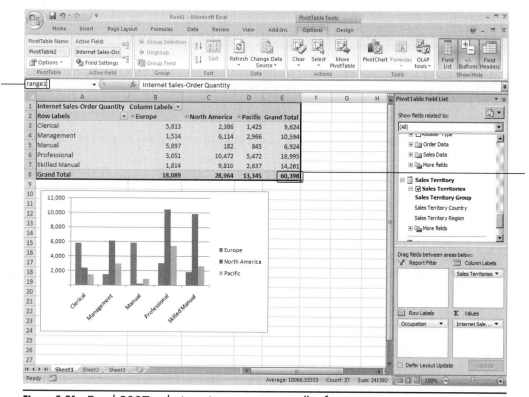

Figure 5-21 *Excel 2007—designating a range or cell reference*

BI TIP

In every BI project it is important to consider the maintenance aspects of the reports and charts. The use of master workbooks, each of which contains reports and charts that pertain to a specific subject area of the organization, helps to avoid the proliferation of spreadsheets that become a challenge to track. These master Excel workbooks are published with item-level permissions that determine who can see which components of the spreadsheets (such as specific PivotTables, charts, and named ranges) through Excel Services for enterprise-wide consumption.

1. Holding the left mouse button down, select the cells that make up the PivotTable (in this case A1–E8).

2. In the spreadsheet Name box, type the name desired for the selected cell reference (in this case **range1**), and press ENTER.

Figure 5-21 shows how easy it is to name a range of cells. Note the Name box has a drop-down control that allows you to quickly select any named range in the spreadsheet and quickly navigate to it. This becomes an important feature in large spreadsheets where users could otherwise spend quite a bit of time scrolling around to find a desired data area—especially since Excel 2007 can hold one million rows of data!

In Figure 5-22 we're going to take a final configuration step that will make sure our Excel report displays refreshed data every time it's displayed in SharePoint Excel Services.

1. Click the Connections icon, in the Connections menu group on the Data tab of the Ribbon menu.

2. Click the Properties control in the Workbook Connections dialog box.

3. Check the checkbox for "Refresh data when opening the file."

4. Click OK.

Now that we've created an Excel report with multiple components and a named range, we're ready to publish it to Excel Services. This is where the process gets more exciting, since it's definitely a new experience to Office users—and please

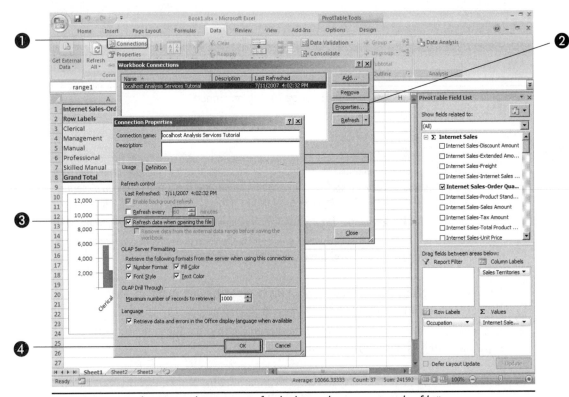

Figure 5-22 *Excel 2007—choosing "Refresh data when opening the file"*

note, publishing to Excel Services requires Excel 2007 stand-alone, or Office 2007 Pro-Plus, Ultimate, or Enterprise on the client—and it requires SharePoint 2007 Enterprise on the server!

Publishing an Excel 2007 Report to SharePoint 2007 Excel Services

In the past Excel users have saved their Excel spreadsheets (we're calling them reports in this discussion) to their local client drives or to public drives for sharing with others. This has always introduced problems in getting people to pick up the latest Excel report for a meeting, for example, so that everyone is working with the same data. Also, people inevitably end up getting the Excel spreadsheet from different locations at different times, and bringing printouts to a meeting where questions arise as to the correct version of the spreadsheet and the validity of the data.

So, in a world where we literally run organizations on spreadsheets, Excel Services offers a new way of doing business with collaborative BI. In an Office and SharePoint 2007 environment, people with permission to publish into designated SharePoint Report Libraries will create and maintain Excel spreadsheets that "live in SharePoint" with version-control and workflow approval processes.

What do we mean when we say the spreadsheet lives in SharePoint? We are saying that the process of "publishing" an Excel spreadsheet to Excel Services results in a copy of the Excel workbook being placed into SharePoint's internal server repository. The SharePoint server Excel workbook then is no longer connected to the original client-based Excel workbook!

This part of the discussion is critical to understanding Microsoft's server-based Excel technology, and it helps to note the following points when planning an implementation of Excel Services.

Fundamental aspects of SharePoint 2007 Excel Services reports:

► Publishing Excel 2007 workbooks to Excel Services places a separate copy of the workbook in the chosen SharePoint 2007 document library.

► An Excel workbook in a SharePoint library has a SharePoint menu choice to Edit In Excel, which uses your local Excel 2007 and saves back to the SharePoint library. The save operation does not overwrite the SharePoint workbook unless you choose to do so by giving it the same filename.

► If the Excel workbook was originally created using an Office Data Connection (ODC) from a SharePoint 2007 Data Connections Library (DCL), then the "published to Excel Services" copy of the workbook in SharePoint will also use the ODC from the SharePoint library.

▶ If an ODC is changed or updated in a SharePoint DCL, then Excel Services workbooks that were created using the ODC will automatically inherit the changes to the ODC from the SharePoint library—if those workbooks are configured to automatically update to the ODC from the DCL.

▶ When an Excel Services workbook with an ODC from the SharePoint DCL refreshes data in a SharePoint browser window, it typically passes the SharePoint user credentials (user ID and password) through the connection to the data for data source authentication—unless a static ID and password were specified in the original ODC configuration.

Figure 5-23 shows how we use the new 2007 top-menu Office button to publish the Excel 2007 PivotTable and PivotChart to SharePoint Excel Services.

1. Click the Office button icon, in the upper left of the screen.
2. Choose the Publish choice in the pop-up menu list.
3. Choose the Excel Services choice in the pop-up menu box.

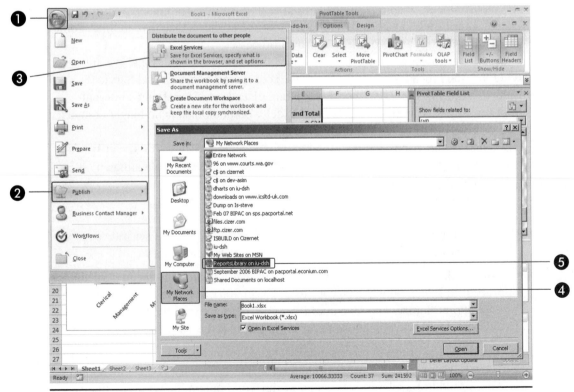

Figure 5-23 *Excel 2007—Publish to Excel Services*

4. Click My Network Places on the left-side pane of the Save As dialog box.
5. Choose the "ReportsLibrary on *your_server_name*" (it has a SharePoint globe-folders-stand icon)—but *don't click Open yet,* since we're going to continue these menu steps using the next screen shot.

Figure 5-23 shows what the Windows Explorer Network Places choices look like in a SharePoint environment where the SharePoint server is known to the network. Your organization will differ, of course, depending on the server and network configurations in place with your environment. However, the concept will be the same—we are publishing an Office piece of content to a network server for collaborative work!

Figure 5-24 continues the Excel publishing procedure from Figure 5-23, as we next use Excel Services Options to look at the various parts of the Excel report.

1. Click the Excel Services Options button, on the Save As dialog box.
2. Choose Items In The Workbook on the drop-down control in the Excel Services Options dialog box.

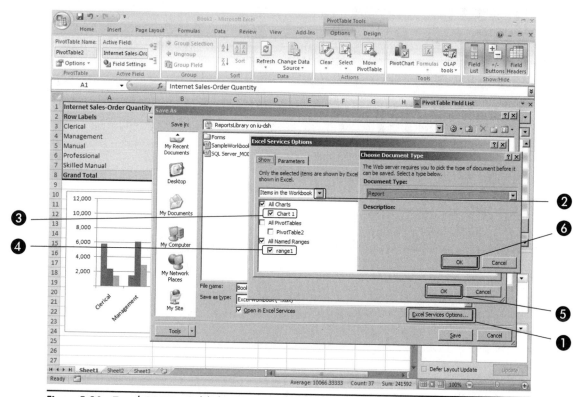

Figure 5-24 *Excel 2007—Publishing to Excel Services Options*

3. Check Chart 1 in the list of Items In The Workbook.

4. Check range1 in the list of Items In The Workbook.

5. Click OK.

6. Leave the Document Type as Report, and click OK.

In Figure 5-24 we are able to see how the Excel Services publishing procedure allows us to see the multiple parts of the Excel workbook; in this case the chart and the range of cells we designated on the spreadsheet. This is a nice element of control for the publishing process, showing the value of using Excel ranges to name various parts of a workbook. The chart and the range will be available as individual items from within SharePoint as well, after we finish the publish process.

Figure 5-25 shows the next step in publishing the Excel workbook, which is automatically copied to the SharePoint server as part of the process.

1. Click the View drop-down control at the upper right of the SharePoint screen.

2. Choose range1 in the pop-up menu list.

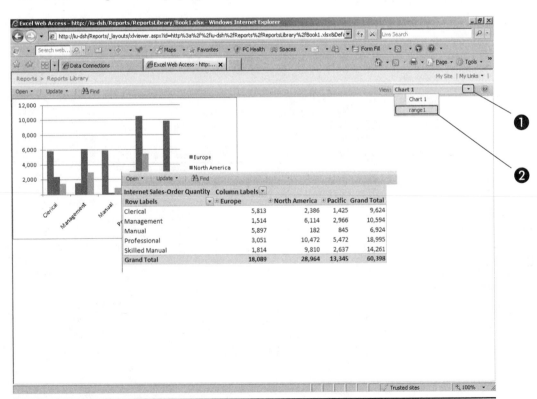

Figure 5-25 *SharePoint 2007 Excel Services showing a published workbook*

In Figure 5-25 we've left the client desktop Excel environment and are now in the server SharePoint environment as Excel Services automatically displays the screen shown. Excel Services is actually rendering the published Excel workbook in a SharePoint window to show the successful upload. And as we mentioned before, we have a View drop-down control that allows us to choose to display the various Excel report components and ranges.

We're now seeing a live Excel spreadsheet/report in a browser window, with no involvement from any desktop Excel client. This is the new experience of Microsoft's server-based Excel!

Figure 5-26 shows the newly published Excel report in the SharePoint Reports Library. Notice the standard look and feel of items in the SharePoint library.

1. Hover over the newly published Excel report (it has a !NEW suffix next to its name), and click the drop-down control.

2. Choose Edit Properties in the pop-up menu list.

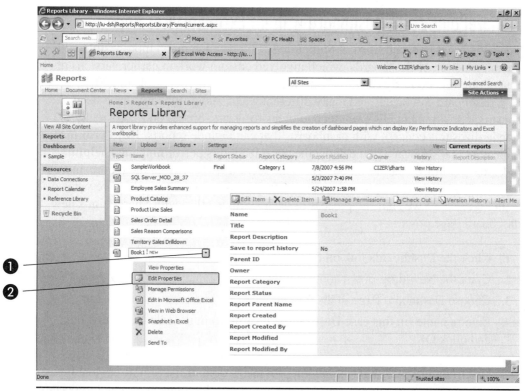

Figure 5-26 *SharePoint 2007 Reports Library with a newly published Excel report*

The SharePoint library in Figure 5-26 is a standard screen that we see throughout the SharePoint experience. That is because all Office spreadsheets, documents, and reports are placed in a SharePoint document library—and then SharePoint exposes the special properties and edit tools that are appropriate for the reports and documents.

This is a great benefit to all of us, since users learn one SharePoint user interface, which handles a wide range of Office content pieces. The same permissions control (who can upload or publish to SharePoint), version control, and live-viewing capabilities apply to all the Office items.

BI TIP

As organizations mature in their use of documents and reports to run their businesses, it becomes important to have a centralized server repository that can handle the wide variety of content generated by today's information workers. This allows us to apply rules of content ownership and versioning, as has been done in the past with programming projects.

A SharePoint 2007 Dashboard with an Excel Services Report

The wide-ranging capabilities of SharePoint 2007 become much more visible with the introduction of dashboards, which involved custom work in earlier versions of SharePoint but are fairly easy to create with the out-of-the-box tools in 2007.

A dashboard can be defined many different ways, and dashboards have been constructed with many different technologies for years. SharePoint 2007 really standardizes this concept with dashboards that can include reports, Key Performance Indicators that show at a glance how the organization is performing, and helpful links to supporting SharePoint content. This section will focus on the reports in a dashboard—where the reports show live refreshed data every time they are viewed.

In Figure 5-27 we start the process of dashboard creation with SharePoint's new dashboard page process.

1. Click the Dashboards link on the left side of the Reports site.
2. Click the New drop-down control at the top of the page.
3. Choose Dashboard Page in the pop-up menu list.
4. Enter a name (in this case **Dashboard Example**) in the File Name text box, and click OK.

Notice in Figure 5-27 that SharePoint provides a default list of new content types for the Reports Library: report, dashboard page, and folder—each of which proceeds

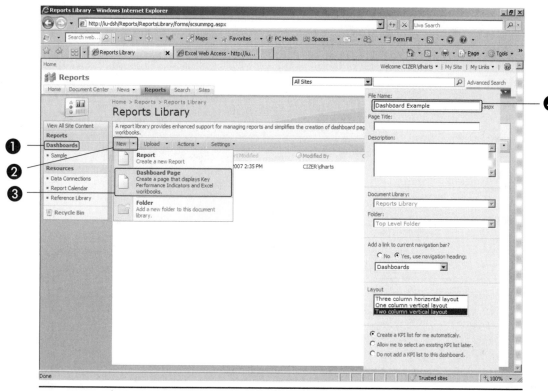

Figure 5-27 *SharePoint 2007—creating a new dashboard page*

to screens that support the particular choice. Once we create a dashboard page, it will appear as an item in the Reports Library—and when we click the dashboard item, it will display our new dashboard page.

Figure 5-28 shows how quickly the dashboard creation process moves along, as we find ourselves immediately in the default SharePoint dashboard screen with helpful hints and links to add content pieces to the dashboard.

1. Click the drop-down control on the Excel Web Access [1] screen section.
2. Choose Modify Shared Web Part from the pop-up menu list.

The process shown in Figure 5-28 quickly becomes familiar to SharePoint designers, since the various pieces of a SharePoint screen are edited through the Modify Shared Web Part menu. Notice also the nice screen layout provided as a default in this case, with a Key Performance Indicators section, a Related Information section (for miscellaneous links), and two Excel Web Access sections, which are designed to hold Excel Services reports.

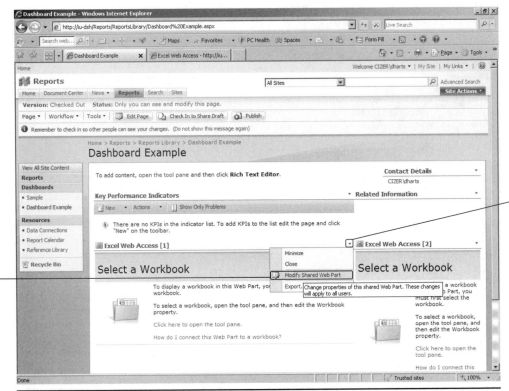

Figure 5-28 *SharePoint 2007—adding an Excel Services report to a dashboard*

Excel Web Access is the Microsoft term for the SharePoint web part that contains an Excel Services report. And "web part" is the Microsoft term for standard SharePoint placeholders that are predesigned to display specific Office content pieces—which in our case consist of an Excel report. The web parts simply display their content in their respective SharePoint screen sections.

Let's look next at the configuration of the Excel Web Access web part, which will hold our newly published Excel report.

1. Click the Workbook text-box browse ellipsis.
2. Choose Reports Library from the pop-up menu list.
3. Choose Book1 from the pop-up menu list.

Figure 5-29 shows how easy it is to add an Excel Services report to an Excel Web Access web part in SharePoint 2007. We're simply browsing to a SharePoint library

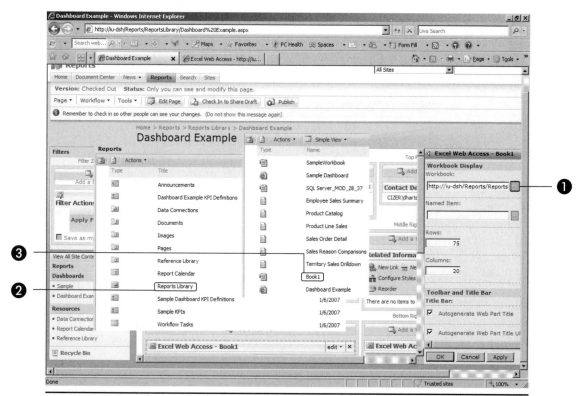

Figure 5-29 *SharePoint 2007—Excel Web Access configuration for an Excel Services report*

that contains all uploaded reports, and choosing an Excel-type report (which has an Excel icon next to its name in the library list).

Figure 5-30 shows the other setting we'll explore for our sample Excel report, which enables us to display the Excel range that was originally designed into the spreadsheet.

1. Click the Named Item text-box browse ellipsis.
2. Enter **range1** in the pop-up list.
3. Click OK.

Figure 5-30 shows that we can select the named range we wish to use for the default display of the Excel report—although we have to remember the name of the range on the spreadsheet.

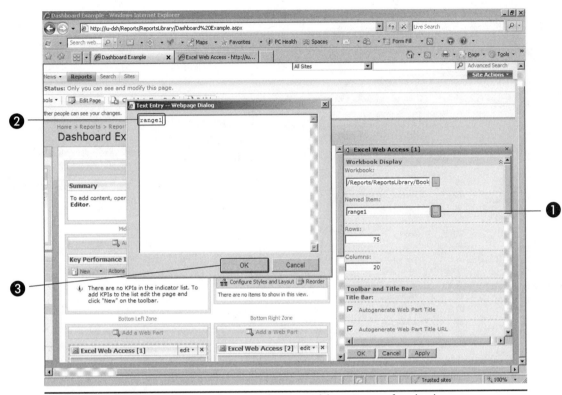

Figure 5-30 *SharePoint 2007—choosing the spreadsheet Range for display*

Figure 5-31 shows the Excel report displaying in the dashboard!

1. Click the PivotTable Row Labels drop-down control.
2. Choose Occupation in the pop-up menu list.
3. Click Filter on the pop-up menu.

In Figure 5-31 we're looking at true server-based Excel, rendering with live data in a browser—which for the purposes of this book is the single most compelling new technology in Office SharePoint 2007. And furthermore, the Excel PivotTable has clickable data filter controls and expand-collapse buttons to dynamically slice and dice the display of data.

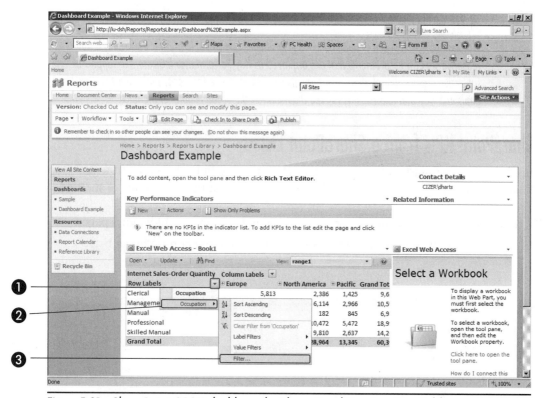

Figure 5-31 *SharePoint 2007 dashboard with an Excel Services PivotTable*

Key Performance Indicators in SharePoint 2007

An important part of SharePoint dashboards is the ability to add Key Performance Indicators (KPIs). KPIs are simply visual numeric indicators of business processes. For example, we might wish to always display the up-to-the-minute number of employees in our organization, or the gross values of orders placed through a corporate web site.

There is an entire body of knowledge surrounding the proper selection of KPIs that help track various parts of an organization. In a "balanced scorecard" scenario KPIs are visually grouped under top-level strategic goals for an organization. Thus we might find KPIs for sales and profit grouped under a "Grow the profitable enterprise" goal, and we might find KPIs for employee retention and hours worked in volunteer organizations grouped under "Maintain a satisfied workforce" goal.

A complete discussion of Key Performance Indicators and balanced scorecards is beyond the scope of this book—but it helps to realize that SharePoint 2007 can support such implementations with the KPI features described in this section.

BI TIP

Although objective business intelligence measurements are valuable in their own right, a well-reasoned set of measurements that are displayed as Key Performance Indicators in support of subjective organizational mission statements can link objective (numeric) and subjective (text) goals in a way that allows users to "see the health of the organization" at a glance.

SharePoint KPIs from a SharePoint List

In Figure 5-32 we start the process of Key Performance Indicator creation with SharePoint's ability to display KPIs that use a SharePoint list as a source of metrics.

1. Click the New drop-down control in the Key Performance Indicators pane.
2. Choose "Indicator using data in SharePoint list" in the pop-up menu list.

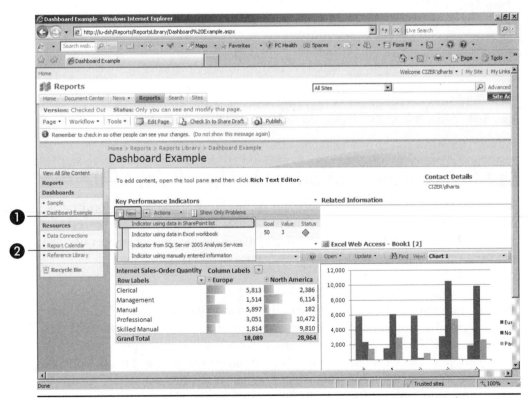

Figure 5-32 *SharePoint 2007 Key Performance Indicator—from a SharePoint list*

Figure 5-32 shows how easy it is to add a KPI. In this case we're going to choose an already existing KPI that has been defined in a SharePoint KPI list library. The KPIs in a list library can actually be manual or derive their data from connections to Excel or Analysis Services. For the current example we'll just follow the process of adding a KPI from a SharePoint list without worrying about the data source.

Figure 5-33 shows how we navigate the SharePoint screen controls and libraries to choose a KPI. This becomes a familiar process—much like the process of navigating Windows File Explorer—as we continue to configure and use SharePoint 2007.

BI TIP

One of the benefits of a standard "portal" technology like SharePoint is that navigation among libraries is similar to navigation among Window File Explorer folders. We quickly come to expect such standard user interface mechanisms in today's business intelligence tools, so that we can go about the work of configuring BI tools without having to relearn different user interface navigation paradigms.

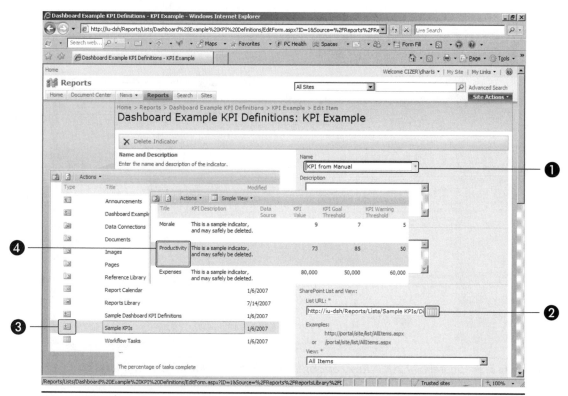

Figure 5-33 *SharePoint 2007 Key Performance Indicator—choosing a SharePoint list*

1. Enter the desired KPI Name.
2. Click the SharePoint List exploration icon.
3. Choose the Sample KPIs SharePoint library.
4. Choose the Productivity KPI, or any desired KPI.

In Figure 5-33 we see that SharePoint 2007 makes the selection of a KPI fairly straightforward. The screen navigation simply leads us to a screen where, on the List URL, we can click the SharePoint exploration icon to find the library and KPI desired.

Figure 5-34 shows the final steps in configuring our KPI. We've simply scrolled down on the KPI configuration screen to see the user interface choices shown.

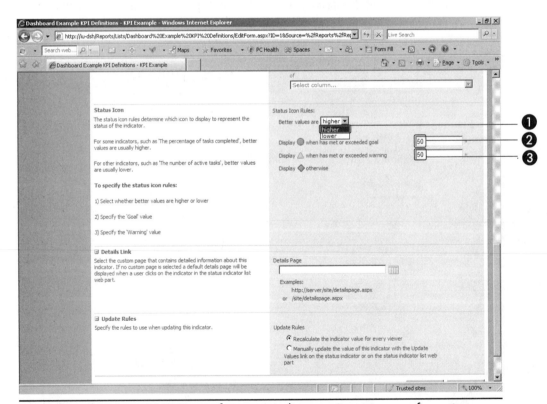

Figure 5-34 *SharePoint 2007 Key Performance Indicator—Status icon configuration*

1. Click the Status Icon Rules drop-down to select "higher," which is better for the KPI.

2. Enter the desired threshold value to display Green.

3. Enter the desired threshold value to display Yellow.

In Figure 5-34 we're able to complete the KPI configuration that we've chosen from the KPI library list. It's clear that this KPI is simple in nature, with hard-coded (manually entered) threshold values that cause the graphical indicator to show yellow and green.

Figure 5-35 shows what the final KPI looks like when we click it, on the dashboard page, to see the details supporting the KPI.

For the sake of completeness, Figure 5-36 shows the location of the configured KPI so that we can see how to find the KPI library—from which we've chosen the KPI for display on the dashboard. Frankly, the more we look at SharePoint

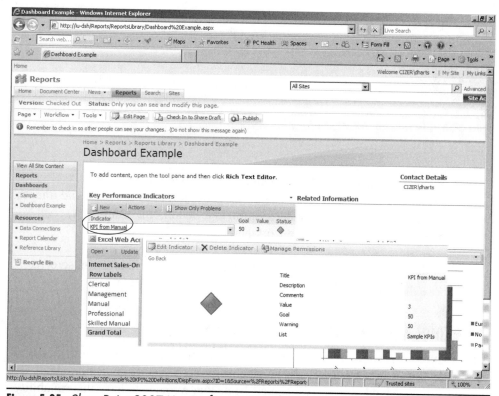

Figure 5-35 *SharePoint 2007 Key Performance Indicator—Details display*

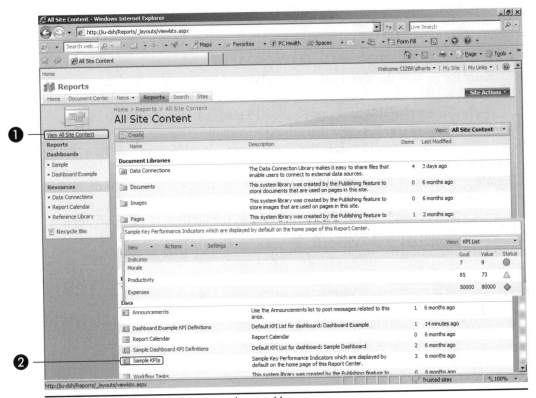

Figure 5-36 *SharePoint 2007 Sample KPIs library*

and understand these document libraries that can hold Word documents, Excel workbooks, KPI definitions, Office Data Connection (ODC) definitions, and images, the more we can appreciate the standardization that SharePoint brings as a server-based repository of Microsoft Office work and content.

1. Click the View All Site Content link at the top left of the SharePoint screen.
2. Choose the Sample KPIs document library.

SharePoint KPIs from an Excel Workbook

Using Figure 5-37, we're going to configure a more interesting KPI—from an Excel workbook. This is important because so much Key Performance Indicator data is only available in stand-alone Excel spreadsheets that we need to have this capability from a practical standpoint.

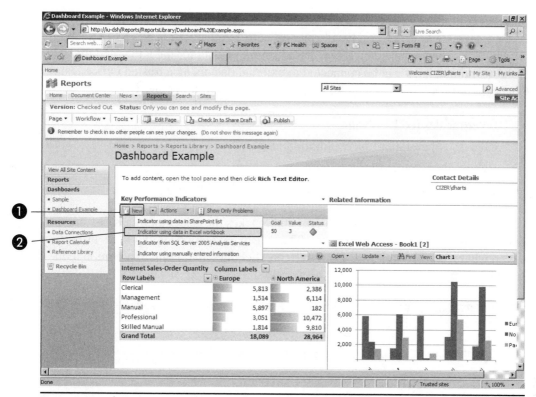

Figure 5-37 *SharePoint 2007 Key Performance Indicator—from an Excel workbook*

BI TIP

Although it could be argued that database servers and cubes provide a most trusted source of KPI data, the fact is, much of our performance measurement data in the real world is in Excel spreadsheets. It makes sense that we should be able to tap into these Excel workbooks for source KPI data to build the Key Performance Indicator portion of SharePoint dashboards.

1. Click the New drop-down control in the Key Performance Indicators pane.
2. Choose "Indicator using data in Excel workbook" in the pop-up menu list.

Figure 5-37 shows how easy it is to add a KPI from Excel. In this case we're going to choose an already-existing Excel spreadsheet that has been uploaded to a SharePoint library. It is significant to note that an Excel workbook in a

SharePoint library can provide a server-based trusted source of KPI data, since it is not dependent on desktop Excel spreadsheets. In other words, the KPI Excel workbook can be considered a server-based source of data for the KPI—and the Excel workbook itself can be connected to external data using a trusted Office Data Connection (ODC) from a SharePoint Data Connection Library (DCL)!

1. Enter the desired KPI Name.
2. Click the SharePoint List exploration icon.
3. Choose the Reports Library SharePoint library.
4. Choose the Book1 workbook, or any desired Excel workbook.

In Figure 5-38 we see that SharePoint 2007 makes the selection of a KPI from an Excel workbook fairly straightforward. The screen navigation simply leads us to a screen where, on the Workbook URL, we can click the SharePoint exploration icon to find the library and Excel spreadsheet desired.

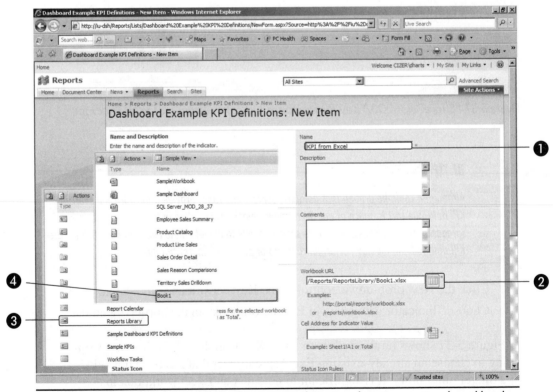

Figure 5-38 *SharePoint 2007 Key Performance Indicator—choosing an Excel workbook*

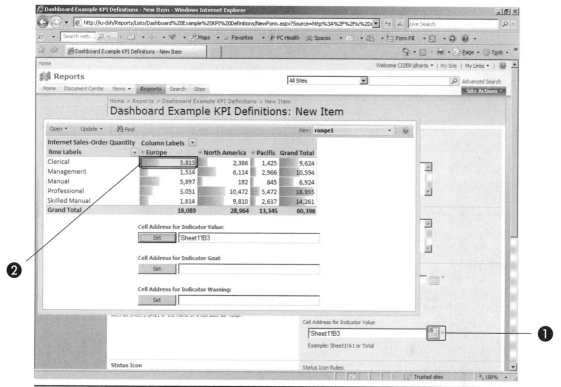

Figure 5-39 *SharePoint 2007 Key Performance Indicator—Excel configuration*

Figure 5-39 shows the final steps in configuring our KPI. We've simply scrolled down on the KPI configuration screen to see the user interface choices shown.

1. Click the Excel exploration icon.
2. Click the desired cell that contains the Indicator Value (in this case B3).

Figure 5-39 brings up the familiar Excel interface—and it's easy to understand that we're selecting a cell of data that represents the actual KPI value. In our example we arbitrarily chose cell B3—but in a planned scenario the Excel spreadsheet would likely exist just for the purpose of providing KPI values.

In Figure 5-40 we're able to complete the KPI configuration that we've chosen from the Excel document library. It's clear that this KPI is simple in nature, with hard-coded (manually entered) threshold values that cause the graphical indicator to show yellow and green. However, if the Excel KPI spreadsheet is configured to

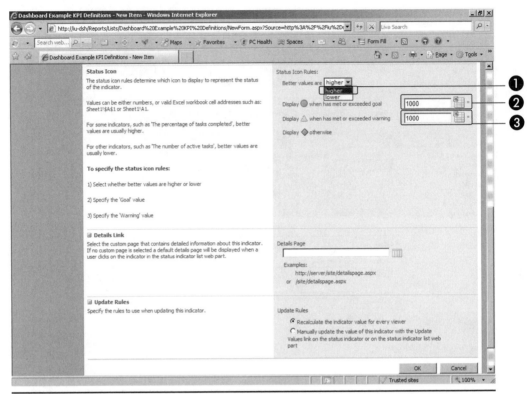

Figure 5-40 *SharePoint 2007 Key Performance Indicator—Status Icon configuration*

contain the threshold values, the Excel exploration icons shown in Figure 5-40 can be used to connect to threshold values that are driven by the Excel workbook that might be connected to external data.

This is significant because it shows that Excel can act as the source of the KPI actual value, and the threshold values!

1. Click the Status Icon Rules drop-down to select "higher," which is better for the KPI.

2. Enter the desired threshold value to display Green.

3. Enter the desired threshold value to display Yellow.

SharePoint KPIs from an Analysis Services Cube

In Figure 5-41 we're going to configure an advanced KPI—from a SQL Server Analysis Services OLAP cube. This is important because the most robust source of Key Performance Indicator data is from SQL Server OLAP cubes, which provide live data actual and threshold values, in addition to trend directions.

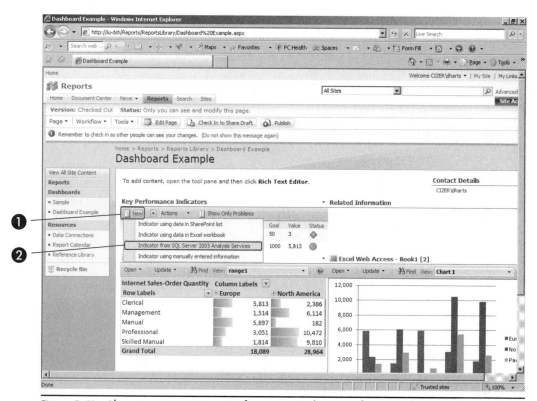

Figure 5-41 *SharePoint 2007 Key Performance Indicator—from Analysis Services cube*

BI TIP

Online analytical processing (OLAP) cubes from SQL Server Analysis Services provide the most advanced source of Key Performance data, not just because the KPIs are server-defined but because the KPI data is automatically available in a hierarchical tree view that can follow organization structures of offices and departments. This supports slicing and dicing of the KPI data when Excel PivotTables are connected to the Analysis Services cube.

1. Click the New drop-down control in the Key Performance Indicators pane.
2. Choose "Indicator from SQL Server 2005 Analysis Services" in the pop-up menu list.

Figure 5-41 shows how easy it is to add a KPI from Analysis Services. In this case we're going to connect to an OLAP cube on a SQL Server 2005 server, which contains an already-defined KPI.

Figure 5-42 shows the SharePoint KPI configuration screen that displays the KPI definition from the cube. Note that there is no text box for the KPI name—it and other properties are already defined in the OLAP cube on the Analysis Services server.

1. Click the Data Connection exploration icon.
2. Choose the desired Analysis Services Data Connection.
3. Choose All KPIs in the KPI drop-down control.

In Figure 5-42, the Data Connection is first configured as shown, and then the KPI drop-down control fills with KPIs that are contained in the Analysis Services cube. When the KPI is displayed in SharePoint, it will be immediately apparent that it provides more information than other KPI sources (notably a trend indication).

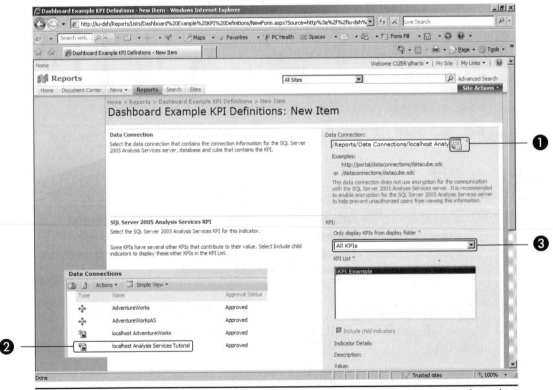

Figure 5-42 *SharePoint 2007 Key Performance Indicator—choosing a server and a cube*

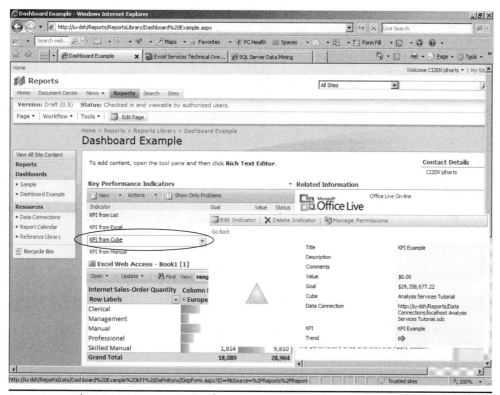

Figure 5-43 *SharePoint 2007 Key Performance Indicator—from cube, properties*

As seen in Figure 5-43, we can click the KPI From Cube link on the SharePoint dashboard page and view a Details screen that shows data provided by the Analysis Services server. With Analysis Services KPIs we do not define thresholds in the SharePoint configuration—because they are driven by live data from the cube!

For the sake of completeness Figure 5-44 provides a brief look at the Visual Studio 2005 configuration of a Key Performance Indicator on an Analysis Services 2005 cube. A full description of this process and the cube KPI features is beyond the scope of this book—but it helps to see the sophistication of the business intelligence design environment that is used to define SQL Server 2005 cube KPIs.

We'll finish the discussion of SharePoint KPIs with the final menu choice in the Dashboard KPI menu—that of a completely manual KPI definition with hard-coded values that are not connected to live data.

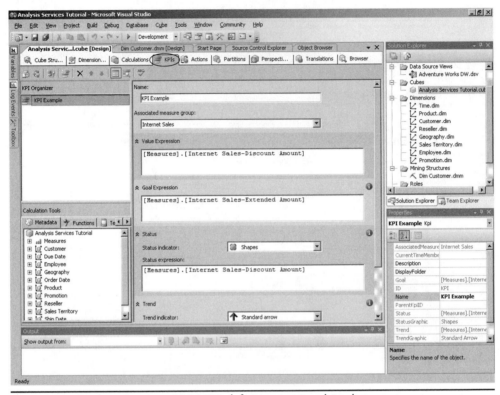

Figure 5-44 *Analysis Services 2005 KPI definition in Visual Studio*

SharePoint KPIs from Manual Entry

In Figure 5-45 we see the SharePoint 2007 selection of a manual KPI.

1. Click the New drop-down control in the Key Performance Indicators pane.
2. Choose "Indicator using manually entered information" in the pop-up menu list.

The screen navigation leads us to a screen where we can enter the static actual and threshold values as shown in Figure 5-46. We've simply scrolled down on the KPI configuration screen to see the user interface choices shown.

1. Enter the desired Name for the KPI.
2. Enter the static value for the Indicator.

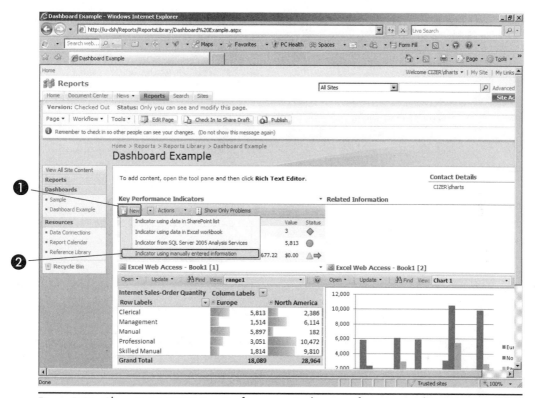

Figure 5-45 *SharePoint 2007 Key Performance Indicator—from manual entry*

3. Click the Status Icon Rules drop-down to select "higher," which is better for the KPI.

4. Enter the desired threshold value to display Green.

5. Enter the desired threshold value to display Yellow.

As we can see in Figure 5-46, the KPI Indicator Value and its Green and Yellow Threshold values are simply entered into the text boxes shown. Although this produces a very simple KPI, it is worth knowing about, since it's very easy and quick to create. This simplicity can often provide the information we need where a KPI is not fast-changing and has no external data source.

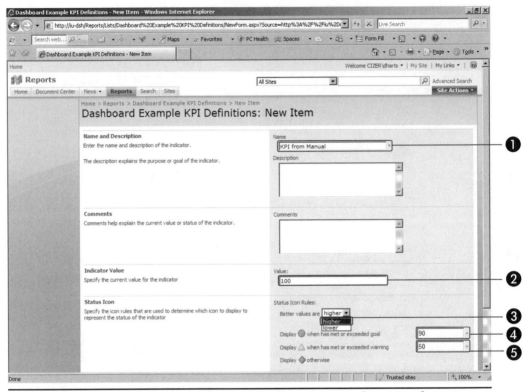

Figure 5-46 *SharePoint 2007 Key Performance Indicator—manual entry configuration*

SharePoint Images and Links

In this section we'll take a quick tour of a few features we'll use to complete our SharePoint 2007 dashboard. In this case we're going to add a link to the Microsoft Office Live web site, and a nice logo for a fresh appearance as shown in Figure 5-47.

1. Click the View All Site Content link at the top left of the SharePoint screen.
2. Choose the Images document library.
3. Click the Upload drop-down control.
4. Choose Upload Document on the pop-up menu.
5. Click the Browse control to locate the desired image file.

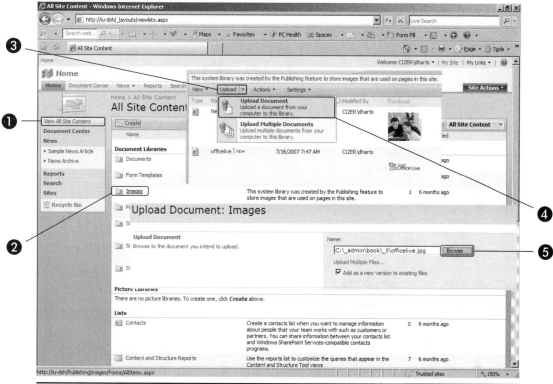

Figure 5-47 *SharePoint 2007—upload an image*

Figure 5-47 shows what is by now a familiar SharePoint navigation library experience. We're viewing "All Site Content" because it's a fast way to access all the SharePoint libraries. In this case we are uploading an image, which will then be available to all SharePoint users that have permission to access the Images library. This can provide a nice repository of high-quality images and organization logos that can be used throughout the SharePoint experience.

Figure 5-48 displays the next step in configuring the on-screen link with an image.

1. Click the drop-down control at the right side of the Related Information pane.
2. Choose Modify Shared Web Part on the pop-up menu.

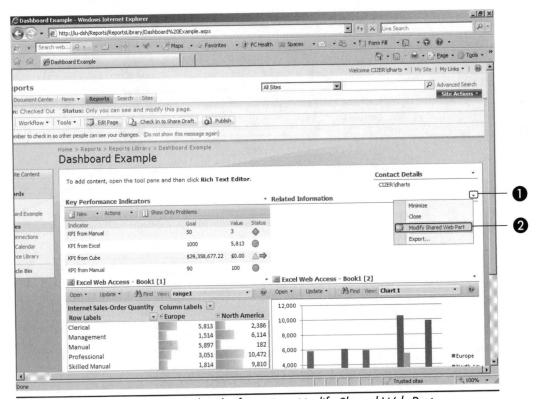

Figure 5-48 *SharePoint 2007—Related Information, Modify Shared Web Part*

In Figure 5-48 we're using the on-screen edit controls, which are available to us as a SharePoint administrator, to enter Modify Shared Web Part experience. This modify web part process is a standard part of the SharePoint configuration process which, in Figure 5-49, allows us to click the New Link screen option to define the external web site link.

Clicking the New Link menu option shown in Figure 5-49 brings up the configuration screen shown in Figure 5-50, where we can either enter the web site URL or browse to it—a familiar experience in Internet Explorer.

1. Enter the desired Title.
2. Enter the desired Link URL, or Browse to an internet web site to choose the URL.
3. Click the Image URL Browse control.

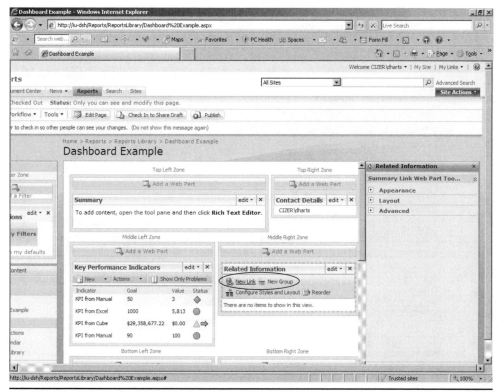

Figure 5-49 *SharePoint 2007—Create a link*

4. Choose the Images SharePoint library.

5. Choose the desired image.

Figure 5-50 shows the configuration option that we can use to define an external web site URL—which is one of the most familiar aspects of a portal to users of company intranet sites. It's nice that SharePoint makes it easy to configure these links, which pertain to the dashboard screen we're designing in our working example.

SharePoint Check In, Version History, and SharePoint Designer

Once we are finished designing the SharePoint dashboard screen, it makes sense that SharePoint requires us to "check in" the results. This is simply an extra step that lets us check our work before making it available to users of the SharePoint site across the enterprise.

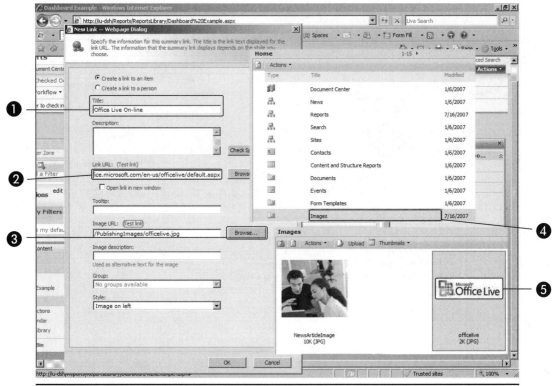

Figure 5-50   *SharePoint 2007—link configure*

As Figure 5-51 shows, SharePoint also maintains a version history of the changes to this dashboard page—so that we can view and even roll back to earlier versions of the dashboard screen if we find a problem with new items or configuration.

1. Click the Check In The Share Draft control on the page menu bar.
2. Click the Tools drop-down on the page menu bar.
3. Choose Version History on the pop-up menu.

Figure 5-51 shows the versions that SharePoint has automatically saved for us during the design process. This is a familiar experience to programmers who have long used the same sort of Check In/Out and Version Control tools to test and publish programs in a controlled manner.

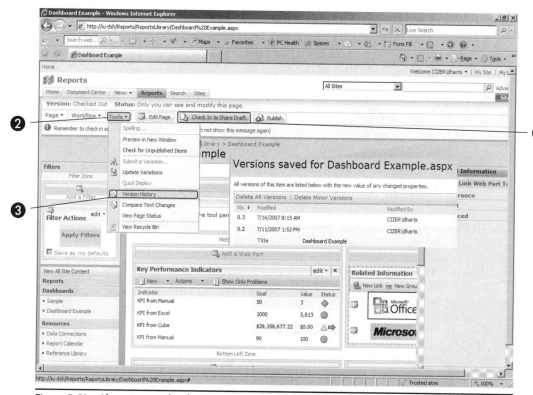

Figure 5-51 *SharePoint Check In, Version History*

BI TIP

In the past business intelligence workers kept separate copies of their work on desktop machines. With today's server-based repositories we can instead "check in" our work and trust the server to keep track of changes that all users have made to uploaded content. This can be termed "configuration management" in the context of group work — and it's becoming a critical part of the Microsoft Office content work process today.

Figure 5-52 shows an advanced option available to SharePoint designers, which supports customization of SharePoint sites and content display in a Visual Studio integrated design environment. This requires the SharePoint 2007 Designer application, which is a separate product in the Microsoft Office suite—normally used by programmers that are tasked to enhance a SharePoint site for organization use.

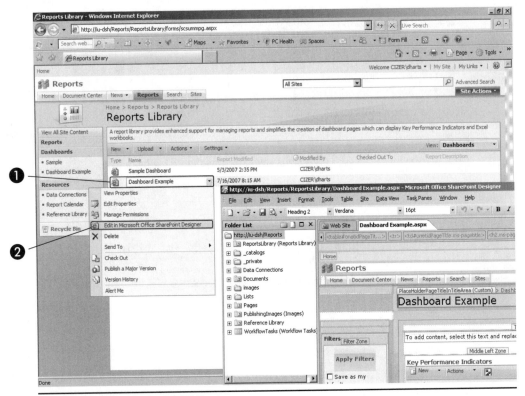

Figure 5-52 *SharePoint 2007 Designer*

Most users will never use SharePoint Designer, but it's good to know that it's available at the "high end" of the feature set supporting SharePoint 2007.

1. Click the "Dashboard Example" drop-down control, in the Reports Library.
2. Choose "Edit in Microsoft Office SharePoint Designer" on the pop-up menu.

Figure 5-52 show what the SharePoint ASP.Net application looks like in Visual Studio—which again, is a toolset that a programmer can use to customize or enhance the SharePoint functionality.

In Figure 5-53 we see the finished result of our work in configuring a SharePoint 2007 dashboard screen.

Note in Figure 5-53 that we've been able to put a live Excel PivotTable into a screen that can be accessed entirely through an end user's browser—there is no

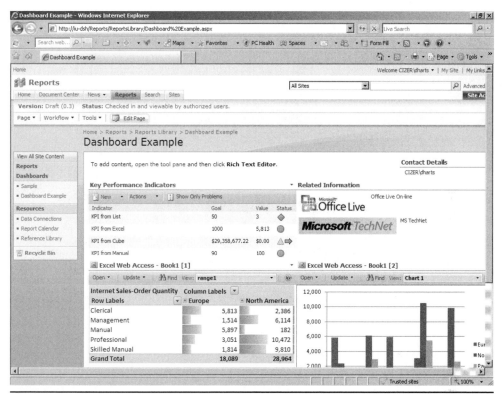

Figure 5-53   *SharePoint 2007—dashboard with Excel Services, KPIs, and links*

client download or installation required of any kind. Using the built-in capabilities of SharePoint 2007, we've configured Key Performance Indicators from different data sources (and static KPIs as well)—and we've added some handy external web site links with images to round out the display.

It's rather amazing that this can be accomplished entirely with the default tools provided in SharePoint 2007—without any programming involved. It is exactly this sort of commercial off-the-shelf (COTS) capability in products that succeeds in the everyday working world—where we need to get a collaboration site up and running to provide a collaborative Microsoft Office working environment.

Excel and Data Mining: Key Influencers, Categories, and Forecasting

This unique chapter explores Microsoft Data Mining technology, which has been hidden in the background of SQL Server Analysis Services for many years. Excel 2007 dramatically changes this by bringing Data Mining to the forefront and making it possible for every Excel analyst to connect to the amazing statistical algorithms produced by Microsoft Research over the last decade. Underlying patterns in multi-hundred-thousand row data sets can be uncovered with Cluster and Dependency analysis, and multiple columns of data can be focused with Regression analysis to produce true forecasting of data trends.

Examples of the following topics will be provided in this chapter:

▶ Analyze Key Influencers and Categories in data patterns in Excel

▶ Fill from Example, Forecast, and Highlight Exceptions in Excel

▶ Goal Seeking and What-If in Excel

▶ Cluster Diagrams in Excel and Visio

BEST REFERENCE

For further research on this topic, go to www.sqlserverdatamining.com.

Technology Positioning Statement

The Microsoft SQL Server 2005 Data Mining add-in for Office 2007 is a freely available download that brings the ease of use of the Office environment to the advanced analytics of data mining. There are two analytical add-ins available for Excel 2007, and a visualization add-in for Visio.

The Table Analysis Tools add-in for Excel enables any Excel user to do some predictive and investigative analysis with a straightforward, task-driven user interface. For example, I can find outlying rows in a table simply by clicking Highlight Exceptions. The Table Analysis tools require no data mining expertise and return results in attractive, easy-to-understand reports.

The Data Mining add-in for Excel is more advanced. It enables the user to select specific algorithms, and it returns results with somewhat more technical data and visualizations than the Table Analysis tools.

(continued)

The intent is to empower as many users as possible with the compelling technologies of predictive analytics, through the familiar environment of Office. Microsoft is aiming for a seamless experience of exploration and discovery, dissolving the traditional barriers between Business Intelligence, Data Mining, and information work.

—Donald Farmer, Microsoft Analysis Services Team

What Is Data Mining?

Data mining is the practice of analyzing sets of data, while connected to the database server or file where the original data resides, to discover anomalies and patterns. This is best understood when thinking about large data sets of thousands or millions of rows, where it's clear a person cannot scan through all the data to find problems or trends.

We've all seen massive Excel spreadsheets where we could seemingly scroll through rows and columns forever. And turning the data into PivotTables and charts provides the first real visualization of what the data represents. But what if there are many different characteristics of the data, not all of which can be represented in graphical form?

The answer is data mining, which has long been known to a special subset of data workers who have access to high-end statistical analysis tools. Their job has been to discover problems with the data that might indicate good or bad things, or to uncover patterns in the data that might yield insight as to how an organization is running. One way to think of this is to ask, Are there certain combinations of the data that, when grouped together, show a particularly large part of the business story behind the data? Some analysts have likened this process to "mental multitasking with rows and columns of data."

The following illustration shows an example of an Excel 2007 Data Mining chart, using the SQL Server 2005 Analysis Services Data Mining algorithms. This chapter will explore the steps used to create the following example Data Mining chart.

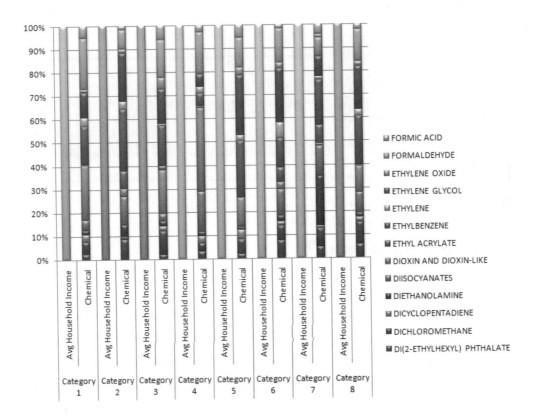

Downloading the Excel 2007 Data Mining Add-In

The free Data Mining add-in application is available from www.microsoft.com/downloads. On the downloads site, search for "Data Mining Add-In" to find the actual download link. Note the Data Mining add-in is published by the Microsoft SQL Server group but is in fact an application to be installed on your Excel desktop client computer. The installation asks for the name of an available SQL Server 2005 Analysis Services server, since it will be using the Data Mining algorithms on the server running SQL Server—and it installs the DMAddinsDB database on that server, which will be used as a temporary working storage area when the Excel tools are connected to SQL Server Analysis Services.

The Excel 2007 Data Mining add-in puts high-end statistical analysis tools (remember the Statistics course everyone "loved" so much in school?) in our hands with a reasonable user interface—all within Excel on the desktop. This embracing of Office users allows people to use Data Mining that would otherwise not even know about the tools.

Figure 6-1   *Excel 2007 Data Mining add-in Analyze tab*

Excel Data Mining tools are divided into two tabs on the Ribbon menu:

▶ **Analyze tab**   Two types of data mining activity described here use Excel tables: one where you will use Key Influencer and Category tools to find deviations and patterns in the data, and another where you will use Forecasting and What-If to intelligently predict future data values and trends. This latter predictive capability can also be used to fill in missing data in a statistically accurate manner, where you have incomplete data sets that you'd like to fill out (see Figure 6-1).

▶ **Data Mining tab**   This is a set of more advanced data mining tools that actually create data mining models that are saved to a SQL Server database. The user interface choices are more sophisticated with these tools, and the resulting visualization supports advanced analysis of the data (see Figure 6-2). Furthermore, the data mining models can be opened in other tools, as you'll see when we show a Cluster Analysis model in a Visio diagram!

Where Does Data Mining Fit in the Microsoft BI Picture?

The accompanying illustration shows a matrix view of Microsoft Business Intelligence technology (often referred to as BI). The Office, SharePoint, and SQL Server applications we see in the marketplace are shown on the left side of the matrix. These applications are used in the real-world activities of reporting, analysis, measurement, and planning as shown across the top of the matrix. The top-down flow of the matrix starts with front-end BI tools we have in Office 2007 at our desktops and extends down

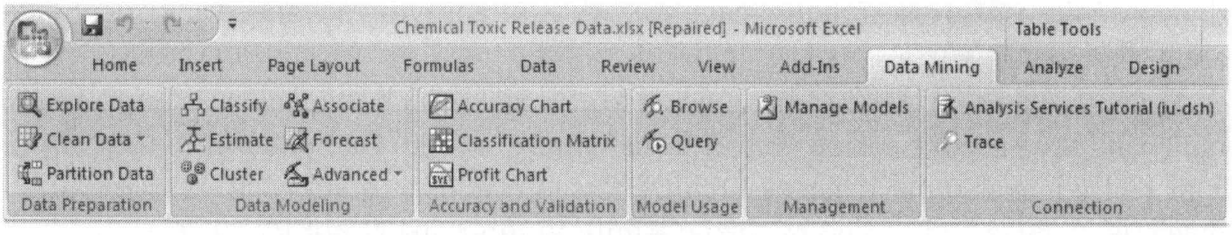

Figure 6-2   *Excel 2007 Data Mining add-in Data Mining tab*

to back-end BI tools that run on servers such as SharePoint 2007 and PerformancePoint 2007, which provide an enhanced experience when connected to Office 2007.

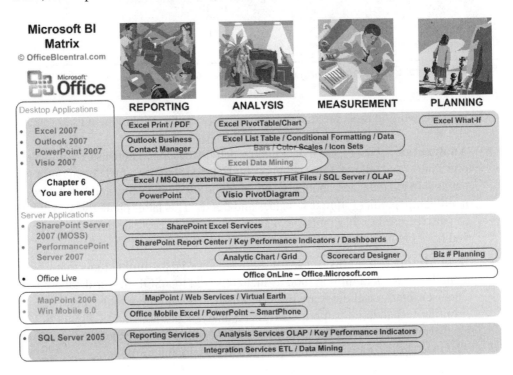

Learning about Data Mining makes more sense if you know where it fits in the Microsoft technology stack, and what it is used for in daily BI activities. The "You are here!" bubble in the illustration shows Excel Data Mining—which fits within the Office 2007 application suite. Data mining makes use of Excel tables, which can be connected to virtually any external data source, both Microsoft and non-Microsoft.

The Excel Data Mining tools require a connection to a SQL Server 2005 Analysis Services server (OLAP cube technology), which houses the advanced data mining algorithms that you'll use to analyze data in Excel. The algorithms come from work done by Microsoft Research to create new ways of applying advanced statistical analysis to data.

We're going use Excel 2007 to connect to external data, bring the data into an Excel table, and then use the various Excel Data Mining tools to find patterns in the data. This really makes sense when you realize this allows us to quickly sift through large data sets that can be handled by the new million row capacity of Excel 2007!

Excel 2007 is perhaps the most commonly used computer application in the world—at least from a business intelligence perspective!—and it takes a giant leap forward in Office 2007 with a Ribbon menu that is more easily extended to hold the new data mining tools. And Excel 2007 can handle one million rows of data! This may be the single most compelling reason that organizations upgrade to version 2007, and then they end up realizing the other benefits that come along with version 2007, such as you'll see in this chapter with Excel analysis tools.

BI TIP

Business intelligence used to be a singular process of running canned reports. Today the tools have evolved, and information workers can greatly enhance their productivity with new tools such as data mining applications that put advanced statistical power at everyone's fingertips. Better tools really do make a difference.

Get External Data from SQL Server

Note that external data can come into an Excel table from almost any database server or file—and Excel has built-in connectors for many kinds of data. We're going to use the External Data connector to SQL Server to bring in data that was originally downloaded from public web sites maintained by the Environmental Protection Agency.

Figure 6-3 shows how we connect Excel to a SQL Server 2005 database server, to bring external data into an Excel table. In our working example we're bringing in toxic chemical release data that has been maintained by the Environmental Protection Agency. The data is pretty interesting because it allow us to see where some of the dangerous chemical releases have occurred in our own states and local areas. U.S. census data has been added to the toxic chemical data on a SQL Server database, which allows us to compare population and land area information to the chemical release data.

The resulting Excel table will have approximately 58,000 rows of data, which is not all the data available on this subject from the EPA but represents a reasonable working set of data that is large enough that a person cannot just browse or group the data to see patterns. It's a good example of meaningful data that affects us in our local neighborhoods and is possibly influenced by the number of businesses in the area, local population statistics, and so forth.

This is exactly the kind of analysis that data mining tools can address, and you'll see that the Excel Data Mining tools can sift through the rows and columns

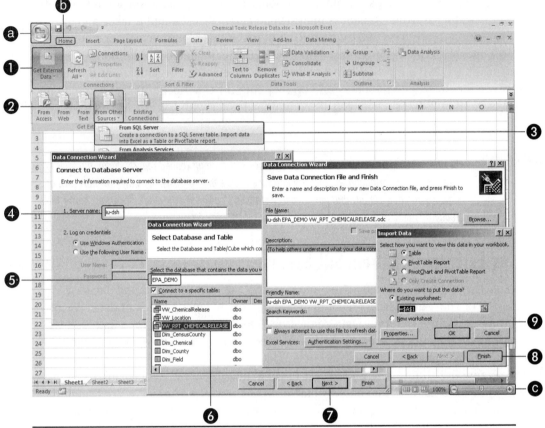

Figure 6-3   *Excel 2007—Get External Data from SQL Server*

quickly and easily. Figure 6-3 shows how we start the process of importing data from SQL Server.

1. Click the Get External Data icon on the Ribbon menu Data tab, to the left of the Connections group of options.
2. Click the From Other Sources icon on the submenu for Get External Data.
3. Choose From SQL Server on the pop-up menu.
4. Enter the Server Name where the database resides, and click Next.
5. Choose the desired database from the drop-down list.
6. Select the desired table or view from the list of data objects for the chosen database.

7. Click Next.

8. Click Finish to accept the default filename for the data connection.

9. Click OK to accept the default Table format and worksheet location.

Figure 6-3 gives us an opportunity to look at the new Excel 2007 menu, especially the Ribbon menu, which is new across the Office 2007 applications. Notice the menu options are logically arranged with helpful icons. Looking at the Get External Data menu group, for example, you can intuitively see several good options for connecting to data—notably SQL Server, and Analysis Services for bringing data into Excel from OLAP cubes.

Excel User Data Mining Interface: Understanding the Screen Components

This is the new 2007 Excel table user interface, and it's where you'll do most of your work in this chapter. The top-level Ribbon menu is divided into tabs that provide a reasonable grouping of menu options. For some work in Excel you'll find that new context tabs become available to the right of the original Ribbon menu tabs—to provide special items needed in working with Excel features that have been selected. This is exactly how the new Office 2007 Ribbon menu is supposed to work; menu tabs with new choices are automatically made available to the user whenever we're working with Excel items that require additional tools. The following explanations correspond to the similarly labeled areas in Figure 6-3.

a. **Office button**   This is where the File, Save, and Open menu choices are found. Also, this holds the menu choice of Prepare | Properties to bring up a dialog box where you can examine or edit the Author, Title, etc., of your workbook.

b. **Ribbon menu tabs**   This is where you can choose groups of menu options for working with workbooks. The Home tab has most of the familiar menu choices for working with data—including Conditional Formatting, which is a great new feature of Excel 2007 (we discuss this in depth in other chapters).

c. **Zoom slider control**   A very useful part of the new 2007 interface is the Zoom slider control that always appears at the lower right of the screen. It's amazing how often we find ourselves using this to zoom the display in or out, to bring whatever we want to see within the viewable screen.

It is worth pausing at this point for a brief discussion of the new Office 2007 menu layout. Microsoft has put a great deal of effort into consolidating the thousands of Office menu commands and choices into this new format. All of the Office 2007 applications use the new Ribbon menu approach for their user interface; notably Excel, Access, PowerPoint, Outlook, and Word.

Our step-by-step instructions in this chapter will primarily use the Ribbon menu icon-based tabbed/grouped interface to accomplish our work, for the purpose of consistency. However, right-click and context-sensitive menus are also a significant part of the Office 2007 interface, and we'll use them whenever we go beyond the immediate options of the Ribbon menu. As you gain familiarity with the new Office 2007 interface, you'll probably develop your own favorite right-click menu paths in everyday work routines.

BI TIP

The new Office 2007 Ribbon menu is a big jump forward for Office applications, and it is perhaps the most important element of commonality to tie together Excel, Access, PowerPoint, Outlook, and Word since the early days of Office integration years ago. For the Excel add-in Data Mining tools it organizes common tasks under the Analyzer tab, and advanced tasks under the Data Mining tab.

The basic elements of the Ribbon menu are straightforward; the Office button, tabs, groups within the tabs, and icons within the groups. Office 2007 sports a much richer set of icons that display across the Ribbon menu and provide an intuitive idea of the actions that can be accomplished by clicking the icons.

Furthermore, many of the icons provide a live preview capability where the on-screen spreadsheet display will change as you hover the mouse over an icon but won't actually change the spreadsheet until you click and choose the icon action. This really makes working with Excel 2007 much faster, since you don't have to keep changing spreadsheet elements back and forth to get visual feedback on formatting and row-column arrangements. In fact, you can mouse over a gallery of choices that may have a large number of options, and very quickly find the appearance you want.

Another helpful aspect of the Office 2007 Ribbon menu design is that the tabs and groups of icons follow your workflow of creating content. So with Excel 2007 we start at the Home tab with the common text and number formatting menu items, followed by the Insert tab, where we can start on a PivotTable / PivotChart inserted onto the spreadsheet, for example.

Subsequent tabs hold groups of icons for more advanced formulas and data work, and at the end of the default Tab strip you find tabs for Review and View to help in the finalization of the workbook. Note you'll always wind up back at the Office button for saving and printing. It also leads to a surprisingly wide range of menu choices for Prepare, Send, and Publish, which hold some important capabilities that allow us to really control workbook content and delivery using e-mail or Microsoft Office SharePoint, for example.

BI TIP

One important thing to note about the new Ribbon menu is the location of the Properties menu item for a workbook. Click the Office button and choose Prepare | Properties to bring up a dialog box where you can examine or edit the Author, Title, etc., of your workbook. This can be significant to avoid surprises when someone else looks at your spreadsheet and sees information you didn't even know was there!

Excel 2007: Data Mining Analyze Ribbon Menu Tools

We're going to jump into data mining with the Analyze tools that make it easy to look for patterns in Excel tables. Excel tables are a big improvement in Excel 2007 and make it easy to turn a spreadsheet of cells into organized rows and columns. The data can be a stand-alone workbook, or it can come from external data sources—as we discuss in Chapter 4.

Given that we have an Excel table of data, we need to connect Excel to any available SQL Server 2005 Analysis Services server to make use of the data mining algorithms that are part of the SQL Server–based application. As Figure 6-4 shows, we'll able to stay within the comfortable world of Excel on our desktop computer but reach out to SQL Server to leverage its data mining capabilities.

1. Click the Analyze tab of the Ribbon menu.
2. Click the <No> Connection icon on the Ribbon menu Analyze tab.
3. Click New to establish a new Analysis Services Connection.
4. Enter the name of the server where Analysis Services is running.
5. Click OK.
6. Click Close to accept the new Analysis Services Connection.

Note the Catalog Name shown in the Connect To Analysis Services dialog box in Figure 6-4. DMAddinsDB was automatically created as part of the Excel Data Mining installation process. It will be used as a temporary working data repository as we use the Excel Analyze tools, although that will be transparent to us and we won't have to worry about it once we have the connection established as shown in Figure 6-4.

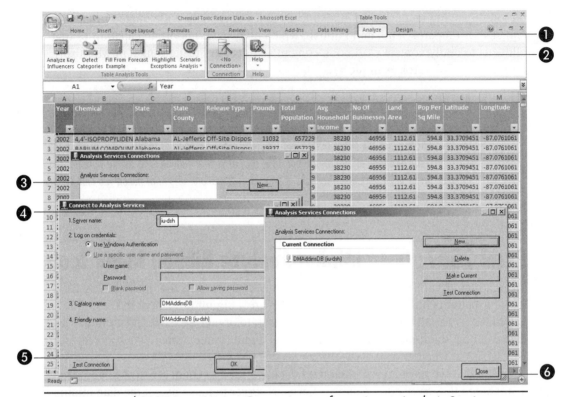

Figure 6-4   *Excel 2007 Data Mining Connection configuration to Analysis Services*

Excel 2007: Data Mining Analyze Tab, Analysis Tools

The Analyze tab is where most people will accomplish data mining within Excel. This is because the data mining tasks are fairly easy to use, and simply need an Excel table of data to work with. Both pattern analysis and predictive analysis can be done with these Analyze tasks, and they don't require any previous knowledge of data mining.

Excel Table: Analyze Key Influencers

Figure 6-5 shows how we start the Analyze Key Influencers data mining task. For reference purposes, this data mining tool uses the Microsoft Research Naïve Bayes algorithm, which calculates the conditional probability between a target column selected, and all other columns (obviously something we can't do manually!).

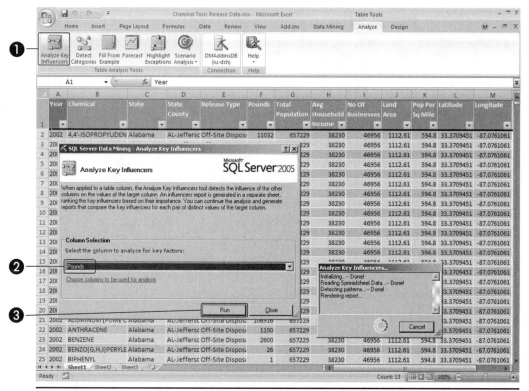

Figure 6-5   *Excel 2007 Data Mining Analyze Key Influencers tool*

The algorithm assumes the columns are independent, with "Naïve" non-knowledge of data associations. This allows the tool to discover new associations in the row column data.

1. Click on the Analyze Key Influencers icon, in the Table Analysis Tools group on the Analyze tab of the Ribbon menu.

2. Choose Pounds on the Column Selection drop-down control, in the SQL Server Data Mining—Analyze Key Influencers dialog box.

3. Click Run to start the Key Influencers analysis process.

In Figure 6-5 note the Analyze Key Influencers pop-up dialog box with the animated green-wheel icon. This provides a visible progress indication of Excel connecting to SQL Server, to analyze the data in the Excel table.

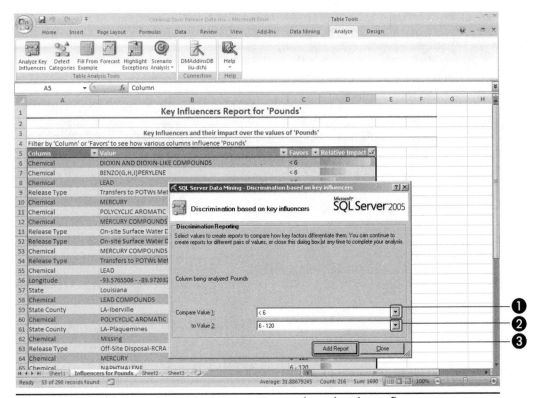

Figure 6-6 *Excel 2007 Data Mining "Discrimination based on key influencers"*

In Figure 6-6 you see the resulting Key Influencers Report for chemical "Pounds" released into the environment, and a secondary dialog box that allows us to add a Discrimination Report to show two columns of contrasting values side by side that influence different groups of the data. You can initially go with the default Compare Value drop-down choices to see what a Discrimination Report looks like—*DON'T click Close yet!* The Discrimination Report will be placed on the Excel worksheet below the Key Influencers Report.

Later in this process you'll choose another set of drop-down values to try a different Discrimination Report.

1. Choose "< 6" in the Compare Value 1 drop-down control.

2. Choose "6 – 120" in the To Value 2 drop-down control.

3. Click Add Report to add a Discrimination Report. *Do not* click Close, since you'll use this dialog box again later in this process!

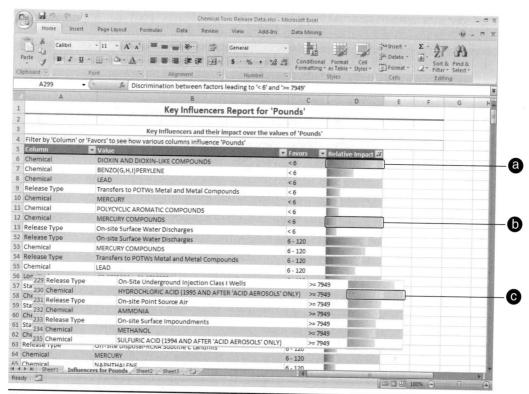

Figure 6-7 *Excel 2007 Data Mining Key Influencers and Relative Impact*

Figure 6-7 shows that in scrolling through the initial Key Influencers Report, we noticed that it might be interesting to contrast the lowest pounds released with the highest pounds released—to see what influences those extreme results!

This is part of the exploration process available with the data mining tools. There is no right or wrong way to do this; and the tools support any way of looking at the data that might catch the interest of the user. In our working example we're interested in what is associated with low and high levels of toxic chemical releases.

In Figure 6-7 the Column column shows groups of data that are associated with (or influence) the pounds released. *The Favors column shows pounds-released groups that have been automatically created by the data mining algorithm*—which lumps the target pounds data into "< 6," "6 – 120", and so forth. The Relative Impact column shows the relative importance of the Value column elements on the pounds-released data groups.

The following can be noted from the Influencers Report in Figure 6-7:

a. DIOXIN has been released in small quantities (< 6) and is a big part of the "< 6" Pounds group.

   b. MERCURY has been released in larger quantities (6 – 120) and is a big part of the "6 – 120" Pounds group.

   c. HYDROCHLORIC ACID has been released in large quantities (>= 7949) and is a big part of the ">= 7949" Pounds group.

Excel Table: Analyze Key Influencers, Discrimination Report

Figure 6-8 shows how we can choose to run a Discrimination Report with Compare Values of Pounds < 6, and Pounds between >= 7949.

1. Choose "< 6" in the Compare Value 1 drop-down control.

2. Choose ">= 7949" in the To Value 2 drop-down control.

3. Click Add Report to continue the Key Influencers analysis process.

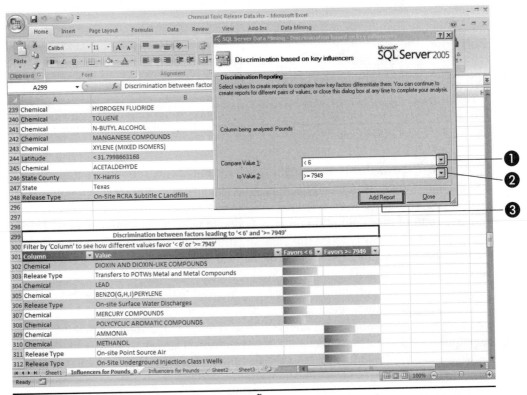

Figure 6-8 *Excel 2007 Data Mining—Key Influencers*

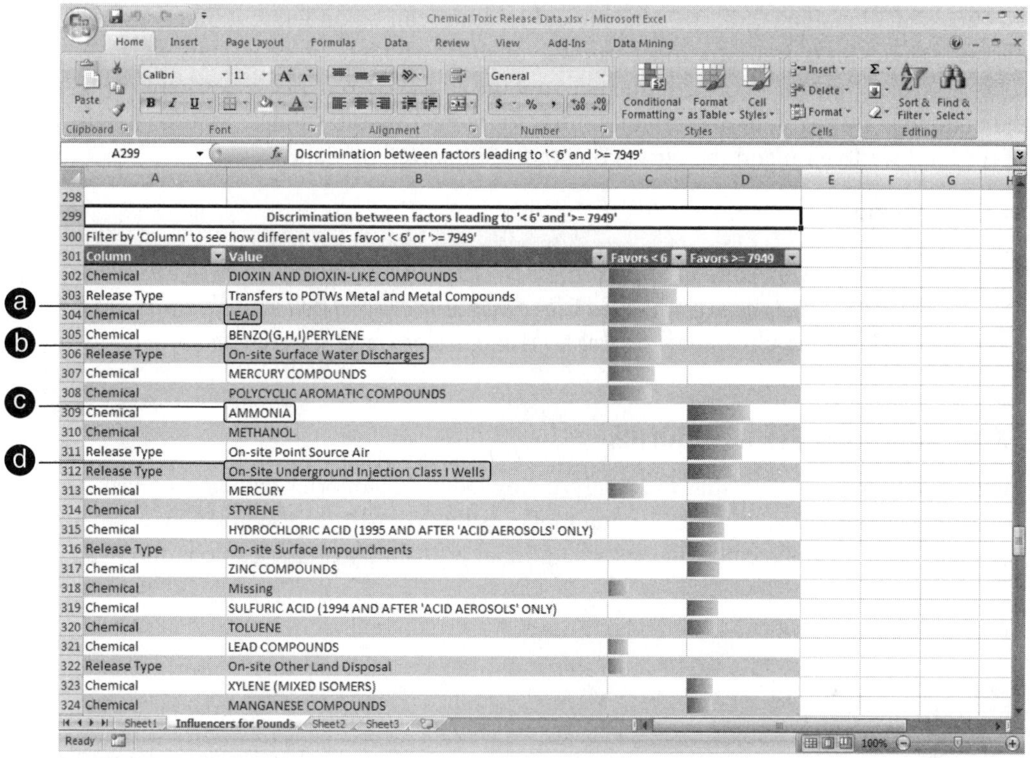

Figure 6-9 *Excel 2007 Data Mining—Key Influencers Discrimination Analysis*

Figure 6-9 continues our data analysis process with a look at the final Discrimination Report that contrasts low-pounds-released chemicals with high-pounds-released chemicals. Again, there is no right or wrong way to go about exploring the data in this fashion. Different people will see different trends or peculiar-looking data—and each person can use their own Key Influencers and Discrimination reports to follow a train of analysis.

The following can be noted from the Discrimination Report in Figure 6-9:

a. LEAD has been released in small quantities (< 6) and is a big part of the "< 6" Pounds group.

b. On-Site Surface Water Discharges are responsible for the LEAD releases.

c. AMMONIA has been released in larger quantities (>= 7949) and is a big part of the ">= 7949" Pounds group.

d. On-Site Underground Injection Class 1 Wells are responsible for the AMMONIA releases.

This is an amazing result; toxic chemical releases can be understood in terms of their impact on our environment, and the means by which the chemicals were released. Now this does not take into account the relative toxicity of the chemical in the quantities released, but it certainly leads to interesting questions about the health of the land we live on and the air we breathe—supported by data!

BI TIP

We should never assume we fully understand the story being told by data just because it's in a spreadsheet that we can group and sort. The advanced data mining tools available to everyone in Excel 2007 can take our understanding to the next level and result in real insight.

Excel Table: Detect Categories

Figure 6-10 shows how to start the Analyze Key Detect Categories data mining task. For reference purposes, this data mining tool uses the Microsoft Research Naïve Bayes algorithm, which calculates the conditional probability of association among all

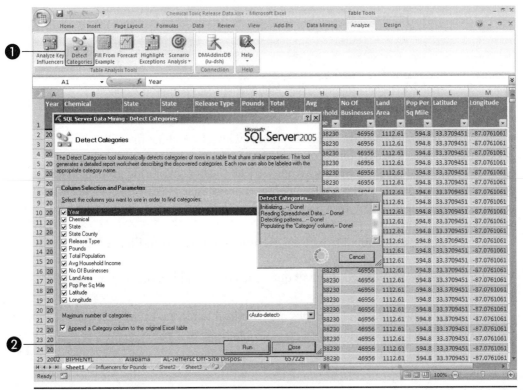

Figure 6-10 *Excel 2007 Data Mining Detect Categories tool*

columns selected (regardless of grouping or sorting that may have been applied!). The algorithm assumes the columns are independent, with "Naïve" non-knowledge of data associations. This allows the tool to discover new associations in the row-column data.

The Naïve Bayes algorithm is less computationally intense than other Microsoft algorithms and therefore is useful for quickly discovering relationships between input columns—and can be run again and again as we explore the data.

1. Click the Detect Categories icon, in the Table Analysis Tools group on the Analyze tab of the Ribbon menu.

2. Click Run on the SQL Server Data Mining—Detect Categories dialog box.

In Figure 6-10 note the Detect Categories pop-up dialog box with the animated green-wheel icon. This provides a visible progress indication of Excel connecting to SQL Server, to analyze the data in the Excel table.

In Figure 6-11 you see the resulting Categories Characteristics Report for all columns in the original toxic chemical spreadsheet. It's really valuable that the

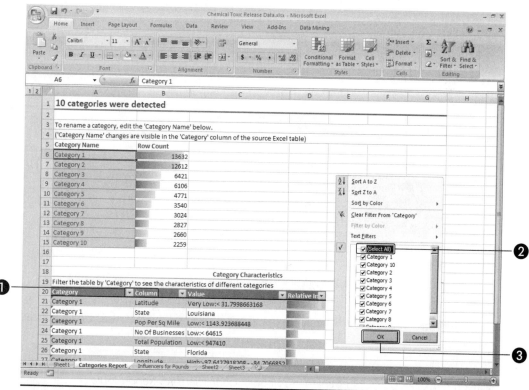

Figure 6-11 *Excel 2007 Data Mining—Categories Report table*

results are placed into an Excel table for us—with data filters at the top of each column. You can click the column data filters and narrow the data display to see the data categories the data mining tool has found.

1. Click the Category drop-down control, in the Category Characteristics table.
2. Choose the desired Categories to display in the pop-up menu.
3. Click OK.

Figure 6-12 shows the continuing thought process of analyzing the Categories Report, as we uncheck values to eliminate data points that are not of interest.

1. Click the Value drop-down control, in the Category Characteristics table.
2. Uncheck various filter items in the pop-up menu.
3. Click OK.

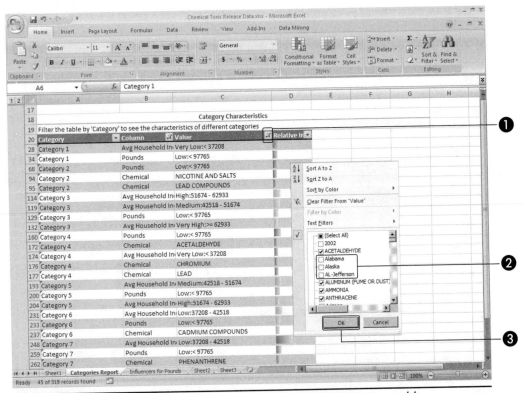

Figure 6-12 *Excel 2007 Data Mining—Category Characteristics Report table*

Notice that the Relative Importance column gives us a visual color gradient indicator to show the importance of the value elements—within the category. This is an example of automatic Excel conditional formatting, which is an important new feature in Excel 2007 (this is discussed in detail in other chapters).

Excel Table: Detect Categories Continuing Analysis

In Figure 6-13 we continue our analysis of the categories of data, by re-running the Detect Categories tool with fewer columns.

1. Click the Detect Categories icon, in the Table Analysis Tools group on the Analyze tab of the Ribbon menu.

2. Uncheck Year and other secondary data elements.

3. Check Chemical as a primary data element.

4. Check Pounds as a primary data element.

5. Click Run on the SQL Server Data Mining—Detect Categories dialog box.

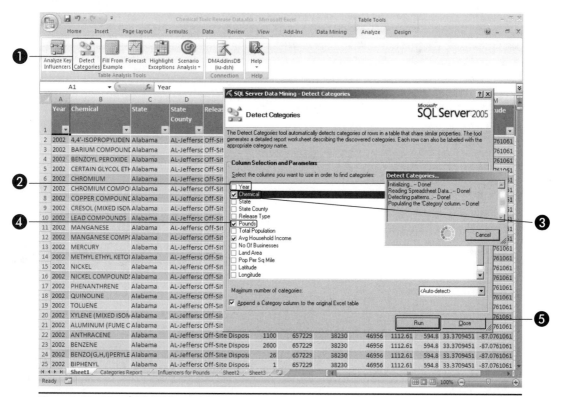

Figure 6-13 *Excel 2007 Data Mining Detect Categories tool, again!*

In Figure 6-13 we're checking only the data columns that we now suspect may play an interesting role in the toxic chemical release data. We then re-run the Detect Categories data mining tool to see the revised results shown in Figure 6-14.

1. Click the Value drop-down control, in the Category Characteristics table.

2. Uncheck the Missing filter items in the pop-up menu.

3. Click OK.

With the cleaner data display shown in Figure 6-14, we can simply uncheck anomalous values, such as Missing data, to see a coherent Excel table of data associations. The Detect Categories task also generates the PivotChart shown in Figure 6-15, which can be manipulated to show a compelling graphical representation of newly discovered data associations.

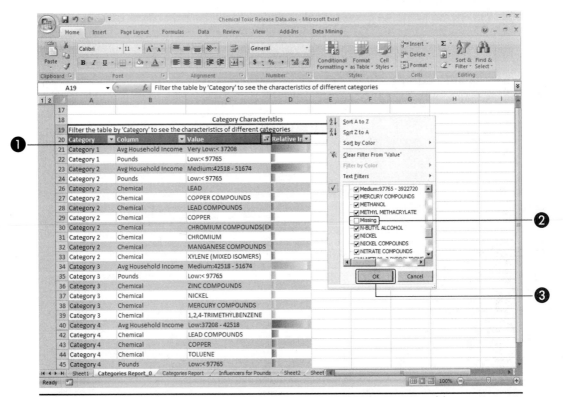

Figure 6-14 *Excel 2007 Data Mining—Category Characteristics Report table, again!*

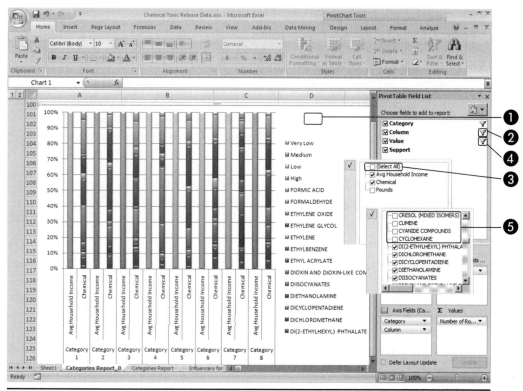

Figure 6-15 *Excel 2007 Data Mining—Category Characteristics Report chart*

1. Click the Chart area to display the PivotTable Field List pane for the chart.

2. Click the Column filter icon (right side of the field list).

3. Uncheck the (Select All) filter item in the pop-up menu, and check "Avg Household Income" and "Chemical".

4. Click the Value filter icon (right side of the field list).

5. Uncheck miscellaneous chemicals to narrow the display to those desired.

Figure 6-15 shows how we can uncheck Column values to control the horizontal axis display, and uncheck Value values to bring our data picture into focus. The result in this case is a coherent display of chemicals that we're concerned about—grouped into categories on the horizontal axis by Avg Household Income.

It's great that Excel 2007 supports this kind of advanced PivotChart with a multi-series data display—and it's automatically generated by the Detect Categories data mining tool. This is a good example of the value of bringing advanced analysis tools into our familiar Excel working desktop environment.

This analysis and display supports a line of questioning that might lend support to the often-mentioned hypothesis that toxic chemicals show up in economically poor areas of the country, where the populace cannot afford to fight polluters.

Figure 6-16 shows how we can edit the generic Category labels to reflect the discoveries we've made in our data association analysis.

1. Click the Category 2 cell of the top-level Category Characteristics report.

2. Enter the desired Category Name **Low Inc; LEAD COPPER** and press ENTER.

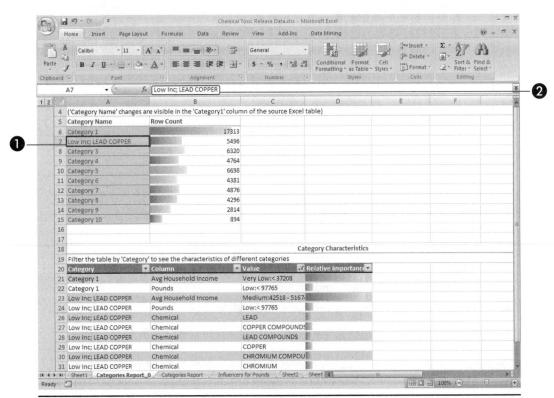

Figure 6-16 *Excel 2007 Data Mining—Category Characteristics Report naming*

In our working example shown in Figure 6-16, we are labeling Category 2 to be "Low Income; LEAD COPPER" data points. Now that we have a direction of reasoning, the Category labels are automatically displayed in the original spreadsheet of data as shown in Figure 6-17.

1. Click the new Category column filter icon, on the original Table data.
2. Check and uncheck desired categories for display.
3. Click OK.

Figure 6-17 shows how we have traveled full circle in our data mining exploration. The Category labels we changed on the Category Name table in Figure 6-16 are linked to the new Category column that has been automatically added to the original spreadsheet data. This is a feature of Excel 2007 tables, where new columns can be added to the table and become part of the coherent columnar display with data filter controls.

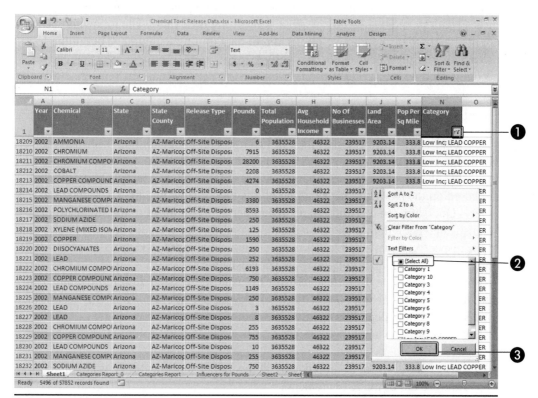

Figure 6-17 *Excel 2007 Data Mining—Category Characteristics table, Category column*

In our working example, we can now select the desired categories to display—and tell quite a story with the data that otherwise might not be discovered. The EPA data can be used in this manner to discover the reasons associated with toxic chemical releases by state and county—which comes home to where we live!

BI TIP

The Key Influencers and Detect Categories tools are probably the best everyday data mining features of the Excel 2007 Data Mining add-in. Given the time-proven 80-20 rule, most people will use these to discover associations with their data in Excel tables—and lend real value to help run their businesses.

Excel 2007: Data Mining Analyze Tab, Predictive Tools

The Analyze tab also has a set of tools with more of a predictive direction, where missing data should be filled in, or actual forecasting is of value. The following sections are not meant to be a complete discussion of data mining techniques, but rather to provide a brief presentation of the complete range of data mining tasks that can be accomplished with Excel 2007 connected to SQL Server Analysis Services 2005.

Excel Table: Fill From Example

Figure 6-18 shows how we start the Fill From Example data mining task. This can be used in two ways: to complete a partially filled column of data values, and to fill in a new column where the user has manually entered a few example values that are based on the row data. An example of this latter use would be where the user enters "Good" in one cell and "Bad" in another cell. The Fill From Example tool is sophisticated enough to pick up on the reasoning for these values based on other data in the respective rows—and to fill in remaining cells with Good and Bad that will correlate with row data throughout the spreadsheet rows.

Fill From Example uses the Microsoft Logistic Regression algorithm, which is a variation of the Microsoft Neural Network algorithm—it creates a neural network model that is equivalent to logistic regression.

In our working example, you'll fill in cells in the Pounds column that are empty.

1. Click the Fill From Example icon, in the Table Analysis Tools group on the Analyze tab of the Ribbon menu.

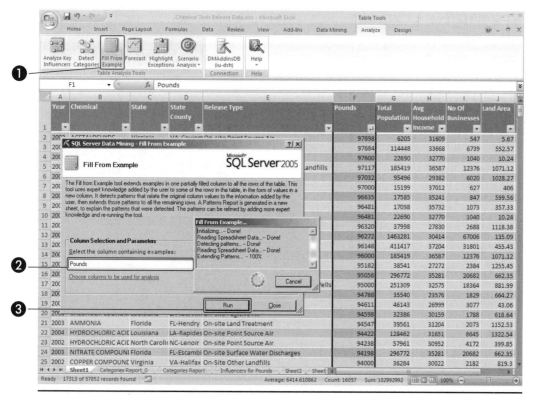

Figure 6-18 *Excel 2007 Data Mining Fill From Example tool*

2. Choose the Column with empty values to be filled in.

3. Click Run on the SQL Server Data Mining—Fill From Examples dialog box.

In Figure 6-18 note the Fill From Example pop-up dialog box with the animated green-wheel icon. This provides a visible progress indication of Excel connecting to SQL Server, to analyze the data in the Excel table.

Figure 6-19 shows the result of this data mining task, where a new column is added to the original spreadsheet to show suggested values for the missing Pounds cells. A Pattern Report is also generated as an Excel table, showing the row data values that influenced the automatically chosen values for empty Pounds cells.

a. A new column has been automatically added to the original spreadsheet, showing suggested Pounds values.

b. As you scroll down, the new values can be seen—where the data mining task has associated known Pounds values from other data rows with the rows shown.

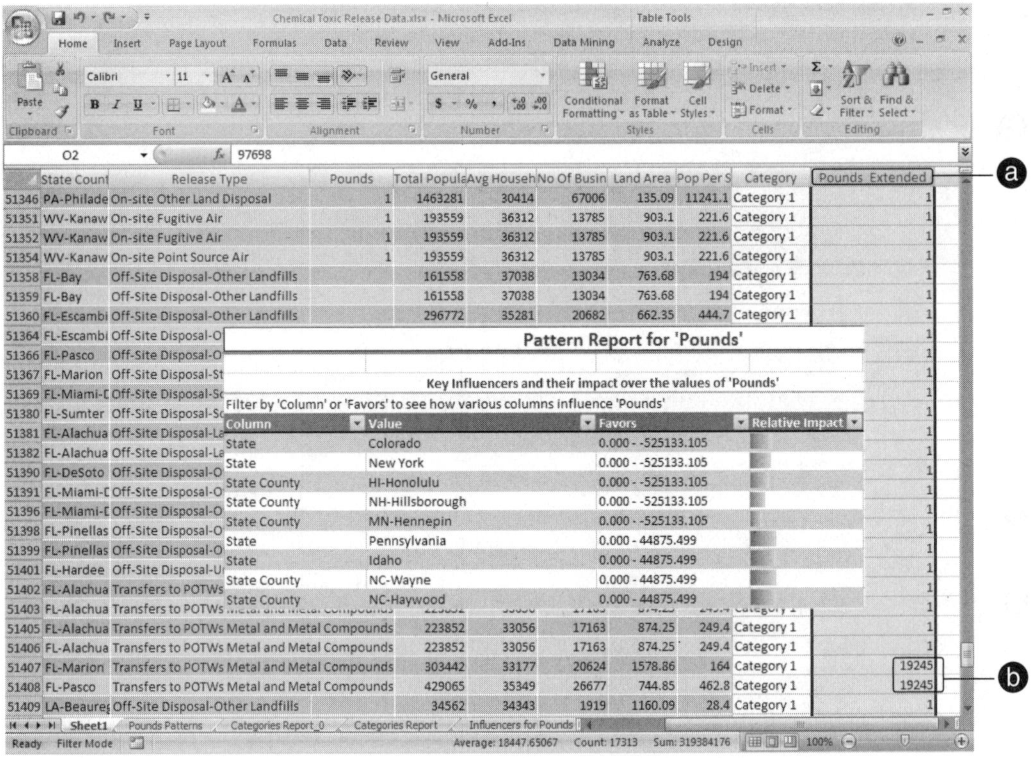

Figure 6-19 *Excel 2007 Data Mining—Fill From Example new column suggested values*

Excel Table: Forecast

Figure 6-20 shows the creation of a smaller table of data for our Forecast example. This is by design, since large data sets (such as tens of thousands of rows) will peg a normal desktop processor and potentially never return forecast data results.

For this reason, we've decided to work with a subset of data to show the concept in action. The Forecast data mining tool is quite powerful and uses the Microsoft Research Time Series algorithm, which is a regression algorithm used to predict continuous columns, such as chemical pounds released, in a forecasting scenario. It does not rely on designated input columns to predict the predictable column; instead, the prediction for the Time Series Model is based only on the trends that the algorithm derives from the original dataset of columns.

1. Holding the left mouse button down, drag the mouse to select the already-filled values of the partially filled column of values.

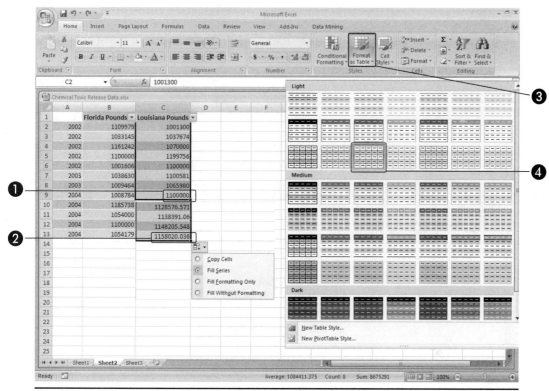

Figure 6-20 *Excel 2007 autofill empty cells with drag and drop*

2. Click the lower-left corner of the selected values, and drag the mouse down to the desired end cell to automatically fill in missing values.

3. Click the Format As Table icon, in the Styles group on the Home tab of the Ribbon menu.

4. Choose the desired table style.

Note that Figure 6-20 uses a simpler Auto-Fill feature of Excel 2007 that is very handy. Simply highlight a cell set and then drag the lower-left corner of the highlighted cell set down over empty cells; Excel will arithmetically generate new cell values based on the previously highlighted cell values. This is much different from the Excel Data Mining Fill From Example tool, which takes all associated row data into account when generating new cell values.

Figure 6-21 shows how we start the Forecast Data Mining task. A time-series column is required, which the Forecast tool will automatically use to generate

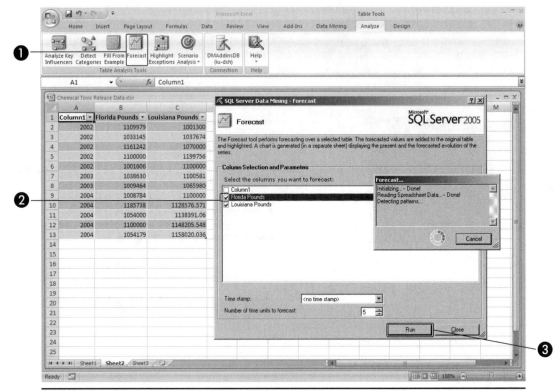

Figure 6-21 *Excel 2007 Data Mining Forecast tool*

future time units. In our working example, Column1 is numeric and shows the Year associated with current values.

1. Click the Forecast icon, in the Table Analysis Tools group on the Analyze tab of the Ribbon menu.

2. Check the desired columns to forecast.

3. Click Run on the SQL Server Data Mining—Forecast dialog box.

In Figure 6-21 note the Forecast pop-up dialog box with the animated green-wheel icon. This provides a visible progress indication of Excel connecting to SQL Server, to analyze the data in the Excel table.

Figure 6-22 shows the result of this data mining task, where new rows are added to the original spreadsheet to show suggested values for the future Pounds cells. *A Forecasting Report is also generated as an Excel chart, showing the projected trend lines of the data values.*

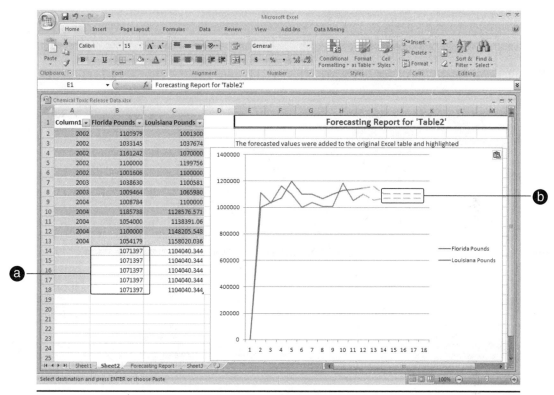

Figure 6-22 *Excel 2007 Data Mining—Forecast Report*

   a. New cell values are predicted for the five future units as selected in the Forecast tool.

   b. A dotted line shows the future predicted values of Pounds Released.

BI TIP

Forecasting is as much an art as it is a science, but the value of a statistically sound tool such as Excel Data Mining is immense in the right context. It can make data prediction a defensible exercise in discussions where people need to make decisions with forecasted data.

Excel Table: Highlight Exceptions

Figure 6-23 shows how we start the Highlight Exceptions Data Mining task. In our working example we'll choose to examine "Pounds" and "Total Population" to find outliers, or data that is too small or large for the row in which it resides.

Figure 6-23 *Excel 2007 Data Mining Highlight Exceptions tool*

This doesn't mean the outliers are wrong—just that we should look at them to understand the data and perhaps make a judgment call as to whether we should include the outliers in our statistical analysis.

Highlight Exceptions uses the Microsoft Clustering algorithm, which is a segmentation algorithm that uses iterative techniques to group cases in a data set into clusters that contain similar characteristics.

1. Click the Highlight Exceptions icon, in the Table Analysis Tools group on the Analyze tab of the Ribbon menu.

2. Check the desired columns to highlight.

3. Click Run on the SQL Server Data Mining—Highlight Exceptions dialog box.

In Figure 6-23 note the Highlight Exceptions pop-up dialog box with the animated green-wheel icon. This provides a visible progress indication of Excel connecting to SQL Server, to analyze the data in the Excel table.

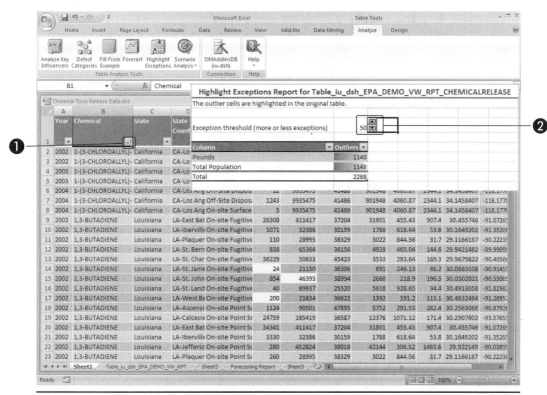

Figure 6-24 *Excel 2007 Data Mining—Highlight Exceptions Report and threshold control*

Figure 6-24 shows the result of this data mining task, where rows are highlighted to show the Pounds and Total Population extreme data values. A Highlight Exceptions Report is also generated as an Excel table, showing the number of outliers found and the statistical probability of the outlier values being wrong.

1. Click the Chemical filter icon, and choose to sort the original data in Ascending order.
2. Click the Up-Down dial control on the Highlight Exceptions Report, and change the Exception Threshold value.

Figure 6-24 shows the value of data mining tools that use Excel to display the results. In this case, the Highlight Exceptions Report provides an interactive Up-Down scroll control that can be used to change the statistical probability used to highlight outlier rows of data.

Changing the scroll control to a lower value immediately results in more cells and rows of data being highlighted in the original spreadsheet. This allows us to play with various levels of statistical outlier accuracy; in this case, we have decided to show all outliers that have a 50 percent probability of being wrong.

Excel Table: Goal Seek

Figure 6-25 shows how we start the Goal Seek Data Mining task. In our working example we'll choose to target "Florida Pounds" and seek a goal of "1008784", which we've chosen from the drop-down control. We also choose a column to vary, in seeking the goal—for which we'll choose "Number of Businesses", and we'll run the Goal Seek on the entire table.

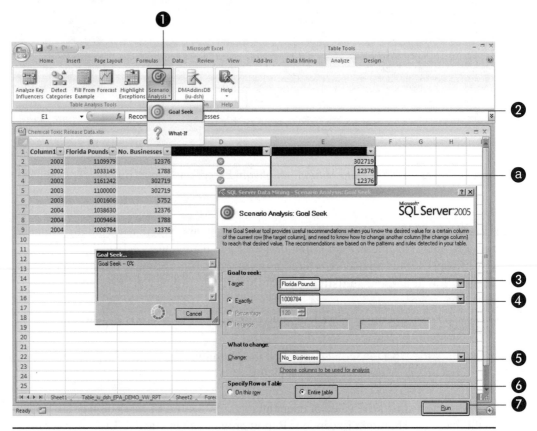

Figure 6-25   *Excel 2007 Data Mining Highlight Exceptions tool*

Goal Seek uses the Microsoft Logistic Regression algorithm, a variation of the Microsoft Neural Network algorithm that creates a neural network model. It relates input columns to the probability that the predictable column will contain specific values.

Note the Goal Seek pop-up dialog box with the animated green-wheel icon. This provides a visible progress indication of Excel connecting to SQL Server, to analyze the data in the Excel table.

1. Click the Scenario Analysis icon, in the Table Analysis Tools group on the Analyze tab of the Ribbon menu.

2. Choose the Goal Seek menu choice on the pop-up menu.

3. Choose the Target column to seek change, from the drop-down control.

4. Choose the Target value in the Exactly drop-down control.

5. Choose the column to Change in seeking the Target, from the drop-down control.

6. Select the Entire Table option button.

7. Click Run.

The result is straightforward, as shown by the annotation *a* in Figure 6-25. A total of 12376 businesses would need to be on the rows shown with green check marks, to achieve the desired pounds released. The red *x* means the Goal-Seek was unable to achieve the desired goal for that row, by changing the change value.

Although this example is simple, it illustrates the power of a statistically sound forecasting tool that can be quickly targeted to specific rows or an entire table. This would greatly assist a discussion of the possible determinants of chemical release amounts—that could be changed by design or public policy.

Excel Table: What-If

Figure 6-26 shows how we start the What-If Data Mining task. In our working example we'll choose to change "Number of Businesses" to 1788 (chosen from the drop-down control), and see what happens to the "Florida Pounds" values for the entire table.

What-If uses the Microsoft Logistic Regression algorithm, a variation of the Microsoft Neural Network algorithm that creates a neural network model. It relates input columns to the probability that the predictable column will contain specific values.

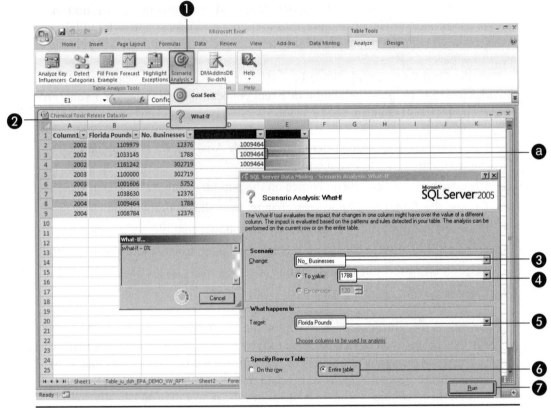

Figure 6-26 *Excel 2007 Data Mining What-If tool*

Note the What-If pop-up dialog box with the animated green-wheel icon. This provides a visible progress indication of Excel connecting to SQL Server, to analyze the data in the Excel table.

1. Click the Scenario Analysis icon, in the Table Analysis Tools group on the Analyze tab of the Ribbon menu.
2. Choose the What-If menu choice on the pop-up menu.
3. Choose the Change column to seek change, from the drop-down control.
4. Choose the target value in the To Value drop-down control.
5. Choose What Happens To Florida Pounds from the drop-down control.
6. Select the Entire Table option button.
7. Click Run.

The result is shown by the annotation *a* in Figure 6-26. A total of 1009464 "Florida Pounds" released would be achieved by changing the "Number of Businesses" to 1788.

Again, although this example is simple, it illustrates the power of a statistically sound What-If tool that can be used to see the effects of changing column values in an Excel table. This is the parallel tool to the Goal Seeker tool and could be a dynamic part of the discussion about what can realistically be changed in the world of toxic chemical handling to reduce the chemical release amounts.

Excel 2007: Data Mining Tab Tools

This is a more advanced area of Excel Data Mining. Although it uses the same connection to SQL Server 2005 Analysis Services to leverage the Microsoft Research statistical analysis tools, it provides a more sophisticated set of menus to configure the data mining experience.

The tools on this Data Mining tab are quite literally a client version of the SQL Server 2005 Data Mining tools. The difference is that we're able to do our work from within Excel instead of Visual Studio, which has long been the Data Mining design environment for SQL Server. These client tools allow us to save our work as "data mining models," which support the reuse of our configurations with new Excel tables. The data mining models are stored on the SQL Server 2005 server. And as you'll see in a later section, the data mining models can be used with Visio 2007 to provide a graphical representation of our work.

The following discussion will just touch on a few of the aspects of this toolset, to get an idea of how we create a data mining model in Excel and show it in Visio.

Excel Model: Explore Data

Figure 6-27 shows how we start the Explore Data task. In our working example we'll choose to examine the Excel table of chemical release data, and look at the Latitude column of data. We could look at any column of data—and it's fairly quick to change to another column—but for the purpose of our discussion we just want to see what the Explore Data task displays.

Note the Outliers pop-up dialog box with the animated green-wheel icon. This provides a visible progress indication of Excel connecting to SQL Server, to analyze the data in the Excel table.

1. Click the Data Mining tab on the Ribbon menu.
2. Click the Explore Data icon in the Data Preparation group.

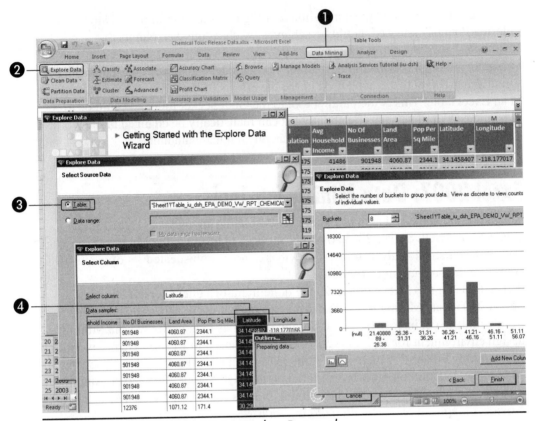

Figure 6-27 *Excel 2007 Data Mining Explore Data tool*

3. Choose the Table to explore from the drop-down control.

4. Choose the desired column to explore, from the drop-down control, and click Run.

The result is shown by the annotation *a* in Figure 6-27. A grouping of Latitudes shows a preponderance of chemical releases occurring around certain geographical areas. Other Latitudes with extreme values, small or large, are shown in the Explore Data chart—and might be considered "outliers" of data. Outliers could be significant or something to be deleted if we think they are incorrect data points.

Excel Model: Cluster

Figure 6-28 shows how we start the Cluster Data Mining task. In our working example we'll choose to examine the Excel table of chemical release data and look at the Chemical, State, and Pounds columns of data.

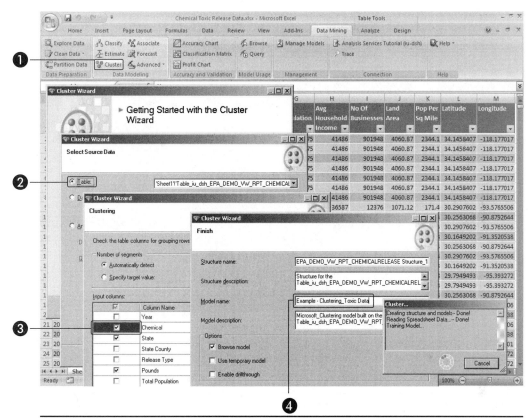

Figure 6-28 *Excel 2007 Data Mining Cluster tool*

We are going to look at the Cluster tool because it is similar to the Detect Cluster tool used earlier in this chapter. This Cluster tool provides a more advanced set of options for configuring the analysis, and the output will be saved as a data mining model.

1. Click the Cluster icon, in the Data Modeling group on the Ribbon menu.
2. Choose the Table to explore from the drop-down control.
3. Check the desired columns to analyze.
4. Enter a name in the Model Name text box, and click Run.

So far, the process of using the Cluster tool is very similar to what we saw with the Detect Cluster tool. However, Figure 6-29 shows some different result screens that support further manipulation of the data.

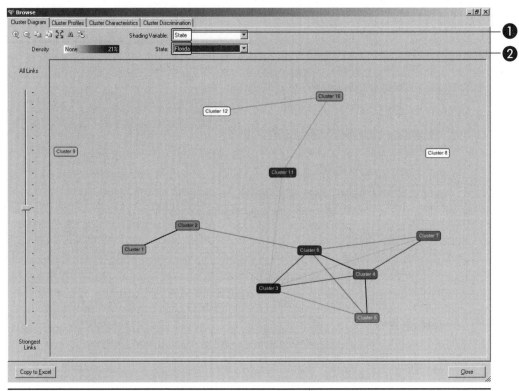

Figure 6-29 *Excel 2007—Cluster diagram*

1. Choose the desired Shading Variable in the drop-down control.
2. Choose the desired State in the drop-down control.

The Cluster diagram in Figure 6-29 shows a graphical representation of the data associations found in the Excel table rows. The significant clusters or nodes of data are shown as rounded rectangles—and the drop-down control at the top allow us to select different columns and values to dynamically see which nodes they influence.

In our working example, the State of Florida does not significantly affect nodes 12 and 8.

Figure 6-30 shows the next tab of the Cluster analysis result display.

1. Click the Cluster Profiles tab in the Cluster Browse dialog box.
2. Click the "Avg Household Income" area in the Attributes Variables list.

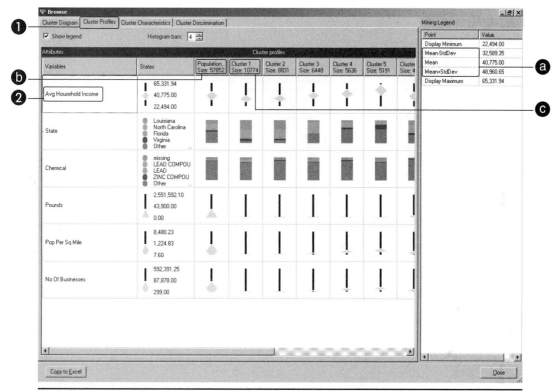

Figure 6-30 *Excel 2007—Cluster Profiles*

In Figure 6-30, selecting "Avg Household Income" results in the statistical analysis values display on the right side of the screen (see *a*). This stat display will change as each area of the Variables column is selected.

Note the annotations *b* and *c*, which point out the number of rows that make up each cluster. The "Population" cluster represents all clusters combined. It's pretty easy to spot useful information right away on this display; for example, the relative placement of Avg Household Income values in Cluster 1, which are lower than the Avg Household Income values across the entire Population data set.

Figure 6-31 shows the next tab of the Cluster analysis result display.

1. Click the Cluster Characteristics tab in the Cluster Browse dialog box.

2. Choose the desired Cluster in the drop-down box.

3. Click Copy To Excel.

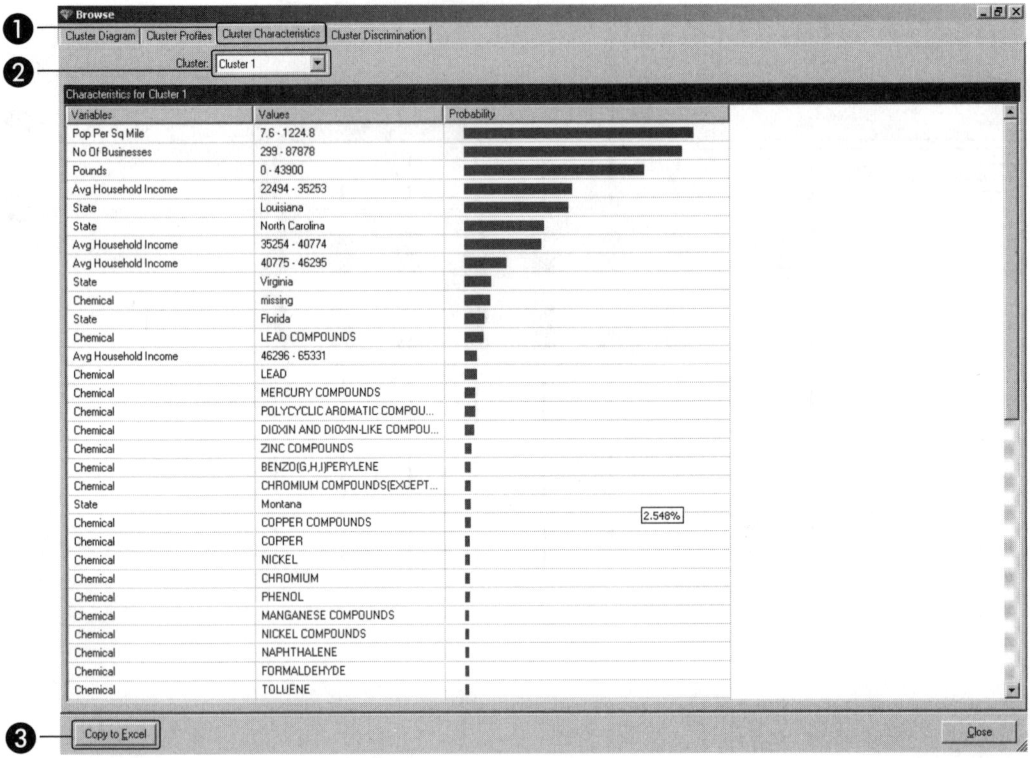

Figure 6-31   *Excel 2007—Cluster Characteristics*

In Figure 6-31, we have a great display of the relative weight of specific data values that determine the clustering of data. This is perhaps the clearest of the display devices in the Cluster tool, since it's so easy to choose the different clusters in the drop-down control and get an immediate sense of the chemical release values that are significant to each Cluster data group.

Figure 6-32 shows the results of using the Cluster display Copy To Excel button.

1.   Click the States column filter icon.

2.   Uncheck miscellaneous values that are not desired in the display.

3.   Click OK.

Chemical Toxic Release Data.xlsx - Microsoft Excel

Home · Insert · Page Layout · Formulas · Data · Review · View · Add-Ins · Data Mining

Explore Data · Clean Data · Partition Data | Classify · Estimate · Cluster | Associate · Forecast · Advanced | Accuracy Chart · Classification Matrix · Profit Chart | Browse · Query | Manage Models | Analysis Services Tutorial (lu-dsh) | Help · Trace

Data Preparation · Data Modeling · Accuracy and Validation · Model Usage · Management · Connection · Help

A1 — *fx* Example - Clustering_Toxic Data

Variables	States	Population (All)	Cluster 1	Cluster 2	Cluster 3	Cluster 4	Cluster 5	Cluster 6	Cluster
Avg Househo		40,775.00	35,873.24	36,749.46	41,981.18	45,455.23	52,219.26	40,851.57	39,94
Avg Househo		8,185.65	6,455.16	6,340.44	6,244.17	8,226.22	10,481.53	8,513.32	1,92
State		11069	43%	41%	12%	7%	1%	21%	
State		10625	33%	33%	28%	14%	9%	20%	
State		6449	9%	10%	21%	14%	11%	18%	
State		4275	11%	8%	1%	6%	21%	10%	
State		3086	0%	0%	0%	0%	0%	0%	
State		1647	0%	0%	0%	0%	0%	0%	
State		1410	0%	0%	0%	0%	0%	0%	
State		1317	0%	0%	0%	0%	0%	0%	
Chemical		2919	8%	4%	6%	5%	8%	2%	
Chemical		2212	5%	1%	8%	2%	8%	1%	
Chemical		2196	3%	5%	3%	6%	3%	5%	
Chemical		1541	2%	2%	3%	4%	3%	2%	
Chemical		1407	1%	5%	1%	3%	1%	7%	
Chemical		1401	2%	2%	3%	3%	3%	2%	
Chemical		1346	3%	2%	2%	3%	2%	2%	
Pounds		43,900.00	61.42	8,086.31	68.85	4,414.53	78.95	110,440.44	25
Pounds	Deviation	835,897.37	95.27	10,626.43	104.19	4,397.90	110.93	117,969.18	33
Pop Per Sq Mile	Mean	1,224.83	110.47	139.9	443.48	1,071.16	1,497.46	697.38	1,28
Pop Per Sq Mile	Deviation	2,418.47	65.59	81.74	204.9	599.04	755.31	645.17	50
No Of Businesses	Mean	87,878.00	4,886.30	6,503.08	25,379.35	54,831.91	80,051.46	33,507.94	53,25
No Of Businesses	Deviation	168,171.00	3,693.06	4,801.79	10,358.32	33,907.53	45,031.02	33,290.11	12,05

Dropdown: Sort A to Z · Sort Z to A · Sort by Color · Clear Filter From "States" · Filter by Color · Text Filters · (Select All) · AMMONIA · California · CHROMIUM COMPOUNDS(E · COPPER COMPOUNDS · Deviation · Florida · Illinois · OK · Cancel

Sheet1 · Cluster Diagram · **Cluster Profiles** · Cluster Characteristics · Cluster Discrimination

Ready   23 of 27 records found   100%

Figure 6-32 *Excel 2007—Cluster Characteristics, copied to Excel*

In Figure 6-32 we see a really advanced Excel table rendition of the Cluster analysis. The States column data filter allows us to easily select the data values for display, which in this case are the chemicals we're interested in exploring. The subsequent columns have Excel conditional formatting, which is one of the most important new features in Excel 2007. Indeed, this Excel table could not have been adequately displayed in earlier versions of Excel.

BI TIP

New versions of software applications we use in our daily work have features that are compelling in their own right—but those new features may be very significant when connected to other applications. Excel 2007 with SQL Server 2005 Data Mining is an example of two applications that work together better than either would alone, and in ways that were not possible with earlier versions.

Visio 2007: Data Mining Cluster Diagram

Visio 2007 provides the final presentation of our SQL Server 2005 Data Mining model. Having used the Excel 2007 Data Mining add-in Client tool to accomplish cluster analysis, we can now display the resulting model that was saved to SQL Server.

Figure 6-33 shows how we start this process with Visio 2007.

1. Click the Cluster icon in the Visio Shapes list, and drag it onto the Visio sheet.
2. Choose the Analysis Services connection used earlier for the Excel Cluster analysis.
3. Choose the Example Clustering_ Toxic Data Mining model saved earlier in the Excel Cluster analysis.

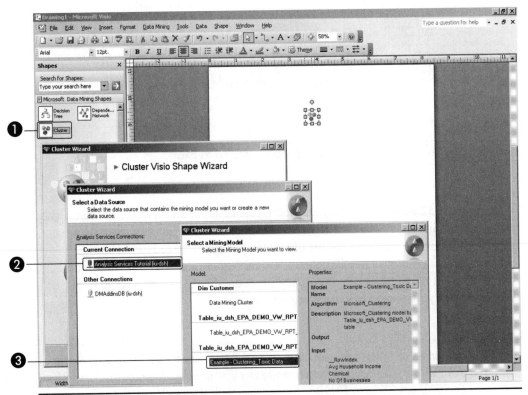

Figure 6-33 *Visio 2007 Data Mining cluster*

In Figure 6-33 you see a set of Data Mining Shapes in the left pane that are part of the Excel and Visio 2007 Data Mining download from Microsoft. In our working example, you'll simply drag the Cluster shape onto the Visio canvas. This proceeds to the steps shown in Figure 6-34, where you'll be able to choose a Cluster display configuration.

1. Check the "Show clusters with characteristics chart" option button, on the Cluster Wizard dialog box.
2. Click Finish.

Note in Figure 6-34 that Visio is connecting to SQL Server 2005 to render the Data Mining cluster—as shown by the green check-icons. The result is shown in Figure 6-35, where you see a Visio Data Mining Cluster diagram with "Characteristics" for all nodes.

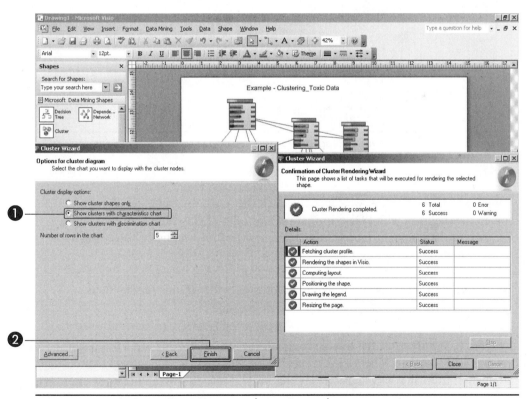

Figure 6-34 *Visio 2007 Data Mining—Cluster Wizard*

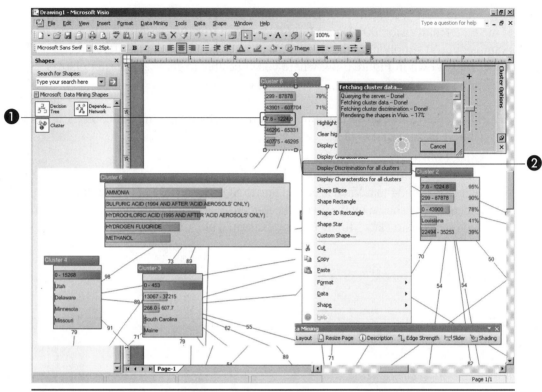

Figure 6-35 *Visio 2007—Cluster diagram, properties and display change*

Figure 6-35 shows how we can right-click the Visio diagram and choose to display the diagram with "Discrimination" for all nodes, which connects to the SQL Server data model to provide a different set of information about each node of associated data on the cluster diagram.

1. Right-click a cluster in the diagram, to display the actions pop-up menu.
2. Choose "Display Discrimination for all clusters".

Figure 6-35 shows off the live-data capabilities of Visio 2007—it's not just a drawing tool anymore! The Visio Cluster Shape is a "data aware" object that displays information from an Analysis Services Data Mining model—which in our example is showing the chemicals and other data elements that make up the nodes of the cluster diagram. This is an example of the benefit of creating a Data Mining model when working with Excel Data Mining—the resulting model can be re-surfaced in other tools as you see with Visio 2007.

Figure 6-36 shows the finished Visio 2007 Cluster diagram, with a Cluster Options control and a floating toolbar for display options.

1. Hold the left mouse button down on the slider control, and move it to see fewer or more cluster connections.

2. Click the Layout icon on the Data Mining toolbar to rearrange the diagram.

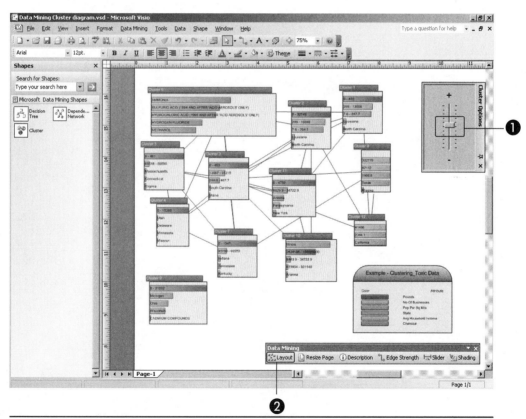

Figure 6-36 *Visio 2007—Cluster diagram, on-screen controls*

In Figure 6-36 the Cluster Options slider control changes the number of connection lines between the nodes within the Cluster diagram. Sliding the control down toward the negative symbol lowers the probability threshold of line connections to display between nodes. Thus a lower threshold displays more lines; a higher threshold toward the positive symbol displays fewer lines—which are those with a higher statistical probability of data similarity between the nodes!

Clicking the Edge Strength icon in the floating toolbar displays the probability (on a scale from 0 to 100) on each connector line between the cluster nodes. This interactive control display in Visio is a capability that really gets the attention of people today—as you realize that Visio 2007 provides an interactive data-connected analysis device that is unique in the world of business intelligence tools!

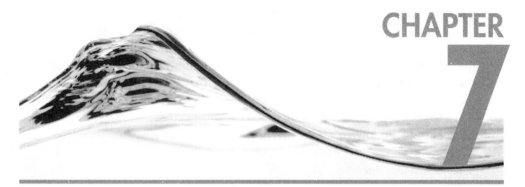

PerformancePoint: Dashboards, Scorecards, and Key Performance Indicators

P erformancePoint server trades on the name of SharePoint, and this is by design since the purpose of PerformancePoint is to bring enterprise-level "Balanced Scorecards" into the SharePoint portal framework. It is really two applications under the banner of PerformancePoint: Monitoring and Analysis (M & A) and Planning, which holds the promise of providing a SQL Server Analysis Services (OLAP)-based model to which Excel planning templates can connect. This is truly part of the future of Microsoft business intelligence.

Examples of the following topics will be provided in this chapter:

▶ Dashboard Designer

▶ Key Performance Indicators and Scorecards

▶ Analytic Charts and Grids

▶ Strategy Maps

BEST REFERENCE

For further research on this topic, go to http://performancepointinsider.com/blogs.

Technology Positioning Statement

PerformancePoint 2007 is a significant new Office technology that puts visual Performance Indicators into an integrated Dashboard display, and delivers them in a secure SharePoint environment. Top-level Dashboard Filters guide the entire display and allow consumers to literally explore the data behind performance metrics shown in the PerformancePoint Scorecards.

With SQL Server Analysis Services as the foundation for Scorecards, we can now offer interactive Key Performance Indicators and live Analytic Grids and Charts to thousands of users across global organizations. And all this is done with Designers that support drag-and-drop access to Cube Measures and Dimensions.

PerformancePoint is quite simply the enterprise front-end display of choice for performance measurement in today's global organizations.

—Steve Handy, Microsoft PerformancePoint Team

What Is a PerformancePoint Scorecard?

PerformancePoint 2007, previously known as Microsoft Business Scorecard Manager, is an improved scorecard design and delivery application—wrapped inside a Dashboard Designer that contains the scorecard and associated charts and grids. Earlier versions of PerformancePoint (Business Scorecard Manager) required significant work by online analytical processing (OLAP) cube designers to generate custom Multidimensional Expressions (MDX) queries in support of the scorecards.

PerformancePoint changes this paradigm, where the integrated Scorecard Designer allows us to drag and drop Key Performance Indicators and SQL Server 2005 Analysis Services cube measures and dimensions onto a design canvas where the resulting hierarchical data cells provide a multidimensional display of actual metric, target, and threshold data.

But first, let's define what we mean when using the term "PerformancePoint Scorecard." A *scorecard* is a display of performance measurements, typically in several columns across a set of time elements such as Calendar Quarters. Most often, the rows represent the hierarchical structure of the organization being measured (office, department, etc.) and the columns show Key Performance Indicator (KPI) Actuals and Targets by time period—with the numeric KPI metrics in the cells of the row-column scorecard. PerformancePoint can support multiple

Key Performance Indicators in a scorecard, either as a top-level row grouping or as a repeating set of columns showing Actual and Target values.

The resulting scorecards can be connected to live data through the SQL Server Analysis Services cube, and we can add *analytic charts* and *analytic grids,* which provide a drill-down experience into the data that supports the scorecard(s). All of this is delivered using Windows SharePoint Services (WSS) version 3 or SharePoint 2007 (which runs on top of WSS), since the PerformancePoint dashboards and scorecards are rendered as SharePoint web pages.

In PerformancePoint, scorecards contain KPIs, which are simply measures that we choose to track our progress or success for any organizational effort. KPIs provide a common basis for working toward organizational goals, and they help teams work in a common direction when everyone can see live-data KPIs on a PerformancePoint scorecard.

Where Does PerformancePoint Fit in the Microsoft BI Picture?

The accompanying illustration shows a matrix view of Microsoft Business Intelligence technology (often referred to as BI). The Office, SharePoint, and SQL Server applications we see in the marketplace are shown on the left side of the matrix. These applications are used in the real-world activities of reporting, analysis, measurement, and planning as shown across the top of the matrix. The top-down flow of the matrix starts with front-end BI tools we have in Office 2007 at our desktops and extends down to back-end BI tools that run on servers such as SharePoint 2007 and PerformancePoint 2007 that provide an enhanced experience when connected to Office 2007.

The "You are here!" bubble in the illustration shows PerformancePoint analytic charts and grids, and also scorecards, which contain Key Performance Indicators. SharePoint is the enterprise delivery technology that allows PerformancePoint scorecards to be published for widescale use. PerformancePoint and SharePoint are server applications from the Microsoft Office group of products.

We're going use the PerformancePoint Dashboard Designer to design a scorecard with KPIs and associated analytic charts and grids—and then we'll "publish" the results to SharePoint. The PerformancePoint scorecards can be designed to use relational data sources, but we're going to focus on SQL Server Analysis Services (SSAS) OLAP cubes as the data source, which is part of the SQL Server 2005 foundation of the BI matrix.

PerformancePoint 2007 is a Microsoft technology that has achieved a new maturity in business intelligence "scorecarding." The challenge of combining Key Performance Indicators with a built-in hierarchical data structure to reflect the organization—with multiple "Target" definitions that can answer real-world questions—has been answered.

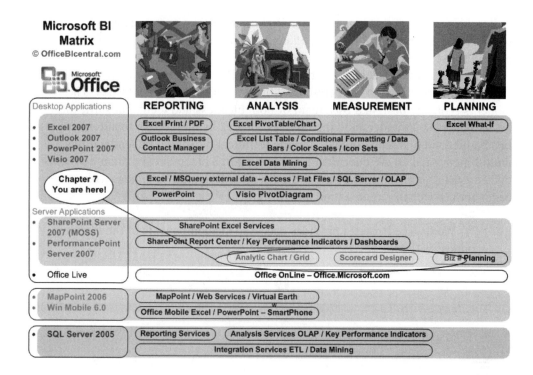

BI TIP

Scorecard applications have been a specialized area of business intelligence for many years. The Microsoft PerformancePoint server changes the market with an off-the-shelf scorecard application that does not require custom programming and is targeted to global enterprises — based on the scalability of SQL Server 2005 Analysis Services OLAP cubes.

PerformancePoint 2007 Planning

PerformancePoint is really made up of two server applications: the Monitoring and Analysis application with its dashboards, scorecards, and analytic charts/grids (which are discussed in this chapter), and the Planning application, which is a unique budgeting and forecasting application. Together, the applications are presented in Microsoft literature as a single platform that supports the monitoring, analysis, and planning processes of organizations that are using business intelligence to both measure and project performance. The acronym "MAP" is sometimes used to headline these discussions.

For the purpose of understanding the PerformancePoint server technology, this section takes a very brief look at the Planning application, but a full exploration is beyond the scope of our discussion.

Figure 7-1 shows the design environment for a Planning *model,* which is a sophisticated combination of hierarchical budget data and business rules. The model is typically designed by a team of both business and technical staff; the business personnel understand the business processes they'd like to automate in a budget and planning context, and the technical personnel understand the multidimensional OLAP cube data that can support a hierarchical planning process in their organization. Note the Visual Studio–like design environment with screen panes for component organization and design.

   a. The Workspace Browser provides access to the components of the Planning application.

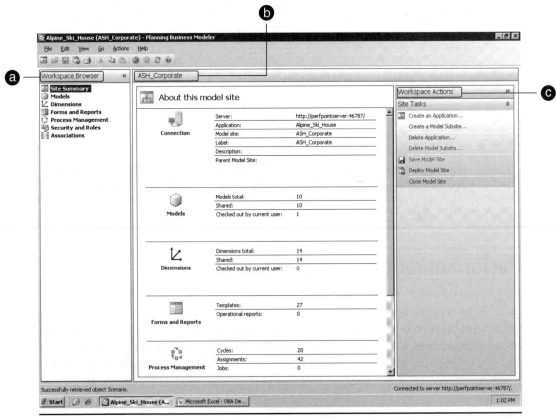

Figure 7-1   *PerformancePoint Planning Business Modeler*

b. The design pane supports the design and configuration of the root model site, model subsites, and components of the planning application.

c. The Workspace Actions pane allows us to start the creation of a planning application and its models.

You can quickly see, in looking at Figure 7-1 and the preceding discussion, that the planning application contains models of budgeting and planning processes, input forms and output reports, and process management workflow rules. This combination is a specialized area of business intelligence. However, it is quite important to large organizations that have been running their planning processes with disconnected Excel spreadsheets. These organizations have a real need to bring a server-based order to their world with an approach such as PerformancePoint Planning that can replace manual planning methods with a centralized repository of formulas and data.

Many organizations have an existing system of independent Excel spreadsheets they use to run their budgeting and planning process and to communicate with geographically dispersed offices or regions. Microsoft PerformancePoint Planning is unique in being able to migrate this existing process to a server-based budgeting, planning, and forecasting model that relies on the SQL Server 2005 Business Intelligence Platform. This server-based Analysis Services Model provides a central repository of hierarchical "plan" data that supports the overlay of business rules and business workflow procedures such as approval and forwarding.

In Figure 7-2 you see an example Excel template that dynamically connects end-users to the server-based model.

a. The PerformancePoint Planning Excel add-in creates a new Ribbon menu context tab for PerformancePoint connections and assignments.

b. The connection to the PerformancePoint server supports dynamic input and output of planning data from within Excel.

c. The PerformancePoint Excel Action pane organizes the assignments, such as an Excel form that is ready for input.

As Figure 7-2 shows, end users who are participating in the planning process use pre-designed Excel Templates interfaces to dynamically connect to the server model. This allows finance-planning personnel to use familiar Excel tools to input data to the server-based Planning model, and to use Excel reports that provide output data from the entire budget, planning, and forecasting solution. In this manner, Microsoft's PerformancePoint server enables Excel users to accomplish "collaborative Excel planning" in both online and offline, with all historical, current, and future data on a secure SQL Server platform.

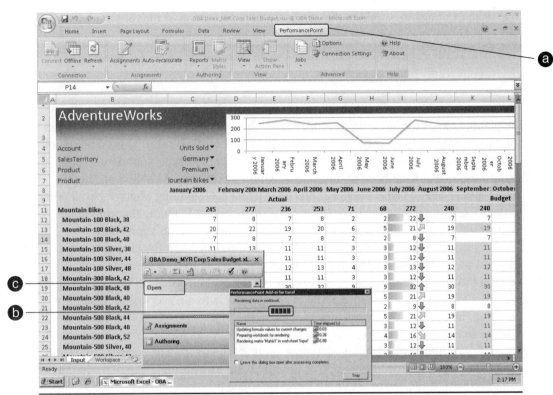

Figure 7-2 *PerformancePoint Planning Excel add-in*

PerformancePoint 2007 Dashboard Designer

From this point forward in the chapter we'll explore the PerformancePoint Monitoring and Analysis application (sometimes referred to as "M & A"). Figure 7-3 shows the PerformancePoint 2007 Dashboard Designer. It uses the Office 2007 Ribbon menu user interface, which gives the immediate look and feel of Microsoft Office applications. The Dashboard Designer is a simplified version of the Visual Studio integrated design environment, with content panes on the left, a design canvas in the center, and "explorer" panes on the right to find all the components of the dashboard design.

1. Click the Office Button icon.
2. Choose Open on the pop-up menu.
3. Browse to the desired dashboard sample, and click Open.

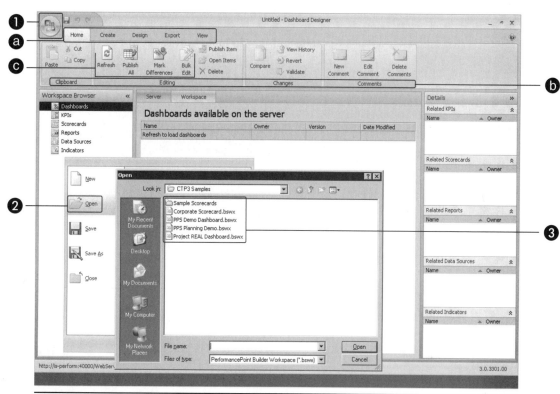

Figure 7-3   *PerformancePoint 2007 Dashboard Designer*

The PerformancePoint screen in Figure 7-3 shows off the new Office 2007 Ribbon menu that provides a consistent user interface experience. There are many pieces to bring together into a PerformancePoint dashboard, and the new design interface intuitively helps understand the connections between dashboards, scorecards, Key Performance Indicators, and reports (analytic charts and analytic grids).

Looking at Figure 7-3, you see the main levels of the new Office 2007 Ribbon menu:

a. Looking at the PerformancePoint Ribbon, you see a top-level tab interface that organizes spreadsheet tasks into common areas: Home, Create, Design, Export, and View.

b. Looking across the tabs, you see a variety of submenu tasks in groups: Clipboard, Editing, Changes, and Comments.

c. Looking within the Editing Tools group, you see a variety of icon menu items for Refresh, Publish All, Mark Differences, and Bulk Edit. The Publish All icon is routinely used to synchronize the Scorecard, KPI, and Report components of the dashboard, which updated the display seen in SharePoint 2007!

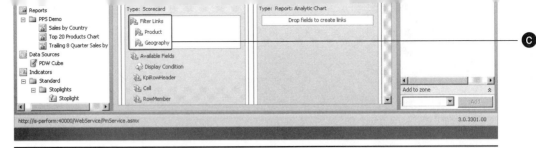

Figure 7-4 *PerformancePoint 2007 Dashboard Designer Summary tab*

Figure 7-4 shows a sample PerformancePoint 2007 dashboard in design mode. Designers can put multiple scorecards, KPIs, and report charts or grids into a dashboard. In this example we'll explore dashboard top-level filters, a scorecard, and an analytic chart that are connected to the top-level filters.

1. Click the PPS Demo Dashboard item in the left-pane Workspace Browser tree list.
2. Click to expand the scorecards, reports, and filters on the right-pane Available Items.

In Figure 7-4 we get our first look at the new PerformancePoint Dashboard Designer. All related components are accessible on the screen, and you can see them at a glance. The following highlights of the Dashboard Designer screen follow the *a, b,* and *c* annotations in Figure 7-3.

a. The Details right-side pane contains the components that are contained in the dashboard. Simply click the Expand and Collapse controls to see the scorecards, reports, and filters that are included in the current dashboard display.

b. The Filters in the Header of the dashboard can be connected to scorecards and analytic charts/grids in the dashboard. The filters are connected to Cube Dimension data elements, which are also designated to be Filter Links in the subsidiary Scorecard and Analytic components.

c. The Filter Links are displayed in the Scorecard pane and the Analytic Chart/Grid pane. This provides an on-screen visual linking mechanism that effectively parameterizes the entire dashboard display.

In Figure 7-5 you can see the Properties of the dashboard.

1. Click the PPS Demo Dashboard item in the left-pane Workspace Browser tree list.
2. Click the Properties tab over the design pane.

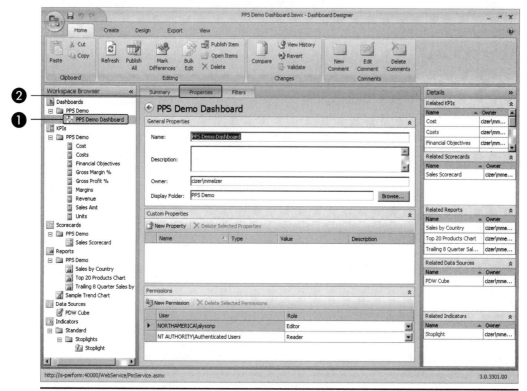

Figure 7-5   *PerformancePoint 2007 Dashboard Designer Properties tab*

Figure 7-5 shows the Properties tab of the Dashboard Designer pane. More important, it shows a Details pane on the right side that helps us see all the components that are associated with this dashboard. Related Data Sources, Related KPIs, Related Scorecards, Related Reports, and Related Indicators are all clickable elements that help navigate to the respective design interfaces.

Note the Workplace Browser left-side pane shows all such components that are available to the dashboard design process—but only the right-side Details pane shows those components that have actually been designed into the dashboard presentation.

Dashboard Filters

Figure 7-6 provides a look at the top-level dashboard filters and their configuration.

1. Click the PPS Demo Dashboard item in the left-pane Workspace Browser tree list.
2. Click the Filters tab over the design pane.

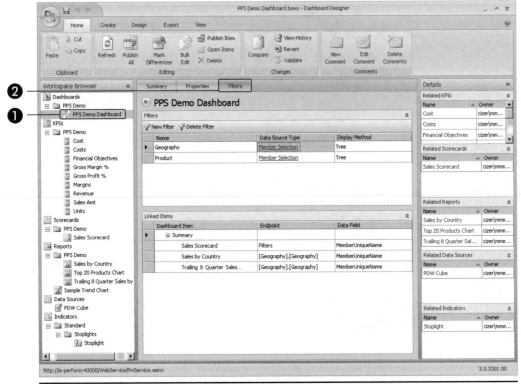

Figure 7-6   *PerformancePoint 2007 Dashboard Designer Filters tab*

In Figure 7-6 you see the Filters tab that allows us to configure the data filters to display at the top level of the dashboard display. Note these dashboard filters are *not connected* to subsidiary scorecard or analytic components until we explicitly define such connections, as we'll discuss later in this chapter.

Figure 7-7 shows the configuration that supports the dashboard filters, which are simply connected to SQL Server Analysis Services 2005 Cube Dimension data elements.

1. Click the Member Selection link in the Filters Data Source Type column.
2. Click Next after viewing the Filter dimension data element Name.
3. Click Next after viewing the Analysis Services cube Name.

In Figure 7-7 you see a concept in PerformancePoint that is important—and that stems from real-world experience with dashboard design projects. Dashboard filters provide a parameterization of scorecards that is critical to their use in everyday

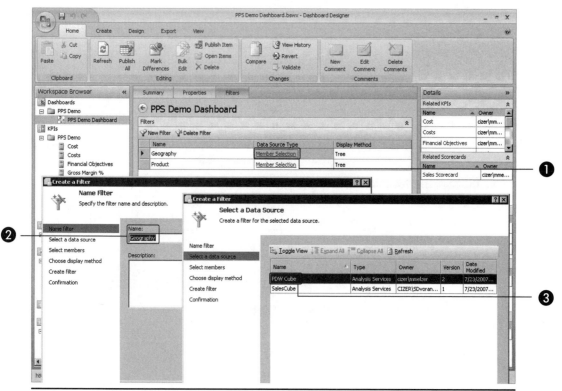

Figure 7-7   *PerformancePoint 2007 dashboard filter data configuration*

working environments. Through filters we can effectively view multiple dashboards (and scorecards) that display data only for chosen departments of the organization. The filter-scorecard experience relies heavily on the hierarchical nature of Analysis Services cubes that can reflect the organizational levels and allows us to show different scorecards that are based on a single master scorecard.

BI TIP

Interactive business intelligence displays that allow us to explore organization hierarchies are best constructed on OLAP multidimensional cubes. The "slice and dice" look at our business processes by program and by department should be constructed on the multidimensional Analysis Services foundation of SQL Server 2005.

Figure 7-8 continues the discussion of dashboard filter design.

1. Click the Select Dimension control in the Filters Select Members dialog box.

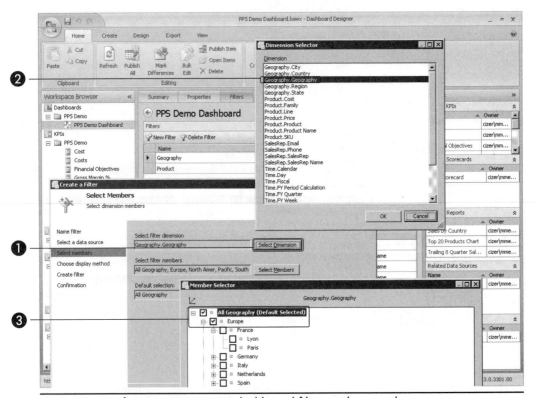

Figure 7-8   *PerformancePoint 2007 dashboard filter—select members*

2. Choose a Dimension from the pop-up list, and click OK.
3. Check the desired Dimension values to be used as filters.

Figure 7-8 shows a browse capability that allows us to explore and choose data values to display in the filters. It's surprising to see how quickly dashboard/scorecard designers learn this process when it becomes apparent that the OLAP cube data values reflect the organization in which they work.

Figure 7-9 shows how we finish the filter design process.

1. Click the Tree icon to choose the display method.
2. Click Next to finish the filter configuration process.

Figure 7-9 shows that we can choose to provide only a SINGLE-SELECT list of filter values, which is appropriate when we want to limit the size or scope of the data

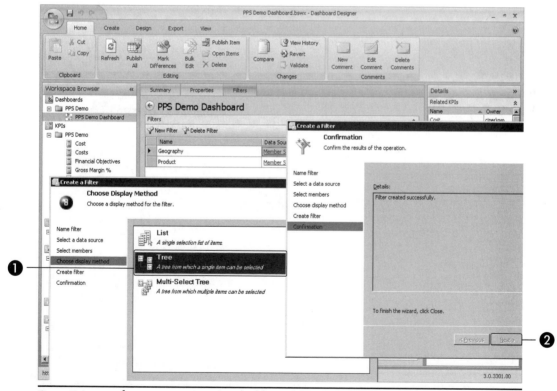

Figure 7-9   *PerformancePoint 2007 dashboard filter—Choose Display Method*

that will be displayed in the scorecards and analytic components. Alternatively we can choose to provide a MULTI-SELECT list of filter values in the Multi-Select Tree control.

Dashboard Display Configuration

Figure 7-10 shows off some of the configurable aspects of the dashboard display.

1. Click the drop-down control at the top of the Sales Scorecard lower-left pane.
2. Choose Edit Item on the pop-up menu.
3. Click the Size tab in the Edit Item dialog box.
4. Choose the Specify Width option button.
5. Enter the desired width as a percentage of the dashboard page.
6. Click OK.

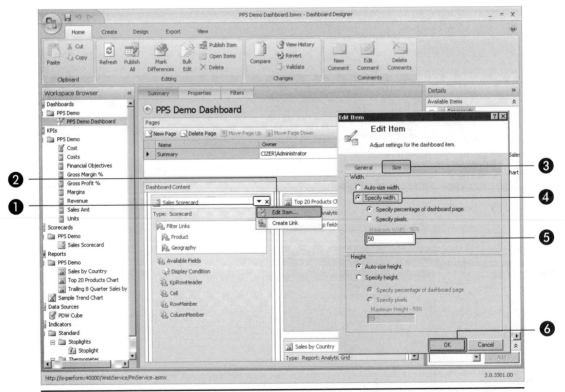

Figure 7-10 *PerformancePoint 2007 Dashboard pane—Specify width*

In Figure 7-10 you see that you can pretty easily control the actual or relative size of scorecard and analytic components within the dashboard display. This is significant because the PerformancePoint Dashboard Design pane provides a straightforward user interface to adjust the sizes of components, which will later be "published" to SharePoint 2007.

To be complete in our exploration of dashboard design, Figure 7-11 shows how we start the creation of a new dashboard.

1. Click the Dashboard icon in the Scorecard Elements group, on the Create tab of the Ribbon menu.

2. Choose the desired dashboard layout.

3. Click OK.

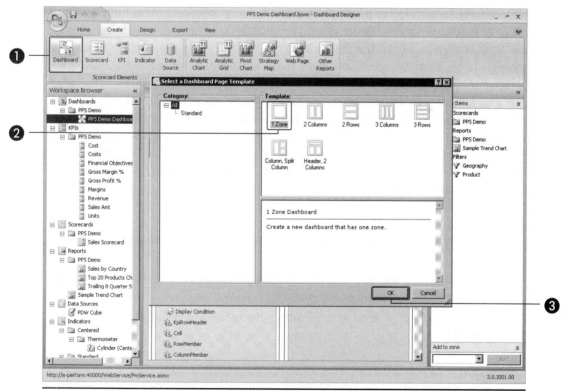

Figure 7-11   *PerformancePoint 2007 dashboard templates*

As you see in Figure 7-11, PerformancePoint provides an out-of-the-box experience with preconfigured dashboard templates that arrange the scorecards with KPIs and analytic components included in the final display.

KPI Design and Configuration

Key Performance Indicators (KPIs) are actually the original reason that Microsoft first published a scorecard product (Business Scorecard Manager). And although KPIs can be displayed in a stand-alone manner through SharePoint, they provide a more compelling presentation when grouped in a scorecard, perhaps by business processes under headings such as Revenue or Employee metrics.

Although the structure of a KPI seems simple at first glance—made up of Actual, Target, and Threshold numbers—it becomes more sophisticated when we realize that we might want to have multiple Thresholds that correspond to multiple levels of achievement, or multiple Targets. Sophisticated KPI structures can be designed into the Analysis Services cube (on the back-end SQL Server that supports the front-end scorecard), but PerformancePoint adds a front-end layer of control that allows us to design a robust KPI display.

KPIs also differ in that an increasing KPI might be good, or a decreasing KPI might be the desired outcome, or a KPI that gets as close to a "center" Target as possible might be appropriate where we don't want the metric to go too far below or above the Target value. Furthermore, the calculation of a KPI's relative performance can be based on a "normalized" value from 0 to 100 percent, or an "actual" value from Worst-Value to Target-Value.

Figure 7-12 shows the initial KPI Workspace screen.

1. Click the folder containing multiple KPIs on the left-pane Workspace Browser tree list.

2. Using the left mouse button, drag the cursor over the KPIs to be configured in the list of KPIs available in the workspace.

3. Click the Bulk Edit icon in the Editing group, on the Home tab of the Ribbon menu.

In Figure 7-12 you see a new feature in PerformancePoint: the ability to bulk-edit KPIs. This is important from a maintenance perspective when faced with possibly hundreds of KPIs that might be available in our workspace (although only the KPIs placed in the scorecard are used in the dashboard display). Bulk-edit basically allows us to change common properties across all KPIs that we've multi-selected in the KPI list pane.

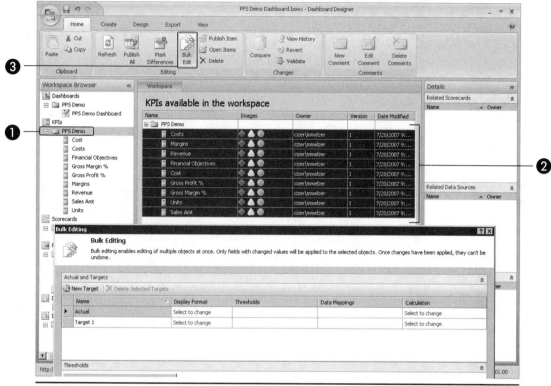

Figure 7-12 *PerformancePoint 2007 KPI bulk edit*

Figure 7-13 shows the menu for formatting the KPI display.

1. Click the KPI to be configured, in the left-pane Workspace Browser tree list.
2. Click the Display Format cell for either Actual or Target.
3. Check the Override Display Format checkbox, and choose the desired formats.
4. Click OK.

As Figure 7-13 shows, the numeric format options we expect with a Microsoft user interface are available within PerformancePoint—and they can be configured for each KPI individually even though the resulting KPIs may appear on one scorecard.

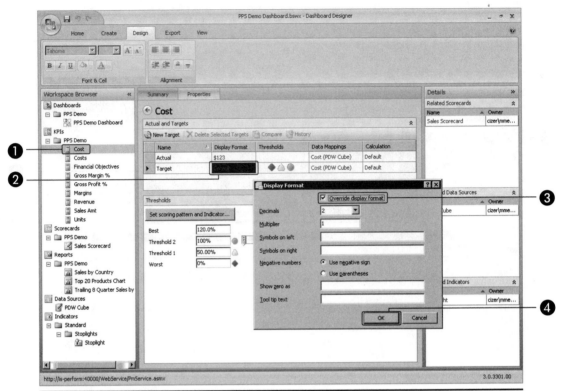

Figure 7-13   *PerformancePoint 2007 KPI display format*

KPI Scoring Patterns and Banding Methods

This section really gets to the important part of KPI configuration: the Scoring Pattern and Banding Method. Figure 7-14 shows how we start this process for an individual KPI.

1. Click the Thresholds cell for the KPI Target.
2. Edit the Threshold levels, or select and drag the visual width bars.
3. Click the Set Scoring Pattern And Indicator control.
4. Click the drop-down to select a Scoring Pattern in the Edit Banding Settings dialog box.

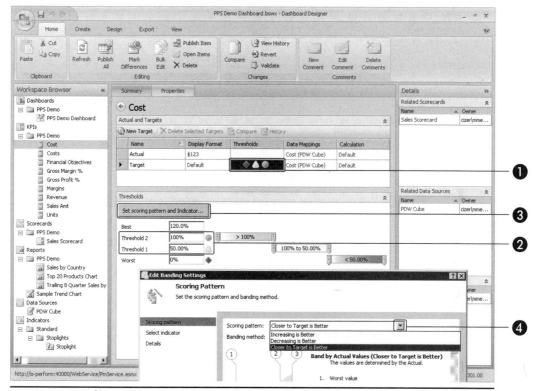

Figure 7-14 *PerformancePoint 2007 KPI thresholds and scoring pattern*

Figure 7-14 shows an interesting Thresholds configuration pane for the selected KPI. Note we can directly enter the Threshold numbers/percentages, or we can use the left mouse button to drag the green-yellow-red slider bars to be smaller or larger. Nice visualization!

The Edit Banding Settings dialog box shows we have choices for the Scoring Pattern:

▶ Increasing Is Better means that a higher percentage or number is better.

▶ Decreasing Is Better means that a lower percentage or number is better.

▶ Closer To Target Is Better means that exactly on Target is better.

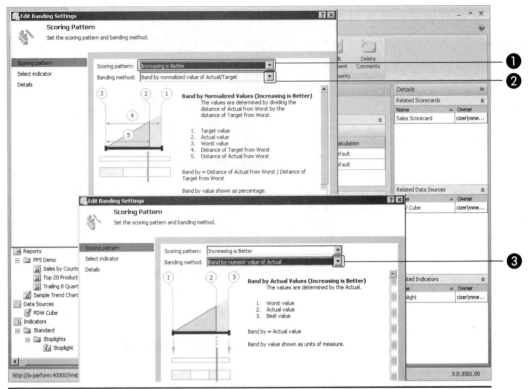

Figure 7-15   *PerformancePoint 2007 KPI scoring pattern and banding method*

Figure 7-15 explores the banding methods that can be matched with the Scoring Patterns.

1. Click the Scoring Pattern drop-down control and select Increasing Is Better.
2. Click the Banding Method drop-down control and select "Band by normalized value of Actual/Target."
3. Click the Banding Method drop-down control and select "Band by numeric value of Actual."

Figure 7-15 shows a helpful graphic that changes on the dialog box as we select different Banding Methods:

▶ Band By Normalized Values uses percentages to measure the success toward Target, based on the total distance to the Target.

▶ Band By Actual Values uses numeric values to measure the actual progress toward the Target.

This combination of Scoring Pattern and Banding Method really sets Performance-Point server apart from other products on the market for high-end scorecarding. It addresses the real-world need to show KPI performance in a way that reflects the business processes being measured.

Figure 7-16 shows how we finish the configuration of a KPI.

1. Click the Toggle View icon to expand the list of Indicators.

2. Choose the desired Indicator.

3. Enter the Worst Value numeric, and click OK.

In Figure 7-16 we are able to select an Indicator graphic from those that we've made available in the current dashboard workspace. There are many Indicator icons (graphics) available that we can add into the workspace, and we'll look at them later in this discussion.

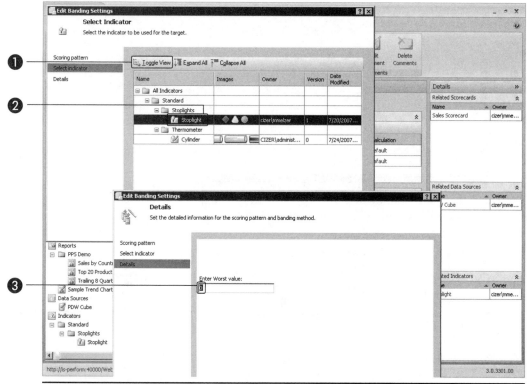

Figure 7-16 *PerformancePoint 2007 KPI configuration—Indicator selection*

KPI Actual and Target Data Mapping

It makes sense that we need to associate numeric values from a data source, with the Indicators in the dashboard workspace. Figure 7-17 shows how we configure the Data Mappings for both Actual and Target values.

1. Click the Data Mappings cell in the KPI Actual row.
2. Click the Select A Measure drop-down control in the Dimensional Data Source Mapping dialog box.
3. Click OK.

In Figure 7-17 we're able to choose an OLAP cube measure to display in the KPI Actual value. Cube measures are hierarchical by design and can support the display of performance metrics with a drill-down hierarchy that reflects your organization.

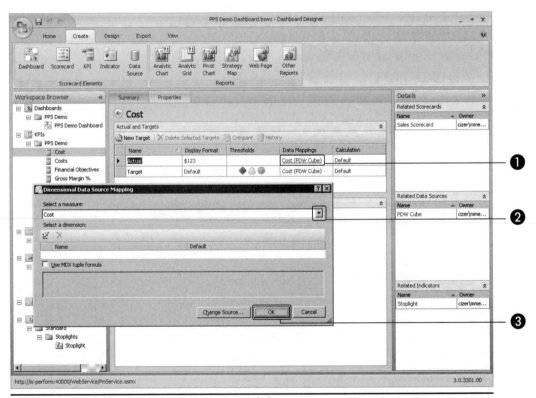

Figure 7-17 *PerformancePoint 2007 KPI actual data mapping*

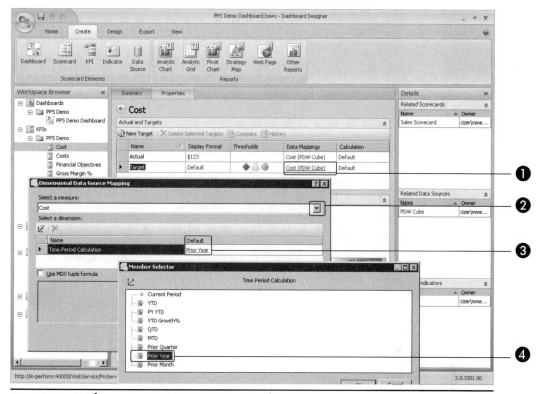

Figure 7-18 *PerformancePoint 2007 KPI target data mapping*

Figure 7-18 shows the next step, where we choose the Target data element.

1. Click the Data Mappings cell in the KPI Target row.
2. Click the Select A Measure drop-down control on the Dimensional Data Source Mapping dialog box.
3. Click the Default value link in the Name row.
4. Choose the desired default value for the KPI Target, from the Member list.

In Figure 7-18 you see the capability to choose an OLAP cube measure for the Target value and to choose a Time Period calculation on which to base the Target. In our working example we're setting the Target to the "Prior Year" Actual value, since it makes sense that we want to display a KPI Actual that shows whether we're over or under the Prior Year value.

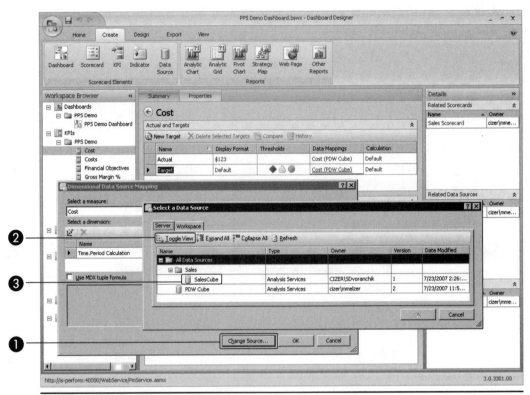

Figure 7-19 *PerformancePoint 2007 KPI Data Mapping—change source cube*

Figure 7-19 shows how we can select or verify the data source for the KPI.

1. Click the Change Source control in the Dimensional Data Source Mapping dialog box.
2. Click the Toggle View icon to display All Data Sources.
3. Choose SalesCube from the list of Analysis Services cubes.

In Figure 7-19 you see an important distinction with the more sophisticated PerformancePoint scorecards that are constructed in the real world—they are based on SQL Server 2005 Analysis Services cubes!

BI TIP

While a scorecard can be designed to show Key Performance Indicators from a wide variety of data sources, including relational and flat-file formats, the really useful scorecards are built against OLAP cube data sources, which support fast data exploration with millions of data elements and can reflect the organization hierarchy in the drill-down user interface experience.

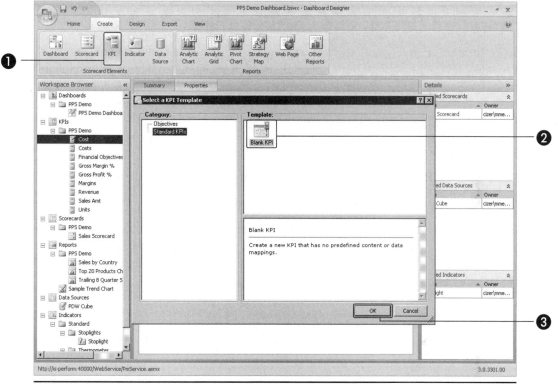

Figure 7-20   *PerformancePoint 2007—creating a new KPI*

Figure 7-20 finishes our KPI discussion by showing how easy it is to create a new KPI.

1. Click the KPI icon in the Scorecard Elements menu group, on the Create tab of the Ribbon menu.
2. Choose the Blank KPI template.
3. Click OK.

Note in Figure 7-20 that we've clicked the Create tab in the Ribbon menu to find all the PerformancePoint components. This is a good example of the Ribbon menu user interface that can bring together many different elements such as dashboards, scorecards, and KPIs in a coherent menu presentation!

Scorecard Design and Configuration

In PerformancePoint, scorecards can also contain dimensional data elements that provide a hierarchical breakout of the KPIs, which are in turn based on hierarchical data elements in a cube. Figure 7-21 shows an already existing scorecard, and to demonstrate this Dimensional model, portrays the "Pivot" capability that is inherently available with such a design.

1. Click the Sales Scorecard in the left-pane Workspace Browser tree list.
2. Click the Pivot icon in the Scorecard Editor menu group, on the Design tab of the Ribbon menu.

Figure 7-21 shows a nice aspect of a dimensional scorecard: the ability to completely pivot the data (swap rows with columns). Notice that the Details tree-view pane on the right side of the screen provides a drag-and-drop supply of all the measures and dimensions available from the OLAP cube data source.

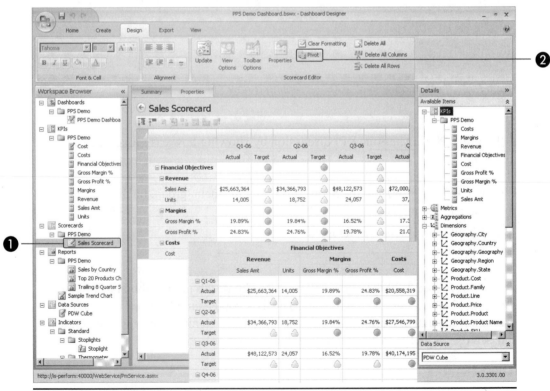

Figure 7-21   *PerformancePoint 2007—Scorecard "Pivot"*

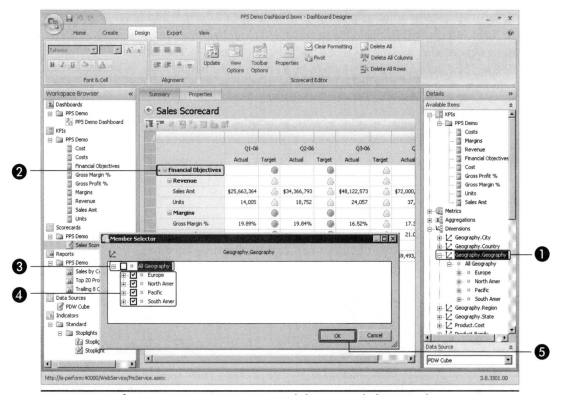

Figure 7-22 *PerformancePoint 2007—scorecard dimensional element selection*

In Figure 7-22 you see how a cube data element can be added to the scorecard.

1. Click the desired dimension data element in the right-side Details pane tree list, and carefully drag it over the scorecard.

2. Slowly move the mouse to hover over the top-left cell, until a *blue* positioning bar appears on the left side of the Financial Objectives cell.

3. Uncheck the All Geography checkbox.

4. Check the desired Geography checkbox values.

5. Click OK.

Figure 7-22 shows that we can simply click a cube data element on the right-side pane and then carefully drag and drop it onto the Scorecard design pane. We say "carefully" because as you drag the data element slowly over the scorecard cells or the left-side margin of the scorecard, you'll see that a *blue line* appears to show where the data element will be placed in the display hierarchy. This becomes fairly intuitive for designers when the data is made up of elements they understand, such that the hierarchical structure is understood to be a reflection of the organization structure.

In Figure 7-23 you see some more top-menu options to control the Scorecard display.

1. Click the Update icon in the Scorecard Editor menu group, on the Design tab of the Ribbon menu.

2. Click the View Options icon in the Scorecard Editor menu group, on the Design tab of the Ribbon menu.

3. Click OK.

Figure 7-23 features a "Rendering" graphic that actually shows the scorecard connecting to the back-end SQL Server Analysis Services cube to refresh the display

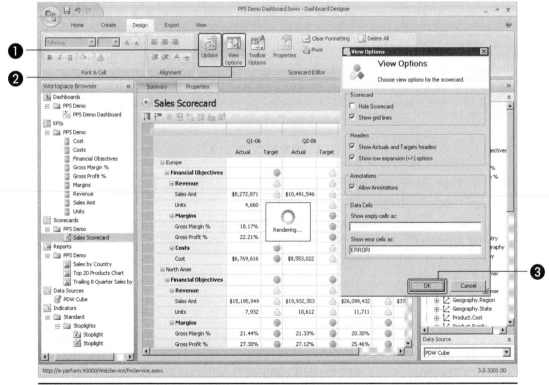

Figure 7-23 *PerformancePoint 2007—Scorecard Update and View Options*

with new elements. The View options are what we have come to expect with a product such as PerformancePoint that comes from the Microsoft Office group.

Figure 7-24 provides a brief look at the Scorecard Properties tab.

1. Click the Properties tab at the top of the Scorecard design pane.
2. Click the Role drop-down control to see the Editor and Reader roles.

Note in Figure 7-24 that we can set permissions on the Scorecard Designer, but these are *not* end-user permissions that guide who can see the dashboard or scorecard in the final SharePoint environment. The Editor and Reader roles are only used to guide who can edit or see the Scorecard Designer in our working example.

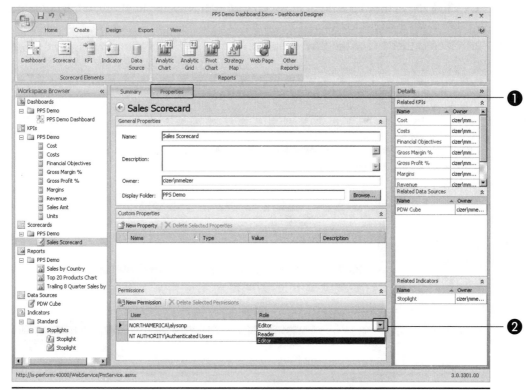

Figure 7-24 *PerformancePoint 2007—scorecard properties and roles*

BI TIP

Well-architected business intelligence presentations do not rely on embedded User-Role permissions to control who in the end-user population can see different dashboards or scorecards, for example. Rather, the end-user permissions to view finished BI presentations such as dashboards are controlled by the authentication process that grants access to a screen such as we see in SharePoint. The end-user permissions to view back-end data are best controlled by the User-Role permissions applied to the database or cube itself—which provides a secured server source of BI data to all front-end applications that connect to the server database or cube.

In Figure 7-25 you see the range of scorecard templates that are available when creating a new scorecard.

1. Click the Scorecard icon in the Scorecard Elements menu group, on the Create tab of the Ribbon Menu.

2. Choose ERP to see the SAP template.

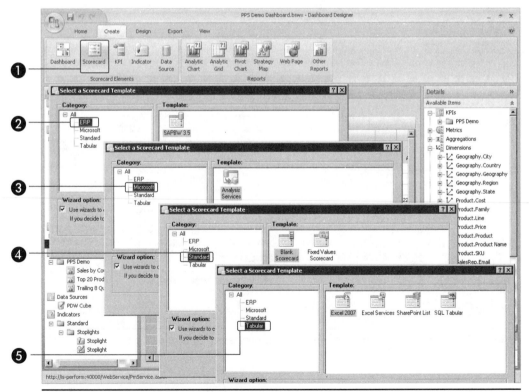

Figure 7-25 *PerformancePoint 2007—scorecard templates*

3. Choose Microsoft to see the SQL Server Analysis Services template.
4. Choose Standard to see the Blank and Fixed Values templates.
5. Choose Tabular to see other templates.

The message here is that the Microsoft SQL Server Analysis Services template is the choice that can support enterprise-capable scorecard presentations. It's great that we can create scorecards against a wide range of data sources (and SAP is compelling because such installations can well use a Microsoft scorecard), but the real-world field work is done with scorecards using Analysis Services cubes as the data source.

Report Design and Configuration

The section of PerformancePoint that falls into the Report area is significant because it's where we find the ProClarity technology that Microsoft recently acquired in the BI marketplace. ProClarity was known for its high-end "slice-and-dice" analytic screen components that provide an intuitive ability to browse the hierarchical data of SQL Server Analysis Services cubes.

Microsoft terms this technology the "Analytics" aspect of PerformancePoint 2007 and refers to the dashboard/scorecard technology as "Monitoring." Together the "Monitoring and Analytics" technology is what we're discussing in this chapter (sometimes referred to by Microsoft as "M & A").

The following section shows off the ProClarity Grid and Chart components that provide drill-down access to the back-end cubes that support the scorecard—and do so purely in the browser without requiring any client installation or download controls.

Analytic Grid Design

Figure 7-26 shows off the live-data display feature of the analytic grid.

1. Click the Sales By Country choice in the left-pane Workspace Browser tree list.
2. Click the Browse control on the Scorecard design pane.
3. Click the Expand and Collapse controls on the Browse Analytic Report dialog box.
4. Click OK.

In Figure 7-26 we're able to click the Browse control to connect to the back-end OLAP cube and interactively drill down through the data. This provides a nice design preview capability that helps us see what the end users will see with this analytic grid.

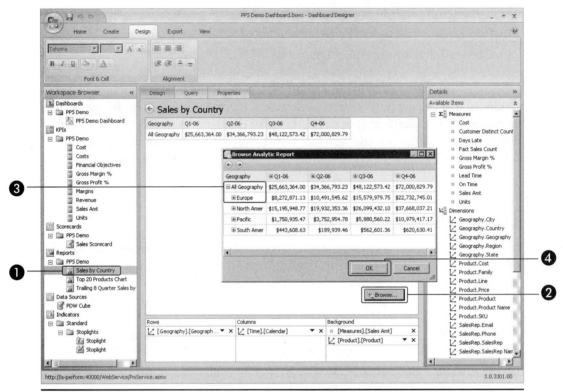

Figure 7-26 *PerformancePoint 2007—Reports: analytic grid*

Figure 7-27 continues this experience as we show how to add a dimensional data element to the grid.

1. Click the desired Dimension data element in the right-pane Details tree list.
2. Holding down the left mouse button, drag the data element to the Scorecard Rows field pane.

Figure 7-27 shows the interactive drag-and-drop capability of the analytic grid, where you can test different cube data elements much as we did with the Scorecard Designer. And just as we noted with the Scorecard Designer, you should *carefully* drag and drop the data elements from the right-side Details tree-view pane into the Rows, Columns, or Background panes to see the *blue line* that shows where the new data element is going to be positioned in the Rows, Columns, or Background lists.

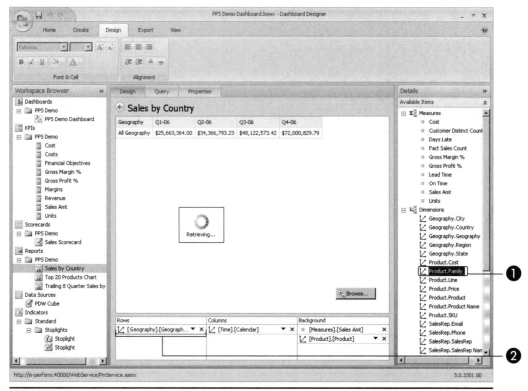

Figure 7-27   *PerformancePoint 2007—Reports: analytic grid—new dimension*

The Background pane is special in two ways: it holds the "Measure," which is the numeric data element from the cube that we wish to see displayed in the Grid cells, and whatever data elements are in the Background pane are available as "dashboard filter" elements.

Dashboard filters can interactively control the overall display of associated analytics grids and charts—if the filter data elements are contained in the Background pane!

Figure 7-28 shows how we can browse the grid data with new elements.

1. Click the Browse control on the Scorecard design pane.
2. Click the Expand and Collapse controls to explore the data in the Browse Analytic Report dialog box.
3. Click OK.

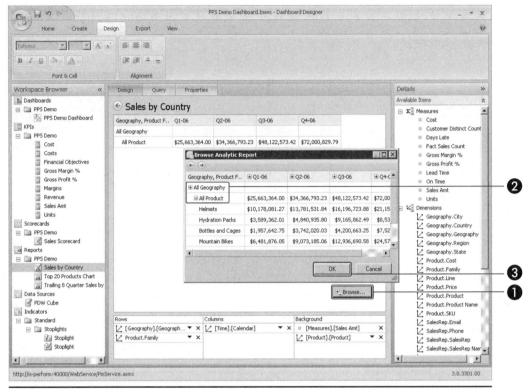

Figure 7-28 *PerformancePoint 2007—Reports: analytic grid—browse the data*

Notice in Figure 7-28 that the Browse preview display automatically places the "Product Family" within the Geography data elements. This hierarchical display of data is provided by the very nature of the back-end Analysis Services OLAP cube, and it illustrates the power of scorecards that are constructed in this manner.

Figure 7-29 shows another feature within the analytic grid; the ability to see the MDX that is being generated behind the scenes.

1. Click the Query tab on the Scorecard design-pane top menu.

2. Click the desired dimension data element in the right-pane Details tree list.

3. Holding down the left mouse button, drag the data element into the MDX query.

In Figure 7-29 you see the Multidimensional Expressions (MDX) query that has been automatically generated by our drag-and-drop grid design. MDX is the SQL-like query language used to access OLAP cubes, and it was invented by Microsoft as part

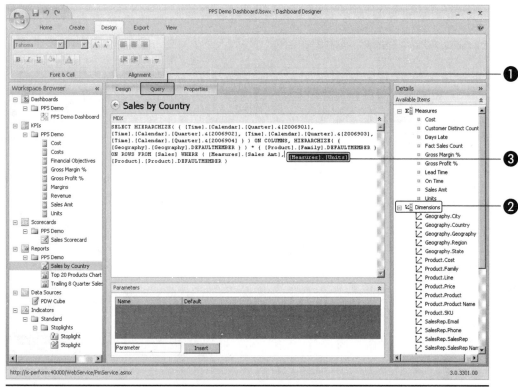

Figure 7-29 *PerformancePoint 2007—Reports: analytic grid—MDX query*

of SQL Server Analysis Services. There are many situations in cube data browsing where we'd like to see the MDX used to achieve the visual results, and this tool provides just that.

You can also drag and drop the cube measures and dimensions onto the MDX Query pane itself if you wish, although this is not recommended for anyone that is not fairly expert in MDX syntax.

Analytic Chart Design

Figure 7-30 shows off the live-data display feature of the analytic chart, which is very similar to the grid.

1. Click the "Trailing 8 Quarter Sales by Product" selection in the left-pane Browse Workspace tree list.

2. Click the desired dimension data element in the right-pane Details tree list.

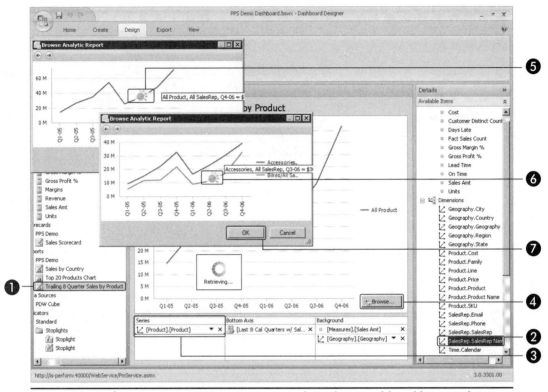

Figure 7-30 *PerformancePoint 2007—Reports: analytic chart—add and browse data*

3. Holding down the left mouse button, drag the data element into the Scorecard design-pane Series pane.

4. Click the Browse control to view the chart.

5. Hover the mouse over a line in the chart, and click it to drill down.

6. Hover the mouse over a line in the subsequent chart, and click to drill down.

7. Click OK.

Figure 7-30 shows several design and navigation steps that can be taken with the analytic chart. You can drag and drop cube data elements into the Series, Bottom Axis, and Background list panes just as we did with the analytic grid.

The Background pane is special just as with the grid: it holds the "Measure," which is the numeric data element from the cube that we wish to see displayed in the chart, and whatever data elements are in the Background pane are available as dashboard filter elements.

In Figure 7-30 we're able to click any line of the chart and drill down to lower levels of the dimensional data—which is of course provided by the back-end OLAP cube structure.

Figure 7-31 shows a nice added benefit of the Analytic Chart Designer, that we can specify the default values to show in the chart.

1. Click the drop-down control in the Scorecard design Series pane to display the Member Selector.
2. Uncheck the All Product checkbox.
3. Check the individual Product category checkboxes for display.
4. Click OK.

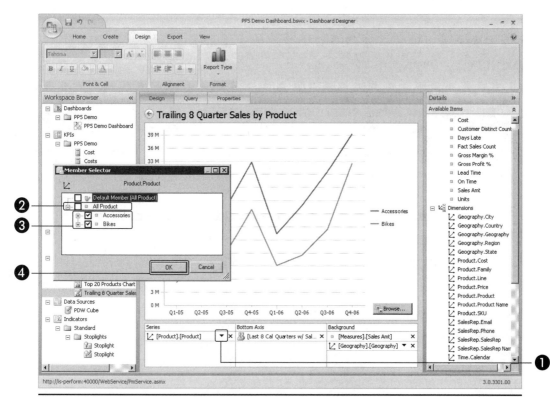

Figure 7-31   *PerformancePoint 2007—Reports: analytic chart—data display selector*

Figure 7-31 shows how we can open up the dimension that guides the Series display (the lines of the chart) and choose to show only certain levels or values at the top Drill Up level of the chart. This is useful when we want to control the chart display to deliver a focused data message and not have end users get confused with too much data at an unnecessarily high level.

Trend Analysis Chart Design: Data Mining

Data Mining is a feature of SQL Server 2005 Analysis Services that is today being used by Excel users with the free Excel 2007 Data Mining download from Microsoft. This high-end Microsoft Research statistics capability is available in PerformancePoint as well, through a special report termed the "Trend Analysis Chart" as shown in Figure 7-32.

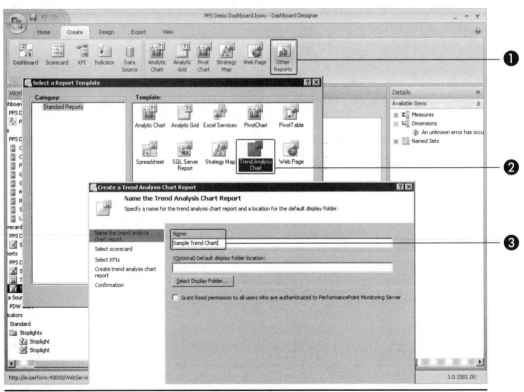

Figure 7-32 *PerformancePoint 2007—Reports: create a new trend analysis chart*

1. Click the Other Reports icon in the Reports menu group, on the Create tab of the Ribbon menu.
2. Click the Trend Analysis Chart icon in the Template dialog box.
3. Enter a Name for the new Chart, and click Next.

In Figure 7-32 we give a Name to the trend chart and proceed to the configuration shown in Figure 7-33.

1. Choose the Sales Scorecard scorecard.
2. Uncheck the top-level dimensional data elements.
3. Check only the Units checkbox data element, and click Finish.

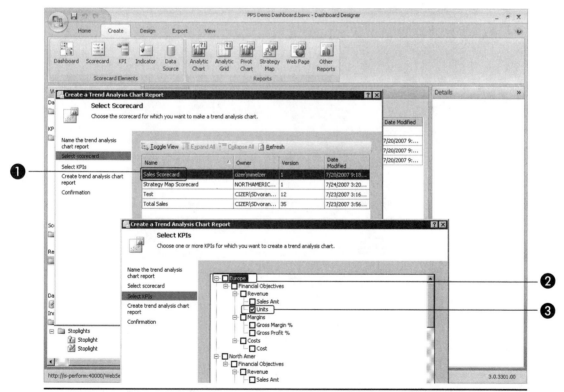

Figure 7-33 *PerformancePoint 2007—Reports: trend analysis chart data element*

Figure 7-33 shows how we can easily select the singular Scorecard KPI "Measure" that we'd like to forecast (or Trend). The Forecast data mining tool is quite powerful and uses the Microsoft Research Time Series algorithm, which is a regression algorithm used to predict continuous data elements, such as units sold, in a forecasting scenario.

The resulting trend forecast chart is shown in Figure 7-34.

1. Choose the Use Selection option button in the Select Time Period pane.
2. Enter **2** in the Time Periods text box.
3. Click the Trend Analysis Chart display pane to render the new chart.

The circular green icon in Figure 7-34 shows PerformancePoint actually connecting to Analysis Services Data Mining to use the Time Series Algorithm in a statistically accurate prediction of units sold.

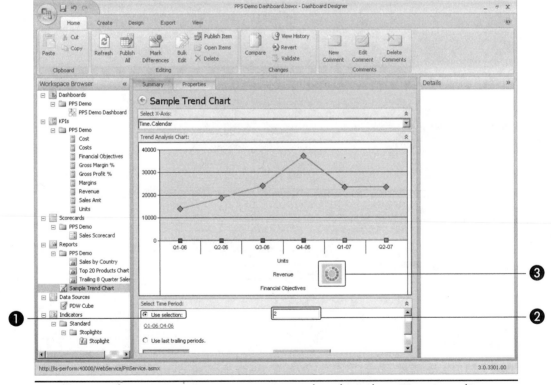

Figure 7-34 *PerformancePoint 2007—Reports: trend analysis chart "Time Period"*

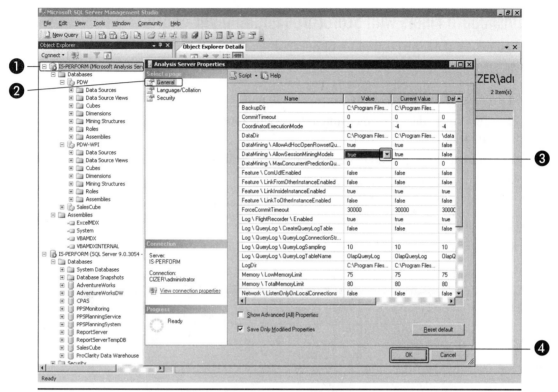

Figure 7-35 *SQL Server 2005 Analysis Services "AllowSessionMiningModels"*

Figure 7-35 is provided for the sake of completeness. It is the Analysis Services server configuration item that must be set to "true" to allow the PerformancePoint trend chart to connect to the Data Mining algorithm that resides only on the Analysis Services server!

1. Right-click the Microsoft Analysis Services tree node, and choose Properties.
2. Select the General menu choice.
3. Click the DataMining \ AllowSessionMiningModels Value drop-down control, and select "true."
4. Click OK.

In Figure 7-35 you see the SQL Server Management Studio, which is the user interface for Analysis Services administrators. In our working example we're using it to access the DataMining setting that allows PerformancePoint to connect in a SessionMiningModel context.

Dashboard Filters with Scorecards and Analytic Charts

Figure 7-36 shows the end result of our dashboard filters connecting to a scorecard and an analytic grid and chart.

1. Click the on-screen drop-down control under the "Product" label.
2. Choose the desired dimensional data value for filtering across the Scorecard and Reports.
3. Click the Expand and Collapse controls to drill down in the analytic grid.
4. Right-click any of the analytic chart lines.
5. Choose Drill Down To to navigate to the dimensional data hierarchy.
6. Choose Geography.
7. Choose Region to filter the chart.

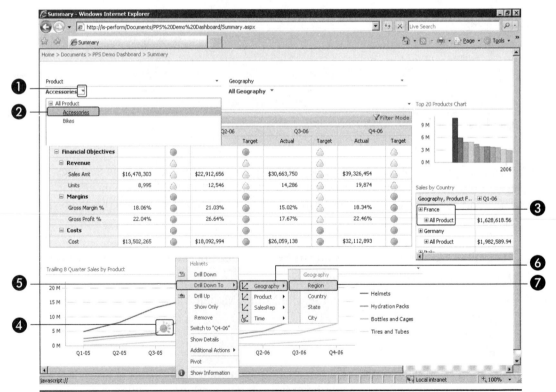

Figure 7-36   *PerformancePoint 2007 filters and drill-down*

In Figure 7-36 you see an intuitive PerformancePoint dashboard display in SharePoint 2007. The top-level dashboard filter controls dynamically change the display of data in the scorecard and analytic grid and chart that have Background data elements that are the same as the dashboard filter data elements.

As we discussed earlier, the dashboard filter data elements have been associated with the Scorecard and Analytic components in the Dashboard Designer.

Note also in Figure 7-36 that you can right-click an analytic chart element (such as the line in a line chart) and use a variety of OLAP cube browse techniques. For simplicity we've shown the Drill Down To process, but note that the right-click pop-up menu also has a Drill Up menu choice that will take the chart back up to the previous dimensional data level.

Data Sources

Figure 7-37 shows the configuration of the Analysis Services OLAP cube that supports our dashboard, scorecard, and analytic grid and chart.

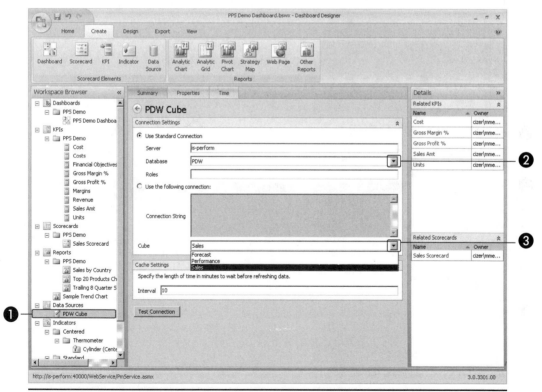

Figure 7-37 *PerformancePoint 2007—data sources; Analysis Services cube*

1. Click the PDW Cube selection in the left-side Workspace Browser pane.
2. Click the Database drop-down control to choose the Analysis Services database.
3. Click the Cube drop-down control to choose the Analysis Services cube.

Figure 7-37 displays a navigation mechanism that is familiar to Analysis Services designers: browsing an OLAP database and the selection of a cube. This is fairly intuitive and is just like the data connection process that is used by Excel 2007 end users when they connect directly to Analysis Services to create a PivotTable!

Indicator Design and Configuration

The creation of *indicators* is straightforward and shown in Figure 7-38.

1. Click the Indicators selection in the left-side Workspace Browser pane.

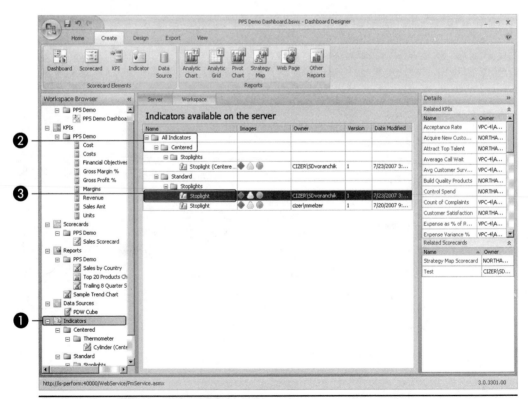

Figure 7-38 *PerformancePoint 2007—Indicators*

2. Click the Expand controls to view all Indicators.

3. Select the Stoplight Indicator row.

Figure 7-39 shows the expanded display of indicators that we've chosen for this dashboard workspace. Centered indicators work with Target value scenarios that should be exactly achieved with Actual data (under or over is Bad). Standard indicators work with Target value scenarios that should be met or overachieved with Actual data (over is Good).

1. Click the Indicator icon in the Scorecard Elements menu group, on the Create tab of the Ribbon menu.

2. Choose a Centered Thermometer in the Category pane.

3. Choose the Cylinder (Centered) icon in the Template pane, and click OK.

Notice in Figure 7-39 that we've chosen an indicator that can display multiple thresholds, as shown by the levels to be defined in the Cylinder (Centered)

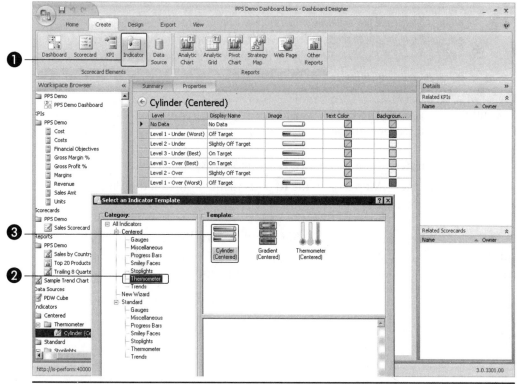

Figure 7-39 *PerformancePoint 2007—Indicators; add a new indicator*

configuration rows. This thermometer has sometimes been called a "color rod" that supports a multiple color-threshold display!

Strategy Map Design

Strategy maps are perhaps the most unique part of PerformancePoint. They provide a hierarchical view of the Key Performance Indicator measures across levels of the organization that is similar to the familiar "org-chart" display of data. This org-chart representation of performance metrics seems to make sense to decision makers that deal with their organizational structures every day.

The other valuable use of strategy maps with PerformancePoint is to group KPIs into areas of concern for the organization. Thus we might find gross revenue and units sold (2 KPIs) grouped under "Financial Performance." And we might find revenue-per-employee and percentage of employees retained each year (2 KPIs) grouped under "Workforce Productivity."

BI TIP

Business Intelligence presentations invariably show numeric data in what we hope is an entertaining manner with charts and color-coded tables. However, the more sophisticated BI presentations also show how the numeric data metrics support the strategic goals of the organization that are articulated in mission statements.

Figure 7-40 shows how we start the process of creating a strategy map within the PerformancePoint Dashboard Designer.

1. Click the Strategy Map item in the left-side Workspace Browser pane.
2. Click the Strategy Map icon in the Reports menu group, on the Create tab of the Ribbon menu.

In Figure 7-40 you find a Ribbon menu icon that starts the process of creating a strategy map. The creation of a strategy map requires Visio 2007, which is playing an increasingly important part in the Microsoft BI application suite. A complete

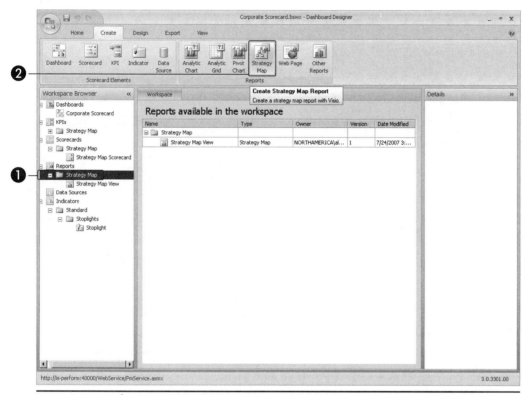

Figure 7-40 *PerformancePoint 2007—create a strategy map*

discussion of strategy map design is beyond the scope of this chapter, but Figure 7-41 shows what the finished map looks like.

In Figure 7-41 you see the finished strategy map on the right, with Financial, Customer Satisfaction, Operational Excellence, and People Commitment regions that directly correspond to the scorecard on the left. The red-yellow-green indicator colors work in parallel for both KPI visualizations.

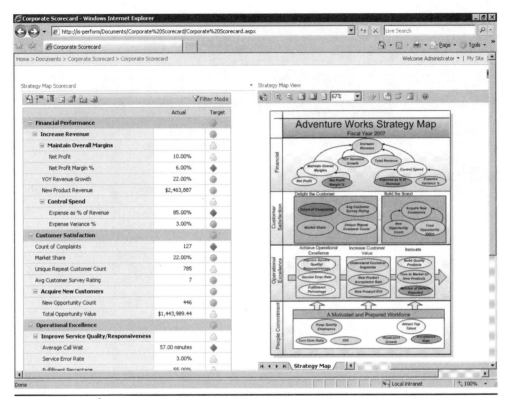

Figure 7-41 *PerformancePoint 2007—create a strategy map*

Strategy maps really push the envelope of performance dashboards—and yet they are surprisingly easy to understand when their pictorial design reflects our organization and goals. This combination of scorecard metrics with strategy goals represents the best of business intelligence today, where we can measure the performance of an enterprise and *understand why* we are measuring the performance with terminology that defines our work as an organization.

Office BI: Office, Visio, Windows Mobile, Office Online, SQL Server, and Virtual Earth

This is the "show and tell" chapter in which we look at all the cool Microsoft Business Intelligence examples we've heard of or seen in commercials and have wondered how they are actually done. From Outlook e-mail access to SharePoint, to PowerPoint's use of Excel charting, to Visio PivotDiagrams (yes, there is actually a Visio PivotTable look-alike that connects to OLAP cubes!), to a comprehensive overview of Windows Mobile Smartphone BI Excel spreadsheets—it's all here in this chapter. Last but not least, we show how to connect Excel to Virtual Earth with real-time interactive maps of our BI location data.

Examples of the following topics will be provided in this chapter:

▶ Outlook view of SharePoint

▶ PowerPoint Excel Charts, Visio PivotDiagram

▶ Word and Excel, Windows Mobile Smartphone Excel, Office Online

▶ SQL Server Integration Services, Analysis Services, Reporting Services

▶ Virtual Earth

BEST REFERENCE

For further research on this topic, go to http://www.microsoft.com/office/community/en-us/default.mspx.

Technology Positioning Statement

Office 2007 is the most diverse suite of applications ever offered in a single published product, and as such, there are monitoring and analysis tangents that are not part of mainstream Microsoft Business Intelligence. The very fact that we can use Outlook to access SharePoint, and that we can display multidimensional data in Visio, hints at the amazing things we can accomplish with "outside the box" thinking.

Using the Office 2007 Ribbon menu we can seamlessly move between Excel and PowerPoint, or Excel and Word—and then publish the results to SharePoint 2007 for collaborative work. At the end of the day, we are connecting the various Office technologies and saving the work results to SharePoint!

(continued)

And as the Windows Mobile Smartphone technology continues to progress, we'll graduate from reading Outlook e-mail on our phones to analyzing Excel reports in a wireless world that is seamlessly connected to the flow and pulse of business around the world, around the clock 24 hours a day.

—Doug VanDyke, Microsoft Field Team

What Are the Other Parts of Office Business Intelligence?

Some people have said there are so many moving parts to Microsoft Business Intelligence that it's hard to explain them in a single presentation. While this is indeed a challenge, we might also say the many moving parts provide an opportunity to connect various components into whatever BI display we desire. This chapter will explore several of these other Office BI components.

In this light you can think about using the BI content created in Excel, to provide a compelling analytic slide in PowerPoint—or a good rendition of an Excel table in Word. This puts the focus on the end user so that you can think about delivering BI value in whatever Office application is most a part of the consumer's everyday working life. It's all about bringing BI to users in applications they are already using!

The delivery of business intelligence content takes on new meaning with the fast-growing availability of SharePoint, which is becoming one of the ubiquitous Microsoft technologies, next to the Windows operating system and Microsoft Office. So it makes sense that the "other parts" of Microsoft BI find a common repository with SharePoint libraries that help us control and share documents, images, and spreadsheets, for example.

And while the number of Microsoft Office users is projected to reach one billion with Office 2007, Microsoft Windows Mobile may reach even more people as a growing operating system of choice on the one billion cell phones sold every year! It just makes sense that familiar Office spreadsheets can be extended to a Windows Mobile Smartphone in the context of business intelligence.

The foundation of the Microsoft Business Intelligence technology is SQL Server 2005, which in this book is positioned as a "BI Server" upon which you can build relational data marts and multidimensional cubes, which in turn support Excel and Visio reports and charts, and SharePoint dashboards and scorecards. The Standard and Enterprise licenses for SQL Server include a free Visual Studio

Business Intelligence Design Environment that is used to access and control the following major BI components of SQL Server:

- ▶ **Integration Services** This is the extraction, transformation, and loading (ETL) technology that can pull in data from flat files, mainframes, database servers, etc. The data pulls can be automated and scheduled to coincide with events in a networked organization, or in accordance with monitored data changes, or in accordance with a recurring calendar day-time basis.

- ▶ **Analysis Services** This is the online analytical processing (OLAP) technology that produces virtual cubes of data. The cubes are multidimensional and can be speedily sliced and diced in Excel and other tools to view time slices of data, or grouped data based on look-up values that are inherently part of the cube design.

- ▶ **Reporting Services** This is the XML reporting technology that can render relational or multidimensional data into HTML, Excel, or PDF reports.

BI TIP

Business intelligence reports, charts, scorecards, and dashboards can be constructed from almost any kind of data — from mainframe COBOL files to PC server-based Oracle, DB2, and SQL Server sources. However, it makes sense to bring this back-end data into a single business intelligence server where it can be cleansed and formatted, and multidimensional cubes can be designed with easy-to-understand ways to slice the data. In the Microsoft context this business intelligence server is a dedicated SQL Server 2005 where you can accomplish the ETL cleansing and OLAP cubing, and where you can place real-time data marts that support the OLAP cubes.

And finally, Visio continues to surprise us with an expanding capability to connect to data and display the results in unique ways. Most people are familiar with the concept of organizational charts that show the hierarchical layout of people and teams, and this carries over into a Visio display of hierarchical data from OLAP multidimensional cubes, as you'll see in this chapter.

Where Do These Other Pieces Fit in the Microsoft BI Picture?

The accompanying illustration shows a matrix view of Microsoft Business Intelligence technology (often referred to as BI). The Office, SharePoint, and SQL Server applications we see in the marketplace are shown on the left side of the matrix. These applications are used in the real-world activities of reporting, analysis, measurement, and planning as shown across the top of the matrix. The top-down flow of the matrix starts with front-end BI tools we have in Office 2007 at our desktops and goes down to back-end BI tools that run on servers such as SharePoint 2007 and PerformancePoint 2007, which provide an enhanced experience when connected to Office 2007.

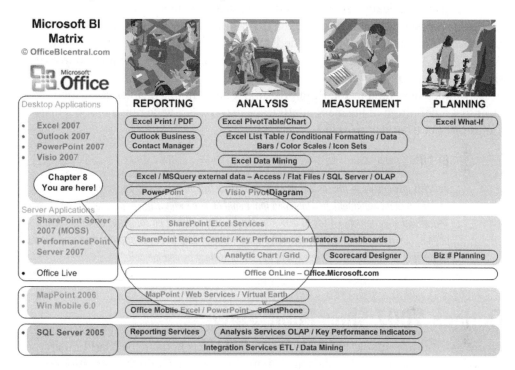

Learning about the other pieces of our BI picture makes more sense if you know where they fit in the Microsoft technology stack, and how they can be included in daily BI activities. The "You are here!" bubble in the illustration shows Visio PivotDiagrams, Office Live, and Windows Mobile, which show up in many different places on the Microsoft BI matrix. This is partly because Office applications such as Visio have a role in BI that is still forming as data connections become available across more of the Office suite. It's important to note that these Office Data Connections can be stored in a SharePoint Data Connection Library, which allows Office users to retrieve trusted predesigned connections to external data, from a trusted server-based repository.

Windows Mobile is a technology that can be used in multiple areas of BI work, since it extends desktop BI displays to our cell phones. This, too, is a BI role that is still forming as the electronic hardware in Smartphones and PocketPC phones advances with better displays, keyboards, processor and memory capability, and wireless access to data networks.

SQL Server 2005 is the foundation for the BI technologies shown in the illustration. This is because a dedicated BI Server can use SQL Server Integration Services to automatically bring data into a coherent data mart(s) from database servers, spreadsheets, flat files, and even mainframes. The resulting data on the BI Server can support every part of the BI matrix technologies, and SQL Server Analysis Services cubes on the same BI Server provide the best-possible source of slice-and-dice data for analysis.

As we look at several of the BI matrix components in this chapter, it becomes clear that a definition of business intelligence can cover a wide range of tools that are part of our everyday working environment.

BI TIP

Business intelligence in the context of Microsoft Office can be defined as any reporting, analysis, performance measurement, and planning that might be done with Office applications in a connected SharePoint environment. These BI activities can be accomplished on computer desktops or cell phones, but at the end of the day they all display working data from our organizations and allow us to manipulate the displays as we explore the business story behind the data.

Outlook 2007 SharePoint View

Figure 8-1 shows Outlook 2007 with a SharePoint Lists node in the Mail Folders tree view, at the same level as the Outlook mail tree node. Outlook integration with SharePoint is one of the two most compelling new collaborative experiences in Office 2007—along with the Excel Services capability that you've previously explored.

1. Click the SharePoint Lists expand control in the Mail Folders tree view.
2. Click the Reports—Reports Library icon under the SharePoint Lists tree node.
3. Click the Send/Receive Outlook icon in the top menu bar.

Notice that Figure 8-1 allows *everyone* to look at SharePoint contents through Outlook. It has been said that Outlook is the most-used part of the Office suite today, which makes sense when we think about how much time we spend on e-mail. When Outlook and SharePoint are connected, the Send/Receive action in Outlook synchronizes new SharePoint contents as well as new e-mail contents.

It's important to note that Figure 8-1 shows off a live-data-connected spreadsheet from Excel, in the Outlook preview pane.

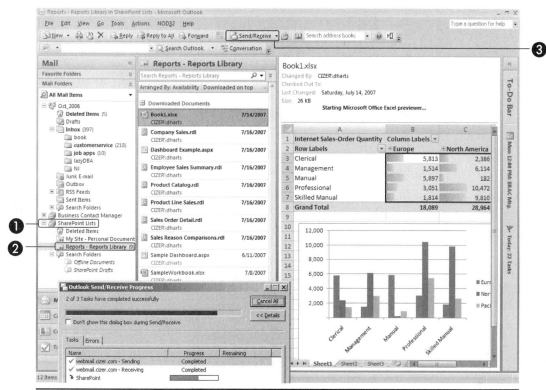

Figure 8-1   *Outlook 2007—displaying SharePoint reports*

BI TIP

Using SharePoint as a repository for Office Excel spreadsheets, Word docs, and PowerPoint slide decks makes sense when viewed in the Outlook 2007 preview pane. This is because we can dynamically view those Office content pieces in Outlook—without having to attach them to innumerable e-mail messages that are hard to organize as communication attachments proliferate throughout the organization.

Connecting SharePoint to Outlook 2007

In Figure 8-2 you see how to start the process of connecting SharePoint to an Outlook client. As you'll see, this is easy to accomplish and can provide access to SharePoint libraries for everyone with Outlook 2007.

1. Click the Actions drop-down menu control on the top menu bar in the desired document library.

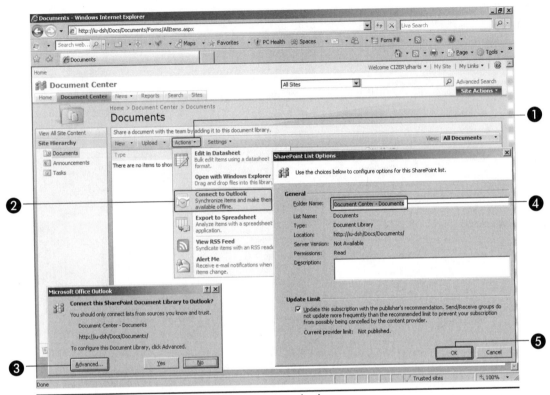

Figure 8-2 *SharePoint 2007—connecting to Outlook*

2. Choose Connect To Outlook on the pop-up menu.
3. Click the Advanced button on the Microsoft Office Outlook dialog box.
4. Enter the desired Outlook Folder Name in the text box.
5. Click OK.

Figure 8-2 is an example of the difference we see in Office 2007 and SharePoint 2007, where the Office applications are ready to connect to SharePoint out of the box. In Figure 8-3 we continue the process of offering connections to the SharePoint libraries.

1. Right-click Reports—Reports Library in the Mail Folders tree view.
2. Choose Share Reports on the pop-up menu.
3. Enter the e-mail address for the desired recipient of SharePoint sharing.
4. Click Send.

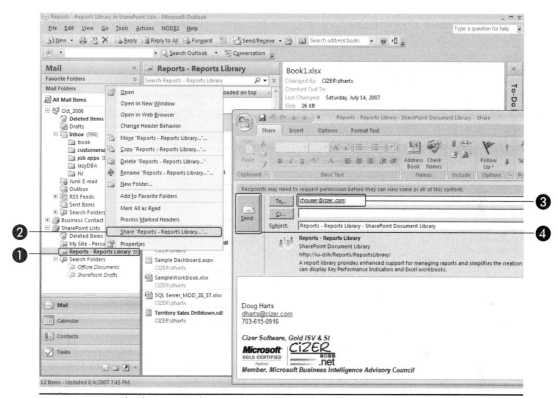

Figure 8-3   *Outlook 2007—sharing the Reports Library with others*

Figure 8-3 displays a familiar Outlook e-mail mechanism, where you simply enter the e-mail address for the recipient(s) of the message offering access to SharePoint 2007. In Figure 8-4 you see the resulting e-mail message that is sent to an Outlook recipient, offering the connection to SharePoint libraries.

1. Click the top link to accept the SharePoint library connection.
2. Click the bottom link to see how to connect Outlook 2003 to SharePoint.

Figure 8-4 shows an Outlook e-mail message that is much like the e-mails we receive every day in our working environments. Users can click the first link and, if they are using Outlook 2007, connect seamlessly to the SharePoint libraries from within Outlook.

A user running Outlook 2003 may get a message that says "You cannot open a Windows SharePoint Services list . . . ." The third link in the e-mail message in Figure 8-4 brings up a Microsoft Knowledge Base article that explains how to finish the SharePoint connection from Outlook 2003. This is important because large

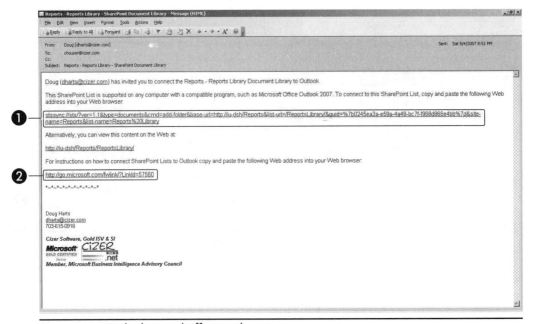

Figure 8-4 *Outlook e-mail offering SharePoint connection*

enterprises have users that are invariably on different version of Microsoft Office—and SharePoint is able to serve the needs of both Office 2003 and Office 2007 users.

This highlights an important point, however—that Office 2007 and SharePoint 2007 can connect to Office 2003 users—but as we travel farther back in Office versions prior to 2003 the integration becomes more challenging and the user interfaces are not as seamless.

BI TIP

Organizations always face the question of when to upgrade to new versions of any software they use. In the case of Microsoft Office 2007, however, the argument is more compelling when viewed in terms of application integration. Office 2007 applications are better integrated among themselves for business intelligence work, and better integrated with SharePoint 2007 for server-based business intelligence repositories that provide trusted sources of data and analysis.

SharePoint Objects in Outlook 2007

Once Outlook 2007 users are connected to SharePoint 2007, the usual actions of Outlook come into play as you see in Figure 8-5. The SharePoint Reports Library is available in the Outlook Mail Folders tree-view pane—in the same place as our

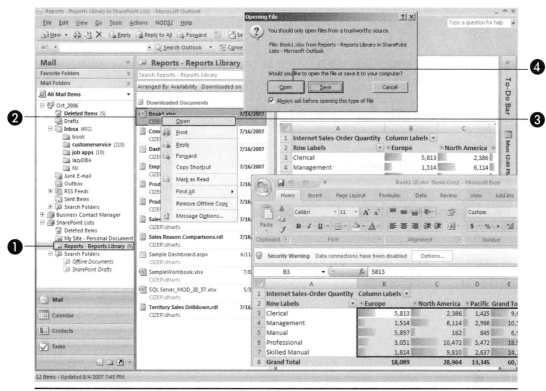

Figure 8-5   *Outlook 2007—opening a SharePoint Excel report*

well-known Inbox. Note this Reports tree view displays the number of new (not yet viewed) reports, just as Outlook does with new (not yet viewed) e-mail messages.

The Outlook preview pane in Figure 8-5 is displaying a live Excel PivotTable that is clickable because it comes from SharePoint, which provides a central repository of Excel spreadsheets as we've discussed in Chapter 5!

1. Right-click Reports—Reports Library in the Mail Folders tree view.

2. Right-click the desired Excel Workbook document in the Library list pane.

3. Choose Open on the pop-up menu.

4. Click Open on the Opening File dialog box to open the Excel spreadsheet.

In Figure 8-5 we're exploring the menu options available in Outlook when viewing Excel Reports from SharePoint. It makes sense that we can click a workbook and open it—which then uses our desktop Excel 2007 to display the workbook in Excel itself.

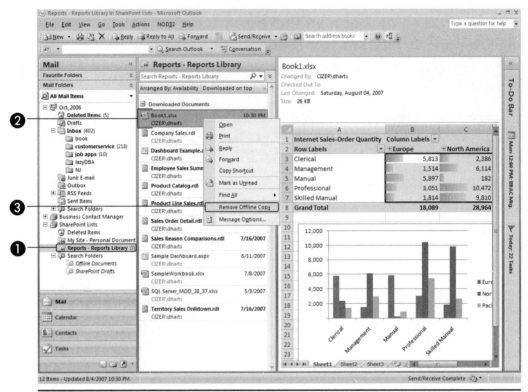

Figure 8-6   *Outlook 2007—removing an offline copy of an Excel report*

In Figure 8-6 we continue our exploration of Outlook-SharePoint menu options.

1. Right-click Reports—Reports Library in the Mail Folders tree view.
2. Right-click the desired Excel Workbook document in the Library list pane.
3. Choose Remove Offline Copy on the pop-up menu.

In Figure 8-6 we're choosing to remove the "Offline" copy of the Excel Services PivotTable and PivotDiagram. This is significant in that we're now working with a copy of the SharePoint Excel spreadsheet that has been downloaded to our Outlook e-mail repository (which can exist on the Exchange server or on our workstation, depending on individual Outlook-Exchange configuration settings).

As Figure 8-7 shows, we can subsequently choose to reload the Excel spreadsheet from SharePoint into Outlook.

1. Right-click the Reports—Reports Library in the Mail Folders tree view.
2. Right-click the desired Excel Workbook document in the Available For Download list.

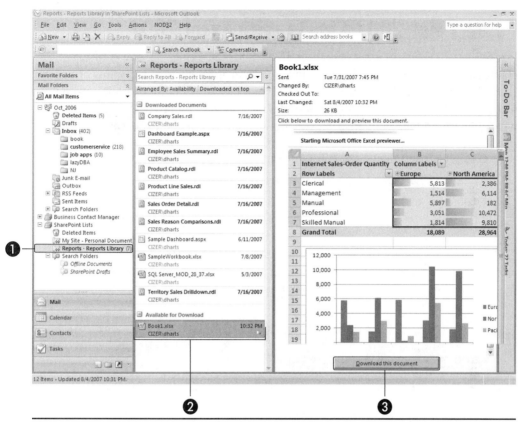

Figure 8-7   Outlook 2007—download a SharePoint Excel report

3. Click the Download This Document button that appears in the Outlook preview pane.

Figure 8-7 shows how we can control Outlook's list of SharePoint content, which in this case will result in new data being displayed in the Excel Services spreadsheet if the SharePoint configuration has specified a data refresh when viewed. If we delete the SharePoint item in our Outlook client, the SharePoint item is removed only from our client, not the SharePoint server. This makes sense when we realize other users in the organization may be accessing the same Excel Services workbook—and they may want to control or delete the workbook content in their Outlook client as well without interfering with SharePoint's server-based content.

PowerPoint 2007 Charts with Excel 2007

PowerPoint 2007 enjoys integration with Excel 2007 that brings the power of Excel charts directly into our PowerPoint design environment. Not surprisingly, this brings up Excel 2007 on our desktop to give us the user interface of Excel for chart design and manipulation. In fact, Excel actually provides the charting engine for PowerPoint, and when you are working with the data, you are working with a real Excel spreadsheet!

1. Click the Insert tab on the Ribbon menu.
2. Click the Chart icon in the Illustrations menu group.
3. Choose a Chart type.
4. Click OK.

As Figure 8-8 shows, the new Ribbon menu of Office 2007 makes it easy to insert an Excel chart into our PowerPoint slide. In our working example we're choosing the default Column chart to see how this process works.

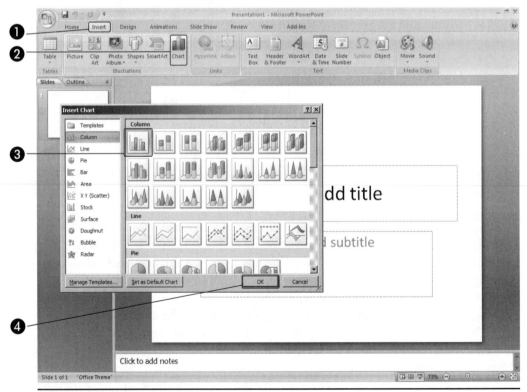

Figure 8-8 *PowerPoint 2007—Insert Chart*

Figure 8-9 shows the automatic start of Excel 2007 in a half-window pane next our ongoing work in PowerPoint.

1. Click any cell in the Excel chart, change the value, and press ENTER.
2. Click the Click To Add Title area on the PowerPoint chart, and enter any desired text.

In Figure 8-9 we're not doing a lot of work because we're simply running through the default options of using Excel to create a PowerPoint chart. PowerPoint and Excel are dynamically connected in Figure 8-9, as we see by changing values in the spreadsheet that are automatically reflected in the accompanying PowerPoint chart display.

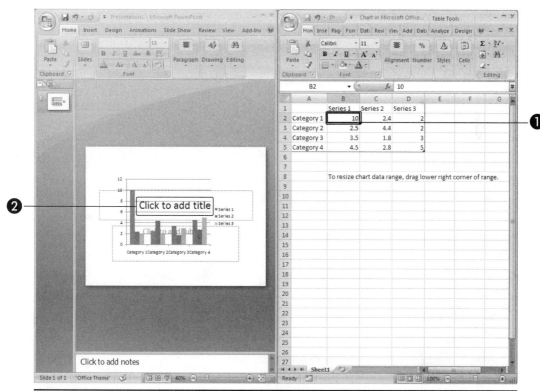

Figure 8-9   *PowerPoint 2007 chart from Excel 2007*

In Figure 8-10 you see a different way to put Excel analytics into PowerPoint—by starting with an existing Excel PivotTable (in Excel 2007) and copying it into PowerPoint.

1. Holding down the left mouse button, select the desired Excel PivotTable.
2. Right-click over the selected cell range, and choose Copy.
3. Click Paste on the PowerPoint Home tab of the Ribbon menu.
4. Choose Paste Special on the pop-up menu.
5. Choose Microsoft Office Excel Worksheet Object in the Paste Special list box.
6. Click OK.

Figure 8-10 shows that Office 2007 offers a better copy-and-paste scenario between Excel and PowerPoint. By choosing the Microsoft Office Excel Worksheet Object in

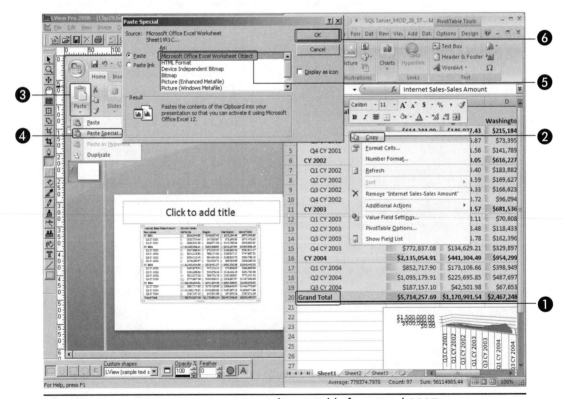

Figure 8-10 *PowerPoint 2007 "Paste Special" PivotTable from Excel 2007*

the Paste Special dialog box, we're able to place a data-connected PivotTable onto a PowerPoint slide. The fidelity of the resulting PivotTable is excellent even though the PivotTable Filter controls do not transfer to PowerPoint.

Figure 8-11 shows how we edit the Excel spreadsheet object that we've placed on a PowerPoint slide.

1. Click the PowerPoint spreadsheet object to select it.
2. Right-click over the selected spreadsheet object, and choose Linked Worksheet Object on the pop-up menu.
3. Choose Edit on the pop-up menu.

In Figure 8-11 we're able to choose to edit the Excel spreadsheet from within PowerPoint, which then automatically opens up Excel 2007 for its PivotTable design interface.

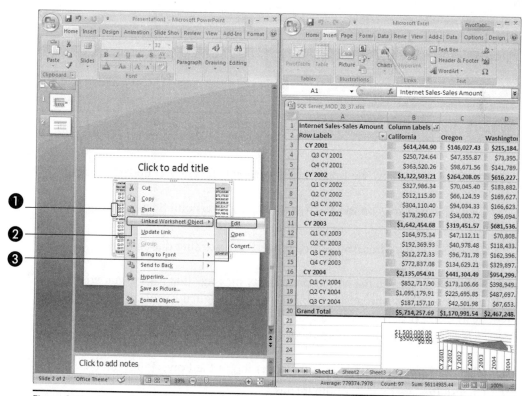

Figure 8-11 *PowerPoint 2007 Linked Worksheet Object—edit in Excel 2007*

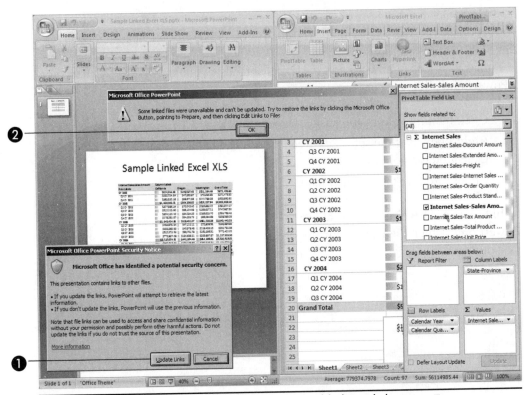

Figure 8-12 *PowerPoint 2007 Update Links to embedded Excel chart*

Figure 8-12 shows how we finish the PowerPoint spreadsheet update process.

1. Click Update Links on the Microsoft Office PowerPoint Security Notice dialog box.
2. Click OK on the Microsoft Office PowerPoint warning dialog box.

In Figure 8-12 you see the Microsoft security message that asks if you wish to update the PowerPoint spreadsheet object from the original Excel spreadsheet. This takes us to the next step shown in Figure 8-13, where you are able to edit the links to files such as an external Excel Workbook.

1. Click the Office Button icon at the upper left of the PowerPoint screen.
2. Choose Prepare on the pop-up menu.
3. Choose Edit Links To Files on the pop-up menu.

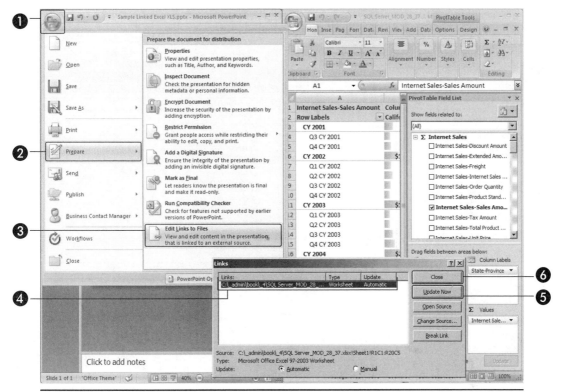

Figure 8-13 *PowerPoint 2007 Edit Links To Files for embedded Excel PivotTable*

4. Click the desired worksheet item in the Links list box.
5. Click Update Now to update the data.
6. Click Close.

Figure 8-13 shows how easy it is to update the PowerPoint Links to an external object such as the original Excel PivotTable. This is a somewhat manual process that is designed to protect embedded Excel objects from a security perspective—not to automatically update PowerPoint slide content.

Publishing PowerPoint 2007 to SharePoint

Figure 8-14 takes us to the next stage of working with PowerPoint 2007, where you can publish the slide deck to SharePoint 2007.

1. Click the Office Button icon at the upper left of the PowerPoint screen.
2. Choose Publish on the pop-up menu.

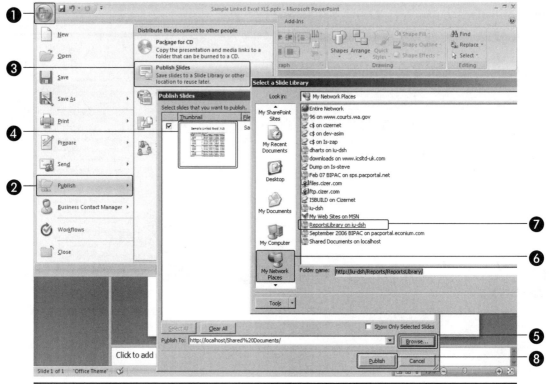

Figure 8-14 *PowerPoint 2007—publish to SharePoint 2007*

3. Choose Publish Slides on the pop-up menu.
4. Click to select the desired slides to publish.
5. Click the Browse button.
6. Choose My Network Places to navigate to the SharePoint library list.
7. Choose Reports Library in the My Network Places list.
8. Click the Publish button to publish the selected slides to SharePoint.

As you see in Figure 8-14, Office 2007 offers an easy-to-use Publish feature that encourages Office users to save content to a server-based SharePoint repository. This certainly makes sense with the multitude of PowerPoint slide decks we invariably create for presentations every day. Having a SharePoint server-based repository of slides is of great benefit so that everyone knows where the latest true version of a

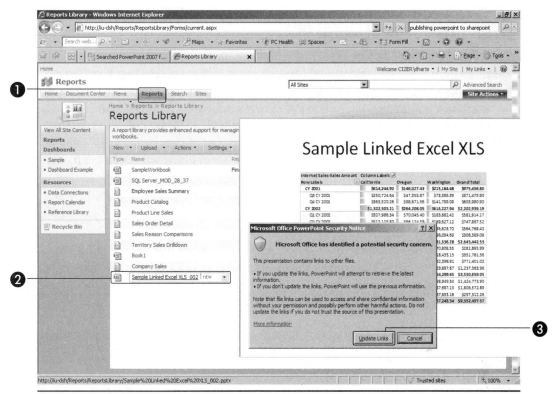

Figure 8-15 *SharePoint 2007—PowerPoint display in the Reports Library*

PowerPoint deck is located—and they can open or download it for presentation use as shown in Figure 8-15.

1. Click the Reports tab in SharePoint.
2. Click the PowerPoint Name in the Reports Library list.
3. Click Update Links on the Microsoft Office PowerPoint Security Notice dialog box.

In Figure 8-15 we are completing the PowerPoint publish-and-retrieve process. In our working example we have an embedded Excel spreadsheet object that has its own embedded data connection—and so SharePoint understandably asks us the same "Microsoft Office . . . security concern" question you saw in the PowerPoint application itself.

Visio 2007 PivotDiagram

It is not widely known that Visio can produce a Pivot diagram of multidimensional data. Rather, it is normally Excel that we use for such a task, where the resulting PivotTables provide an amazing ability to slice and dice the data with automatic cross-tab subtotaling. The subject of Excel PivotTables is handled in depth in Chapter 2 of this book.

For the purpose of demonstration, we'll proceed with a simple PivotDiagram to show how we're able to arrange the hierarchical display of data using Visio's unique shapes drag-and-drop design interface. Figure 8-16 shows how we start this process.

1. Click the Getting Started choice in the Template Categories list pane.
2. Choose the PivotDiagram template.

In Figure 8-16 we're able to use a PivotDiagram template that has the ability to connect to external data. The connection to external data is a fast-growing feature set for Visio—where people can bring relational or multidimensional data into Visio and arrange the visual results in a way that provides an informative display.

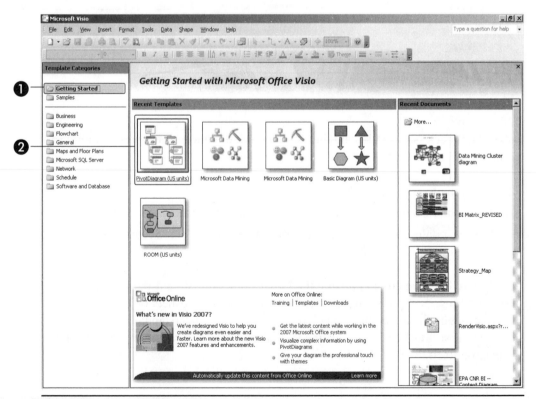

Figure 8-16 *Visio 2007 template PivotDiagram*

Figure 8-17 shows how we finish the process of connecting the Visio 2007 PivotDiagram to an external data source.

1. Using the left mouse button, select and drag the Pivot Node shape onto the Visio drawing pane.
2. Choose Previously Created Connection on the Data Selector dialog box.
3. Click Browse on the subsequent Data Selector dialog box.
4. Choose Data Connection Library in the Existing Connections dialog box.
5. Choose Localhost Analysis Services Tutorial in the Existing Connections list.
6. Click Finish.

In Figure 8-17 we're showing off something of real value with Visio's external data connection—which is the ability to use an already-existing Office Data Connection (ODC) from a SharePoint 2007 Data Connection Library. This allows us to bring data into Visio without having to figure out the connection settings for a

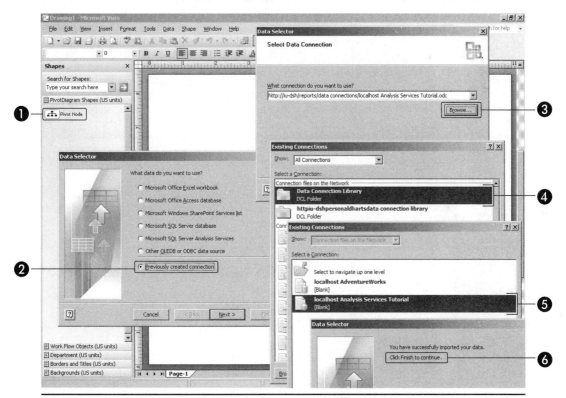

Figure 8-17 *Visio 2007 PivotDiagram—choosing an Office Data Connection*

particular data source, because someone that understands the data source has already captured the connection settings in an Office Data Connection and stored it as an ODC in a SharePoint library for others to use!

BI TIP

As we create business intelligence displays, it becomes clear that we can better focus on the visual presentation to the user if a database person with a good understanding of the back-end data has preconfigured data connections for us. This allows many BI presentation designers to use the work of one database engineer, and it allows people with front-end skill sets to focus on the creation of professional quality reports and charts.

Figure 8-18 shows what the SharePoint 2007 Data Connections Library looks like—which is a subject that is handled in depth in Chapter 5.

1. Click the Reports tab in SharePoint.
2. Click the Data Connections link in the Resources pane.

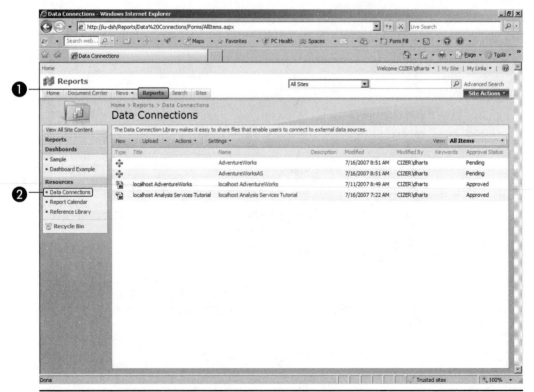

Figure 8-18   *SharePoint 2007—Data Connections Library*

In Figure 8-18 you see the new SharePoint 2007 interface, which is easier to use than previous versions of SharePoint. And the new SharePoint comes preconfigured with libraries that are ready to hold reports, data connections, and other content generated by Office knowledge workers.

Figure 8-19 shows the actual design of a PivotDiagram using the Office Data Connection we retrieved from SharePoint.

1. Choose Internet Sales—Order Quantity in the Add Total list pane.
2. Click Customer: Country—Region in the Add Category list pane.
3. Click Customer: Education in the Add Category list pane.

In Figure 8-19 you see a Pivot design interface that is similar to Excel, but with a slightly different process for choosing and arranging the data elements. It allows us to choose dimensions and measures from list panes that are labeled Categories and Totals, respectively.

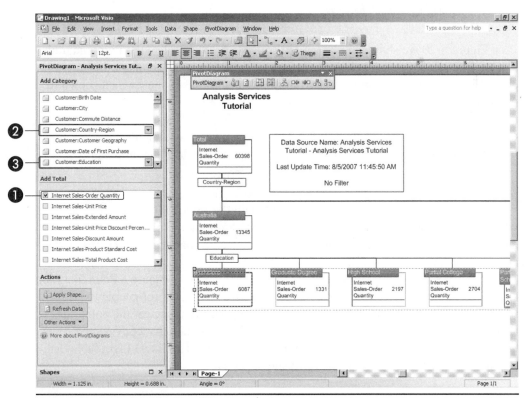

Figure 8-19 *Visio 2007—PivotDiagram design*

We've chosen a single total (measure) because it's easy to see on the Visio display; however, multiple measures can be chosen and will display in the same Visio rectangles shown in Figure 8-19. The order in which we choose the categories (dimensions) determines the hierarchical arrangement on the Visio screen; in our working example we chose Region and then Education, which places Education as the lowest-level data element in the Visio data tree arrangement.

It's interesting to note that Visio's org-chart, or tree-leaf, display of hierarchical data is easier to understand for some people than is Excel's PivotTable display. This is because everyone recognizes the multilayer arrangement in the Visio PivotDiagram, and it just makes sense when we see the data elements in such a display!

BI TIP

A business intelligence data presentation that is intuitively understood by consumers is of prime importance. The best way to create an "intuitively understood" display is with familiar screen mechanisms that people already understand from everyday working life — and the Visio PivotDiagram is an example of such a display because it is similar to the organization charts we've all worked with for years.

In Figure 8-20 we show a quick way to collapse or consolidate the PivotDiagram display by merging peer-level elements into a single element. Although this might be challenging to explain in narrative text, it immediately makes sense when shown in the Visio tree view.

1. Click to select the left-most Education display component, and CTRL-click the remaining components to multi-select all Education display components.
2. Click the Merge icon in the PivotDiagram floating toolbar.

Figure 8-20 shows that we've multi-selected all the Education data rectangles, which can be done with CTRL-clicks or by simply dragging the mouse over all the data elements. The result is shown in Figure 8-20 as the changed PivotDiagram that appears to the upper-right of the original diagram.

The ability to consolidate data elements is critical in Visio because a PivotDiagram so quickly stretches across a huge design area—which is harder for people to grasp because they have to scroll to see the entire display. This emphasizes the point that a PivotDiagram is best suited to a consolidated display of data that conveys the hierarchical relationship of data dimensions—in contrast to an Excel PivotTable that can display much more detailed data in a single screen.

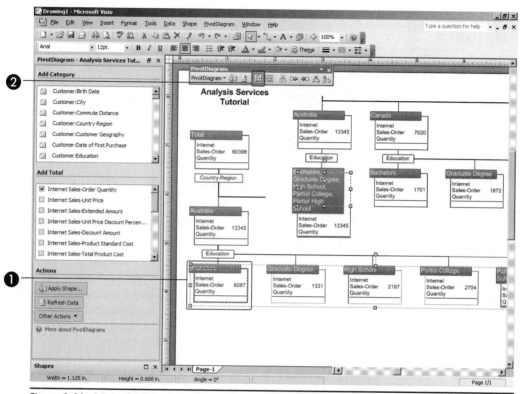

Figure 8-20 *Visio 2007—PivotDiagram Merge Category*

In Figure 8-21 we continue our process of consolidating the PivotDiagram by choosing specific dimensional data values to be displayed.

1. Right-click Customer: Education in the Add Category list pane.
2. Choose Configure Dimension in the pop-up menu.
3. Click the Configure Level button in the Configure Dimension dialog box.
4. Choose "begins with" in the Filter drop-down list.
5. Enter **bachelor** in the text box for the first filter.
6. Choose "or" in the Filter drop-down list.
7. Choose "begins with" in the Filter drop-down list.
8. Enter **graduate** in the text box for the second filter, and click OK.
9. Right-click any object in the drawing pane.

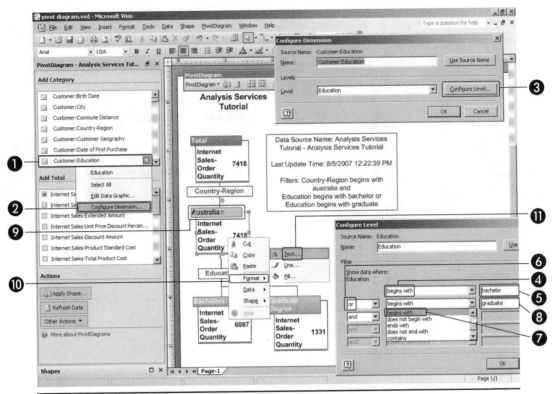

Figure 8-21 *Visio 2007—PivotDiagram Configure Dimension*

10. Choose Format in the pop-up menu.
11. Choose Text to configure the font and color.

Figure 8-21 shows how quickly we can change with the Visio presentation—by choosing the data values to display and by formatting the fill colors and text. A designer with a good eye can create a stunning display of data this way, using Visio's Configure Dimension feature and the built-in formatting tools that are common to all Microsoft Office applications.

In Figure 8-22 you see how easily the PivotDiagram can be "pivoted" or changed from a top-down to a left-to-right arrangement.

1. Holding the left mouse button down, click and drag to multi-select all objects in the PivotDiagram.

2. Click the Arrange icon in the floating PivotDiagram toolbar.

3. Choose Left-To-Right on the pop-up menu.

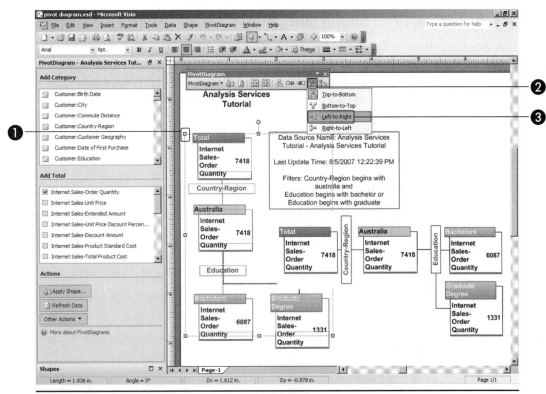

Figure 8-22 *Visio 2007—PivotDiagram Left-to-Right*

Figure 8-22 shows that we've multi-selected all the diagram rectangles—which can be done with CTRL-clicks or by simply dragging the mouse over all the data elements. The result is shown in Figure 8-22 as the changed PivotDiagram that appears to the upper-right of the original diagram.

It's interesting to note that the two displays shown in our working example are very common to good data displays because people are used to looking at information from top to bottom, or from left to right.

BI TIP

A good data presentation makes it easy for consumers to "read" the data story from top to bottom, or left to right. This avoids the need to jump around visually in the business intelligence display, which is confusing and leads to presentations that are perceived as too complicated. People are more comfortable with an intuitive flow of data visualization that follows the way we've learned to read in a top-down and left-to-right paradigm—with color or shapes being used to emphasize "blocks of data" in the same way paragraphs of text are arranged for easy reading.

Saving Visio 2007 to SharePoint

It makes sense that we finish our Visio PivotDiagram discussion by saving the results to SharePoint. Although Visio allows us to save diagrams as JPG or GIF graphics, it is more useful to save the actual Visio format to SharePoint's central repository so that other Visio users with permission to edit the Visio diagram can retrieve it from a library of business intelligence content.

Figure 8-23 shows the process of saving our PivotDiagram to SharePoint.

1. Click the File choice on the top Visio menu bar.

2. Choose Save As on the pop-up menu.

3. Choose My Network Places in the Save As dialog box.

4. Choose Reports Library in the My Network Places list.

5. Click Save.

6. Enter the desired Report Description in the text box for the SharePoint Reports Library.

7. Click OK.

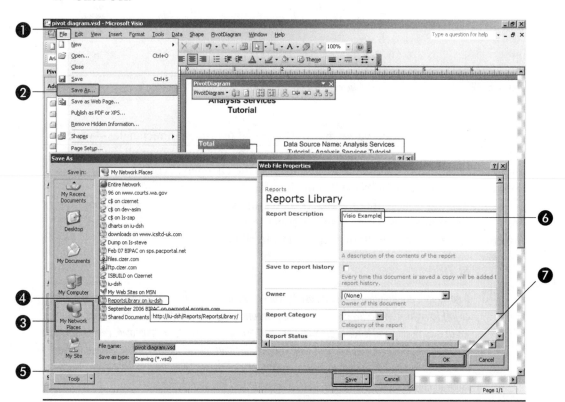

Figure 8-23 Visio 2007—saving to SharePoint 2007

Note in Figure 8-23 that you don't see the Office 2007 Ribbon menu interface—so we use the traditional File | Save As procedure. The next version of Visio will have the new Ribbon menu, which will use a "Publish to SharePoint" mechanism that makes full use of the enhanced integration between Office and SharePoint.

Figure 8-24 shows how we access the Visio PivotDiagram through the SharePoint user interface.

1. Click the Reports tab in SharePoint.

2. Click the Visio object in the documents list.

3. Click OK to open the Visio diagram as Read Only.

Note in Figure 8-24 we're able to open the Visio diagram—although it does require that we have the Visio application on our desktop machine. The SharePoint library knows that our working example is a Visio object—and as such SharePoint automatically associates the Visio object with Visio on our client computer for editing purposes. In fact, SharePoint has a web part for Visio that supports the placement of a Visio diagram next to an Excel spreadsheet—all on the same page in SharePoint!

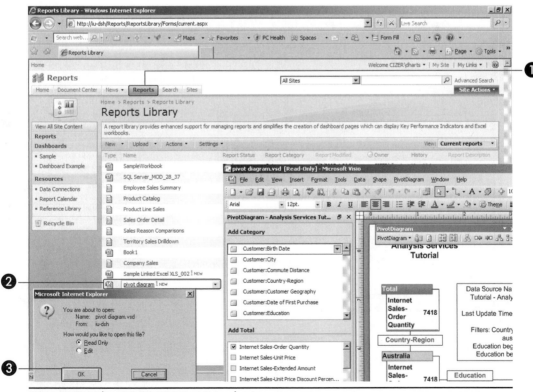

Figure 8-24 *SharePoint 2007—Visio document*

Word 2007 and Excel 2007 PivotTables

One might ask why Word is included in a discussion of business intelligence tools; the answer is that many real-world reports are produced in Word doc format, which is always easy for people to read. Additionally, narrative elements of a BI presentation can be included in Word using the phenomenal power of its editing tools.

We will look briefly at the interaction between Word and Excel, and Figure 8-25 shows how we start the simple process of copy and paste.

1. Using the left mouse button, drag the mouse to select the desired PivotTable.
2. Right-click over the selected PivotTable, and choose Copy on the pop-up menu.

In Figure 8-25 we've simply selected an example Excel 2007 PivotTable and proceeded to copy it to the Office clipboard. Figure 8-26 show how we complete this process.

1. Click Paste on the Word Home tab of the Ribbon menu.
2. Choose Paste Special on the pop-up menu.

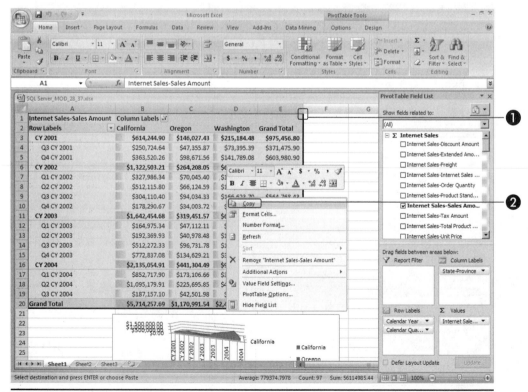

Figure 8-25 *Excel 2007—copy*

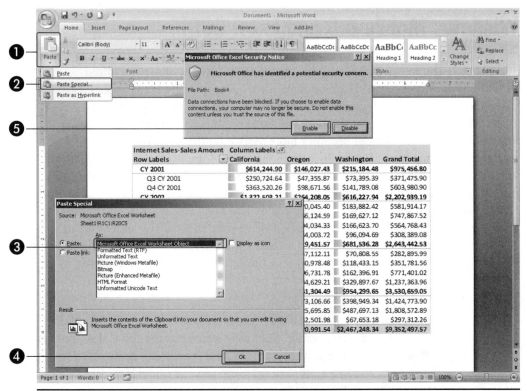

Figure 8-26 *Word 2007 Paste Special—Excel PivotTable*

3. Choose Microsoft Office Excel Worksheet Object in the Paste Special list box.
4. Click OK.
5. Click Enable to enable the PivotTable data connection.

In Figure 8-26 we use the Paste Special capability of Office to place a data-connected Excel Worksheet Object into a Word document. Since the Excel object has its own embedded Office Data Connection, Word asks us the same "Microsoft Office . . . security concern" question you saw in the PowerPoint application when we accomplished the same Paste Special operation.

The resulting PivotTable looks quite good, and the conditional formatting of Excel 2007 carries over into Word. The PivotTable Filter controls are not available, since we don't have a native Excel engine capability in Word—but the spreadsheet will show refreshed data in the Word document if we choose to Update Links as we explained in the earlier section of this chapter "PowerPoint 2007 Charts with Excel 2007."

Windows Mobile 6.0 and Excel 2007

Windows Mobile is one of the most fascinating areas of business intelligence available to explore, partly because it's changing so fast. As observers of our industry have remarked, the number of Windows users worldwide is approaching one billion—but the wireless industry sells one billion cell phones every year!

As Windows Mobile becomes more available on these billion phones, we find that Microsoft Office content becomes more visible on the same phones. This is a world that is changing as fast as the cell phone technology itself—and this chapter will explore what can be done today with Excel 2007 and the Windows Mobile 6.0 operating system on a cell phone.

As you'll see in this section, you can deploy and view Excel 2007 spreadsheets to a Windows Mobile Smartphone fairly easily—but you really cannot edit it. A Windows Mobile PocketPC phone has edit capability for Excel spreadsheets through its touch-sensitive screen, but it is limited by the actual screen area.

BI TIP

Many consumers of business intelligence do not need to manipulate or edit the reports and charts they receive; they simply need to see the "health of the organization at a glance." A well-designed BI presentation can convey enough information to be of use in a read-only context. This is the state of the art we find today with cell phone technology, where we can see BI presentations that help us keep our finger on the pulse of the business minute-by-minute.

Note that Windows Mobile 6.0 on a Smartphone (not a touch-sensitive screen) will display the Windows logo in the lower-left part of the Home screen, while a Windows Mobile 6.0 PocketPC phone will show the Windows logo in the upper-right part of the screen.

Copying the Excel Spreadsheet to a Smartphone

Figure 8-27 shows how we accomplish the copy-and-paste of a file to our Windows Mobile 6.0 Smartphone. For the purpose of our working example we'll use a T-Mobile Dash Smartphone with Windows Mobile 6.0 and the Documents to Go cell phone application from T-Mobile that allows us to view Excel, Word, PowerPoint, and PDF files.

1. Right-click the desired Excel 2007 file in desktop Windows Explorer, and choose Copy.
2. Click the Explore icon in Microsoft ActiveSync.
3. Right-click in Windows Mobile File Explorer, and choose Paste.

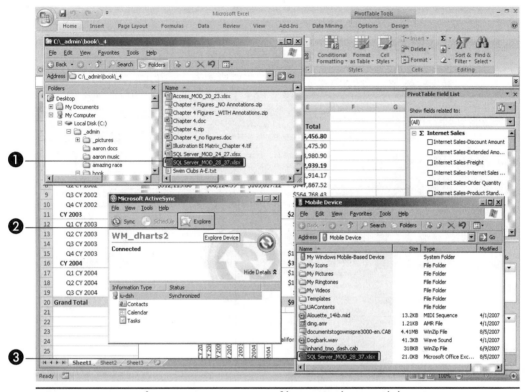

Figure 8-27 *Microsoft ActiveSync 4.5—copy file to Windows Mobile 6.0*

In Figure 8-27 we are making use of the free Microsoft ActiveSync application on our desktop computer to transfer a file to our cell phone. ActiveSync automatically starts up when it senses that we've connected a cell phone to the desktop or laptop computer through a USB cable or a Bluetooth connection.

As Figure 8-27 shows, we are really just using the familiar copy-and-paste procedure to copy our Excel 2007 file (with an XLSX file extension) to the mobile device. Figure 8-28 shows how we display the spreadsheet once it's on the cell phone.

1. Click Start on the Windows Mobile Home screen, or click the Spreadsheet icon in the recently used applications toolbar at the top of the screen.

2. Choose Open and File on the Windows Mobile Open File screen.

3. Choose Open on the pop-up menu.

4. Choose the Excel file in the Mobile File Explorer.

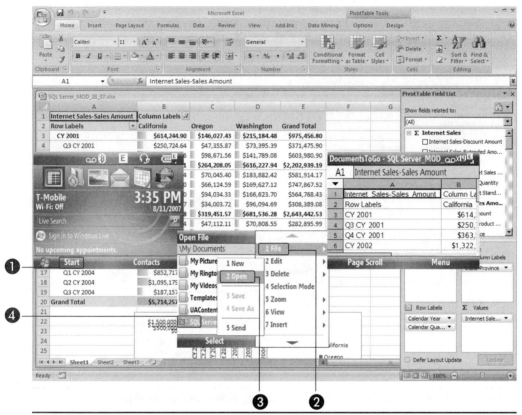

Figure 8-28 *Windows Mobile 6.0—File I Open I Excel 2007 xlsx*

Figure 8-28 shows cell phone screenshots against the backdrop of our desktop Excel PivotTable spreadsheet. It's worth noting that the Windows Mobile user interface works in much the same way as our desktop user interface—with a Start menu option on the lower-left of the screen, for example. This is a real benefit to modern-day knowledge workers that need to extend their desktop Office environments to their mobile phone, since the Windows interface and menu options work as we expect within the limitations of the cell phone display and keyboard.

In Figure 8-29 we are continuing the experience of working with our Excel 2007 spreadsheet on the cell phone by opening the chart in the spreadsheet.

1. Choose View on the Windows Mobile Menu screen.

2. Choose Chart In Sheet on the pop-up menu.

3. Choose Chart 1 on the pop-up menu.

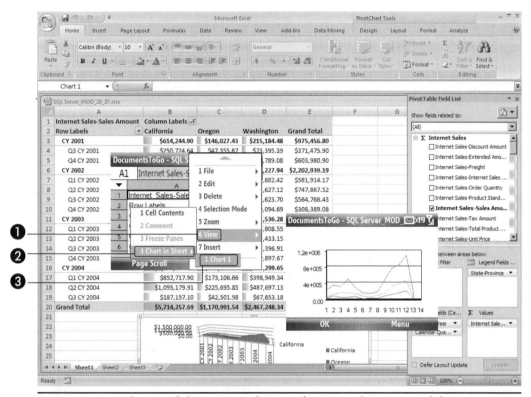

Figure 8-29 *Windows Mobile 6.0—Excel 2007 xlsx, view objects in worksheet*

As Figure 8-29 shows, it is a straightforward process to view various components of the Excel spreadsheet. In our working example we are using the Windows Mobile menu options to view an individual workbook object, which works nicely within the context of our cell phone display.

The logical next question is to ask how we can synchronize the Excel file that we've copied to our mobile device. The answer is with the Microsoft ActiveSync application that runs on our desktop computer. ActiveSync will automatically update the cell phone file with the latest version of the same file from our desktop computer—whenever the Smartphone cell phone is connected to the desktop through a USB cable or Bluetooth connection.

Figure 8-30 shows how we configure this File Sync with Microsoft ActiveSync.

1. Click Tools | Options on the Microsoft ActiveSync screen on your desktop.
2. Check Files as a sync option.

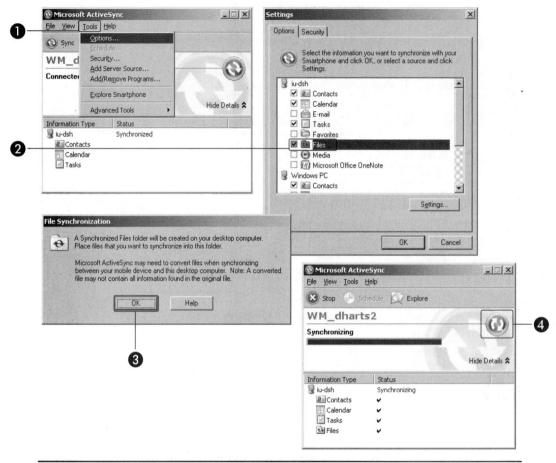

Figure 8-30 *Windows Mobile 6.0—ActiveSync Files*

3. Check OK on the File Synchronization dialog box.
4. Click the green Sync icon on the Microsoft ActiveSync screen.

In Figure 8-30 we are configuring the automatic update of our cell phone files, realizing the files originate from our desktop computer. The greatest benefit of this desktop-to-mobile synchronization methodology is that our original content is always on the desktop or laptop computer—and all Microsoft Outlook contacts, calendar items, tasks, and files (such as our example Excel file) are simply replicated to the mobile cell phone!

This is really quite important, since the mobile device may fail or be lost—and we can easily replicate the original names, phone numbers, and all associated information to a replacement phone.

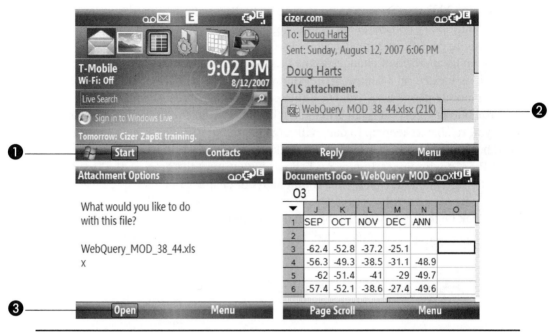

Figure 8-31   *Windows Mobile 6.0—open e-mail attachment XLSX file*

Figure 8-31 shows how we can receive our business intelligence spreadsheet as an e-mail attachment and view it on a Windows Mobile cell phone.

1. Click Start on the Windows Mobile Home screen, or click the E-Mail icon in the recently used applications toolbar at the top of the screen.

2. Click the e-mail attachment.

3. Choose Open from the Windows Mobile 6.0 menu.

In Figure 8-31 you see how a truly mobile workforce can be "live connected" to a Microsoft Office environment that can stream business intelligence content to us around the clock, around the world. The resulting connection to reports, charts, and Key Performance Indicators allows a mobile workforce to be "in the know" about business developments and alerts that are increasingly needed with modern global organizations.

SharePoint Alerts of Spreadsheet Changes to a Smartphone

The logical continuation of the mobile BI story is with the synchronization of our Excel 2007 spreadsheet content with our Windows Mobile 6.0 Smartphone.

SharePoint 2007 can be configured to automatically send e-mail notifications of SharePoint library content changes to designated users. This does not result in an automatic update of the spreadsheet that we've copied to the Smartphone, but it does keep us apprised of changes to the original spreadsheet that in a best-practices scenario is located on a central SharePoint server.

As a mobile phone user, you can either copy the new spreadsheet to your Smartphone or receive it as an e-mail attachment on your Smartphone. In either case you're able to keep up to date with organizational Excel business intelligence workbooks that are being used by colleagues around the world in a collaborative SharePoint environment. Figure 8-32 shows how to start the process of SharePoint 2007 configuration, to enable SharePoint alerts of changes to Excel spreadsheets.

1. Click Outgoing E-Mail Settings on the SharePoint Central Administration screen.

2. Click Configure Outgoing E-Mail Settings on the SharePoint configuration screen.

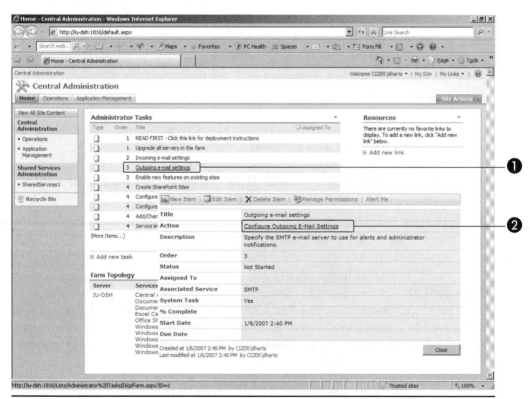

Figure 8-32 *SharePoint 2007 outgoing e-mail configuration*

In Figure 8-32, the SharePoint server Central Administration screen is used to enable outgoing e-mail alerts from the SharePoint server itself. Note this is normally the job of a SharePoint administrator, but we're including it in this SharePoint alert discussion to show a complete picture of the server-based settings that will result in automatic notifications to mobile phone users.

Figure 8-33 shows the options available on the final SharePoint Central Administration screen for enabling e-mail alerts.

1. Enter the organization's SMTP server in the Outbound SMTP Server text box.

2. Enter appropriate From and Reply-To e-mail addresses.

3. Click OK.

In Figure 8-33 you see an example of the e-mail server information that SharePoint will use to send alerts through an Exchange E-Mail Server. A complete discussion of this SharePoint configuration is beyond the brief treatment of the subject in this

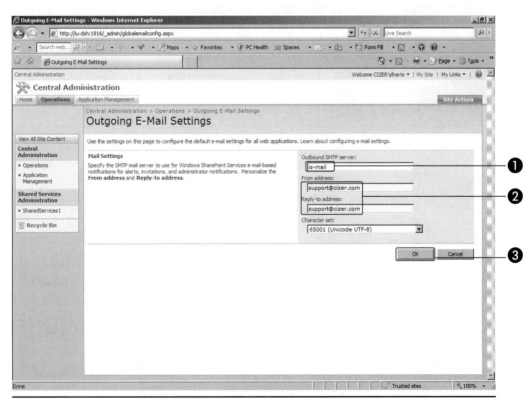

Figure 8-33 *SharePoint 2007 outgoing e-mail settings*

section, but it's clear that SharePoint 2007 has a flexible server-based mechanism to keep all users, including mobile users, up to date with SharePoint content.

In Figure 8-34 we return to the SharePoint library to configure alerts of library changes.

1. Click the Actions drop-down menu in the Reports Library.
2. Choose Alert Me in the pop-up menu.

In Figure 8-34 you see the familiar SharePoint Library menu structure, which we're using to configure e-mail alerts of content changes. This SharePoint menu structure is becoming well known across organizations that are using SharePoint to manage business intelligence content and keep users up to date with content changes. In Figure 8-35 we finish the configuration of alerts for changes to our Reports Library.

1. Enter the desired e-mail Alert Title in the text box.

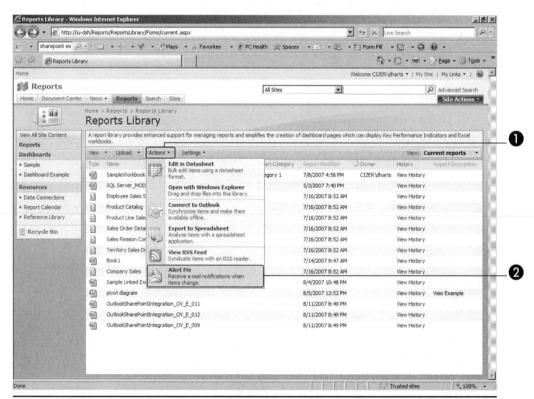

Figure 8-34 *SharePoint 2007 library Alert Me menu options*

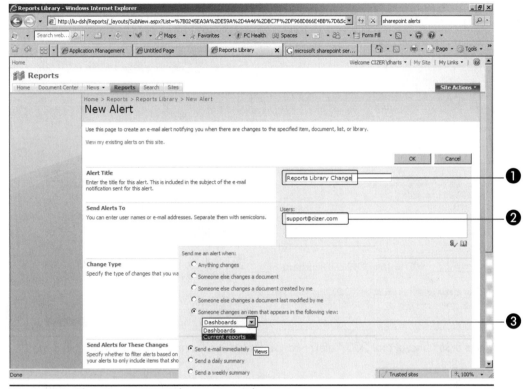

Figure 8-35 *SharePoint 2007 Library New Alert menu options*

2. Enter the desired Users e-mail addresses in the text box.
3. Choose the desired View from the drop-down list.

In Figure 8-35 you see a variety of menu choices that allow SharePoint alert notifications to be automatically sent to users that are working with library content documents (or spreadsheets). Multiple alerts can be configured for the various libraries that an organization uses to maintain central repositories of Office content, such as Excel spreadsheets, Word documents, and PowerPoint slide decks.

In Figure 8-36 you see the end result of SharePoint e-mail communication with business users, and in particular with Windows Mobile users.

As you see in Figure 8-36, the worlds of desktop and mobile Office knowledge workers are easily connected from a SharePoint server. This allows people to stay apprised of the latest business intelligence reports, both in the office and out of the office. In today's global economy where workers are located in time zones

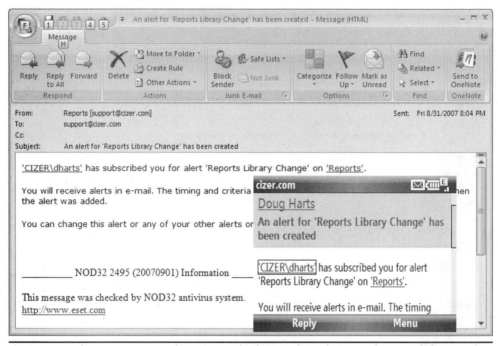

Figure 8-36 *SharePoint 2007 alert—to Outlook e-mail, and to Windows Mobile e-mail*

around the world, we can look to SharePoint as a central source of BI truth that can be accessed from any device that can receive Microsoft Office spreadsheets, documents, and PowerPoint slide decks. The result is an extension of collaborative SharePoint business intelligence to everyone at all levels of the organization.

BI TIP

If we describe "collaborative business intelligence" as the ability for multiple people to access a central repository of real-time reports and charts, then the next step is to provide "collaborative and ubiquitous business intelligence" to mobile users that can use BI tools while they are on the go around the world, around the clock, 24 hours a day.

Office Online

One might ask why our discussion of business intelligence would proceed to an Office web site; the answer is that an online community is available today to help everyday business users learn about and use Office 2007 tools—in fact all the tools and technologies covered in this book are supported from this central Internet location.

Microsoft has termed this Office Online, and it's so popular that people that hear about it think it's a product!

Office Online is not a product; it is instead a community web site where we can find free tutorials, video recordings, and newsgroups that explain Office tools. Figure 8-37 shows how easy it is to access Office Online with nothing more than an Internet connection.

1. Enter **Office.Microsoft.com** in the Internet Explorer address text box.
2. Click the "Check for updates" link in top menu of "Office Online."

In Figure 8-37 you can glimpse of the Office Online experience; Figure 8-38 provides a bit more exploration into the areas that can help everyone use the new features of Office 2007.

1. Click the Help And How-To tab on the Office Online top menu bar.
2. Choose Excel in the Office Discussion Groups list.

Figure 8-37 *Office Online—Home page*

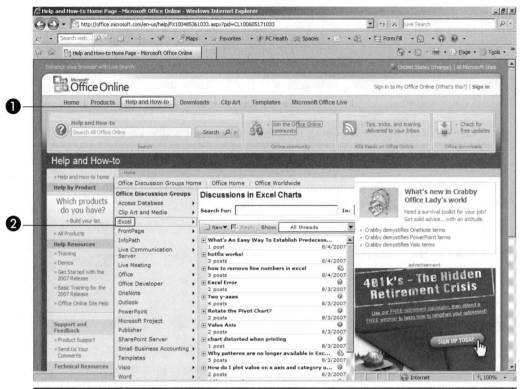

Figure 8-38 *Office Online—Office Discussion Groups*

In Figure 8-38 you see how to navigate to the Office Discussion Groups—most notably the Excel Discussion Group. Here we can search for help with how-to questions that are posted by Excel users from all over the world. It makes sense that our questions are probably not unique and may be answered in these newsgroups, where Microsoft experts provide e-mail answers to users that frequent the online community.

In Figure 8-39 you see an easy way to navigate from the Office Online community to the Microsoft Business Intelligence subsite.

1. Enter **business intelligence** in the Search text box.
2. Click the Search icon.
3. Choose Microsoft Business Intelligence in the search results list.

As Figure 8-39 shows, Microsoft provides a good deal of information in support of the Microsoft Business Intelligence technologies. While much of the associated

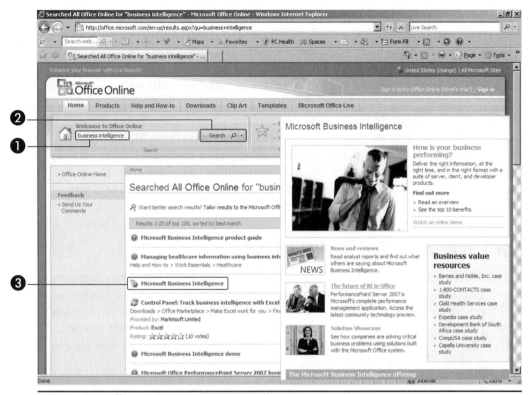

Figure 8-39 *Office Online—"Business Intelligence" search*

content is highly technical in nature, it can be a good starting point when searching for knowledge-base articles on the design and implementation of SQL Server and Office Business Intelligence products.

SQL Server Business Intelligence Platform Technologies

The simplest way to start this discussion is to say the foundation of Microsoft Office 2007 business intelligence applications is SQL Server 2005. And although in principle this is a correct statement, it must be noted that Office BI applications can present reporting, analysis, and measurement displays—while directly connected to a wide variety of data sources, including Oracle, IBM's DB2, and even mainframe data. This is because Excel, for example, can use an Office Data Connection to these non-Microsoft data repositories.

However, a fully functioning BI solution needs more than just a connection to these back-end data sources. A modern BI solution is best implemented with a dedicated BI server that brings data together from the wide variety of data sources, which include Oracle and DB2, for example. If the dedicated BI server uses SQL Server 2005, then we are able to take advantage of three major BI technologies that are included with every SQL Server database server license: Integration Services, Analysis Services, and Reporting Services.

Please note that this section does not attempt to explain these SQL Server BI technologies in depth—our purpose here is to provide a high-level understanding of how they support the front-end Office BI applications such as Excel. This helps business users to understand where the data comes from when they are doing reporting and analysis in a SharePoint Office environment.

SQL Server Integration Services (SSIS)

An understanding of the SSIS design environment is the first step to understanding the architecture of Integration Services, and the way components can be connected at two levels (which we can think of as the Control level and the Data level) to create a flow of data from source to destination. Note that the Visual Studio 2005 Integrated Design Environment (IDE) is used as a development "frame" within which we can create, debug, and deploy a SSIS package.

This is consistent with Microsoft's direction to use VS as a "frame" for programmers working with code in languages such as C# and VB.Net, and for database developers and administrators working with extraction, transformation, and loading (ETL). In fact, the VS IDE is also where we can create online analytical processing (OLAP) cubes using SQL Server Integration Services (SSAS), which are based on Fact-Dimension tables that often are populated with data from a SSIS package.

BI TIP

The value of a consistent user interface that supports database administrators, programmers, and business intelligence developers is immense. It allows IT shops to learn and use the same design paradigm in support of application development that makes use of coding, database, and reporting disciplines.

Figure 8-40 shows an example SSIS project in the Visual Studio design environment. At first glance users often find this interface very busy; sometimes called "VS blur." But in fact, over time the interface makes good sense as we realize that components

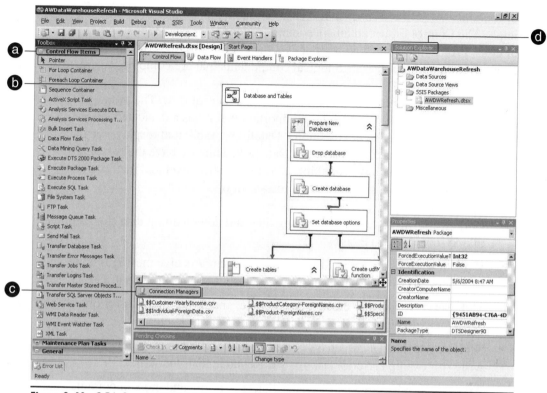

Figure 8-40 *SQL Server 2005 Integration Service (SSIS) control flow*

in the left panes are dragged into the central design screen—and all components associated with our work are displayed in the right-side tree-view Explorer pane.

a. The Toolbox dynamically provides different content elements, depending on the design tab chosen in the central design pane.

b. A tabbed interface allows multiple design processes to be accomplished in the Visual Studio IDE.

c. The Connection Managers show the various data connections that have been configured by the SSIS designer, for both input and output data.

d. The Solution Explorer provides a familiar file-explorer interface to navigate among the multiple components that make up a SSIS project.

Figure 8-40 also shows the top level of a SSIS project (we can refer to this as the Control level). A SSIS package consists of a "Control Flow" that is made up of *containers, tasks,* and *constraints.* These components do just what their names imply. The Control Flow containers contain for loops, for each loops, and sequences of tasks. From a program flow perspective, these Control Flow containers provide a top-level grouping of the SSIS logical components that are combined to create an ETL data flow.

Control Flow tasks are the "units of work" in a control flow. The primary task is the Data Flow task, which is so important that it has a dedicated tab in the SSIS Designer (see the next section, "Data Flow Tab") that displays the data transformations that make up a selected Data task. Thus we have the two levels of the SSIS Designer, which we can think of as the Control level and the Data level.

Other Control Flow tasks can be categorized into:

▶ **Data preparation tasks** for copying files and downloading data (for example, File System task, FTP task)

▶ **Workflow tasks** that run SSIS packages and send/receive messages between packages (for example, Execute Package task, Execute Process task)

▶ **SQL Server tasks** that create, read, update, and delete SQL Server objects and data (for example, Bulk Insert task, Execute SQL task, etc.)

▶ **Scripting tasks** that extend SSIS functionality with program code that you write (for example, Script task for VB.Net code that you write)

▶ **Analysis Services tasks** that create, delete, modify, and most important, process SQL Server Analysis Services (SSAS) cubes (Analysis Services Processing task)

▶ **Maintenance tasks** for SQL Server database backups, rebuilding indexes, etc. (for example, Back Up Database task, Check Database Integrity task)

▶ **Custom tasks** that you create with as COM objects, using Visual Basic or C#, for example

Figure 8-41 shows the next tab of the central SSIS design screen. At this second level (we can think of this as the Data level), a SSIS package consists of a "Data Flow" that is made up of *sources, transformations,* and *destinations.* The sources and destinations extract data from, and load data to, OLE DB—connected databases, flat files, and Excel (and to a special destination, a SSAS cube Dimension Processing). These make up the extraction and loading of an ETL data flow.

a. The Toolbox for the Data Flow (central design pane tab) shows the Data Flow Sources that can be incorporated into a SSIS project.

b. The Toolbox also shows the Data Flow Destinations for a SSIS project.

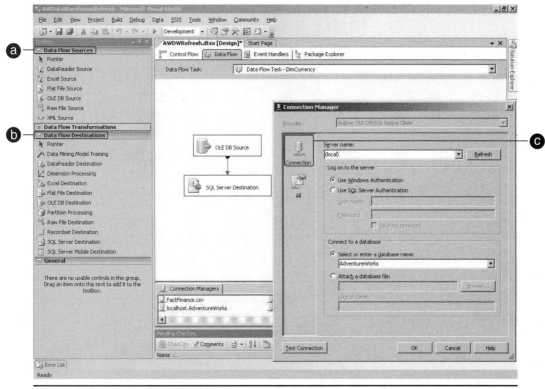

Figure 8-41 *SQL Server 2005 Integration Services (SSIS) data flow sources and destinations*

   c. The Connection Manager supports configuration of database locations and ID-password permissions for the various data connections that have been configured by the SSIS designer, for both input and output data.

In Figure 8-41 note that Data Flow Sources and Data Flow Destinations rely on Data Connections that are configured in the Connection Manager pane of the Visual Studio SSIS Designer.

Figure 8-42 shows the Transformations that are the data manipulation components, within a Data task, that aggregate, merge, distribute, and modify data. In an ETL data flow, these transformations compose the "transformation" part of extraction, transformation, and loading.

   a. The Toolbox for the Data Flow (central design pane tab) shows the data transformations that can be incorporated into a SSIS project.

   b. In the central design pane, we've clicked a Data Conversion component in the SSIS project.

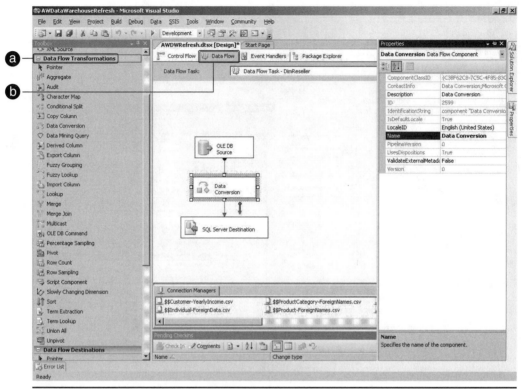

Figure 8-42 *SQL Server 2005 Integration Services (SSIS) data flow transformations*

As a final part of our brief discussion of SSIS, note that Figure 8-42 shows SSIS transformations that can be categorized into

▶ **Business intelligence transformations** that clean and mine data (for example, Fuzzy Grouping transformation, Fuzzy Lookup transformation)

▶ **Row transformations** that update column values (for example, Character Map transformation, Copy Column transformation)

▶ **Rowset transformations** for aggregating and sorting (for example, Aggregate transformation, Sort transformation)

▶ **Split and Join transformations** to split/join data and perform data lookups (for example, Conditional Split transformation, Union All transformation)

▶ **Other transformations** for exporting/importing data and auditing (for example, Export Column transformation, Import Column transformation)

▶ **Custom transformations** that you create using Visual Basic or C#, for example

SQL Server Analysis Services (SSAS)

The SSAS design environment is similar to the SSIS design interface, in that it uses the Visual Studio Integrated Design Environment (IDE) to present the architecture and design elements of OLAP cubes. OLAP is an acronym for online analytical processing, which is really just the analysis we do with Excel spreadsheets when we examine columns and rows of data, scrolling up, down, and across the data.

If the Excel spreadsheet is connected to a SQL Server OLAP cube, as we showed in Chapter 3, we're able to scroll through the data and subtotal it on the fly with PivotTable, which can slice and dice up to a million rows in Excel 2007, which accesses live data from a billion or even a trillion rows in the server-based cube! The OLAP cube can be literally thought of as a cube in computer memory on the server, with sides to the cube that allow us to select date-time slices of data, and perhaps city-state regions of data—in an Excel PivotTable that quickly subtotals the chosen numeric data (perhaps gross sales or tax revenue).

Business intelligence developers design these OLAP cubes in the SSAS design environment shown in Figure 8-43, with data automatically drawn into the cube from relational data sources that reside on their own relational database servers.

a. The tabbed interface allows multiple design processes to be accomplished in the Visual Studio IDE.

b. The Measures pane provides a tree-view list of numeric data in the cube.

c. The Dimensions pane provides a tree-view list of text data (or descriptive data) in the cube.

d. The central design pane shows the data relationship between measures (in the center Fact table) and the dimensions (in the surrounding Dimension tables).

e. The Solution Explorer provides a familiar file-explorer interface to navigate among the multiple components that make up a SSAS project.

In Figure 8-43 you see the Cube Structure tab, which is the default tab for manipulating the cube, where we can make high-level changes to the overall cube. Note the Measure and Dimension panes to the left and the central pane that shows the structure for this cube. In this example the Fact table has a yellow header title, and the Dimension tables have blue header titles. A complete discussion of SSAS dimensional modeling is beyond the scope of this section (there are entire books that have been written in support of this area), but you can at least appreciate the organized nature of cube design by looking at these figures.

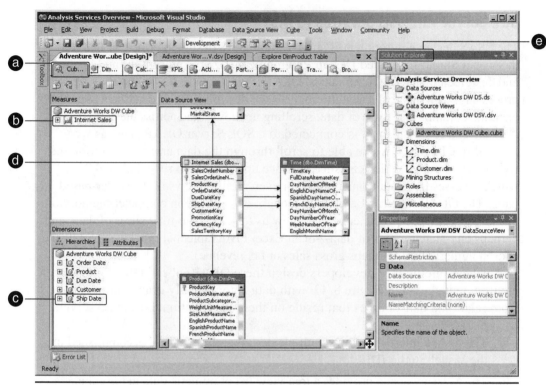

Figure 8-43 *SQL Server 2005 Analysis Services (SSAS) cube design*

Figure 8-44 shows how the OLAP cube designer can browse the Fact and Dimension data elements of the cube, in much the same manner as end users do in Excel 2007 PivotTables.

a. The tabbed interface allows multiple design processes to be accomplished in the Visual Studio IDE.

b. The Measures are numeric data elements that can be dragged and dropped into the central browse data pane.

c. The Dimensions are descriptive text elements that can be dragged and dropped into the central browse data pane, to group the measures by row and by column.

d. The central browse data pane provides a PivotTable interface for the designer to explore and validate cube data measures and dimensions.

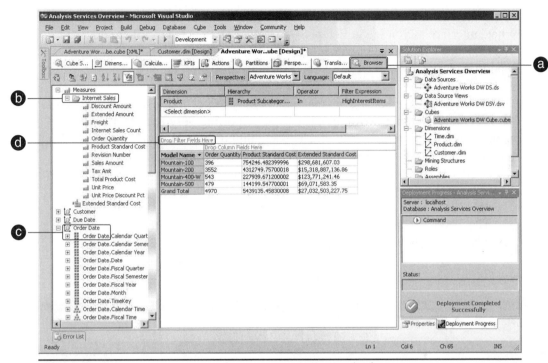

Figure 8-44 *SQL Server 2005 Analysis Services (SSAS) cube browser*

In Figure 8-44 the cube developer can slice and dice by any of our dimensions. The numbers can be split out by the levels of dimension hierarchies. And data can be filtered to display desired subsets of the cube.

At this point it should be clear that the Visual Studio SSAS Integrated Design Environment allows a business intelligence developer to work with cube data in much the same way business users will be able to see it from their Excel 2007 client machines. In this manner, the SSAS design environment allows the BI developer to visually design the server-based OLAP cube data to work properly with the front-end Microsoft Office reporting and analysis tools that everyone can use to slice and dice hierarchies of real-time multidimensional data!

SQL Server Reporting Services (SSRS)

The SSRS design environment is similar to the SSIS and SSAS design interface, in that it uses the Visual Studio Integrated Design Environment (IDE) to present the architecture and design elements of Reporting Services reports. Reporting Services is Microsoft's answer to reporting servers that have been on the market for some time—but which lacked an integrated designer with the power of Visual Studio.

The Visual Studio Reporting Services designer uses a traditional "banded report writer" interface as you see in Figure 8-45. Report Designers are able to drag and drop table and column data fields into the central design pane. The design pane uses Report Header, Body, and Report Footer sections to support the visual construction of a report.

It should be noted that there are many third-party report design tools on the market today that allow people to design these same Reporting Services reports without having to use or learn Visual Studio. This highlights the real value of Microsoft's Reporting Services—that it's a server-based report design standard with many market-driven choices of report designers from Microsoft partner companies, that allow reports to be designed in many different ways.

a. The Datasets pane provides a tree view of table and column elements that are available to the report designer.

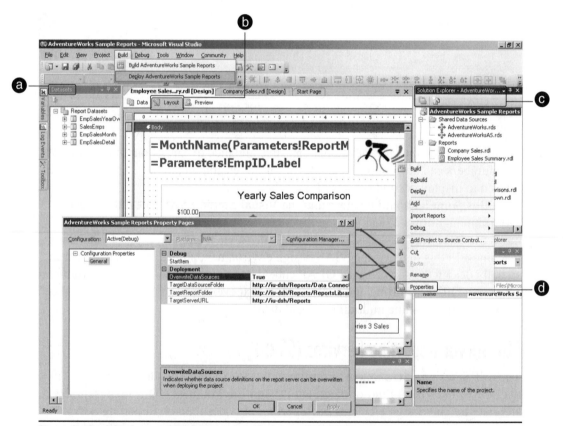

Figure 8-45 *SQL Server 2005 Reporting Services (SSRS) Report Designer*

b. The tabbed interface allows multiple design processes to be accomplished in the Visual Studio IDE.

c. The Solution Explorer provides a familiar file-explorer interface to navigate among the multiple components that make up a SSRS project.

d. The designer can right-click a component of the SSRS project and choose Properties to configure elements of the report.

As you see in Figure 8-45, the Microsoft method of designing reports is much like other reporting writing tools that have been on the market for years. There are two notable differences with Reporting Services, however: it is included with SQL Server 2005 at no extra cost, and it uses an openly published XML design structure for all Reporting Services reports. While a discussion of XML and report structures is beyond the scope of this section, it's worth noting that XML by design produces report data that is non-proprietary and can be used in both Microsoft and non-Microsoft business intelligence applications!

Virtual Earth in a Business Intelligence Context

We're going to use Microsoft's Virtual Earth technology to wrap up this Office Business Intelligence book on an interesting note: the extension of BI to real-time maps! If we agree that good BI presentations provide a compelling visual display, then it makes sense that maps can be used to show BI data locations when we have city, county, and country information that can be incorporated into the data picture.

The Microsoft Virtual Earth web site and maps are freely available for non-commercial use at local.live.com. Internet users will recognize the browser mapping and directions capability that we've come to expect in using online maps—but we're going to briefly explore the use of Virtual Earth, from Excel, to display locations with a custom pushpin icon.

Figure 8-46 shows an Excel spreadsheet with a few latitude and longitude data elements, and associated cities and land areas in square miles. Our Excel–Virtual Earth example uses an Excel macro to send these locations to Virtual Earth through an Internet connection. Virtual Earth will then display a map of the United States with our custom "chemical flask" icon as pushpins over Los Angeles, Denver, and Duval—and the city and land mass will appear as tool-tip text when the mouse is hovered over each city.

1. Save the Excel 2007 spreadsheet as an XLSM format that can contain macros.
2. Click the Macros icon on the View tab of the Ribbon menu.

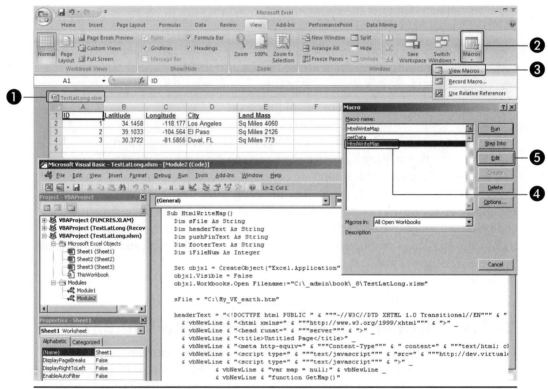

Figure 8-46 *Excel 2007 Visual Basic for Applications (VBA) macro*

3. Choose View Macros from the pop-up menu.
4. Choose the HTMLWriteMap macro in the list of macros.
5. Click Edit to view the macro.

Please note in Figure 8-46 the use of Excel's macro capability. This section is meant to show what the macro menu looks like—without actually explaining the contents of the macro itself, which is written in the Visual Basic for Applications (VBA) language. Microsoft provides excellent Help (both within Excel and through the Microsoft web site) to anyone who would like to learn how to automate Office processes, such as we're doing to connect Excel to Virtual Earth.

For the purpose of our discussion, it's worth understanding that VBA can be used to create programs that automate or extend Microsoft Office applications, including Excel, Word, and Visio. There are books and web sites dedicated to VBA and Office programming in support of people who work with this technology to automate business processes with the Microsoft toolset. Most business users will never need to work with VBA—but it helps to have seen it in Figure 8-46 in the context of Excel.

Figure 8-47 takes a leap forward in this discussion by showing the result of running the macro that takes location information from Excel and displays it in a Virtual Earth online map.

1. Click the message bar at the top of the browser window to allow the Virtual Earth ActiveX control to run.

2. Click Allow Blocked Content to enable the Virtual Earth content.

3. Click Yes to allow Virtual Earth to render the map.

Figure 8-47 shows the security that is built into Internet Explorer, which protects us from malicious or unwanted content on the Internet. In this case we're confident in accessing Microsoft's Virtual Earth application, so we allow the content to display.

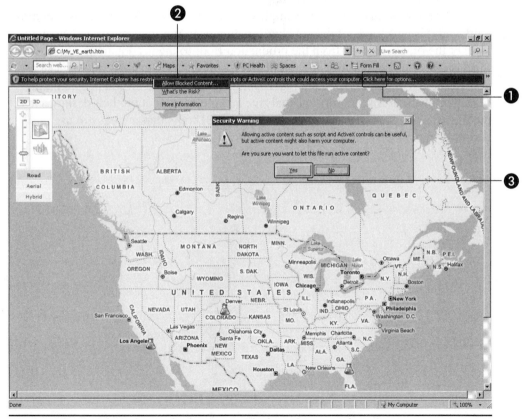

Figure 8-47 *Virtual Earth—in the browser with data-driven pushpins*

The resulting map in Figure 8-47 is a live, clickable display that can be zoomed in and out with a few mouse clicks—we can even click our custom pushpin icons to zoom in on Los Angeles, Denver, or Duval to see imagery at the local level of buildings and streets!

This scenario is familiar to Internet users worldwide; in our case we're connecting the familiar map visualization to display data from our Office 2007 business intelligence data. In this context it's easy to think of business intelligence uses for online maps; for example, we could display many locations simultaneously to show the relative concentration of our BI data, in a geographic setting across the country or on a state-by-state basis.

The use of geo-location technology has recently become inexpensive and widely available, which is leading to innovative color-coded displays of business intelligence data in the same way that charts have been used for so many years to present pictures of data. It really brings business intelligence home to people who work with Excel, to see data displayed "where we live" and to see it come alive in the personal context of our own neighborhoods, cities, and states.

It has been said that this is an example of "BI for the masses" where everyone can work with visualizations of data in charts and maps to run their businesses at every level of the organization—from the production floor to the headquarters office. If this vision is fulfilled through the use of Microsoft Office Business Intelligence as you've seen in this book, then it's reasonable to expect that a billion people on the planet will benefit from reporting, analysis, and measurement on their desktops and mobile Smartphones with the expanding use of BI tools that are easy to use and real-time in their delivery of actionable information.

Index